UTAH'S
Favorite Hiking Trails

WARNING:
HIKING INVOLVES RISK!

Hiking is a sport, not a pastime, and like all sports it involves an element of risk. There have been several instances in recent years of people suffering injury while hiking in Utah's backcountry and then filing a lawsuit against a person or organization that gave them information about the hike. This is a disturbing trend with serious implications for everyone involved in the sport.

The author and publisher of this book will not assume responsibility for any mishap that may occur as a result of information present or not present in this book. It is assumed that anyone attempting any of the hikes described in the following pages is already aware of the potential risks, has made all the necessary preparations, and has had sufficient experience to assume responsibility for himself.

Furthermore, while the author has done his best to assure that the information herein presented is accurate, he cannot guarantee its accuracy. Hikers using the information in this book should make allowance for the possibility that it may not be correct.

UTAH'S

Favorite Hiking Trails

Text and Photography
by
David Day

Rincon Publishing Company
1465 West 1700 North
Provo, Utah 84604
www.UtahTrails.com

first edition: 1998
second edition: 2002

All of the photographs in this book were taken by the author. Leasing agreements are available on request.

front cover: Little Wild Horse Canyon, San Rafael Swell
back cover: Timpanogos Basin, Mount Timpanogos Wilderness Area
    page 1: Chesler Park, Canyonlands National Park
    page 3: Unnamed lake below Hayden Peak, High Uintas Wilderness Area
    page 5: White Pine Lake, Bear River Mountains

Library of Congress Catalog Card Number: 00-133941
ISBN: 0-9660858-1-7

Printed by Art Printing Works, Kuala Lumpur, Malaysia

Published by:

Rincon Publishing Co.
1465 West 1700 North
Provo, Utah 84604

(801) 377-7657
www.UtahTrails.com

to Lily,

Who is always sad
when she can't
go with me.

Contents

Trailhead Locations
(turn to the indicated page numbers for complete descriptions of the trails)

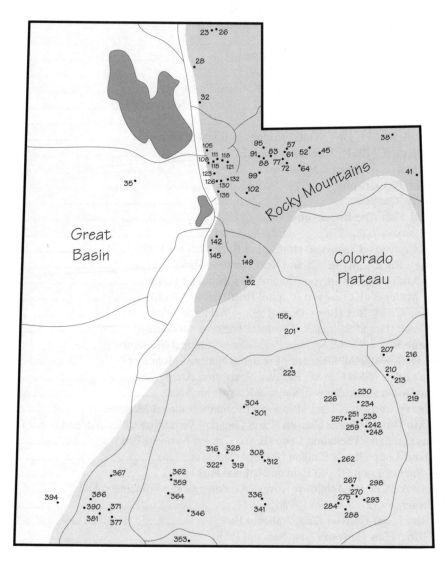

Preface

Before I say anything else, I would like to express my sincere thanks to all of you who took the trouble to contact me with your comments about the first edition of *Utah's Favorite Hiking Trails*. Your response has been phenomenal. I always knew Utah was a great place for outdoor activities, but I never expected that people from all over the U.S. and even Europe and Asia would be so interested in Utah's hiking trails. Many of the revisions in this edition are a direct result of the comments and suggestions I have received.

Some of the information you provided about specific trails was very timely, and I often felt it was a shame we had no way of passing it on to others who might be planning a hike on the same trail. Well, I am happy to inform you that now we do have a way to pass on current information to other hikers. We have included a bulletin board on our web site at www.UtahTrails.com where you can read what other people have said about the hikes and post your own comments about trails you have recently been on.

UtahTrails.com also contains many useful links to other helpful sites where you can obtain up-to-the-minute information about local weather forecasts, river flow rates, road conditions, rules and regulations for backcountry camping, and much more. The site has been set up specifically to help people who are planning trips into Utah's backcountry. Check it out!

As with the first edition of this book, I have rated each of the trails on a scale of one to five stars according to how much I personally enjoy that hike. The best rating is five stars ☆ ☆ ☆ ☆ ☆ , which means that that hike is one of the twelve most enjoyable hikes in the state. These ratings are only my personal opinion, however, and I am sure many of you will disagree with my assessments. If you have been on a particular hike and agree or disagree with my rating I hope you will post a comment on UtahTrails.com and let us all know what you think. Also, please let me know if you have any favorite hikes that you think should be included in the next edition of *Utah's Favorite Hiking Trails*.

May the wilderness remain forever wild!

David Day
Provo, Utah
davidday@utahtrails.com

Introduction

In the past fifty years the state of Utah has emerged as one of the premier hiking destinations in North America. Situated as it is in the heart of the American West, it combines the rugged splendor of the Rocky Mountains with the colorful sandstone canyons of the Colorado Plateau and the remote deserts of the Great Basin. And many of the most scenic spots can only be reached on foot.

In addition to magnificent scenery, many of Utah's hiking trails also provide fascinating glimpses into the region's colorful past. A few of the trails retrace the footsteps of Mormon pioneers who settled the state in the mid-1800s. Some trails pass by turn-of-the-century gold mines and cowboy camps, and others visit homestead cabins from the early 1900s. But perhaps most interesting of all are the 800-year-old Anasazi Indian dwellings in the canyons of Southern Utah. When hiking in these canyons it is hard not feel the presence of the ancient ones who once called them home.

Another factor that makes hiking in Utah so attractive is the presence of so much wide open space, uncluttered with fences, roads, and other man-made obstacles that inhibit one's freedom. Utah's population is still relatively small, and only a tiny percentage of the state's 84,899 square miles is privately owned. In many areas hikers can literally walk for days without seeing any sign of man at all. Sixty-three percent of the state is owned and administered by the federal government, with most of the best areas being preserved in twelve national parks and monuments, and fifteen wilderness areas.

Unfortunately not all of the best areas are currently protected. It has been more than seventeen years since the last wilderness area was created in Utah, and as this book goes to press a battle is raging over how much, if any, additional federal land should be designated as wilderness. Utah's economy and population have been booming in recent years, and many residents are opposed to limiting the expansion by imposing more regulations on the state's publicly owned land. The mining, logging, and ranching industries are especially sensitive to such regulation, and it is they who are leading the fight against the designation of more Utah wilderness areas. Today, as a result of this opposition, Utah has fewer acres of wilderness than any of the other ten intermountain western states.

Geology

Geologically, Utah can be divided into three broad provinces: the Colorado Plateau, the Rocky Mountains, and the Great Basin. Each of these three geologic areas includes a large swath of land that spans across several states, but Utah is unique because it contains all three. The three regions meet at a vaguely defined point somewhere near the center of the state, with the Colorado Plateau occupying the southeastern sector, the Rocky Mountains occupying the northeastern sector, and the Great Basin lying in the west.

The Colorado Plateau

The Colorado Plateau is Utah's most famous geological province. It is a large, mostly desert region covering parts of Arizona, New Mexico, Colorado, and Utah, that was uplifted and eroded some ten million years ago to its present elevation of 3,000 to 6,000 feet above sea level. It was named

Devils Garden, Arches National Park

after the Colorado River, which drains most of the region. The plateau is composed almost entirely of sedimentary rock, predominantly sandstone, that has been cut into a myriad of deep, meandering canyons by the Colorado River and its tributaries. The most famous of these canyons are Arizona's Grand Canyon and Utah's Zion Canyon, both of which are now national parks.

Like most of the southwestern United States, the Colorado Plateau is an arid region, receiving an average of only about ten inches of rain annually. As a result, a great deal of the plateau's bedrock is exposed, and to a large degree it is the exposed sandstone that makes the scenery so dramatic. Perhaps Edward Abbey described it best in his book, *Desert Solitaire*:

... here all is exposed and naked, dominated by the monolithic formations of sandstone which stand above the surface of the ground and extend for miles, sometimes level, sometimes tilted or warped by pressures from below, carved by erosion and weathering into an intricate maze of glens, grottoes, fissures, passageways, and deep narrow canyons.

. . . each groove in the rock leads to a natural channel of some kind, every channel to a ditch and gulch and ravine, each larger waterway to a canyon bottom or broad wash leading in turn to the Colorado River and the sea.[1]

All of Utah's national parks are located on the Colorado Plateau: Zion, Arches, Bryce, Canyonlands, and Capitol Reef. And about half of the hikes in this book are located there. It is a naturalist's paradise, filled with strange and wonderful rock formations,

---

[1] Edward Abbey, *Desert Solitaire, a Season in the Wilderness*, Simon & Schuster, New York, 1968. (with permission)

frequently called Utah's Redrock Country because of the ruddy appearance of the stone. The shades of red, pink, and yellow are created by tiny particles of iron oxide trapped within the rock. The colors are usually subtle, but become very pronounced in the reddish light of the late afternoon. Early morning and late afternoon are the "golden times" for desert hiking, as desert scenery that may appear harsh and unappealing in the middle of the day can become surprisingly beautiful when the sun is low.

Rocky Mountains

The Rocky Mountains in Utah consist primarily of the Wasatch Range and the Uinta Range in the northeastern corner of the state. It is an area about as different from the Colorado Plateau as one can imagine, with high alpine lakes, glaciated valleys, and snow-capped peaks being the dominant features of the landscape.

White Pine Trail, Wasatch Mountains

The Wasatch Range is a long narrow range of mountains running for about 200 miles in a north-south direction from the Idaho border to the center of the state. The western side of the range, known locally as the Wasatch Front, is one of the state's most prominent landmarks. Here the mountains rise dramatically above the western desert with very few foothills in between. Most of the ski resorts for which Utah is so well known are in the Wasatch Mountains, and the Wasatch peaks are popular hiking destinations.

Most of Utah's major population centers are located along the western side of the Wasatch Front; hence the trails in these mountains are well traveled. Seven of the state's wilderness areas are located in this range, with four of them lying in the forty miles between Provo and Salt Lake City. Residents of this area are blessed by their close proximity to several hundred miles of the states finest hiking trails.

Unlike the Wasatch Range, the Uinta Mountains run in an east-west direction parallel to the Wyoming border. They span a distance of about 150 miles, finally ending in the Wasatch Range east of Salt Lake City. The Uintas are particularly interesting because they are so high. The area above timberline in the Uinta Mountains exceeds that of any other range outside Alaska in the United States. The hiking trails seldom dip below 9,000 feet, and many of the range's hundreds of alpine lakes remain partially frozen until mid-August. Kings Peak (13,528 ft.), the Uintas' most famous summit, is the highest point in Utah.

The centerpiece of the Uinta Mountains is the 456,000 acre High Uintas Wilderness Area, which was created by Utah's last wilderness bill in 1984. An extensive network of trails in the wilderness area make it possible to walk for days without ever coming to a road. The longest route, the Highline Trail, is over sixty miles long. It follows the east-west summit ridge, remaining more than 10,000 feet above sea level for most of the distance.

The Great Basin

Immediately to the west of the Wasatch Mountains lies a vast, dry desert province known as the Great Basin. It is one of the most prominent geological features in the West, occupying an area of nearly 200,000 square miles and extending all the way through Nevada to the Sierra Nevada Mountains in California. The Great Salt Lake, which lies on the eastern edge of the Great Basin, is a remnant of the huge prehistoric Lake Bonneville that once covered most of northwestern Utah. But today there are few sources of fresh water in the province; hence few people live there.

The Great Basin is mostly barren land, but it is certainly not featureless. Interestingly, the flat desert country is broken up by a large number of small linear mountain ranges, all oriented in a north-south direction. Most of the mountains have no permanent rivers and, with a few notable exceptions, none exceed 10,000 feet in elevation. An old geological survey likens the ranges to "a group of caterpillars, all crawling irregularly northward". Surrounded as they are by desert, the small mountain ranges form biological "islands", and many contain unique species of plants and animals. Consequently, they are of great interest to biologists.

Deseret Peak, Stansbury Mountains

The arid nature of the region and the general lack of population mean that there are few established hiking trails in Utah's Great Basin. Some hikers enjoy the solitude of the area so much that they don't mind the lack of water and the long dusty drives to the Basin's interior desert ranges, but the most popular hiking opportunities are in two less isolated areas near its eastern boundary. Good trails can be found in the Stansbury Mountains, about 40 miles west of Salt Lake City, and in the Pine Valley Mountains, between Saint George and Cedar City.

Ecology

The Deserts

Utah, with its average annual precipitation of only 13 inches, is essentially a desert state. The only state in the U.S., in fact, that receives less rainfall is Nevada. Most of the hikes in this book lie within a desert ecological zone known to biologists as the Upper Sonoran Life Zone that extends across the Colorado Plateau and the Great Basin. The zone is characterized by plants resistant

Loafer Mountain, Wasatch Mountains

when hiking in these areas.

The Foothills

The Upper Sonoran Life Zone normally extends to about 5,500 feet, above which lies the Transition Life Zone. This region defines the transition between the desert and the mountain ecosystems. Open forests of ponderosa pine are usually common in the Transition Zone, with pinion pine, juniper, and sagebrush scattered between. In northern Utah, however, the ponderosa pine are more often absent—a fact that has long puzzled botanists.

In the canyons one is likely to find dense thickets of Gamble oak, scrub maple, and mountain mahogany. At the higher elevations, the pinion pine and juniper are replaced by Douglas fir. Squirrels and chipmunks also thrive in the Transition Zone, along with cottontails, jackrabbits, skunks, coyotes, mule deer, and the occasional mountain lion.

to drought and salty soil. On the valley floors one can find a variety of desert grasses intermingled with cactus, shadscale, greasewood, Mormon tea, rabbit brush and saltbush, and growing at slightly higher elevations is that ubiquitous western shrub, the sagebrush.

In areas where the annual rainfall exceeds 12 inches you might also find scattered groves of pinion pine and juniper along with the resident squirrels and chipmunks that feed on the pinion nuts. Other Upper Sonoran animals include prairie dogs, kangaroo rats, desert cottontails, jackrabbits, skunks, and coyotes. Mule deer are quite common, and occasionally you might be lucky enough to see a pronghorn antelope or a bighorn sheep. There are also bobcats and mountain lions in the desert canyon country, but they are rarely seen. The Upper Sonoran Zone is the favorite habitat of rattlesnakes, so be on the lookout for them

The Mountains

Above about 8,000 feet the Transition Life Zone gives way to an ecosystem known as the Canadian Life Zone. This is the zone that contains most of the hiking trails in the Wasatch and Uinta Mountains. Here the forests are usually dominated by Douglas fir, although in the Uintas lodgepole pine prevail. Deer, elk and moose can often be seen grazing in the meadows of the Canadian Zone and, among the smaller animals, gophers, marmots, and pikas are common.

As one goes higher in elevation Engelmann spruce and subalpine fir begin to dominate. Then above 10,000 feet one enters the Hudsonian Life Zone, where a short growing season and harsh winter conditions prevent the trees from reaching full size. The highest trees in most of Utah's mountains are usually stunted Engelmann spruce, sometimes reaching only a few feet in height.

Timberline, the maximum elevation at which trees will grow, varies a great deal from mountain to mountain, but in Utah it rarely exceeds 11,000 feet.

--- **History** ---

Prehistoric Cultures

The ancestors of the American Indians resided in Utah for at least ten thousand years before the arrival of the first white men, and the remnants of their most recent cultures can still be seen along many backcountry hiking trails. The most notable artifacts belonged to the Anasazi Indians, who left behind hundreds of archeological sites in southeastern Utah. Almost every major canyon in this part of the state contains traces of prehistoric Anasazi occupancy.

Archeologist have divided the Anasazi culture into six distinctive periods: the Basketmaker I, II, and III periods and the Pueblo I, II, and III periods. The Basketmaker II period, which began around the time of Christ, marks the time when the early nomadic Indians first began to learn the secrets of agriculture. Corn, introduced by other Indians living in Mexico, was probably their first crop. During the Basketmaker III phase they farmed extensively and lived in large, subterranean pit houses. It was also during this time that the bow and arrow were invented.

The Pueblo I, II, and III periods, lasting from about 700 until 1300 A.D., mark a time of increasing technological skill in building above-ground stone houses. It was during the last 150 years of this time, the Pueblo III period, that the famous Anasazi cliff dwellings were built in the four corners area of Arizona, New Mexico, Colorado, and Utah. The best preserved Pueblo III ruins are now located in Colorado's Mesa Verde National Park, but Utah has a greater number of Anasazi sites than any of the other three states.

There must have been many thousands of Indians living in southeastern Utah at that

Anasazi Cliff Dwelling, Grand Gulch

Big Man Pictograph, Grand Gulch

Utah—the Anasazis, the Fremonts, and the Archaic Peoples that preceded them—produced prodigious quantities of rock art. Most of it is in the southeastern part of Utah where the Indian populations were largest, but some rock art can be found in almost every corner of the state. The largest rock art panel in the United States is in the Horseshoe Canyon section of Canyonlands National Park, near Hanksville. Here, decorating the smooth canyon wall, are a series of intriguing red, brown, and white ghostlike pictographs that may be as much as 8,000 years old.

Early White Settlers

The last half of the nineteenth century saw a massive migration of pioneers into Utah from the eastern and midwestern states. The Mormons, led by Brigham Young, first arrived in what is now Salt Lake City in 1847, and almost immediately began fanning out to settle the rest of the state. The following year gold was discovered in California, and soon there was a huge exodus of people traveling westward through Utah in hopes of getting rich. In 1849 alone some 6,000 wagons journeyed through the state carrying an estimated 40,000 people to the west coast. The new Mormon settlers made a thriving business of selling supplies to the wagon trains, and many cattle and sheep ranches got their start during that time.

time, because now it seems that almost every canyon in the region contains at least one or two Anasazi ruins. Discovering these ancient structures while traveling alone in the wild canyon country of Southern Utah, far away from the tourists, park rangers, asphalt trails and interpretive plaques of the national parks, is an awesome experience. Some of the most interesting hikes in this book are in the canyons where the Anasazis once lived.

North of the four corners area you may occasionally come across remnants of the Fremont Indians. These people occupied parts of eastern Utah from about 700 to 1250 A.D. There were particularly large concentrations of them along the Green River and the Fremont River, after which they were named, but there numbers were never as large as the Anasazis. Nor were they as advanced. They lived in caves and simple shelters, and, although they did build stone granaries, they never developed the elaborate cliff dwellings that distinguish the Anasazis.

All of the prehistoric Indian cultures of

A number of the hiking trails in Utah follow routes originally established by the early migrants and settlers. Others were made by prospectors that decided to stay on in Utah and try their luck. And still others were made by the ranchers who worked the area. Some of the trails pass by old homesteads and cabins as well as old mines and discarded mining equipment. Some of them visit old cowboy camps, where cowboys once stayed while tending their cattle. Many of these camps have signatures and other graffiti carved in the sandstone canyon walls by the workers who lived there.

Helpful Hints for Hikers

Dozens of books have been telling hikers and backpackers in great detail what they should wear, what they should eat, where they should sleep, how they should walk, what they should carry, and a thousand other minutia. But let me assure you, you don't have to be a scholar to enjoy this sport. Hiking is really just an excuse to get out and enjoy the great outdoors, and the most important prerequisites are nothing more than common sense and a love of nature. If you have never done any hiking I suggest you get out and do some now, and read the books later. Start with the easy trails first. Then after you have completed a few hikes go ahead and read what the experts have to say.

Having said that, let me now caution you that successful hikes require a large amount of planning. Before you set out try to think through what the journey entails. How long is the trail? Is the route well marked? How long will you be gone? How much water will you need? What kind of clothing should you wear? Most of these questions can easily be answered with a modicum of common sense, but it is important that you ask them. Make the entire trip in your mind before you actually start, checking to see that you have packed what you will need for each phase of the journey. The longer your hike is the more adversely you will be affected by your mistakes, so be sure to try a few easy ones before you go for the big ones.

Access

The first thing to consider in planning a hike is how to get to the trailhead. An ordinary car is all you need most of the time, but occasionally a good four-wheel-drive vehicle can come in very handy. In some cases you can avoid the necessity of a 4WD by using a mountain bike for the last few miles to the trailhead, and sometimes, if the roads are dry, a 2WD with high clearance will do nicely. There are only three hikes in this book that you absolutely cannot do without a 4WD vehicle: The Maze, The Chocolate Drops, and the Green & Colorado River Overlook, all located in the Maze District of Canyonlands National Park. These hikes require seven hours of off-highway driving, the last 14 miles of which is extremely rough. If you don't have a 4WD vehicle with high clearance you won't make it.

Quite often a hike does not end at the same trailhead where it started, and in these cases you will need a plan for getting back to where your vehicle is parked. Again, a bicycle often fills the bill nicely. Of course the best way to handle this situation is with two cars, one parked at the end of the hike and one at the beginning, but this is often inconvenient. If you are a serious hiker I suggest that you invest in a bicycle rack, and carry a mountain bike on your car on all of your backcountry trips. You will be surprised how often it comes in handy.

Finally, let me point out that there are a few items you should always carry in your car when driving to remote trailheads:

  ◇ several gallons of extra water
  ◇ a hundred feet of rope
  ◇ a good spare tire
  ◇ a bicycle pump
  ◇ a few basic tools
  ◇ a shovel

When driving to an unfamiliar trailhead for the first time I also like to carry a logbook with me. It is useful to write down the odometer reading at various points along the way so you can keep track of where you are and how far you have come.

Clothing

The most important item of clothing on a hike is, of course, your foot wear. Your shoes must be comfortable and durable, and they must give your feet the protection they need. Many of the trails in Utah are very rocky, and on these trails boots are the only practical thing to wear. Some trails, however, are over slickrock or sand, and on these many people prefer to wear sneakers. When planning your hike be sure to find out if it will be necessary to wade across any streams. If so, you should wear some sort of wettable shoes. Walking for long distances with wet feet can cause blisters, but on hikes that require a lot of wading there may not be any other alternative.

Some hikers carry an extra pair of shoes in their pack for use around the camp or for wading streams, but for me it is more important to keep my weight down. Carrying extra socks, however, is a very good idea. A clean pair of socks each day will go a long way towards preventing blisters.

Walking generates a lot of body heat, especially if you are climbing. So you will probably want to wear jackets and sweaters that you can easily take off and put back on. Most hikers prefer to wear several layers of clothing rather than a single heavy jacket, but on long trips the weight of additional sweaters and shirts can add up fast.

In my opinion, shorts are impractical in most hiking situations. Your legs need protection from brush, from insects, and from the sun. If there is any doubt about what the trail conditions are going to be like, always opt for long pants. I also prefer to wear a long sleeved cotton shirt, even in the summer time, just for the protection it offers. Never go hiking without a hat. In hot weather it protects you from the sun and in cold weather it keeps your head warm. The most practical kind of headgear is a cheap, wide rimmed, foldable, canvas hat.

Catherine Pass Trail, Wasatch Mountains

A special mention should me made here about the hazards of skin cancer in Utah. This state has one of the highest incidents of skin cancer in the United States. Since exposure to the sun is the largest single cause of skin cancer, hikers should choose clothing that will minimize their exposure and use a high SPF sunscreen lotion on those parts of the body that cannot be covered.

Drinking Water

Water is one of the most important items to consider when planning a hike. Water is necessary for almost all of our body functions, and without it we cannot survive for more than a few days. When it is hot our bodies need prodigious amounts of water to function normally—a gallon a day or more in Utah's desert country in the summertime. This is not a problem on day hikes, but on longer hikes water can become a matter of serious concern. Fortunately it is usually possible to find water along the trail, so it need not all be carried from the trailhead. But caution is advised. There is always a possibility getting sick from ingesting contaminated water.

Opinions vary widely on the subject of when water is safe to drink. If you listen to the rangers in our national parks you will come away with the opinion that untreated water is *never* safe to drink. Yet I have known people who routinely drink from desert potholes, filled with tadpoles and mosquito larva, with no ill effects. Some people use inexpensive halogen tablets to treat their water in the backcountry, and others, claiming that the pills cause cancer, insist on carrying expensive filter pumps with them wherever they go. Again, common sense is the key. No one can guarantee that you will never get sick, but there is no need to be paranoid about the possibility. With a little common sense the risk can be minimized significantly.

First, it is important to remember where the germs that carry human disease come from. Generally, they are carried by other humans and animals that associate with humans, i.e. cows, sheep, horses, pigs, cats, dogs, etc. Beaver should also be included in the list, since they have been known to carry the microbes that are responsible for giardia. Second, bear in mind that most microbes can't swim very far; hence they are only likely to be found downstream from the contamination point. Knowing this, we can formulate a few basic rules:

◇ The closer you get to the source of a stream, the safer is the water.

◇ Stream water should be treated if humans or their animals frequent areas upstream in the watershed.

◇ Running water is safer than still water, since microbes tend to be washed down-

stream before they can multiply.

◇ Always treat the water if their are signs of beaver in the area.

Untreated spring water can be consumed with very little risk, but you should always treat the water you get from ponds and lakes. On rare occasions, especially in the desert, you may come across water that is contaminated with naturally occurring, sometimes poisonous minerals, such as salt, sulfur, or even arsenic. This is generally not a problem, since the taste of contaminated water is usually so bad no one would want to drink it anyway. But if you are in doubt check for insects or frogs living in the water. If the water is lifeless and has a peculiar taste, don't drink it under any circumstances.

There are three commonly used ways of treating water to kill or remove microbes: halogen tablets, boiling, or filtering. Using halogen (iodine or chlorine) tablets is the

Zion Narrows

Bowman Fork Trail, Wasatch Mountains

most convenient and inexpensive method. As stated earlier, some studies indicate that prolonged use of these tablets can cause cancer, but for short term use the risk is infinitesimal. If you are boiling the water, be sure to boil it for at least several minutes. Above 8,000 feet you should boil it for a full five minutes, since at higher elevations water boils at a lower temperature. If you don't mind spending the extra money and carrying a little extra weight, filter pumps are probably the best way to purify your drinking water.

Finally let me say that in my opinion the danger in drinking untreated water in the wild has been vastly overstated. Even if you drink indiscriminately, the chances are good that you won't get sick. And in most circumstances, even if you do get sick it will not be a life threatening illness. On the other hand, dehydration can easily lead to a life threatening situation, especially in desert areas. If you are threatened with dehydration, a muddy pool of untreated water could well save your life.

Minimum Impact

There was a time in the West when there were so few people using the backcountry that human impact was not a problem. That is no longer the case. The detrimental effect of man on the environment is becoming increasingly obvious, and it is up to each one of us to minimize it as best we can.

Probably the greatest amount of environmental destruction by hikers and backpackers is caused from incidents involving campfires. Many acres of prime forest land in the West have been destroyed by people who were careless with their fires. But fires adversely affect the environment even when they are carefully tended. The ugly marks from fires built in arid areas can last for years, and in places where wood is scarce campers often ravage the land for firewood, burning everything in sight. A much better solution is to carry a small camp stove. They are inexpensive, convenient, and weigh only a pound or two. Furthermore, open fires are now illegal in many of our national parks and forests. A small camp stove should be an integral part of every backpacker's standard equipment.

Another area of concern is garbage. There is nothing more disheartening to a nature lover than to walk through a pristine wilderness area that has been littered with trash. The slogan "Pack it in, pack it out" is a good one to follow. Some organic material, such as unwanted food or body wastes can be buried, but only if it is deposited at least six inches below the surface and covered with well packed dirt. But do not bury your toilet paper. Furthermore, nothing should be buried near a lake or in a stream bed, where it might pollute the surface water.

Utah's desert areas require special consideration from backcountry hikers. Most people don't realize how fragile the arid ecosystems are, but it can take years for the desert to recover from the impact of a careless hiker. Old campfire sites, refuse deposits, and even foot prints seem never to go away. Desert soils are filled with an array of dry, thread-like microscopic plants that nitrogenate the soil and bind it together, and once these plants are crushed or burned it can take up to twenty years for them to grow back. Without this component of the soil, called the cryptobiotic crust, the desert would be a barren place indeed. Most shrubs and grasses can not thrive without it. So when hiking off-trail in the deserts of Southern Utah try to stay on the slickrock or in the sandy bottoms of washes as much as possible, especially in the national parks and other areas where there is a lot of foot traffic.

One of Southern Utah's greatest treasures is the incredible prehistoric cliff dwellings that were left behind by the Anasazi Indians some 700 years ago. It is impossible to describe the thrill of discovering one of these archeological gems, far from any road in a wild desert canyon. Yet the ancient ruins have received more abuse than any of Utah's other backcountry attractions. Most of the damage was inflicted many years ago, when indiscriminate excavation and pot hunting were legal, but even today the ancient dwellings are still being abused. Occasionally they are intentionally vandalized; more often damage is inflicted as a result of carelessness. If you visit one of these ruins remember that they are very fragile and can be easily damaged. Do not walk over them or climb on them. And do not remove any pottery shards, corn cobs, or other objects from the sites. Treat them just as you would treat an exhibit in a museum, because that is exactly what they are.

Crack Canyon, San Rafael Reef

Maps

There is no substitute for a good map of the area in which you are hiking. The maps provided in this book should be sufficient to complete the described hikes, but if possible you should take along a more detailed map of the area you plan to visit. Part of the joy of hiking is exploring and taking side trips on your own that may not have been part of the original plan, and it is much easier to do this if you have a good map with you. Also, it is sometimes useful to know exactly where you are on the trail. A good map will help you plot your course with greater accuracy.

The best topographic maps available are the 7.5 minute series, published by the United States Geological Survey. They are large scale (about $2^5/_8$ inches per mile, with contour lines at 40 foot intervals), and they are widely available in ranger stations, national park visitor centers, and stores that sell camping supplies.

Unfortunately, many of the 7.5 minute USGS maps do not accurately depict the trail locations. The best trail maps are produced by Trails Illustrated, of Evergreen, Colorado. Most of the Trails Illustrated maps are only about $^1/_2$ to $^1/_4$ the scale of the detailed 7.5 minute maps, but they do give much more information about the hiking trails and trailheads.

You will find your map much more useful if you also carry a compass and a watch. The watch will help you estimate how far you have gone since the last landmark (most people walk about 2 miles per hour on level ground). When using your compass to determine a direction, bear in mind that the magnetic declination throughout Utah is generally about 15 degrees east. In other words, your compass needle will always point 15 degrees east of the direction of true north.

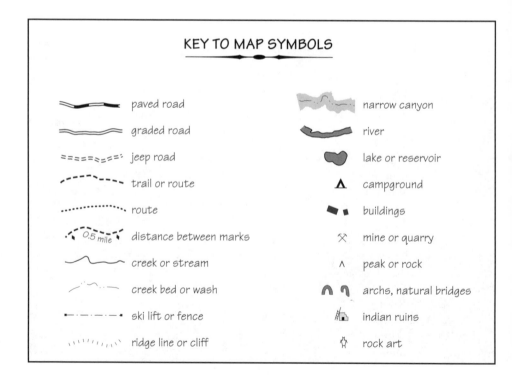

KEY TO MAP SYMBOLS

paved road		narrow canyon	
graded road		river	
jeep road		lake or reservoir	
trail or route		campground	
route		buildings	
distance between marks		mine or quarry	
creek or stream		peak or rock	
creek bed or wash		archs, natural bridges	
ski lift or fence		indian ruins	
ridge line or cliff		rock art	

Naomi Peak

Distance:	6.4 miles (round trip)
Walking time:	4¹/₂ hours
Elevations:	1,920 ft. gain/loss
	Tony Grove Trailhead (start): 8,060 ft.
	Naomi Peak: 9,978 ft.
Trail:	Good trail most of the way
Season:	Midsummer through mid-fall. Parts of the trail are usually covered with snow from November until the end of June.
Vicinity:	Near Logan
Maps:	Naomi Peak *(USGS)*
Information:	http://www.utahtrails.com/naomi.html *(Utah Trails)*
	http://www.fs.fed.us/wcnf/ *(Wasatch-Cache Nat. Forest)*
	phone: (435) 755-3620 *(Logan Ranger District)*

Drive north of Logan on Highway 89 towards Bear Lake. After 22 miles you will see a sign directing you to Tony Grove Lake and Campground. Turn here and follow the signs for 6.9 miles to Tony Grove Lake. There is a parking area at the end of the road just above the lake, and the trail head is on the north side of the parking lot.

Naomi Peak is the highest point in the Bear River Mountains of northern Utah and southern Idaho. While the limestone range is not very high it is extremely rugged, and the views from the top of Naomi are outstanding. Many of the most interesting peaks in the range can be seen from the summit.

If you are hiking in late July or August you will also be able to enjoy another highlight of the Bear River Range: wildflowers. Nowhere else in Utah will you see them in such staggering abundance. A colorful profusion of geraniums, paintbrushes, columbines, lupines, daisies, and mountain sunflowers stretch for miles across the meadows north of Tony Grove Trailhead. It is a shame that these meadows were not included in the 1984 Utah Wilderness Bill that created the Mount Naomi Wilderness Area. Snowmobile operators frequent the area in the winter, and they lobbied successfully to have the watershed east of the peak excluded from the bill. This hike touches only briefly on the eastern boundary of the wilderness area.

From the trailhead at Tony Grove Lake the trail climbs gently uphill for about 400 yards before coming to a forest service sign-

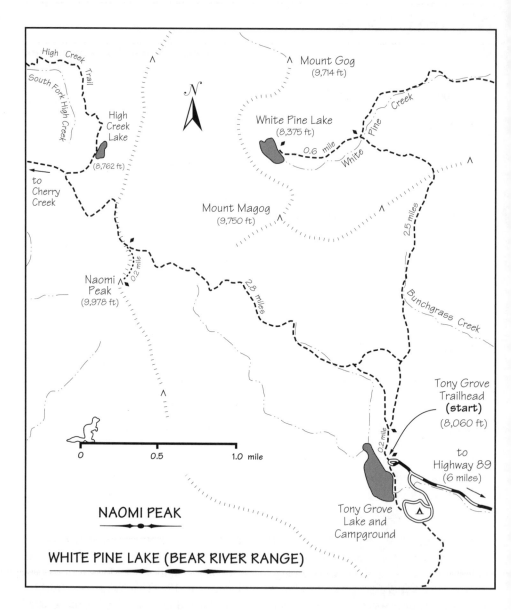

High Creek Trail

South Fork High Creek

to
Cherry
Creek

High
Creek
Lake
(8,762 ft)

N

^ Mount Gog
(9,714 ft)

White Pine Creek

White Pine Lake
(8,375 ft)

0.6 mile

White Pine

^

Mount Magog
(9,750 ft)   ^

2.5 miles

Naomi ^
Peak
(9,978 ft)

0.2 mile

2.8 miles

Bunchgrass Creek

^

Tony Grove
Trailhead
(start)
(8,060 ft)

0.2 mile

to
Highway 89
(6 miles)

0   0.5   1.0 mile

Tony Grove
Lake and
Campground

NAOMI PEAK

WHITE PINE LAKE (BEAR RIVER RANGE)

board where it forks. Bear left here, as the trail goes into a long turn to the west towards Naomi Peak. The wildflower section of the trail continues for only about 0.5 mile beyond the sign before the grade gets steeper and the rocky soil becomes less supportive of ground cover.

As the trail ascends toward the summit ridge you will climb onto two narrow benches, each about 250 feet above the preceding one. The path climbs out of the meadow and onto the first bench about 0.8 mile from the trailhead. Then after a brief respite the route becomes steep again until the second bench is reached 0.8 mile farther along. From the second bench the trail makes its third and last steep climb up to the summit ridge just north of the peak.

Once you reach the summit ridge it will be necessary to leave the trail and strike out along the top of the ridge for the last 0.2 mile to the peak. The Mount Naomi Wilderness Area boundary line also follows the ridge, and you will see a forest service sign at the boundary

see color photo, page 161

just before the point where you must leave the trail. It is an easy ten-minute scramble along the summit ridge to the top of Naomi Peak. The peak is only 140 feet higher than the pass, and there is no vegetation to impede the way.

The view from the top of Naomi Peak is striking. Smithfield Canyon, a deep gorge through the mountains, dominates the view to the west. The dome-shaped peak 1.5 miles to the northwest, on the other side of Smithfield Canyon, is Cherry Peak. Cherry Peak is easily accessible from the Cherry Creek Trail which you can see about 400 feet below its summit. The distinctive peak one mile east of Naomi Peak is Mount Magog. White Pine Lake, lies just out of sight on the north side of Magog.

High Creek Lake

If you still have energy to spare after climbing Naomi, you might want to visit the nearby High Creek Lake . This side trip will add 2.4 miles to the hike's total distance and about a thousand feet to the elevation gain and loss. To get there just continue west on the trail below Naomi as it crosses the summit ridge. After 0.9 mile the trail splits again, with the right fork leading to High Creek Lake and the left fork leading to Cherry Creek. High Creek Lake is a small but very scenic lake nestled against the steep western side of the summit ridge. There are several groves of large Engelmann spruce around the lake, and a few fine camp sites along its southern shore.

Mount Magog, as seen from Naomi Peak

White Pine Lake, Bear River Range

☆ ☆ ☆ ☆   **day hike**

Distance:	6.6 miles (round trip)
Walking time:	4¼ hours
Elevations:	1,250 ft. gain/loss
	Tony Grove Trailhead (start): 8,060 ft.
	Highest point: 8,840 ft.
	White Pine Lake: 8,375 ft.
Trail:	Good trail all the way
Season:	Summer through mid-fall. Parts of the trail are usually covered with snow from November until early June.
Vicinity:	Near Logan
Maps:	Naomi Peak *(USGS)*
Information:	http://www.utahtrails.com/whitepinebear.html *(Utah Trails)*
	http://www.fs.fed.us/wcnf/ *(Wasatch-Cache Nat. Forest)*
	phone: (435) 755-3620 *(Logan Ranger District)*

Drive north of Logan on Highway 89 towards Bear Lake. After 22 miles you will see a sign directing you to Tony Grove Lake and Campground. Turn here and follow the signs for 6.9 miles to Tony Grove Lake. There is a parking area at the end of the road just above the lake, and the trail head is on the north side of the parking lot.

This is one of the most scenic hikes you will find anywhere, especially if it is done around the first of August when the wildflowers are at their peak. The first two-thirds of the trail pass through a series of alpine meadows that are filled with acres and acres of pink, blue, purple, yellow, and white flowers. No other trail in this book offers the abundance of wildflowers you will see on the White Pine Lake trail. You might want to stop at the Forest Service Ranger Station in Logan and buy a guide to the wildflowers on your way

see map, page 24

to the trailhead. As you leave Logan you will see it on the right side of Highway 89 just 2.1 miles after you leave Main Street.

Given the natural beauty of White Pine Lake and its environs, it is unfortunate that it is not a part of the Mount Naomi Wilderness Area. The lake lies about a mile outside of the wilderness area's eastern boundary. It is a popular destination among snowmobile sportsmen during the winter months, and it was their lobbying effort that led to its exclusion when Ronald Reagan signed the

Utah Wilderness Bill into law in 1984. White Pine Lake is still pristine, but there is no guarantee that it will not be developed in the future. There already exists a jeep road within 0.6 mile of the lake.

From Tony Grove Lake the trail climbs gently uphill for a quarter mile to the junction with the Naomi Peak trail. Turn right here and continue climbing for another 1.9 miles until you reach the highest point on the hike, some 780 feet above the trailhead. Up to this point the trail goes through open meadows with occasional groves of Engelmann spruce and limber pine. The limber pines are the trees with large clusters of needles near the ends of the twigs that look almost like tufts of fur. They get their name because the branches are so limber they can be bent double or even tied in knots without breaking.

Finally, 2.1 miles from the trailhead the trail starts down into White Pine Basin. The prominent peak west of this point is Mount Magog and, although you cannot see it yet, the lake is located just north of this peak. When you reach the bottom of the basin you will come to another trail junction where you must turn west for the last half mile to White Pine Lake.

see color photo
page 161

The lake itself is small and very shallow, but the beauty of its setting makes up for its deficiencies. It is situated directly between two 9,700 peaks, Mount Magog and Mount Gog, with a magnificent stand of spruce on one side. There are a number of good camp sites above the eastern shore, and if you have the time it is a very pleasant place to spend a night.

White Pine Lake

Wellsville Ridge

 ☆☆

Wellsville Mountains Wilderness Area
shuttle car or bicycle required
day hike

Distance: 7.5 miles
(plus 6.5 miles by car or bicycle)

Walking time: 5³/₄ hours

Elevations: 2,960 ft. gain, 2,520 ft. loss
Deep Canyon Trailhead (start): 5,420 ft.
Stewart Pass: 8,380 ft.
Wellsville Cone: 9,356 ft.
Coldwater Canyon Trailhead: 5,860 ft.

Trail: Good trail all the way

Season: Summer through mid-fall. Parts of the trail are usually covered with snow from November until mid-June. Also, the road to Coldwater Canyon Trailhead is unmaintained and inaccessible in wet weather.

Vicinity: Near Wellsville and Logan

Maps: Honeyville *(USGS)*

Information: http://www.utahtrails.com/wellsville.html *(Utah Trails)*
http://www.fs.fed.us/wcnf/ *(Wasatch-Cache Nat. Forest)*
phone: (435) 755-3620 *(Logan Ranger District)*
phone: (801) 538-4700 *(Utah Division of Wildlife Resources)*

Take Exit 364 from I-15, 55 miles north of Salt Lake City, and drive east through Brigham City on Highway 89 towards Logan. After driving 17 miles you will come to the junction with Highway 23, where you must turn right towards Wellsville and Mendon. You will arrive at the farming community of Mendon after 7 miles. Turn into Mendon and find the corner of Center and Main Street, then drive south on Main Street. After 0.5 mile the road crosses the highway again, and another 200 yards will bring you to a sign that says "National Forest". Turn right onto a gravel road and continue following the signs to the national forest. 1.2 miles after leaving the pavement you will pass the national forest boundary, and 2.2 miles later you will reach the Coldwater Canyon Trailhead at the end of the road (a total of 4.0 miles from Center Street in Mendon). This is where the hike will end and where you must leave your shuttle. (Note: the last two miles of the road to the trailhead is very rough, but with care it can usually be negotiated with an ordinary car.)

In order to get to Deep Canyon, where the hike begins, you must drive west out of Mendon on 3rd North. After 3rd North crosses the highway it continues almost due west for 2.0 miles and ends at the trailhead. The road is graded gravel—much better than the road to Coldwater Canyon. There is a small parking area at the end of 3rd North but, unfortunately, no signs to let you know where the trail is. You will see two primitive roads leaving the parking area: one continues west along the fence, and the other forks off to the south. Walk down the road to the south, and within a few hundred yards it will end where the trail begins.

The Wellsville Ridge is very well known among Utah's bird watchers. It is probably the best place in the state to see such birds of prey as the Cooper's hawk and the red tailed hawk. These raptors are especially prevalent on windy days during the fall migration, when they can be seen riding the updrafts along the western side of the ridge. There are also a number of fine views from the top of the narrow summit ridge. The fertile Cache Valley lies below the mountains on the east side, with its settlements of Logan, Mendon, and Wellsville. On the west side the meandering Bear River makes an interesting picture, as it winds its way lazily toward the Great Salt Lake.

The people who live below the Wellsville Mountains should be remembered for their valiant efforts in the early 1940s to save their beloved mountains. At that time the grass-covered ridges were suffering from decades of overgrazing, and much of the vegetation in the lower canyons had been burned out. In 1941 a few concerned citizens in Cache County formed the Wellsville Area Project Corporation, and soon, even as the United States was becoming embroiled in World War II, private contributions to save the mountain began to accumulate. The money was used to purchase land, which was then deeded over to the Forest Service for protection. The Wellsville project was a huge success, and in 1984 a final tribute to its participants was paid by the U.S. Congress with the creation of the Wellsville Mountains Wilderness Area. Now 23,850 acres of wilderness stand as a monument to a group of people who, fifty years ago, cared deeply about their environment and their children's heritage.

From the trailhead the trail climbs steadily up Deep Canyon for a distance of 3.2 miles, finally reaching a small saddle on the summit ridge after an elevation gain of 2,700 feet. The trail splits at the saddle, with the southern branch going to Stewart Pass and the northern branch proceeding along the ridge to the top of a small unnamed peak 0.7 mile away. This peak is supposed to be an especially fine place to watch the hawks, but in fact if the conditions are right they can be seen almost everywhere along the ridge. The best time to see the hawks is during the fall migration on days when there is enough wind to create good updrafts on the western side of the mountain.

The Wellsville Ridge is surprisingly devoid of vegetation. Perhaps the dry winds that blow across the mountain from the Great Basin desert leave the rocky soil too dry for the forest to flourish. Whatever the reason, the absence of trees along the ridge makes for some marvelous views of the valleys below.

From the saddle above Deep Canyon the main trail proceeds southward for 1.7 miles to Stewart Pass. Along the way the route traverses around the west side of Scout Peak (8,687 ft.), another good place for hawk watching. There are no signs to let you know when you arrive at Stewart Pass, but there is a stone monument marking the place. This is where the ridge trail intersects the Coldwater Canyon Trail, and where you must start your descent back to your shuttle car.

Deep Canyon Trailhead
(start) (5,420 ft)

to Logan
(9 miles)

300 North

2.0 miles

Pole Canyon

Deep Canyon

3.2 miles

Fiddlers Hollow

Mendon

Highway 23

Main Street

Kidman Canyon

Baker Canyon

Stauffer Canyon

Straight Hollow

Thimbleberry Canyon

3.4 miles

to
Wellsville
(4 miles)

(8,585 ft)

0.7 mile

Bird Canyon

Gibson Canyon

Coldwater Canyon

Mendon
Peak
(8,766 ft)

Big   Canyon

Scout
Peak
(8,687 ft)

Old Logway Canyon

North Fork Hell Canyon

Coldwater Canyon
Trailhead
(5,860 ft)

Limekiln Canyon

1.7 miles

Hell Canyon

Coldwater Lake

Stewart
Pass
(8,380 ft)

Coldwater Canyon

2.6 miles

1.6 miles

Three Drag Road Canyon

Jim May Canyon

Shumway Canyon

Two Jump Canyon

Wellsville Cone
(9,356 ft)

Brushy Canyon

Cottonwood Canyon

0.9 mile

WELLSVILLE RIDGE

_N_

Box
Elder
Peak
(9,372 ft)

Precipice Canyon

0   0.5   1.0 mile

Stewart Pass is the lowest point on the Wellsville Ridge between Scout Peak and the Wellsville Cone.

The hike down through Coldwater Canyon is much like the hike through Deep Canyon, except the trail is slightly steeper. You will loose 2,500 feet

see color photo, page 161

in 2.6 miles. About 0.6 mile before you reach the trailhead you will pass by Coldwater Lake, a small pond about 100 feet long.

Wellsville Cone

If time permits, you really should make a side trip to the top of the Wellsville Cone before starting down the Coldwater Canyon Trail from Stewart Pass. The Wellsville Cone is 1.6 miles from Stewart Pass, over an excellent trail, with an elevation gain of 980 feet. The side trip to Wellsville Cone and back will add about 2.5 hours onto your total hiking time.

Wellsville Cone, which can be clearly seen from the top of Stewart Pass, looks like an old volcanic cinder cone with its northern side eroded away. The mountain is made of sedimentary limestone, however, so the cone could not have been formed by a volcano. The Cone has two summits with the eastern peak being the higher one. The ridge trail passes between the two peaks. You will probably see another faint trail coming up through the bowl below Wellsville Cone on the west side of the mountain. This trail originates at the bottom of West Coldwater Canyon, but it is little used now and hard to follow.

For still more ambitious hikers it is only another 0.9 miles from the Wellsville Cone along the last part of the ridge to Box Elder Peak (9,372 ft.). Box Elder is the highest point in the Wellsville Mountains, but the views are not much different than the views from the summit of the Wellsville Cone.

Wellsville Ridge, as seen from the Wellsville Cone

Mount Ogden

day hike

Distance:	10.0 miles (round trip)
Walking time:	7 hours
Elevations:	4,730 ft. gain/loss
	Malans Peak Trailhead (start): 4,840 ft.
	Malans Peak: 7,080 ft.
	Mount Ogden: 9,570 ft.
Trail:	There is no trail for most of the last mile. Furthermore, this part of the route is very steep, gaining 1,600 feet in one mile. It is a very strenuous climb.
Season:	Summer through mid-fall. The upper parts of the trail are usually covered with snow from mid-November through mid-June.
Vicinity:	Near Ogden
Maps:	Ogden *(USGS)*
Information:	http://www.utahtrails.com/mtogden.html *(Utah Trails)*
	http://www.fs.fed.us/wcnf/ *(Wasatch-Cache Nat. Forest)*
	phone: (801) 625-5112 *(Ogden Ranger District)*

Drive east on 27th street in Ogden until the road ends. The trail begins just beyond the barrier at the end of the pavement.

Mount Ogden is a popular hike primarily because it is so close to the city of Ogden. The trailhead is only a three mile drive from Weber State University. The lower part of the climb, across Malans Peak and into Waterfall Canyon, is very pleasant, but beyond that the route to the top of the mountain is extremely strenuous. There are some gorgeous views from the peak, not only of the city of Ogden, but also of the Snow Basin ski area and Pineview Reservoir. Unfortunately, however, the summit is now marred by the presence of a microwave transmitting tower. Mount Ogden can also be reached from its east side by way of a jeep road that ascends from Snow Basin to a saddle 0.2 mile south of the peak.

There may be some confusion near the trailhead because of the existence of many

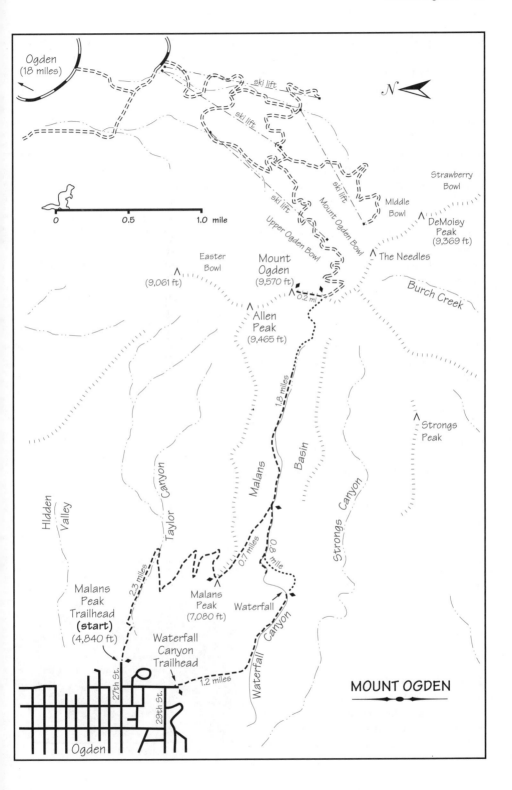

Ogden
(18 miles)

ski lift

ski lift

ski lift

ski lift

ski lift

Mount Ogden Bowl

Upper Ogden Bowl

Middle Bowl

Strawberry Bowl

DeMoisy Peak
(9,369 ft)

The Needles

Easter Bowl
(9,061 ft)

Mount Ogden
(9,570 ft)

0.2 mi.

Burch Creek

Allen Peak
(9,465 ft)

1.8 miles

Strongs Peak

Malans Basin

Taylor Canyon

Strongs Canyon

Hidden Valley

2.3 miles

0.7 miles

0.8 mile

Malans Peak Trailhead
(start)
(4,840 ft)

Malans Peak
(7,080 ft)

Waterfall

Waterfall Canyon

Waterfall Canyon Trailhead

1.2 miles

27th St.

29th St.

Ogden

MOUNT OGDEN

N

intersecting ATV and motorcycle trails. Just make sure that the path you choose heads east, toward the obvious mouth of Taylor Canyon. After you enter the canyon, 0.3 mile from the trailhead, you won't encounter any more ATV roads.

The trail follows a picturesque stream through the bottom of Taylor Canyon for about 0.5 mile before turning south to begin its ascent up Malans Peak. Next, a series of wide switchbacks ascend through a forest of Douglas fir to an elevation of about 7,000 feet, where the trail finally reaches the top of the ridge separating Taylor Canyon from Waterfall Canyon. As it crosses the ridge the path passes by the summit of Malans Peak. As you will see from this perspective, Malans is not really a peak at all, but rather just a prominent knob on the end of the long ridge that comes down the western slope of Mount Ogden. From Malans Peak the trail continues south into the bottom of Waterfall Canyon.

Once you reach Waterfall Canyon turn east and follow the drainage all the way to a saddle just south

see color photo, page 162

of the summit. For the first mile you can walk on a primitive trail on the left side of the stream, but at about the same time the water disappears the trail also disappears. From there on it is a steep, strenuous climb up the dry, rocky streambed to the saddle. Once you reach the saddle, just south of the peak, there is a good 0.2-mile trail to the top. The summit is clearly visible for most of the last two miles. It seems so close while you are on the trail, but so far when the trail runs out.

Lower Waterfall Canyon

An alternative to the Taylor Canyon-Malans Peak trail is to make the first part of the hike up through the lower part of Waterfall Canyon. To reach the Waterfall Canyon

Trailhead, drive to the end of 29th Street, then turn right onto a dirt road that leads to a large public parking area. The parking lot is on the east side of a highrise apartment building. A sign at the back of the parking lot marks the beginning of a 1.2-mile-long trail to the Waterfall Canyon Waterfall.

This is a good trail as far as it goes, but once you reach the 200-foot waterfall you must exit the canyon and do some steep, off-trail climbing to get around it. About 100 feet to the right of the waterfall there is a notch in the side of the canyon through which you can climb out. The route is very steep and there are a lot of loose rocks, but it isn't dangerous if you are careful. Some hand-over-hand scrambling is necessary in a few places. After about 600 vertical feet of climbing you will cross over a ridge and see the upper part of Waterfall Canyon again below you. If you drop back down into the canyon at this point you will find a primitive trail that leads upstream to a junction with the Malans Peak Trail.

A lot of hikers make a loop hike up Waterfall Canyon, across Malans Peak, and down Taylor Canyon, with Mount Ogden as a possible side trip. If you do this I recommend you go up Waterfall and down Taylor—not the other way around. It is much easier and less dangerous to climb up the detour around the waterfall rather than down.

Above Lower Waterfall Canyon

Deseret Peak

☆ ☆ ☆

Deseret Peak Wilderness Area
day hike

Distance:	8.4 miles (loop)
Walking time:	6³/₄ hours
Elevations:	3,613 ft. gain/loss Mill Fork Trailhead (start): 7,418 ft. Deseret Peak: 11,031 ft.
Trail:	Most of the trail is well maintained and easy to follow. A portion of the return path, however, is not well maintained and can occasionally be confusing.
Season:	Midsummer through mid-fall. The upper parts of the trail are usually covered with snow from November through late June.
Vicinity:	Deseret Peak Wilderness Area, west of Salt Lake City
Maps:	Deseret Peak East, Deseret Peak West *(USGS)*
Information:	http://www.utahtrails.com/deseret.html *(Utah Trails)* http://www.fs.fed.us/wcnf/ *(Wasatch-Cache Nat. Forest)* phone: (801) 943-1794 *(Salt Lake Ranger District)*

Drive west from Salt Lake City on I-80 for about 20 miles, then turn onto *Highway 36 (exit 99) and drive south towards Tooele for 3.5 miles. When you* *reach Mills Junction, turn west onto Highway 138 and drive another 11 miles* *to Grantsville. On the west side of Grantsville you will see a sign directing* *you to South Willow Canyon. Turn left here and continue for 5.1 miles, then*
turn right onto South Willow Canyon Road. South Willow Canyon Road ends after 7.3 miles, *the last 4 miles of which are unpaved. At the end of the road, just beyond the Loop Camp-* *ground, you will see a parking area and a sign marking the Mill Fork Trailhead.*

Most of the western side of Utah is occupied by an interesting geographical area known as the Great Basin. The Great Basin is a vast, semiarid desert that extends from the Wasatch Front, across Nevada, to the Sierra Nevada mountains of California. The desert is not unbroken, though. It contains a number of narrow, isolated mountain ranges, running mostly in a north-south direction and separated by long desert valleys. The mountain ranges of the Great Basin are of great interest to evolutionary biologists because of their isolation. Life has developed in slightly different ways in each of the secluded ranges, making them ideal natural laboratories for the study of evolution.

In Utah the best known and most accessible of the Great Basin mountain ranges is

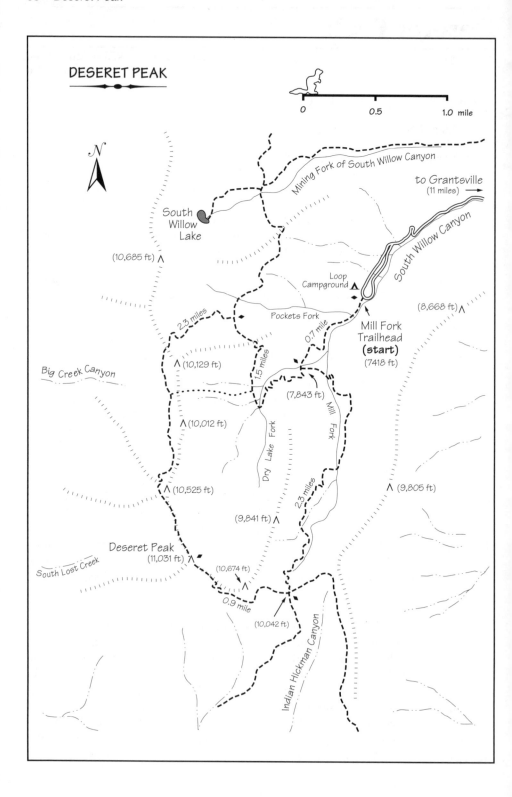

DESERET PEAK

0   0.5   1.0 mile

N

Mining Fork of South Willow Canyon

to Grantsville
(11 miles) →

South
Willow
Lake

(10,685 ft) ∧

South Willow Canyon

Loop
Campground ∧

(8,668 ft) ∧

2.3 miles

Pockets Fork

0.7 mile

Mill Fork
Trailhead
(start)
(7418 ft)

∧ (10,129 ft)

1.5 miles

Big Creek Canyon

(7,843 ft)

Dry Lake Fork

Mill Fork

∧ (10,012 ft)

∧ (10,525 ft)

2.3 miles

(9,841 ft) ∧

∧ (9,805 ft)

Deseret Peak
(11,031 ft) ∧

South Lost Creek

(10,674 ft)
∧

0.9 mile

(10,042 ft)

Indian Hickman Canyon

the Stansbury Range, in which Deseret Peak is the highest point. The Stansbury Mountains are almost the only Great Basin range in Utah with a good system of hiking trails. The uniqueness of the mountains was recognized in 1984, when a 25,500-acre area, including Deseret Peak, was selected for the creation of the Deseret Peak Wilderness Area.

From the Loop Campground the trail proceeds up South Willow Canyon for 0.7 mile to Mill Fork. Here the trail splits, with the right fork leading to the Willow Lakes and the left fork to Deseret Peak. Take the Deseret Peak fork. For the next 2.3 miles the path meanders up Mill Fork, realizing an elevation gain of 2,200 feet and finally crossing the ridge at the head of the valley.

At the top of the ridge you will encounter a four-way junction in the trail with signs marking the way to Deseret Peak, Bear Fork, Antelope Canyon, and Loop Campground. The Deseret Peak Trail climbs again up the south side of another intersecting ridge and finally reaches the peak after 0.9 mile.

Many of northern Utah's most prominent features can be seen from the top of Deseret Peak, including the Great Salt Lake and the Wasatch Front. Stansbury Island, 25 miles north in the Great Salt Lake, is thought to be an extension of the Stansbury Mountains. On most days it isn't difficult to see Mount Nebo, 60 miles to the southeast on the southern end of the Wasatch Mountains. And in the west more of the Great Basin ranges can be seen, including the Cedar Mountains, 20 miles away.

From the peak the loop trail continues northward, staying on the top of the summit ridge for about 0.4 mile and then dropping down 200-300 feet below the ridge on the west side. The trail is not as well maintained here and there may be some confusion at times. But there are few trees at this altitude, and you can occasionally see parts of the trail far ahead.

Finally, 1.6 miles after leaving the summit of Deseret Peak, the trail makes an abrupt turn to the right, crosses to the east side of the ridge, and starts down again towards Mill Fork Canyon.

see color photo, page 170

About 0.7 mile after leaving the ridge the trail intersects the Willow Lakes trail, where you should turn right. From that point the path is much more distinct.

As shown on the map, it is possible to cross the summit ridge and drop down towards Mill Fork about 0.4 mile before the main trail does so. Doing this saves about a mile of walking, but is unlikely to save any time as it is much easier to walk on the trail. You will recognize this alternative route because the Forest Service has placed an 8-foot-high juniper pole on the ridge at the point where the route departs from the main trail.

After you meet the Willow Lakes trail it is an easy walk back to Mill Fork, from where you can retrace your steps for the last 0.7 mile to the Mill Fork Trailhead.

Looking north from Deseret Peak

Little Hole

☆

Flaming Gorge National Recreation Area
shuttle car or bicycle required
day hike

Distance:	6.9 miles (plus 8.9 miles by car or bicycle)
Walking time:	3¾ hours
Elevations:	220 ft. loss Boat ramp parking area (start): 5,780 ft. Little Hole: 5,560 ft.
Trail:	Very popular, well maintained trail. Because of its popularity with fishermen the Little Hole Trail has been designated as a National Recreation Trail.
Season:	Spring, summer, fall. There is snow on the trail during the winter months.
Vicinity:	Flaming Gorge National Recreation Area, near Vernal
Maps:	Dutch John, Goslin Mountain *(USGS)* Flaming Gorge *(Trails Illustrated, #704)*
Information:	http://www.utahtrails.com/littlehole.html *(Utah Trails)* http://www.fs.fed.us/r4/ashley/ *(Ashley National Forest)* phone: (435) 784-3445 *(Flaming Gorge Ranger District)*

Drive north of Vernal on Highway 191 for 41 miles until you reach the Flaming Gorge Dam. Continue on past the dam for another 0.3 mile until you see a road leaving on the right near a sign that says "River Access". Turn here and continue another 0.9 mile to a large parking lot above the boat launching area. A short foot path descends from the parking area to the boat ramp, where the Little Hole Trail begins.

To get to Little Hole, where the hike ends, you must return to Highway 191 and continue driving north. After 2.3 miles you will come to a junction where the Little Hole Road begins. Turn right here and drive another 5.9 miles to the Little Hole parking area. This is where you should leave your shuttle car or bicycle.

The Little Hole trail is an exceedingly scenic walk that winds through the bottom of Red Canyon on the north shore of the Green River. The canyon's brilliant colors so impressed John Wesley Powell on his ex-

pedition down the Green River in 1869 that he named it the Flaming Gorge. A century later, in 1964, the Flaming Gorge Dam submerged most of Powell's spectacular canyon with water, but a small section of it, Red

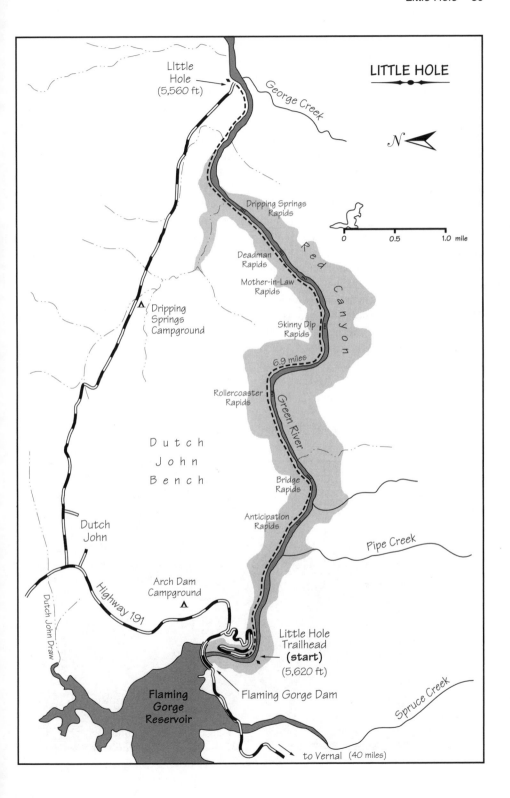

LITTLE HOLE

LIttle Hole (5,560 ft)

George Creek

N

0   0.5   1.0 mile

Dripping Springs Rapids

Red Canyon

Deadman Rapids

Mother-in-Law Rapids

Skinny Dip Rapids

Dripping Springs Campground

6.9 miles

Green River

Rollercoaster Rapids

D u t c h
J o h n
B e n c h

Bridge Rapids

Anticipation Rapids

Pipe Creek

Dutch John

Arch Dam Campground

Highway 191

Little Hole Trailhead **(start)** (5,620 ft)

Dutch John Draw

Flaming Gorge Dam

Flaming Gorge Reservoir

Spruce Creek

to Vernal (40 miles)

Canyon, still remains below the dam to remind us of how the Flaming Gorge got its name.

In the past thirty years, since the creation of the Flaming Gorge National Recreation Area, the Forest Service has developed Red Canyon as a premier sport fishing area, and you are likely to encounter dozens of fishermen along the Little Hole Trail. If you crave solitude this is the wrong hike, but, for me, watching the fly fishermen ply their skill is an added bonus. Few rivers offer a more perfect setting for fishing than the Green, and Red Canyon is kept abundantly stocked with rainbow and brown trout. Trout as large as 22 pounds have been caught here.

This hike can be done in either direction. The west-to-east route described here is best if you are hiking in the afternoon, as the sun will then be at your back. If, however, you are planning a morning hike, you can avoid having the sun in your face by starting at Little Hole rather than the dam.

From the boat ramp parking lot below

Flaming Gorge Dam a sign will direct you to a small footpath, about 0.2 mile long, that descends to the boat ramp. You will find the Little Hole trailhead just beyond the boat ramp on the downstream side. The scenery starts almost immediately, as the red shale and sandstone cliffs of the Mancos Formation soar on either side of the river to a height of about 600 feet. For the next four miles the elevation of the | *see color photos, page 170* | canyon rim steadily increases, finally reaching a height of 1000 feet above the water.

A series of small rapids breaks the monotony of the clear water, with whimsical names like Rollercoaster, Skinny Dip, and Mother-in-Law. The rapids are usually not particularly hazardous, but it is fun to watch the boaters negotiate them. After the first two miles there is a noticeable decline in the number of fishermen, but their numbers begin to pick up again along the last two miles of the trail. Finally, after six miles, the river emerges from Red Canyon and widens somewhat as it approaches Little Hole.

Red Canyon of the Green River

Jones Hole

☆ ☆ ☆   **Dinosaur National Monument**
day hike

Distance:	8.0 miles (round trip)
Walking time:	4³/₄ hours
Elevations:	540 ft. loss/gain Jones Hole Trailhead (start): 5,560 ft. Green River: 5,020 ft.
Trail:	Easy, year-round trail descending along Jones Hole Creek to the Green River.
Season:	Spring, summer, fall. Hiking is also sometimes possible in the winter, if the road is open.
Vicinity:	Dinosaur National Monument, near Vernal
Maps:	Jones Hole *(USGS)* Dinosaur National Monument *(Trails Illustrated, #220)*
Information:	http://www.utahtrails.com/joneshole.html *(Utah Trails)* http://www.nps.gov/dino/ *(Dinosaur Nat. Monument)* phone: (435) 789-2115 *(Visitor Center)*

Drive east out of Vernal on 500 North Street. The road forks about a mile from town; take the left fork and follow the signs to Jones Hole. After six miles you will pass the turn off to Island Park. Do not take this turn, but continue straight on the paved road for another 33 miles to the Jones Hole Fish Hatchery. The trail starts at the south end of the Fish Hatchery, about two hundred yards from the visitors parking area.

Jones Hole is the name given to a 2,000-foot-deep gorge that runs along the border between Utah and Colorado in Dinosaur National Monument. Jones Hole Creek, in the bottom of the gorge, is fed from a number of small springs at the head of the canyon and along its sides. The trail begins just below the first spring, at the Jones Hole Fish Hatchery, and winds pleasantly along the creek for about four miles to join the Green River in Whirlpool Canyon. The creek bed is a lush green oasis surrounded by the semi-arid land of Dinosaur National Monument. At times the trail climbs away from the water into the sagebrush and pinion-juniper forest that surrounds it, but mostly it stays very close to the canyon floor where boxelders, cottonwoods, and other water-hungry trees prevail. The creek is also an important source of water for the monument's wildlife, and it is not uncommon to see deer—especially in the early hours of the day.

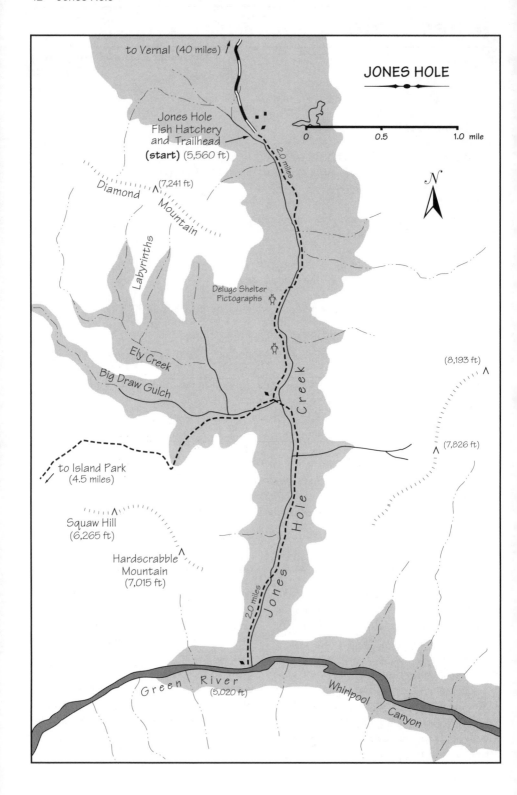

to Vernal (40 miles)

JONES HOLE

Jones Hole
Fish Hatchery
and Trailhead
(start) (5,560 ft)

0   0.5   1.0 mile

2.0 miles

N

Diamond Mountain (7,241 ft)

Labyrinths

Deluge Shelter
Pictographs

(8,193 ft)

Ely Creek

Big Draw Gulch

Creek

(7,826 ft)

to Island Park
(4.5 miles)

Jones Hole

Squaw Hill
(6,265 ft)

Hardscrabble
Mountain
(7,015 ft)

2.0 miles

Green River (5,020 ft)

Whirlpool Canyon

Jones Hole Creek, above Ely Creek

From the visitors parking area of Jones Hole Fish Hatchery walk downstream for a few hundred feet, past the fish tanks, to the southern end of the complex. Here you will see a sign on the east side of the creek marking the trailhead. The trail stays on the same side of the creek for just over a mile. For most of the way the path is very near the water, although at see color photo, page 171 one point it leaves the creek to meander briefly through the pinion-juniper forest on the left bank. The vegetation changes dramatically just a short distance from the water's edge.

After a half-hour walk the trail crosses a small footbridge, giving hikers the opportunity to see two interesting archeological sites on the west bank. Excavations at the Deluge Shelter site in 1965-67 showed that Jones Hole has been occupied intermittently by at least fifteen separate Indian cultures over the past 7000 years. The cultural layers exposed by the excavation proved to be unusually well defined, and the information gained has contributed significantly to the puzzle of America's prehistoric past.

Both of the Jones Hole archeological sites contain well preserved examples of prehistoric Indian rock art, which, although many hikers use this trail, are remarkably unvandalized. Enjoy the centuries-old art, but please watch that no one in your group does anything to deface the precious remnants of our past. Don't even touch them, as the oils in our fingers can cause significant damage.

Shortly after passing the second archeological site you will come to the confluence of Ely Creek and Jones Hole Creek. There is a small camping area here for overnighters. This is the only place in Jones Hole where camping is permitted, but permits must be obtained in advance from the Dinosaur National Monument Visitors Center. Ely Creek is also worth exploring. It flows out of an area known as the Labyrinths, a rugged maze of backcountry canyons, only

Pictographs at Deluge Shelter

about a mile northwest of the confluence.

Sharp-eyed hikers may notice a change in the geological structure of Jones Hole as they pass Ely Creek. Above this point the canyon cuts through the Weber Sandstone formation, while below Ely the canyon floor enters an older formation of limestone and shale. This 200-million-year-old sedimentary formation bears testimony to the existence of an ancient sea that once covered the area, and fossil remains of the sea's inhabitants can often be found in the limestone.

The trail ends two miles below Ely Creek where Jones Hole Creek joins the Green River. If you are hiking in the summer you will probably see at least one party of river runners here. The Green River is very popular with rafters, and Jones Hole is a favorite overnight stop. There are several camp sites nearby, but the sites are reserved for rafters and are off limits to hikers.

Island Park

An interesting extension to this hike, for those wishing to sample the semidesert en-vironment above Jones Hole, is the trail connecting Jones Hole to Island Park. This trail leaves Jones Hole from the backpacker's campground and follows Ely Creek for about a half mile. It then climbs 800 feet up the south side of Big Draw Gulch to the plateau above and continues in a generally southwesterly direction. Beyond this climb the trail is not difficult, but ample water should be carried as it is a hot, dry walk. The trail ends in Island Park near Ruple Ranch, 6.5 miles from the Ely Creek Campground. With a little advance planning a car can be spotted at Ruple Ranch for the drive back to the trailhead at Jones Hole Fish Hatchery. An 18-mile-long gravel road leads from Ruple Ranch to the paved Jones Hole Road, and from there it is another 33 miles back to the fish hatchery.

The first two miles of the trail from Jones Hole to Island Park are well defined. Unfortunately, however, the Park Service no longer maintains the trail, and in a few places above Big Draw Gulch it can be difficult to follow. If you want to do this hike I recommend you take along a compass and a good map of the area (the USGS Jones Hole and Island Park quadrangles are ideal). The area is fairly flat and obstacle-free, so loosing the trail is not a serious problem if you have a compass and a good map.

One of the things that makes the Island Park hike so interesting is the extremely large number of deer in the area—especially in the spring. In the spring of 1995 I counted more than 50 deer (mostly doe with their newborn fawns) within a mile of Ruple Ranch!

One final note: Their seems to be a large disagreement over the distance from Jones Hole to Ruple Ranch. One Park Service signs says 8.0 miles, another says 4.7 miles, and a popular map says 7.7 miles. I stand by my estimate of 6.5 miles.

Kings Peak

☆ ☆ ☆ ☆ ☆

High Uintas Wilderness Area
4-day hike

Distance:	31.6 miles (round trip)
Walking time:	day 1: 5¼ hours
	day 2: 5¼ hours
	day 3: 8½ hours
	day 4: 4 hours
Elevations:	5,080 ft. gain/loss
	Henrys Fork Trailhead (start): 9,430 ft.
	Dollar Lake: 10,785 ft.
	Gunsight Pass: 11,888 ft.
	Anderson Pass: 12,700 ft.
	Kings Peak: 13,528 ft.

Trail: The trail is well marked and easy to follow as far as Anderson Pass. There is no trail, however, for the last 0.8 mile from Anderson Pass to the summit. The final assent to the peak requires a tiring scramble up about 800 feet of talus.

Season: Midsummer to mid-fall. The upper parts of the trail are usually covered with snow from mid-November until mid-July. The most pleasant time for the climb is late August, when the days are still relatively long but the meadows have dried out and the mosquitoes have abated.

Vicinity: North slope of the High Uintas Wilderness Area, near Evanston, Wyoming

Maps: Gilbert Peak, Bridger Lake, Mount Powell, Kings Peak *(USGS)*
High Uintas Wilderness *(Trails Illustrated, #711)*

Information: http://www.utahtrails.com/kingspeak.html *(Utah Trails)*
http://www.fs.fed.us/wcnf/ *(Wasatch-Cache Nat. Forest)*
phone: (307) 782-6555 *(Mountain View Ranger District)*

Drive east of Evanston, Wyoming, on I-80 for 35 miles, then take exit 39 south onto Highway 414. Drive south on Highway 414 for 6 miles to the town of Mountain View, where you must turn right on Highway 410 towards the farming village of Robertson. 6.8 miles from Mountain View, just before you reach Robertson, you will come to a junction where Highway 410 makes an abrupt *bend to the west and a wide gravel road continues straight ahead to the south. Continue south at this point on the gravel road. 12.3 miles after leaving the highway you will come to a major fork in the road. The right fork leads to China Meadows while the left fork leads to Henrys Fork Trailhead. Bear left at this point and continue for another 10.7 miles, following the signs to the Henrys Fork Trailhead.*

As you probably know, Kings Peak is the highest point in Utah, and as you might imagine, this hike is a very popular one. According to Forest Service estimates the Henrys Fork Basin receives about 5,000 visitors annually. Many come for the express purpose of climbing Utah's highest mountain, but many more come just to enjoy the abundant scenic beauty of the area and perhaps do a little fishing in the basin's half dozen lakes. Late summer is the most popular time to visit Henrys Fork, but some visitors also enjoy cross country skiing in the basin in the winter months. Henrys Fork Trailhead is one of the few trailheads on the north slope of the High Uintas that is accessible all year round.

Although the climb to the top of Kings Peak is very strenuous it is not technically difficult, and | see color photos, page 167 | about the only requisite for the trip is good physical condition. Furthermore, the view from the top is extraordinary. Even if it were not the highest point in the state, the assent of Kings Peak would still be one of Utah's best hikes.

Henrys Fork is the closest trailhead to Kings Peak; hence it is the most popular place to begin the hike. But many variations of this hike are also possible. If you spend an hour on the summit in mid-August you will probably meet other climbers who have walked up from every direction. Many hikers approach Kings Peak from the south slope along Yellowstone Creek or the Uinta River. Others come from Hoop Lake or Spirit Lake on the eastern side of the Uintas. And a surprising number of people begin their hike at Mirror Lake, 40 miles to

the west. Looking down from the top with a good pair of binoculars you can usually see hikers far below inching their way east or west along the Highline Trail towards Anderson Pass, just north of the summit.

Day 1 (7.1 miles)

From the trailhead parking area the trail follows along the west side of Henrys Fork, climbing ever so gently at a grade you will hardly notice. The creek, usually about 20 feet below the trail, is pristine, and the forest is densely wooded with lodgepole pine. It is a very pleasant walk.

The first major point of interest along the way is Alligator Lake, located at the end of a short spur trail about an hour and ten minutes from the trailhead. Watch for a large pile of rocks on the south side of a wooden boardwalk that crosses a small drainage. At that point you will see the trail to Alligator Lake branching off to the right of the main trail. The Lake is 0.4 mile up the drainage at the end of the spur. Alligator is a surprising large lake, about 600 yards long by 150 yards wide. There are a number of fine campsites on the lake's south shore, and it is a good place to spend the night if you are getting off to a late start.

5.5 miles from the trailhead the trail breaks out of the trees on the northern end of a large meadow. There is a major trail junction here between the Henrys Fork Trail, which runs south along Henrys Fork, and the North Slope Trail, which crosses it in an east-west direction. The junction is called Elkhorn Crossing.

At Elkhorn Crossing you have a choice of two trails: you can either proceed south on the Henrys Fork Trail or you can turn right

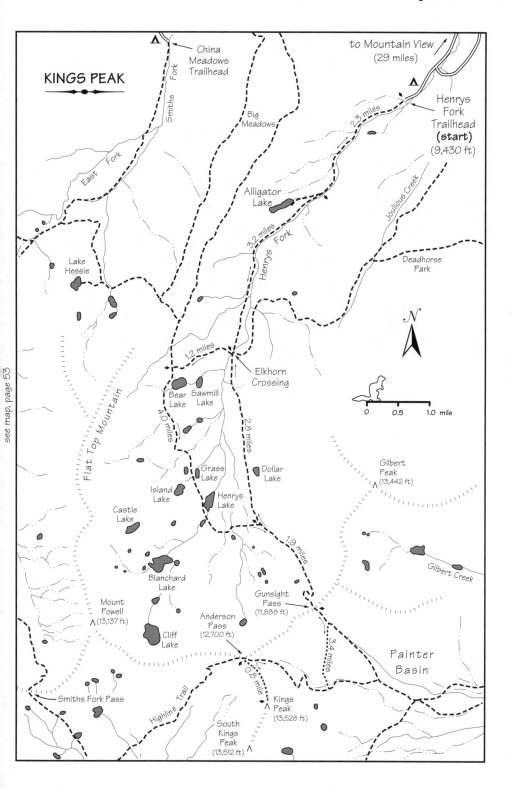

KINGS PEAK

China Meadows Trailhead

to Mountain View (29 miles)

Henrys Fork Trailhead **(start)** (9,430 ft)

2.3 miles

Smiths Fork

Big Meadows

East Fork

Joulious Creek

Alligator Lake

3.2 miles

Henrys Fork

Deadhorse Park

Lake Hessie

N

see map, page 53

Flat Top Mountain

1.2 miles

Elkhorn Crossing

Bear Lake   Sawmill Lake

0   0.5   1.0 mile

4.0 miles

2.8 miles

Gilbert Peak (13,442 ft)

Grass Lake   Dollar Lake

Island Lake

Henrys Lake

Castle Lake

1.9 miles

Gilbert Creek

Blanchard Lake

Gunsight Pass (11,888 ft)

Mount Powell (13,137 ft)

Cliff Lake

Anderson Pass (12,700 ft)

3.4 miles

Painter Basin

Smiths Fork Pass

Highline Trail

0.8 mile

Kings Peak (13,528 ft)

South Kings Peak (13,512 ft)

Unnamed lake on the West Side Loop Trail

and follow the North Slope Trail for a short distance to the West Side Loop Trail. The two routes converge again just below Gunsight Pass; hence you can get to Kings Peak by following either trail. For the sake of diversity I suggest you take the West Side Loop Trail on your way up the peak and use the Henrys Fork Trail for your return trip. If you choose to do this, then turn right at Elkhorn Crossing and proceed west on the North Slope Trail (Forest Service Trail #105).

About half an hour after leaving Elkhorn Crossing you will arrive at the West Side Loop Trail junction. Turn south here and proceed towards Bear Lake and Henrys Fork Lake. There are several signs in this area indicating that you are now on the Highline Trail, but these signs are in error. The real Highline Trail (Forest Service Trail #25) is still many miles to the south. You won't reach it until you have crossed the Uinta divide at Gunsight Pass.

Five minutes after leaving the junction

between the North Slope Trail and the West Side Loop Trail you should see the calm waters of Bear Lake flickering through the trees on the left. There is no trail to the lake, but it is only 100 yards off the trail. There are many good campsites around Bear Lake and it is a fine place to stop for the day. You can also visit Sawmill Lake, a slightly smaller lake 200 yards farther down the drainage from the east end of Bear Lake.

Day 2 (6.8 miles)

Between Bear Lake and the bottom of Gunsight Pass you will pass by several more picturesque lakes, the largest of which is Henrys Fork Lake. 0.3 miles after leaving Henrys Fork Lake the trail passes by a tiny cabin that has been used for many years as a sheep herders' bivouac. Henrys Fork Basin is heavily grazed during the summer months and you will almost certainly see sheep while you are there. Many hikers are offended by the sights and sounds of domestic animals in this high wilderness valley. They do contaminate the water sources and destroy the wildflowers, but for me the sounds of their bells and their baa-a-a-as drifting through the alpine valley seem to add a certain tranquility to the pastoral scene.

Finally, 3.8 miles from Bear Lake, the West Side Loop Trail crosses Henrys Fork Basin to end at Henrys Fork Trail. The elevation at this point is 11,000 feet, just above timber line, and there are few trees. A mile southeast you can see Gunsight Pass, a deep notch in the Uinta Crest where the trail crosses to the South Slope. And south, above the basin you can see Anderson Pass and Kings Peak. Your route to the summit will be along the ridge south of Anderson Pass.

Next the trail climbs slowly up the east side of Henrys Fork Basin until it reaches the top of Gunsight Pass. If it is late in the day you might want to establish a camp on

Henrys Fork Basin and Gunsight Pass

the northern side of Gunsight Pass rather than continuing into Painter Basin. There is a flat grassy area beside a small pond just below the northern side of the pass. The elevation here is 11,460 feet, about 430 feet below the top of the pass. If time permits, however, I suggest you continue another 2.0 miles across the pass and into Painter Basin where you will find a better place to camp.

About 0.6 mile below the south side of Gunsight Pass you will see a less distinct trail veering off to the right along the foot of the cliffs. The main trail continues southeast across Painter Basin for 1.0 mile before doubling back to the west, so you can save a lot of time by taking the less distinct shortcut south through the basin below the bottom of the cliffs. This shortcut trail eventually fades and disappears, but that isn't a problem. Just continue due south in the grassy meadow along the base of the talus slope. About 0.7 mile after leaving the main trail you will see a fresh water spring flowing out of the rocks at the edge of the meadow. This area is an excellent place to stop and make camp for the night.

Day 3 (10.1 miles)

Painter Basin is only 2.9 miles from the top of Kings Peak, but you still have a 2,120-foot elevation gain to deal with as well as some off-trail scrambling. There is no trail for the last 0.8 mile. Also, remember you can't walk as fast at the high altitude. Leave your packs at your camp and get an early start so you will have plenty of time for a leisurely lunch at the top.

From the spring continue walking south along the western side of Painter Basin, across a small drainage, until you reach a place where there is grass growing on the rocky slopes above you and there appears to be an easy way up. Turn west here and start working your way up the southern side of

Painter Basin

the small drainage. After about 0.3 mile you should run into the Highline Trail, and from there it is only 1.6 miles further to the top of Anderson Pass.

At Anderson Pass you must leave the trail and start picking your way up the ridge to the top of the peak. There are cliffs on the west side of the ridge, but the slopes are more gradual on the east. You will see occasional cairns, but they really don't do much good. It is pretty obvious where you are going, and there is really no easy way. It is just a matter of making your way slowly upward over the jumble of jagged boulders, and if you are persistent the goal will be reached in about an hour.

One of the most astonishing features of the view from Kings Peak is the vastness of the panorama. Other than a few thread-like trails in the basins below there are virtually no signs of human activity. The nearest road is ten miles away and the nearest town is twice that distance. Another striking fea-

ture is the number of lakes that can be seen. More than a dozen large lakes in Garfield, Henrys Fork, Atwood, and Painter Basins are visible. But probably the most notable characteristic is the amount of land that is above timberline (about 11,000 ft.) and devoid of trees. In fact the Uintas have more square miles of land in the Arctic-Alpine Tundra Life Zone than any other mountain range, outside Alaska, in the United States.

The descent from Kings Peak back to Anderson Pass is even more tricky than the assent, so be careful. There are many loose rocks, and I can't think of a worse place to break a leg. Once you reach the pass, however, it is a very pleasant walk back to Painter Basin. Some people spend a second night at the Painter Basin campsite, but if you want to complete the trip in the allotted four days you should pack your belongings and walk down to Dollar Lake for the third night.

Dollar Lake is probably the most beautiful of all the lakes in Henrys Fork Basin.

Unfortunately it is heavily used by campers, and many other hiking books encourage you to camp elsewhere. But if you can find a site it really is an exquisite place to spend the night. The lake is surrounded by a grove of tall Engelmann spruce, and there is a marvelous afternoon view of Kings Peak from its southern shore.

The lake is not visible from the trail and there is no established trail leading to it; consequently it is easy to miss. When you reach the trail junction below Gunsight Pass where the West Side Loop Trail departs, make a note of the time and continue straight ahead on the Henrys Fork Trail. After about 15 minutes you will leave the meadow and enter into a large grove of spruce. Within ten minutes after entering the trees you should see one or two small cairns on the right side of the trail. Leave the trail at this point and walk due east for 200 yards and you will run into the lake. The main trail continues north for another 300 yards before entering the meadow again. If you come to the point where the trail leaves the trees it means you have gone too far.

Day 4 (7.6 miles)

From Dollar Lake back to the trailhead is only 7.6 miles and it is downhill all the way. There are no more lakes to explore, but there is plenty of otherwise fine scenery. The first 2.0 miles follow the east side of the meadow to Elkhorn Crossing. This is prime moose habitat and you probably have at least a fifty-fifty chance of seeing one if you are observant. At Elkhorn Crossing the trail crosses to the west side of Henrys Fork. Look for the footbridge about 100 yards downstream from the point where the main trail fords the creek. Once you are back on the west side of Henrys Fork you can simply retrace your original footsteps back to the trailhead.

Kings Peak, from Anderson Pass

Red Castle Lakes

☆ ☆ ☆ ☆   **High Uintas Wilderness Area**
                                                        3-day hike

Distance:	25.0 miles (round trip)
Walking time:	day 1: 7³/₄ hours
	day 2: 3³/₄ hours
	day 3: 6¹/₄ hours
Elevations:	3,010 ft. gain/loss
	Cache Trailhead (start): 9,340 ft.
	Bald Mountain Ridge: 11,530 ft.
	Lower Red Castle Lake: 10,760 ft.
	Red Castle Lake: 11,300 ft.
Trail:	Trail is generally well marked and easy to follow.
Season:	Midsummer to mid-fall. The trails around the Red Castle Lakes are usually covered with snow from mid-November until July.
Vicinity:	North slope of the High Uintas Wilderness Area, near Evanston, Wyoming
Maps:	Lyman Lake, Mount Powell *(USGS)*
	High Uintas Wilderness *(Trails Illustrated, #711)*
Information:	http://www.utahtrails.com/redcastle.html *(Utah Trails)*
	http://www.fs.fed.us/wcnf/ *(Wasatch-Cache Nat. Forest)*
	phone: (307) 789-3194 *(Evanston Ranger District)*

Drive west from Kamas on the Mirror Lake Highway (Highway 150) toward Evanston, Wyoming. After driving 47 miles you will pass the Bear River Ranger Station on your right, and another 2.2 miles will bring you to a well marked gravel road leading to Lyman Lake and the Blacks Fork River. This is Forest Road No. 58, popularly known as the North Slope Road. Turn right here and stay on Road No. 58 for the next 18.6 miles, following the signs to East Fork Blacks Fork. The road is used by logging trucks and is badly washboarded in a few places, but it is still suitable for ordinary cars. After 18.6 miles you will see another road branching off to the right (Road No. 65) with a sign that says "East Fork Blacks Fork Trailhead, 6 miles". Turn right here and drive for 4.9 miles to another sign that says "Bear River-Smiths Fork Trail". This trail crossing, sometimes called the Cache Trailhead, is where the hike begins. The small dirt road on the left leads to a convenient parking area near a gravel pit about 100 yards from the main road. The trail runs about 150 feet to the south of the gravel pit.

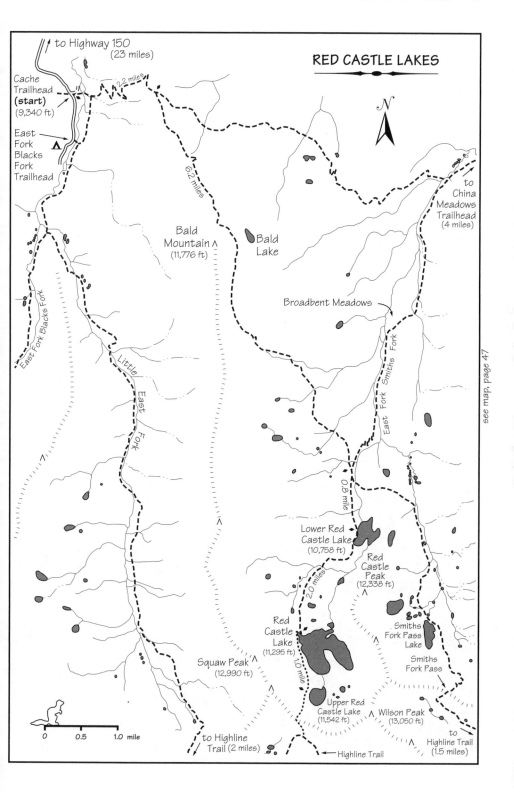

to Highway 150
(23 miles)

RED CASTLE LAKES

Cache
Trailhead
(start)
(9,340 ft)

0.2 miles

N

East
Fork
Blacks
Fork
Trailhead

to
China
Meadows
Trailhead
(4 miles)

6.2 miles

East Fork Blacks Fork

Bald
Mountain ∧
(11,776 ft)

Bald
Lake

Broadbent Meadows

East Fork Smiths Fork

Little East Fork

see map, page 47

0.8 mile

Lower Red
Castle Lake
(10,758 ft)

Red
Castle
Peak
(12,338 ft)

2.0 miles

Red
Castle
Lake
(11,295 ft)

Smiths
Fork Pass
Lake

1.0 mile

Smiths
Fork Pass

Squaw Peak ∧
(12,990 ft)

0   0.5   1.0 mile

Upper Red
Castle Lake
(11,542 ft)

∧ Wilson Peak
(13,050 ft)

to Highline
Trail (2 miles)

to
Highline Trail
(1.5 miles)

Highline Trail

Hikers planning a trip to the scenic Red Castle Lakes on the north slope of the High Uintas generally have two different trails to choose from: the East Fork Smiths Fork Trail or the Bald Mountain Trail. The first route, beginning at China Meadows and following the East Fork Smiths Fork all the way to its source, is the most popular route. The East Fork Smiths Fork Trail is very well maintained and has a total elevation gain (to Lower Red Castle Lake) of only about 1,280 feet. The Bald Mountain Route, on the other hand, is much more strenuous. It begins at East Fork Blacks Fork and climbs over Bald Mountain Ridge before reaching the lower lake, achieving an elevation gain of 2,190 feet. Both trails are within a quarter mile of the same length.

I have chosen here to describe the Bald Mountain route to the Red Castle Lakes, primarily because it is the most scenic of the two. The additional 900 feet of elevation gain is compensated for by the fine views

that can be had from Bald Mountain Ridge. The trail follows the grassy, treeless ridge at an elevation of 11,500 feet for almost two miles before dropping down to the East Fork Smiths Fork drainage, and Red Castle Peak occupies a prominent place on the skyline for almost the entire distance.

The most interesting way to see the Red Castle Lakes is to hike in on the Bald Mountain Trail and hike out on the East Fork Smiths Fork Trail to China Meadows. Not many people do this, however, because the two trailheads are 50 miles apart. (See pages 45-46 for instructions on how to get to China Meadows.)

Day 1 (9.2 miles)

From Cache Trailhead the Bear River-Smiths Fork Trail heads east and, after about 200 yards, crosses the East Fork Blacks Fork Creek. It will be necessary to get your feet wet here, as there is no bridge and no stepping stones crossing the creek. Normally

Bald Mountain Ridge

the water is only ankle deep, but if there has been a lot of rain you might want to consider beginning your hike 0.6 miles farther down the road at the East Fork Blacks Fork Trailhead, where the Forest Service has constructed a bridge. There is a convenient connecting trail joining the east side of the bridge with the Bear River-Smiths Fork Trail. Of course, if you do this the hike will be 0.6 miles longer.

Once it crosses the river the trail almost immediately starts upward, gaining a little over a thousand feet in the next two miles. After reaching the top of the ridge it temporarily levels out and meets the Bald Mountain trail junction. Bear to the right here, as indicated by the sign. Soon the path begins to climb again and within a mile you will be above timberline. Bald Mountain (11,776 ft.) is the large, gently sloping dome in front of you.

At its highest point the trail passes within 0.3 miles of the top of Bald Mountain. If you want to make a detour to the summit it is an easy off-trail walk, with only 250 feet of elevation gain. On the other side of the trail, about 300 yards to the east is Bald Lake. The lake is so close it almost seems as though you could hit it from the trail with a rock, but because it is 450 feet lower it is seldom visited.

From Bald Mountain the trail continues to meander along the top of Bald Mountain Ridge for another 1.3 miles before dropping into the East Fork Smiths Fork drainage. The remaining three miles to Lower Red Castle Lake is a beautiful walk through scattered forest and meadow land, with lots of water and good camping spots. If you got off to a late start you won't have any problem finding a place to spend the night. This is also a summer grazing area for sheep ranchers, and you will probably see signs of sheep if not the sheep themselves.

Finally, a mile after the trail reaches East Fork Smiths Fork, you will come to Lower Red Castle Lake. There are several good camping spots near the trail on the west side of the lake, and the views of Red Castle Peak are fabulous. After supper you will probably want to spend an see color photos, page 166 hour beside the lake watching the reflections while the last rays of sunset transform the Castle into a glowing ember of red.

Day 2 (6.0 miles)

From Lower Red Castle Lake it is a pleasant 6-mile round trip hike to the two upper Red Castle Lakes. The scenery is excellent, but there are no good camping spots at Red Castle or Upper Red Castle Lake, so leave your camp at the lower lake. The trail continues up the west side of Lower Red Castle Lake, then bends around the west side of the Castle, finally reaching Red Castle Lake on its northern side. Red Castle Lake is 537 feet higher than Lower Red Castle which places it well above timberline. Consequently, there are no trees whatsoever around the higher lake.

From this vantage point you can see that the Red Castle Peak is actually the end of a short spur that extends northward from Wilson Peak on the Uinta Crest. The forma-

Sheep herder on Bald Mountain Ridge

tion seems oddly out of place, because although the Uinta Crest is composed almost entirely of gray colored Precambrian quartzite the Red Castle is composed primarily of sandstone and shale based material. As a result the castle-shaped peak is not only a different color than the other surrounding peaks, but it has eroded into an entirely different form. Because of the contrast, this rugged peak is probably the most picturesque summit in the entire range.

On the northwestern corner of Red Castle Lake you will find a well cairned trail leading up the talus slope toward Upper Red Castle Lake. The route is not difficult, and the elevation gain to Upper Red Castle is only 247 feet. Upper Red Castle Lake is a small, rocky lake, about 200 yards in diameter. It is fed entirely from the melting snows on the higher slopes of Red Castle Basin and it is not very deep; hence its size varies a great deal from year to year.

The primitive trail from Red Castle Lake does not stop at Upper Red Castle Lake, but continues upward to a small pass on the ridge 628 feet above Upper Red Castle. The extensive Highline Trail is only 0.2 mile south of this low point on the ridge; hence there are many possibilities for extended backpacking trips from Upper Red Castle Lake. Squaw Pass, for instance, is 3.5 miles west along the Highline Trail, and from there it is possible to walk back along the Little East Fork Trail to Cache Trailhead where the hike began. Another possibility: Kings Peak, the highest point in Utah, is only ten miles east along the Highline Trail.

Day 3 (9.2 miles)

The hike back to Cache Trailhead from Lower Red Castle Lake is just the reverse of Day 1. The return is much less tiring, however, since the elevation gain required to get back on Bald Mountain Ridge is only 770 feet, and from there the hike is all downhill.

The Red Castle, behind Red Castle Lake

Amethyst Lake

Distance:	13.0 miles (round trip)
Walking time:	day 1: 4¼ hours day 2: 4 hours
Elevations:	1,950 ft. gain/loss Christmas Meadows Trailhead (start): 8,790 ft. Amethyst Meadows: 10,360 ft. Amethyst Lake: 10,740 ft.
Trail:	Reasonably good trail most of the way, but very rocky in places. Can also be muddy in spots, especially in the early summer before all of the snow has melted. A compass is useful for finding Ostler Lake.
Season:	Midsummer through mid-fall. The higher parts of the trail are usually covered with snow from November until mid-July.
Vicinity:	The High Uintas Wilderness Area, near Evanston, Wyoming
Maps:	Christmas Meadows *(USGS)* High Uintas Wilderness *(Trails Illustrated, #711)*
Information:	http://www.utahtrails.com/amethyst.html *(Utah Trails)* http://www.fs.fed.us/wcnf/ *(Wasatch-Cache Nat. Forest)* phone: (307) 789-3194 *(Evanston Ranger District)*

Drive east from Kamas on Highway 150 towards Evanston, Wyoming. 6 miles from Kamas you will pass a Forest Service booth where you must purchase a recreation pass to hike in the area ($3.00/day for each vehicle). You will pass the Mirror Lake turnoff about 31.5 miles from Kamas. Continue on past this turnoff for another 14.3 miles to a small bridge where Highway 150 crosses *the Bear River. 0.4 mile beyond the bridge, on the right, you will see the road to Christmas Meadows Campground. (Do not be confused by the turnout to Stillwater Campground, nearer the bridge.) Take the Christmas Meadows turnout and drive 4.3 miles to the end of the road, where you will see the Christmas Meadows (Stillwater) Trailhead and parking area.*

Easily accessible from Salt Lake City, the hike to Amethyst Lake and Basin is probably the most popular hike into the rugged, north-slope drainages of the High Uintas. The Uinta Mountains are bisected by a long, winding spine of Precambrian rock that runs for about a hundred miles in an east-west direction across northern Utah. The north and south

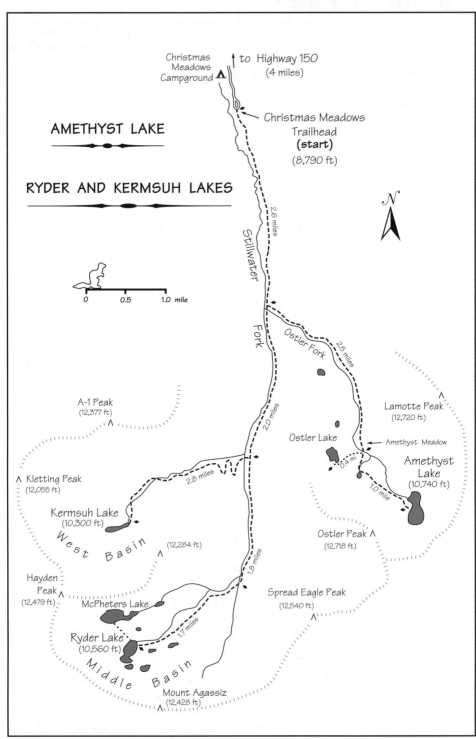

AMETHYST LAKE

RYDER AND KERMSUH LAKES

Christmas Meadows Campground

to Highway 150 (4 miles)

Christmas Meadows Trailhead **(start)** (8,790 ft)

Stillwater

N

2.6 miles

Fork

Ostler Fork

2.5 miles

A-1 Peak (12,377 ft)

Lamotte Peak (12,720 ft)

Amethyst Meadow

2.0 miles

Ostler Lake

Amethyst Lake (10,740 ft)

Kletting Peak (12,055 ft)

0.4 mi

2.8 miles

1.0 mile

Kermsuh Lake (10,300 ft)

West Basin

(12,284 ft)

Ostler Peak ∧ (12,718 ft)

Hayden Peak (12,479 ft)

McPheters Lake

1.8 miles

Spread Eagle Peak (12,540 ft)

Ryder Lake (10,560 ft)

1.7 miles

Middle Basin

Mount Agassiz (12,428 ft)

0   0.5   1.0 mile

see map, page 78

facing slopes of this ridge are punctuated by more than twenty glacier-carved valleys that all end abruptly against the quartzite cliffs of the central spine. It is in the back of one of these glaciated valleys, the Stillwater Drainage, that Amethyst Basin and Amethyst Lake, are located. There are several other alpine lakes within the Stillwater Drainage, but Amethyst Lake is the largest.

Day 1 (5.9 miles)

For the first two miles the trail to Amethyst Lake meanders along the east side of Christmas Meadows, a pleasant, open grassland surrounding Stillwater Creek. This is a popular fishing area, and there are usually a few fly fishermen along the creek. The meadow is also favored by grazing animals, and it is not uncommon to see deer and moose grazing nearby. So many people visit Christmas Meadows now that in the last 20 years the moose have become almost tame.

Shortly after leaving Christmas Meadows you will encounter a forest service sign

Amethyst Meadow and Ostler Peak

informing you that you are entering the High Uintas Wilderness Area, and five minutes later the trail forks. A smaller sign has been nailed to a tree at the fork instructing hikers that they should take the left fork, leading away from Stillwater Creek, to reach Amethyst Lake.

Soon after leaving Stillwater Creek the trail abruptly becomes much steeper, gaining 600 feet in the first half mile. The route is also very rocky here, and hikers carrying a backpack should take care not to twist an ankle. The monotony of the tiring climb is broken by several picturesque cascades along Ostler Creek only a few feet from the trail. After the first half mile the grade decreases, and the trail settles down to a more gradual but steady climb upward. Occasionally the path breaks briefly out of the trees to give hikers fine views of Ostler and LaMotte Peaks, which lie just above the lake. Then, 2.5 miles after leaving Stillwater Creek, the trail passes Amethyst Meadow, a picturebook wetland with a stunning view of Ostler Peak on its south side.

Amethyst Meadow is an ideal place to make camp, and I suggest you pitch your tent here. Although the lake itself is only another mile up the trail, it is much harder to find good camp sites at Amethyst Lake. Furthermore, you are more apt to have a good night's sleep at the meadow, which is 400 feet lower and better protected than the lake. In consideration of others, however, please pitch your tent at least a few hundred feet from the trail and away from the water.

You will probably have a little time left for some afternoon exploring after you have selected a camp site and taken off your packs. I suggest you save Amethyst Lake for the morning and check out Ostler Lake. If you have your camera along you can get a magnificent picture of Ostler Peak from across Ostler Lake in the late afternoon sun.

At the edge of Amethyst Meadow, just beyond the point where the trail crosses

Ostler Peak, behind Ostler Lake (mid-June)

Ostler Creek, you will see a sign that says "Ostler Lake, ¹/₂ mile". Unfortunately there is no reliable trail to Ostler Lake, but it isn't too hard to find if you have a compass. From the sign, head straight into the woods along a compass bearing of about 240 degrees (slightly south of magnetic west). After walking about 0.3 mile and gaining about 240 feet of elevation you will cross a rocky ridge and be greeted by Ostler Lake. The lake is roughly circular in shape, about 700 feet in diameter. If you can arrange to be on the north shore of the lake about an hour before the sun goes down, and if the wind is calm, you will see an unforgettable reflected view of Ostler Peak in the shaded water.

Day 2 (7.1 miles)

Before returning to the trailhead you will want to visit Amethyst Lake, the highlight of the trip. Leave your packs in the meadow; the lake is only 30 minutes away and you can pick them up on the way back down. After the trail crosses Ostler Creek it con-

tinues south for about 0.2 mile along the west side of a smaller stream. Don't cross the stream until you arrive at the unnamed lake from which the stream flows. This small but scenic lake (400 feet in diameter) is also a good place to camp if you prefer to spend the night next to a lake. Upon reaching the unnamed lake the trail crosses the stream and heads east into the basin. Amethyst Lake is about 0.8 mile further. The trail may be hard to follow in the early summer when snow covers parts of it, but don't worry too much about staying on the trail. Just proceed into the basin, keeping the talus slopes of Mount Ostler on your right, and as the valley gets narrower you will soon run into the lake. Amethyst Lake lies in

see color photo, page 165

the extreme southern corner of Amethyst Basin at an elevation of 10,740 feet. The lake is quite large—850 feet across and a half mile long—and is enclosed on three sides by the rocky slopes of the 12,000-feet-high Ostler-LaMotte ridge.

Ryder and Kermsuh Lakes

☆ ☆ ☆ ☆   **High Uintas Wilderness Area**
                                                          3-day hike

Distance:	22.6 miles (round trip)
Walking time:	day 1: 6¹/₂ hours day 2: 5 hours day 3: 4 hours
Elevations:	1,770 ft. gain/loss Christmas Meadows Trailhead (start): 8,790 ft. Ryder Lake: 10,560 ft. Kermsuh Lake: 10,300 ft.
Trail:	Good trail, but very rocky in places. Can also be muddy in spots, especially in the early summer before all of the snow has melted. A compass is useful for finding McPheters Lake.
Season:	Midsummer through mid-fall. The higher parts of the trail are usually covered with snow from November through mid-July.
Vicinity:	The High Uintas Wilderness Area, near Evanston, Wyoming
Maps:	Christmas Meadows, Hayden Peak *(USGS)* High Uintas Wilderness *(Trails Illustrated, #711)*
Information:	http://www.utahtrails.com/ryder.html *(Utah Trails)* http://www.fs.fed.us/wcnf/ *(Wasatch-Cache Nat. Forest)* phone: (307) 789-3194 *(Evanston Ranger District)*

Drive east from Kamas on Highway 150 towards Evanston, Wyoming. 6 miles from Kamas you will pass a Forest Service booth where you must purchase a recreation pass to hike in the area ($3.00/day for each vehicle). You will pass the Mirror Lake turnoff about 31.5 miles from Kamas. Continue on past this *turnoff for another 14.3 miles to a small bridge where Highway 150 crosses the Bear River. 0.4 mile beyond the bridge, on the right, you will see the road to Christmas Meadows Campground. (Do not be confused by the turnout to Stillwater Campground, nearer the bridge.) Take the Christmas Meadows turnout and drive 4.3 miles to the end of the road, where you will see the Christmas Meadows (Stillwater) Trailhead and parking area.*

Ryder and Kermsuh Lakes are the other two major lakes, besides Amethyst Lake, that lie within the Stillwater Drainage of the High Uintas Wilderness Area. When ancient gla- ciers were carving the glove-shaped valley during the past ice age, three large fingers were gouged out of its southern flanks. To- day we call these depressions Amethyst Basin, West Basin, and Middle Basin. These high mountain basins became natural places for the formation of lakes when the glaciers melted; hence the presence of Ryder, Kermsuh, and Amethyst lakes. Amethyst Lake, of course, is located in Amethyst Basin. Kermsuh Lake is in West Basin and Ryder is in Middle Basin. All are surrounded almost entirely by the billion-year-old Precambrian quartzite cliffs that define the Uinta Crest.

see map, page 58

Day 1 (8.1 miles)

For the first 2.6 miles the trail to Kermsuh and Ryder Lakes is the same as the trail to Amethyst Lake (page 57). The path winds lazily along the eastern side of Christmas Meadows. Moose are common in this area, and if you gaze out into the meadow from time to time there is a good chance of seeing at least a moose cow or young bull. Don't count on seeing an older bull, however, as they are much more reclusive than the younger males. There are also a lot of beaver in the meadow as evidenced by the fallen aspen along the way. Beaver seem to prefer aspen to the other trees—probably because the wood is softer and less resinous.

After about two miles Christmas Meadows and most of the quaking aspen are left behind; the canyon floor narrows, and the creek begins to run a little faster. At this point the forest is predominantly lodgepole pine, with some scattered Engelmann spruce. Soon you will encounter a forest service sign informing you that you have crossed the northern boundary of the High Uintas Wilderness Area, and a few minutes later you will see the trail to Amethyst Lake leaving on the left. Keep to the right here, continuing to follow along the left bank of the Stillwater Creek.

The trail continues on for another 2.0 miles, climbing very gradually along the canyon floor until it comes to the next trail junction. As you walk you will begin to see glimpses of A-1 Peak through the trees on your right and Mount Agassiz straight ahead. These rocky peaks, reaching 3,000 feet above the Stillwater Creek, are a preview of what lies ahead. Finally, at a point that is directly magnetic east of A-1 Peak, the trail forks again and a small sign on a tree indicates the way to Kermsuh Lake on the right. You should make a mental note of this trail junction because you will be taking the Kermsuh Lake trail on the return from Ryder, and it is easy to miss the sign when walking in the opposite direction. For now, however, continue straight ahead along the creek.

The trail continues for another 1.8 miles beyond the Kermsuh Lake trail junction before leaving Stillwater Creek. Finally, at an elevation of 9,870 feet, the path crosses the creek and begins climbing for the last 1.7 miles into the Middle Basin. But when you reach this point you will probably want to pause for a while before continuing because the scenery is delightful. A clearing in the forest presents you with an marvelous view of Mount Agassiz across a grassy meadow. If it is late summer the meadow will be filled with wildflowers.

From Stillwater Creek the trail climbs rather steeply for 0.5 mile, then levels out for another beautiful, gentle walk through the high alpine meadows towards the back of the basin. It is a stunning approach to the lake. For almost 360 degrees around you you can see the rocky cliffs that surround Middle Basin, and as you progress westward you will see Hayden Peak rising up on your right. Finally, after passing several ponds, you will cross a small rise in the land to see the large lake in front of you. Ryder Lake is some 600 feet wide

see color photos, page 165

and a third off a mile long. It is surrounded by Engelmann spruce, and there are some very nice camping sites on the eastern side. Frequently there are no other people camping at the lake, and if you are there on one of those days it will feel as if you own the entire Middle Basin.

Day 2 (7.1 miles)

If you have time after breaking camp, you should take a short side hike to McPheters Lake, only 0.4 mile northwest of Ryder. If you have a compass, select a heading due northwest of Ryder. If you don't have a compass just head for the lowest point in the ridge east of Hayden Peak. You should see the lake after a fifteen-minute walk and an elevation gain of about 240 feet. McPheters, about the same size as Ryder, is reputed to be deeper and there are said to be some large fish in the bottom of the Lake. There are not many trees around the lake, however, and the camping is far nicer at Ryder.

From the Middle Basin you must backtrack to Stillwater Creek and down to the Kermsuh Lake Trail, which you passed on the way to Ryder. Again, the trail to Kermsuh Lake rises rather steeply for about 0.5

mile after leaving Stillwater, but soon settles down to a very pleasant walk through a series of meadows to the back of West Basin. Finally, 2.8 miles from Stillwater Creek and 920 feet higher in elevation, you will come to Kermsuh Lake. Kermsuh is somewhat smaller than either Ryder or McPheters Lakes—about 400 feet wide and 1700 feet long. There are no camp sites here quite as nice as those at Ryder; you may prefer to camp in one of the meadows you passed just below Kermsuh. There is, however, a marvelous view of Hayden Peak from Kermsuh. Although you can't see it, McPheters Lake is only a mile away on the other side of the ridge between West Basin and Middle Basin.

Day 3 (7.4 miles)

From Kermsuh Lake it is an easy downhill walk back to Stillwater Creek and on through Christmas Meadows to the trailhead. The total distance is 7.4 miles, and the elevation loss is 1,510 feet.

Mount Agassiz above Stillwater Fork

Brown Duck Mountain Loop

☆ ☆

High Uintas Wilderness Area
bicycle useful
4-day hike

Distance: 34.0 miles (loop)

Walking time: day 1: 5³/₄ hours
                  day 2: 4³/₄ hours
                  day 3: 6¹/₄ hours
                  day 4: 6¹/₂ hours

Elevations:

4,320 ft. gain/loss	
Lake Fork Trailhead (start):	8,200 ft.
Atwine Lake:	10,160 ft.
Cleveland Pass:	11,200 ft.
Tworoose Pass:	10,660 ft.

Trail: The trails are generally well maintained and well marked.

Season: Midsummer to mid-fall. Because of the high elevations, the trails are usually covered with snow from mid-November until July.

Vicinity: High Uintas Wilderness Area, near Duchesne

Maps: Kidney Lake, Tworoose Pass, Explorer Peak, Oweep Creek *(USGS)*
High Uintas Wilderness *(Trails Illustrated, #711)*

Information: http://www.utahtrails.com/brownduck.html *(Utah Trails)*
http://www.fs.fed.us/r4/ashley/ *(Ashley National Forest)*
phone: (435) 722-5018 *(Roosevelt Ranger District)*

Take Highway 40 east of Heber for 70 miles (or Highway 191 north of Helper for 44 miles) until you reach the town of Duchesne. From Duchesne take Highway 87 north for 16 miles, then turn left on the paved road leading to Mountain Home and Moon Lake. The road ends at the Moon Lake Campground 34 miles from Duchesne.

The Brown Duck Trail leaves Lake Fork Trail just outside the Moon Lake Campground, and ideally the Lake Fork Trailhead would also be located adjacent to the campground. But because of the large number of horseback riders using the trails the Forest Service has established a separate trailhead and parking area 0.8 mile back down the road from the camping area. Long term car parking is not allowed in the camping area, but if you have a bicycle you can save a few extra steps by riding it to a point nearer the Brown Duck Trail. The best place to lock up your bicycle for a few days is at the lakeshore access parking area.

From there a short connecting trail follows the shoreline for 0.2 mile to the well marked junction where the Brown Duck Trail begins.

This hike is perfect for fishing enthusiasts looking for an extended trip into a high alpine wilderness area. The trail passes by no fewer than nine good fishing lakes, with short side trips leading to at least ten more. The route circles Brown Duck Mountain (11,866 ft.), passing through Brown Duck Basin, East Basin, and Squaw Basin, and features many fine views of the mountain's rocky peaks and cold, clear lakes. Most of the lakes lie at elevations of around 10,400 feet. The highest point is at the top of Cleveland Pass where the trail climbs out of East Basin and drops down into Squaw Basin. Cleveland Lake, frozen most of the year, lies near the top of the pass at an elevation of 11,172 feet.

Brown Duck Mountain is a favorite destination for horseback riders, so if you are put off by piles of horse manure along the trail and in the meadows then this is not the best hike for you. The most popular location for campers with pack animals is East Basin (day 2), a lush, green area with gorgeous meadows and a half dozen small lakes. It is not unusual to see twenty or thirty horses and mules grazing in the meadows beside the East Basin lakes. Fortunately there are other off-trail places to camp in the basin that are just as pretty, but without the livestock.

Day 1 (6.8 miles)

As explained earlier, the easiest place to begin this hike is the lakeshore access parking area adjacent to the Moon Lake Campground. From there a small trail leads west along the side of the lake for 0.2 mile to the Lake Fork Trail. Soon after you reach the Lake Fork Trail you will see a small sign

Cleveland Pass

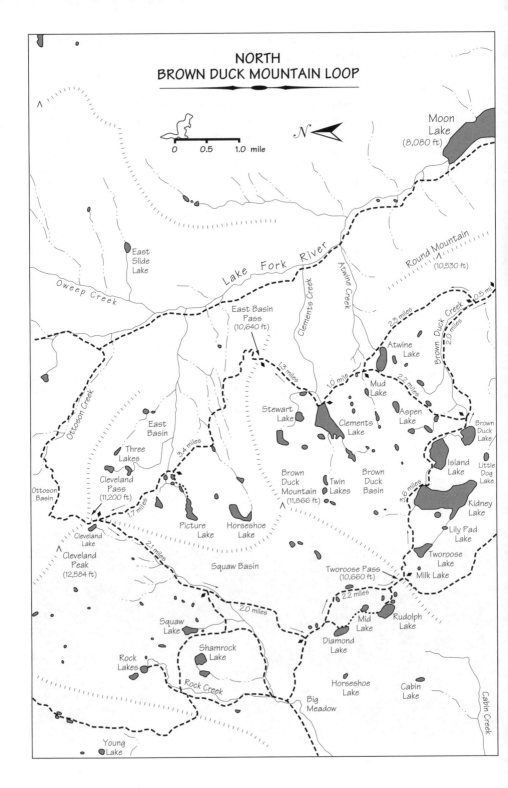

NORTH
BROWN DUCK MOUNTAIN LOOP

0   0.5   1.0 mile

N

Moon
Lake
(8,080 ft)

East
Slide
Lake

Oweep Creek

Lake Fork River

Atwine Creek

Clements Creek

Round Mountain
(10,530 ft)

Brown Duck Creek

0.5 mi

East Basin
Pass
(10,640 ft)

2.3 miles

2.0 miles

Atwine
Lake

1.3 miles

1.0 mile

Mud
Lake

2.2 miles

Ottoson Creek

East
Basin

Stewart
Lake

Clements
Lake

Aspen
Lake

Brown
Duck
Lake

Three
Lakes

3.4 miles

Brown
Duck
Mountain
(11,866 ft)

Twin
Lakes

Brown
Duck
Basin

Island
Lake

Little
Dog
Lake

Cleveland
Pass
(11,200 ft)

3.6 miles

Kidney
Lake

Ottoson
Basin

1.7 miles

Picture
Lake

Horseshoe
Lake

Lily Pad
Lake

Cleveland
Lake

2.1 miles

Twooroose
Lake

Cleveland
Peak
(12,584 ft)

Squaw Basin

Twooroose Pass
(10,660 ft)

Milk Lake

2.2 miles

2.0 miles

Squaw
Lake

Shamrock
Lake

Diamond
Lake

Mid
Lake

Rudolph
Lake

Rock
Lakes

Rock Creek

Horseshoe
Lake

Cabin
Lake

Cabin Creek

Big
Meadow

Young
Lake

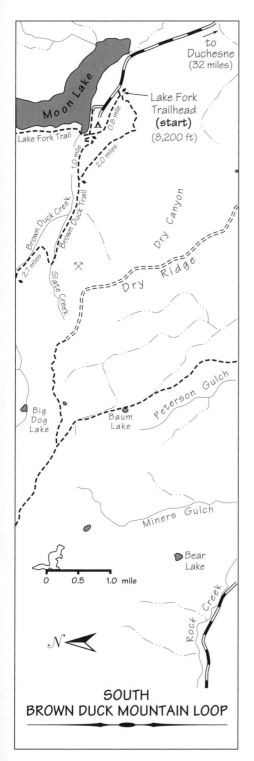

to
Duchesne
(32 miles)

Lake Fork
Trailhead
(start)
(8,200 ft)

Lake Fork Trail

Moon Lake

1.0 mile

2.0 miles

0.8 mile

Brown Duck Creek

Brown Duck Trail

2.7 miles

Slate Creek

Dry Ridge

Dry Canyon

Peterson Gulch

Big
Dog
Lake

Baum
Lake

Miners Gulch

Bear
Lake

Rock Creek

0   0.5   1.0 mile

N

SOUTH
BROWN DUCK MOUNTAIN LOOP

marking the beginning of the Brown Duck Trail on the left.

If you are starting from the official Lake Fork Trailhead, 0.8 miles down the road from the campground, you will see another sign directing you along an old jeep road that eventually meets the Brown Duck Trail higher up the mountain. Don't take this route. You will do better to follow the Lake Fork Trail in a direction parallel to the road for 0.8 mile, then turn left onto the Brown Duck Trail when you reach the trail junction just described. The hike along the jeep road is 0.2 mile further and the scenery is much less interesting.

The first 0.5 mile of the Brown Duck Trail, from where it leaves the shore of Moon Lake, is the steepest part of this entire hike. After making two long switch backs and climbing about 400 feet above the lake the trail settles down to a gradual incline that will continue for most of the first day. Initially the trail is immersed in a forest of lodgepole pine, but as you gain elevation you will see the trees gradually replaced with Engelmann spruce and subalpine fir, which seem to do better above 10,000 feet.

After 1.0 mile the trail merges with the old jeep road that originated at the Lake Fork Trailhead and follows it for another 1.3 miles. Then, almost immediately, the road ends and a foot trail begins. If you are observant you will see the tell-tale signs of mining activity above the end of the road— an indication of what the road was originally built for. Thank goodness the High Uintas is now a protected wilderness area, and prospecting is no longer allowed.

Just beyond the end of the jeep road the trail swings north to cross Slate Creek and soon afterward crosses the official boundary of the High Uintas Wilderness Area. From that point on the Brown Duck Trail never strays far from the south shore of

Brown Duck Creek.

About a half hour after leaving the wilderness boundary you should see a trail junction marked by a small wooden sign nailed to a tree on the right. This is the beginning of the trail to Atwine Lake and you must leave the Brown Duck Trail here. You will have to cross the river at this point—the only place on the entire hike where you must get your feet wet. Be sure to find a good strong stick to help with the river crossing. The current is often strong, but it is seldom more than knee deep.

The Atwine Lake Trail is not nearly as well frequented as the Brown Duck Trail; consequently it may be difficult to follow in places. Basically it heads uphill for a half mile until it reaches the rocky base of Round Mountain, and then turns northwest along more level terrain towards the lake. The trail passes by the north side of two small meadows before reaching the lake. Try not to make noise as you approach the meadows and you may be lucky enough to see an elk, deer, or moose. If there are any large grazing animals in the meadows they will usually be found along the perimeter near the edge of the forest.

The trail first reaches Atwine Lake on its northeastern shore, which is also the best place to make camp. If there are any other campers at Atwine they will probably be on the west side, near the better used trail to East Basin. Atwine is a large, relatively undisturbed lake with heavy timber growing right to the water's edge. The lake has never been dammed and it appears to be in pristine condition. Furthermore, since there are no good pastures around the lake it is seldom used by campers with pack animals. Most visitors to Brown Duck Basin prefer to make camp at the better known Kidney, Island, Brown Duck, or Clements Lakes, but Atwine Lake is by far the prettiest of the basin's five major lakes.

Day 2 (7.0 miles)

From the trail junction on the northwest side of Atwine Lake continue northward towards East Basin. After only a half hour you will come to Clements Lake, a large lake about twice the size of Atwine with an earthen dam across its eastern side. Clements is a popular fishing lake, well stocked with cutthroat and brook trout, but it is not a particularly scenic lake. Like all dammed lakes its water level fluctuates with the seasons and the shoreline is marred by dead trees and mud flats. All of Brown Duck Basin eventually drains into Moon Lake Reservoir, an important reservoir used by the farmers of Duchesne County, and most of the Brown Duck Basin lakes have been dammed in order to increase the water storage capacity of Moon Lake. It is now illegal to build dams in a designated wilderness area, but these dams were built long before the 1984 creation of the High Uintas Wilderness Area.

1.3 miles beyond Clements Lake the trail climbs out of Brown Duck Basin, crosses East Basin Pass (10,630 ft.), and drops down again into the East Basin. The climb to the top of the pass is so gradual you will scarcely know you are going uphill. As you start down the other side, however, the trail gets much steeper and more rocky. Then, when you break out of the trees you will suddenly be confronted with a marvelous view of fifty square miles of

see color photos, page 168

Uintas wilderness. Cleveland Peak (12,584 ft.), the next day's destination, is clearly visible four miles to the northwest, and beyond that is the long line of 12,000- and 13,000-foot peaks that form the Uinta Crest.

From the bottom of East Basin Pass it is an easy 3.4-mile walk to the center of East Basin. Along the way you will pass by a small meadow wedged between the trail and the steep rocky slopes of Brown Duck

Mountain. The last time I was on this trail I saw a moose cow and her calf grazing in this meadow—they must have felt a sense of security knowing that their habitat was protected on at least one side by the mountain. I am sure the young moose calf would have made a tasty meal for a mountain lion.

Before starting up the slope towards Cleveland Pass the trail passes by the east side of an exceptionally pretty group of small lakes surrounded by the lush green East Basin Meadows. This area is a fine place to stop for the night, but unless you are very lucky you will probably find the meadows filled with pack horses and the best camp sites already occupied by their owners. As mentioned earlier, the East Basin area is an extremely popular destination among campers with pack animals.

If you crave solitude, don't despair. Just 0.8 mile off the trail is a seldom visited lake that may be the prettiest spot in the entire Brown Duck Mountain loop. It is called Picture Lake, and it is well named because it lies in a setting that is truly picture perfect. The lake is surrounded by timber with a small, wooded island in the center, and it lies just below an 11,789 foot peak of Brown Duck Mountain. There is usually snow on the mountain until late in the summer, sometimes extending down the slopes almost to the water. Best of all, horses cannot easily get to the lake, and since it is not on the main trail you are likely to have the lake all to yourself.

Although there is no path leading to Picture Lake, it is only a twenty-minute walk from the main trail. Just follow the drainage uphill from the southwest side of the lower group of lakes. After skirting around the last meadow and climbing 130 feet you will cross a low ridge, just beyond which is the lake. Picture Lake is about 150 yards wide by 500 yards long, and it lies at an

Picture Lake

elevation of 10,731 feet. There are a few small but pleasant campsites along its northern shore. If you want to spend more time exploring the area there is another lake of similar size and elevation called Horseshoe Lake about 0.8 mile south of Picture Lake along the base of Brown Duck Mountain. I have never visited this lake, but it must also be very scenic. It lies directly north of the highest peak on Brown Duck Mountain. On the map it looks like an interesting cross-country hike would be to walk south from Picture Lake to Horseshoe lake, and then follow the drainage from the southern side of the lake back to the East Basin Trail.

Day 3 (9 miles)

From East Basin Meadows the trail climbs north for another 1.5 miles to the top of Cleveland Pass , the highest point on the hike. There is a small lake near the summit of the pass, but the most notable point of

Squaw Basin

interest is Cleveland Peak, just north of the pass.

When you descend from Cleveland Pass you will be following the Squaw Basin Trail which follows Squaw Basin Creek down the west side of the mountain. It is also possible to make another loop hike back to Moon Lake by continuing north from Cleveland Pass on the Ottoson Basin Trail. That trail eventually runs into the Lake Fork Trail which follows Lake Fork River back to Moon Lake. The hike described here is much more scenic, though. Once you drop into Lake Fork Canyon there isn't much to see except tall trees.

2.1 miles after leaving Cleveland Pass you should see another sign where the Two Ponds Trail joins Squaw Basin Trail. If you want to make a side trip to Squaw Lake or do some exploring elsewhere in Squaw Basin you should keep to the right at this point and continue walking down the Squaw Basin Trail. Otherwise turn left at the junction onto the Two Ponds Trail. The Two Ponds Trail is basically a shortcut to the Brown Duck Basin. It is a relatively new trail and is not shown on most of the older maps, but it cuts about 2.2 miles off the total distance to Brown Duck Basin.

The Two Ponds Trail is about 2.0 miles long, ending when it reaches the trail to Tworoose Pass and Brown Duck Basin. Turn left when you reach the junction and proceed towards the pass, 2.2 miles away. Over the next 5.8 miles the Tworoose Pass Trail passes by no fewer than 6 lakes, so this is a good time to start thinking about where you plan to pitch camp for the night. In my opinion the best choices for a small group of backpackers are the first two lakes: Diamond and Rudolph. The short spur trail to Diamond Lake is 0.6 miles from the Two Ponds Trail junction. The trail is easy to see, but unfortunately there is no sign marking it. Just proceed along the Tworoose Pass

Trail for about fifteen minutes and then start watching the right side of the path closely for the trail junction. The spur trail is about 0.3 mile long, and there are some small campsites near the north end of the lake. The trail to Rudolph Lake is 1.9 miles from the Two Ponds Trail junction, or 0.2 mile before you reach the top of Tworoose Pass. This short trail is marked by a small sign at the junction, but it is easy to miss so keep your eyes open. The trail to Rudolph Lake is 0.4 mile long.

Day 4 (11.2 miles)

From Rudolph Lake to the Lake Fork Trailhead and the end of the hike is 11.2 miles, but it is nearly all downhill and should be easy walking. Almost the only part that is uphill is the 200-foot climb to get from Rudolph Lake to the top of Tworoose Pass.

Beyond Tworoose Pass the trail gradually descends into Brown Duck Basin, soon passing by Tworoose Lake. Tworoose Lake is not easily visible from the trail and there is no spur trail leading to it, but it isn't difficult to reach. Just walk down the trail from the top of the pass for 15 minutes, then turn south and walk downhill through the woods for another 150 yards. From there you should be able to see Tworoose Lake.

The next lake the trail passes is Kidney Lake, quickly followed by Island Lake and Brown Duck Lake. All three of these lakes have been dammed and made into reservoirs; hence they are not as scenic as many of the other lakes on this hike. Like Clements Lake, the fluctuating water levels have left their shores marred with dead trees and lifeless, piles of bleached white rocks. Nevertheless, the lakes are well stocked with game fish and are very popular with campers. Leaving Brown Duck Lake the trail follows the south side of Brown Duck Creek for another 6.4 miles to Moon Lake, and then turns south for the final 15 minutes to the trailhead.

Rudolph Lake

Grandaddy Basin

☆ ☆ ☆ ☆

High Uintas Wilderness Area
overnight hike

Distance:	16.1 miles (loop)
Walking time:	day 1: 5³/₄ hours day 2: 5 hours
Elevations:	940 ft. gain/loss Grandview Trailhead (start): 9,700 ft. Hades Pass: 10,640 ft. Grandaddy Lake: 10,300 ft. Governor Dern Lake: 9,980 ft.
Trail:	The trails in Grandaddy Basin are extremely popular. Most are well maintained and well marked with signs.
Season:	Midsummer to mid-fall. Because of the high elevations, the trails are usually covered with snow from mid-November until July.
Vicinity:	High Uintas Wilderness Area, between Heber and Duchesne
Maps:	Grandaddy Lake, Hayden Peak *(USGS)* High Uintas Wilderness *(Trails Illustrated, #711)*
Information:	http://www.utahtrails.com/grandaddy.html *(Utah Trails)* http://www.fs.fed.us/r4/ashley/ *(Ashley National Forest)* phone: (435) 738-2482 *(Duchesne Ranger District)*

Take Highway 40 east of Heber for 52 miles (or west of Duchesne for 17 miles) to the intersection with Highway 208. Turn onto Highway 208 and drive north for 10.3 miles to Highway 35. When you arrive at Highway 35 turn left (west) and drive for another 12.9 miles, through the towns of Tabiona and Hanna, until you reach a clearly marked, paved road on the right leading up the North Fork of the Duchesne to Grandaddy Basin. Turn here and proceed north. After 4.2 miles the *pavement ends and becomes a graded gravel road. After 6.5 miles you will encounter a fork in the road with a sign pointing the way to Grandview Trailhead on the right (road 315). The road dead ends at the trailhead, 5.8 miles beyond the fork.*

The High Uintas Wilderness Area is a paradise for sport fishermen. More than a thousand lakes lie within the boundaries of the wilderness area, and according to Utah's Department of Wildlife Resources some 650 of them contain significant populations of game fish. The 170-acre Grandaddy Lake is one of the largest of the Uintas lakes, and

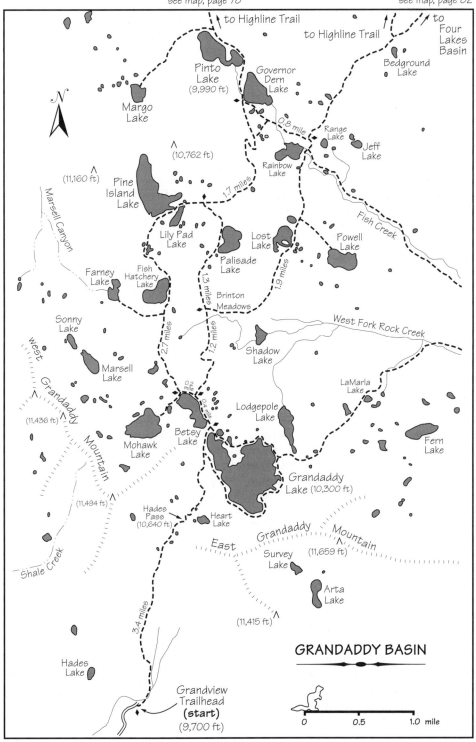

see map, page 78
see map, page 82

to Highline Trail

to Highline Trail

to
Four
Lakes
Basin

Bedground
Lake

Pinto
Lake
(9,990 ft)

Governor
Dern
Lake

Margo
Lake

N

0.8 mile

Range
Lake

Jeff
Lake

∧
(10,762 ft)

Rainbow
Lake

∧
(11,160 ft)

Pine
Island
Lake

1.7 miles

Fish Creek

Marsell Canyon

Lily Pad
Lake

Lost
Lake

Powell
Lake

Palisade
Lake

Farney
Lake

Fish
Hatchery
Lake

1.3 miles

1.9 miles

Brinton
Meadows

Sonny
Lake

2.7 miles

1.2 miles

West Fork Rock Creek

Shadow
Lake

west

Marsell
Lake

LaMarla
Lake

Grandaddy

∧
(11,436 ft)

0.2
mile

0.4 mile

Lodgepole
Lake

Fern
Lake

Mohawk
Lake

Betsy
Lake

Mountain

Grandaddy
Lake (10,300 ft)

∧
(11,494 ft)

Hades
Pass
(10,640 ft)

Heart
Lake

East   Grandaddy   Mountain

Shale Creek

Survey
Lake

∧
(11,659 ft)

3.4 miles

Arta
Lake

∧
(11,415 ft)

Hades
Lake

GRANDADDY BASIN

Grandview
Trailhead
(start)
(9,700 ft)

0   0.5   1.0 mile

also one of the most popular. It is very scenic, easy to get to, and generally well stocked with cutthroat and brook trout.

Unfortunately, there are usually so many campers around Grandaddy Lake it is not possible to enjoy a real wilderness experience there. But there are many other less well visited lakes nearby. There are over twenty lakes within a two-hour walk of Grandaddy. The fishing is good in most of them, and excellent campsites are easy to find.

There are also numerous other trails in Grandaddy Basin, and many variations of this hike are possible. The route outlined here is a loop tour of

see color photos, page 169

nine of the better known lakes. The minimum recommended time for the trip is two days, but one could easily spend a week in the basin—especially if catching fish is on the agenda. If you have more time to spare I suggest you establish a camp at one of the lakes and explore the other lakes on day trips.

Day 1 (8.4 miles)

From Grandview Trailhead the trail climbs gently upward through the lodgepole pine and Engelmann spruce forest for 2.2 miles before reaching Hades Pass, the entryway into Grandaddy Basin. At 10,640 feet above sea level—940 feet above the trailhead—Hades Pass is the highest point on the hike. The slope on either side of the pass is so gradual, however, that you will scarcely know you have reached the summit. Just beyond the pass Heart Lake comes into view, nestled at the foot of East Grandaddy Mountain, and soon afterward you will reach Grandaddy Lake. Don't be discouraged at the number of hikers you encounter between the trailhead and Grandaddy Lake. On some summer weekends there may literally be hundreds of hikers on this trail, but the great majority of them never go beyond Grandaddy Lake, 3.4 miles from

the trailhead.

On the northwestern side of Grandaddy the trail splits, with the right fork going to LaMarla Lake and beyond, and the left fork continuing north into Grandaddy Basin. Bear to the left here and continue northward along the eastern shore of Betsy Lake. Then after 0.4 mile you will reach another junction. This is the beginning of the loop trail to Governor Dern Lake. The direction in which you walk the loop doesn't matter much, but for the sake of discussion I will assume that you turn left here onto the Pine Island Lake Trail.

Notice the side trail going to Mohawk Lake as the main trail leaves the north end of Betsy Lake. Mohawk is a little larger than Betsy, but still only about a third the size of Grandaddy. The spur trail is only 0.4 mile long over level ground, and there are some nice campsites near the lake. It is a good alternative if you are looking for a secluded spot near Grandaddy Lake.

From Betsy Lake, the main trail continues north for 1.1 miles to Fish Hatchery Lake. The abundance of grass along the shore of Fish Hatchery is a good indication of the reduced number of campers here as compared to Betsy and Grandaddy. Just before you reach Fish Hatchery you will also see another spur trail leading to Farney Lake, 0.6 mile away. There are some fine camping sites around Farney Lake, but unfortunately it is too shallow for fish to survive the winter. Two other small lakes, Sonny Lake and Marsell Lake can also be reached by walking from Farney Lake through the timber for about 20 minutes along a bearing slightly west of magnetic south. The forest floor is quite level here and quite open, so the lakes are easy to find. They are both nestled against the north side of a low ridge that runs east of West Grandaddy Mountain.

Back on the Pine Island Loop Trail, the route next passes between Pine Island Lake

Grandaddy Lake

and Lily Pad Lake. Again, Lily Pad is too shallow for good fishing, but this is not true of Pine Island Lake. Pine Island (80 acres in area) is the second largest lake in the basin and the fishing is good. Unfortunately, Pine Island Lake is a favorite destination for groups with pack horses, and the best camping area on the southern end of the lake is littered with horse manure.

0.3 miles after leaving Pine Island Lake you will come to the Palisade Lake Trail that heads south to Palisade Lake and Brinton Meadows. This trail offers a shorter return loop for those not wishing to continue to Governor Dern Lake. Palisade Lake, located 0.4 mile from the main trail is a very pretty lake with some good camping sites.

1.4 miles farther north from the junction with the Palisade Lake Trail is another shortcut trail leading to Rainbow Lake. Don't even consider taking this trail, because if you do you will miss Governor Dern Lake, which in my opinion is the prettiest of all the

Grandaddy Basin Lakes. Governor Dern is much more open than most of the other lakes, with fine views of Mount Agassiz on the main ridge of the Uintas, 4 miles further north. The lake is also completely surrounded with grass and has many fine campsites. Unfortunately Governor Dern Lake is rather shallow, and the fishing is not as good as at Pine Island and some of the other lakes in the vicinity.

Day 2 (7.7 miles)

There are a number of nice day hikes in the vicinity of Governor Dern Lake if you have the time to spend a few nights there. Pinto Lake is only 0.4 mile north, and the Highline Trail is only 2.5 miles farther along the Pinto Lake Trail.

One particularly interesting day hike from Governor Dern involves walking around a loop, past Pinto Lake, Margo Lake, Pine Island Lake, and back to Governor Dern Lake. A primitive trail leads to Margo Lake from the north side of Pinto. After you reach Margo, work your way around to the south side of the lake and then walk cross country for about 0.4 mile along a heading slightly east of magnetic south until you reach the top of a wide saddle. Pine Island Lake is 0.2 mile below the saddle on the south side. Once you reach Pine Island, it is an easy walk around its eastern side back to the Pine Island Lake Trail and on to Governor Dern Lake. The total distance of this loop is 5.5 miles.

Another nice day hike from Governor Dern Lake is along the trail to the Four Lakes Basin. The trail leaves from Rainbow Lake, 0.8 miles south of Governor Dern, and proceeds along a gentle uphill slope for 2.5 miles to Jean Lake (10,753 ft.) and its three companion lakes: Daynes, Dale, and Dean. Nestled against the southern side of the Uintas ridge amidst scattered stands of Engelmann spruce, these glacial lakes are very picturesque. The fishing is also good and there are plenty of good campsites in the basin, but it is difficult for most people to get a good night's sleep at this altitude. If you don't want to return the same way you can go north another 1.2 miles to the Highline Trail, then west to the Pinto Lake Trail, and south again, past Pinto Lake, to Governor Dern Lake. Total distance: 8.7 miles.

see maps,
pages 78, 82

When you leave Governor Dern Lake you will be walking back to Grandaddy Lake via Rainbow Lake, Lost Lake, and Brinton Meadows. Bear right at the two major trail junctions near Rainbow Lake and head due south on the Hades Trail towards Lost Lake. Just before reaching Lost Lake you will notice another spur trail leading to Powell Lake, about 0.6 mile away—another possible side trip.

1.2 miles after passing Lost Lake you will arrive at Brinton Meadows and the Palisade Lake Trail junction. For twenty years the Forest Service maintained a guard station at Brinton Meadows, but under pressure from the Sierra Club they were forced to remove the station in 1995. The law forbids permanent dwellings within a designated wilderness area, so, although the guard station was little more than a tent with a wooden floor, it had to go. This is a shame because rangers staffing the guard station during the summer months provided a valuable service in cleaning up camp sites, monitoring and controlling damage to the ecosystem, and providing emergency assistance. Grandaddy Basin is so heavily impacted by backpackers and pack horses that the absence of the Brinton Meadows Guard Station is now sorely missed.

From Brinton Meadows it is another 1.2 miles back to Betsy Lake, from where you can retrace your steps past Grandaddy lake, over Hades Pass, and back to your car at the Grandview Trailhead.

Governor Dern Lake, Grandaddy Basin

Naturalist Basin

☆ ☆ ☆ ☆ ☆

Distance: 19.0 miles (round trip)

Walking time: day 1: 5 hours
day 2: 5³/₄ hours

Elevations: 1,370 ft. gain/loss
Highline Trailhead (start): 10,350 ft.
Packard Lake: 9,980 ft.
Jordan Lake: 10,630 ft.
Faxon Lake: 10,980 ft.

Trail: Naturalist Basin is a very popular destination, and the trails to the lower part of the basin are well maintained. A small portion of this hike, however, is in the upper part of the basin where there are no trails. The upper basin is all above timber line and the route is easy, but you should carry a compass.

Season: Midsummer to mid-fall. Because of its high elevation, Naturalist Basin is usually covered with snow from mid-November until July.

Vicinity: The High Uintas Wilderness Area, near Kamas

Maps: Hayden Peak *(USGS)*
High Uintas Wilderness *(Trails Illustrated, #711)*

Information: http://www.utahtrails.com/naturalist.html *(Utah Trails)*
http://www.fs.fed.us/wcnf/ *(Wasatch-Cache Nat. Forest)*
phone: (435) 783-4338 *(Kamas Ranger District)*

To get to the trailhead drive west from Kamas on Highway 150 towards Mirror Lake. 6 miles from Kamas you will pass a Forest Service booth where you must purchase a recreation pass to hike in the area ($3.00/day for each vehicle). 35 miles from Kamas, or 3.0 miles after passing Mirror Lake, you will see a well marked turnout on the right side of the highway leading to the Highline Trailhead.

The High Uintas are famous for their gorgeous alpine basins, but none of them can beat the memorable scenery of Naturalist Basin. In my opinion, this small collection of lakes and meadows, nestled together against the southern slopes of Mount Agassiz and Spread Eagle Peak, is the crown jewel of the High Uintas Wilderness Area. Unfortunately, Naturalist Basin is also one of the most popular backpacking destinations in the

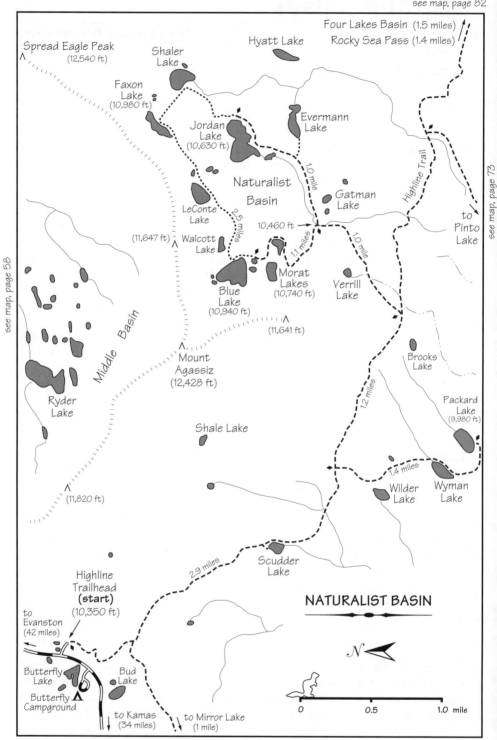

see map, page 82

Four Lakes Basin (1.5 miles)
Rocky Sea Pass (1.4 miles)

Hyatt Lake

Spread Eagle Peak
(12,540 ft)

Shaler
Lake

Faxon
Lake
(10,980 ft)

Evermann
Lake

Jordan
Lake
(10,630 ft)

Highline Trail

see map, page 73

Naturalist
Basin

Gatman
Lake

1.0 mile

to
Pinto
Lake

LeConte
Lake

2.5 miles

10,460 ft

(11,647 ft)   Walcott
Lake

1.1 miles

1.0 mile

Verrill
Lake

see map, page 58

Morat
Lakes
(10,740 ft)

Blue
Lake
(10,940 ft)

(11,641 ft)

Brooks
Lake

Middle Basin

Mount
Agassiz
(12,428 ft)

Packard
Lake
(9,980 ft)

Ryder
Lake

Shale Lake

1.2 miles

(11,820 ft)

1.4 miles

Wilder
Lake

Wyman
Lake

Scudder
Lake

NATURALIST BASIN

Highline
Trailhead
(start)
(10,350 ft)

2.9 miles

N

to
Evanston
(42 miles)

Butterfly
Lake

Bud
Lake

Butterfly
Campground

0   0.5   1.0 mile

to Kamas
(34 miles)

to Mirror Lake
(1 mile)

see map, page 85

High Uintas, so if you are looking for solitude you had better choose another hike. But most hikers tend to congregate around Jordan Lake and the Morat Lakes, where the best fishing can be found, so if you are willing to camp elsewhere it is still possible to enjoy a measure of privacy.

Few hikers venture onto the upper plateau of Naturalist Basin, where 2.5 miles of this hike are located. Five icy lakes cling tenaciously to the talus slopes in the top of the basin, just below the 11,000-foot contour line and just above timberline. Hiking across the stark, sparsely vegetated terrain that separates the small lakes can be an almost otherworldly experience. It is an environment where most life ceases to exist during the wintertime, but during the two or three months of summer a few dormant species suddenly burst forth to quickly mature and reproduce before the arctic cold again forces them into submission. By the end of July, after most of the snow has melted, the thin, rocky soil is usually covered with a colorful carpet of tiny blossoms as the hardy plants begin another cycle of their precarious existence.

Day 1 (8.6 miles)

From the Highline Trailhead the trail meanders gradually downhill through a forest of Engelmann spruce and lodgepole pine. At the higher elevations the forest is almost entirely spruce, but more and more lodgepole pine begin to appear as elevation is lost. After walking for an hour you will see your first lake, Scudder Lake, glinting through the trees. This lake is popular with day hikers, although it is too shallow for good fishing. It can be accessed over a short spur that branches off to the right of the main trail.

From Scudder Lake it is another half hour walk to the Packard Lake Trail junction. Once you reach this junction you are only

Wyman Lake, Just Off the Highline Trail

2.2 miles from Naturalist Basin, so unless you got off to a late start you will probably want to take a short side trip to see Wilder, Wyman, and Packard Lakes. They are all on the 1.4-mile-long Packard Lake Trail. There is also a nice view of the Uintas near the end of the trail. Packard Lake is situated only a hundred yards north of the rim of a 600-foot-deep canyon, in the bottom of which runs the East Fork of the Duchesne River.

Back on the Highline Trail, 1.2 miles beyond the Packard Lake Trail, you will see a sign directing you to Naturalist Basin. Turn left here and proceed north. The path climbs very gradually for about a mile before emerging from the trees on the edge of a wide green meadow with the picturesque cliffs of the Uinta Crest behind it. From the scene in front of you, it should be immediately obvious that you are entering into a very special place.

As you enter Naturalist Basin turn right, across the stream, and start looking for a camp site. If you want to camp by a lake you can try Jordan Lake, about 0.9 miles from the entrance. Jordan is the largest lake, but it is also the most popular. If there are no spaces available at Jordan, or if you want more privacy, then Everman Lake is your best bet. Everman is a beautiful place to camp only 0.7 miles from the entrance, but it is slightly off the main trail and many people don't even know of its existence. Proceed eastward from the entrance of the basin, along the edge of the meadow, for about 0.5 mile until you reach a point where the trail crosses a small drainage, turns north, and starts climbing. Leave the main trail here and continue east along the drainage. You will run into Everman Lake within 0.2 mile.

Day 2 (10.4 miles)

Before leaving this beautiful spot be sure to visit the lakes in the upper part of the basin. The 4.6 mile tour around the basin's 8

major lakes takes only 2½ hours, and since it is a loop you can leave your backpack in camp. The route is easy, but there is no trail so you should have a compass.

Continue on the trail along the southern side of Jordan Lake until the trail disappears at the eastern end of the lake. From there you will have to do some minor scrambling to get to the top of the plateau above the lake. After you have gained about 200 feet in elevation the terrain levels off and the walking is easy. If you walk along a bearing 25 degrees east of magnetic north (slightly east of Spread Eagle Peak), for about fifteen minutes you will run right into Shaler Lake. There are very few trees at this elevation and your view is relatively unobstructed, so you can't miss the lake.

Next, Faxon Lake is almost due west of magnetic north from Shaler Lake, just to the left of a saddle on the ridge between Spread Eagle Peak and Mount Agassiz. It is only 0.3 mile away, so you should be there in ten minutes. From Faxon it is easy to find LeConte, Walcott, and Blue Lakes. They are all situated at about the same elevation along a line at the base of the Uinta crest, so just follow the base of the ridge in an easterly direction towards Mount Agassiz and you will run into them in succession. Again, they are all less than 0.3 mile apart, so you don't have to walk long.

see color photo, page 169

There are at least some fish in all of the upper lakes of Naturalist Basin, with the possible exception of Walcott Lake. There isn't much to eat in these high lakes, however, so they cannot sustain a very large population of fish. It never ceases to amaze me how much difference a few hundred feet at these altitudes can make to an ecosystem. The difference in elevation between the upper and lower parts of Naturalist Basin is only 350 feet, yet their ecologies are worlds apart.

Jordan Lake, Naturalist Basin

From the south side of Blue Lake a primitive trail leads down to the twin Morat Lakes. The trail is vague at first, but soon becomes more distinct as it begins to descend into the lower basin. As you make the short descent you will be treated to a nice view of the two Morat Lakes, with the wide expanse of the Uintas below them. Thank goodness this magnificent land is now protected as a wilderness area. From Morat Lakes a good trail will take you the remaining 0.6 mile back to the bottom of the lower meadow, and from there you can easily retrieve your backpack for the walk back to the Highline Trailhead.

Four Lakes Basin

For those who want to get farther away from civilization than Naturalist Basin and still enjoy the serenity of a beautiful basin on the south slopes of the Uinta crest, Four Lakes Basin provides a good alternative. The fishing is also excellent there–especially in

Jean and Dean Lakes.

To get to the Four Lakes Basin continue eastward on the Highline Trail for 2.8 miles beyond the junction with Naturalist Basin Trail. There you will come to another junction with the trail to Four Lakes Basin departing on the right. Turn south here, and after another 1.2 miles you will arrive at Jean Lake, the first of the basin's four lakes. The total distance to Jean Lake from Naturalist Basin is 5.0 miles, one way, or from the Highline Trailhead it is 8.1 miles. The route is clearly marked with Forest Service signs.

The best camp sites are at Dean Lake, immediately northeast of Jean at the base of the Uinta Crest. There is no proper trail to Dean Lake but it is easy to get to. Just walk along the southern shore of Jean for about 0.3 mile, and a few hundred feet beyond the eastern end of the lake you will come to Dean Lake. Both lakes are situated against the southern base of the Uinta Crest, about 1.5

miles south of the Rocky Sea Pass. The water is deeper along the north shore of the lakes; hence the chances of hooking a larger fish are better, but the fishing is also good on the more easily accessible south shore.

If you feel like exploring, there is an old airplane crash a short way up the slope from the eastern end of Dean Lake. The unfortunate pilot was only about 500 feet too low to clear the ridge when he crashed. The other two lakes, Dale and Daynes, are another 0.5 miles south of Jean Lake on the east side of the main trail. There are a number of good camp sites around these two lakes as well, but they aren't quite as scenic as Jean and Dean.

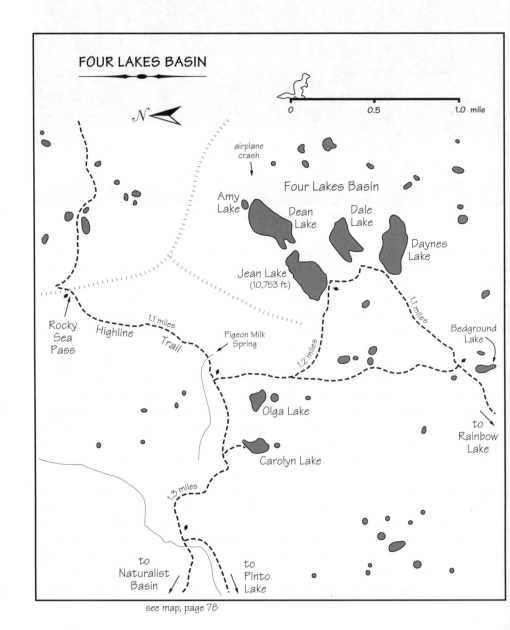

see map, page 78

Notch Mountain Trail

☆ ☆   **shuttle car or bicycle required**
day hike

Distance: 10.5 miles
(plus 4.1 miles by car or bicycle)

Walking time: $6^1/_2$ hours

Elevations: 1,130 ft. gain, 2,070 ft. loss
Bald Mountain Trailhead (start):   10,760 ft.
Meadow Lake: 9,820 ft.
The Notch: 10,590 ft.
Trial Lake Trailhead: 9,820 ft.

Trail: Well marked, well maintained trail

Season: Midsummer through mid-fall. The trail is generally covered
with snow from mid-November through late June.

Vicinity: Near Heber and the High Uintas Wilderness Area

Maps: Mirror Lake *(USGS)*
High Uintas Wilderness *(Trails Illustrated, #711)*

Information: http://www.utahtrails.com/notch.html *(Utah Trails)*
http://www.fs.fed.us/wcnf/ *(Wasatch-Cache Nat. Forest)*
phone: (435) 783-4338 *(Kamas Ranger District)*

Drive east of Salt Lake City on Highway 80 for 30 miles to Wanship and the *junction with Highway 32, then turn south on Highway 32 and drive for another 17 miles to Kamas. Turn left in the center of Kamas and drive west on Highway 150 (the Mirror Lake Highway). After 6 miles you will pass a Forest Service booth where you must purchase a recreation pass ($3.00/vehicle for one day, or $6.00 for a week). 26 miles from Kamas there is a well-marked gravel road on the left leading to Trial Lake. Take this turn and follow the signs for 0.3 miles to the fisherman's parking area near the Trial Lake Dam. This is where the hike will end and where you should leave your shuttle car.*

To reach the Bald Mountain Trailhead where the hike begins return to highway 150 and continue driving east for 3.8 miles to the top of the Bald Mountain Pass. At the summit of the pass you will see a sign directing you to the Bald Mountain Trailhead Picnic Area. Turn left here and drive the final 0.1 mile to the trailhead.

The Notch Mountain Trail is a delight-   ful path on the western side of the Uinta

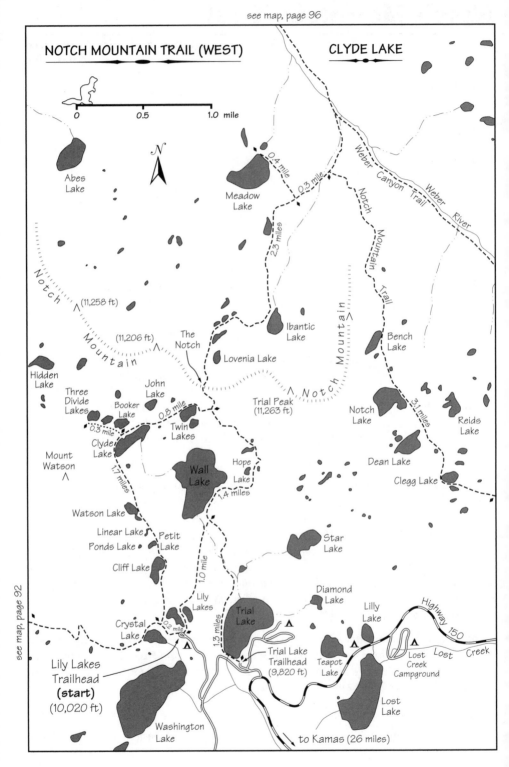

see map, page 96

NOTCH MOUNTAIN TRAIL (WEST)

CLYDE LAKE

0   0.5   1.0 mile

N

Abes Lake

Meadow Lake

0.4 mile

0.3 mile

Weber Canyon Trail

Weber River

Clyde Lake

2.3 miles

Notch Mountain Trail

(11,258 ft)

Notch Mountain

(11,206 ft)

The Notch

Ibantic Lake

Bench Lake

Lovenia Lake

Hidden Lake

Three Divide Lakes

John Lake

Booker Lake

0.8 mile

Notch Mountain

Trial Peak (11,263 ft)

Notch Lake

3.1 miles

Reids Lake

0.3 mile

Twin Lakes

Clyde Lake

Mount Watson

Wall Lake

Hope Lake

Dean Lake

1.7 miles

1.4 miles

Clegg Lake

Watson Lake

Linear Lake

Petit Lake

Ponds Lake

Cliff Lake

Star Lake

1.0 mile

Diamond Lake

Lily Lakes

Lilly Lake

Highway 150

Crystal Lake

0.2 mile

Trial Lake

1.3 miles

Trial Lake Trailhead (9,820 ft)

Teapot Lake

Lost Creek Campground

Lost Creek

see map, page 92

Lily Lakes Trailhead (start) (10,020 ft)

Washington Lake

Lost Lake

to Kamas (26 miles)

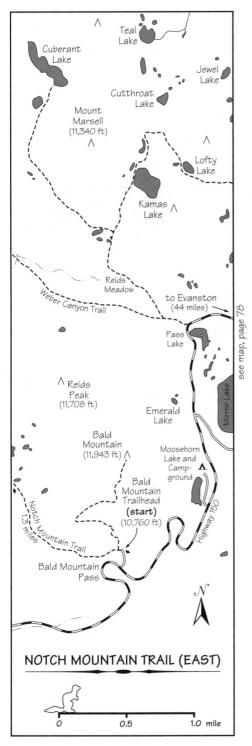

NOTCH MOUNTAIN TRAIL (EAST)

Mountains that winds lazily through the subalpine forest west of Bald Mountain and eventually returns to the Mirror Lake Highway through the notch in Notch Mountain. It is an area strewn with lakes and talus covered mountain peaks—all shaped and sculpted by the glaciers of the last Ice Age. A hundred thousand years ago this area was a sea of ice, broken only by the island peaks of Bald Mountain, Notch Mountain, Mount Watson, Haystack, and a few other summits. At least four separate glaciers came together on the slopes of Bald Mountain, with long fingers extending for up to twenty miles down the north and south slopes of the range. As the glaciers moved they gouged deep pockets into the earth and rock, and today the result is a landscape punctuated by scores of picturesque lakes.

The trail begins on the south side of Bald Mountain and proceeds westward along its rocky base. A hundred yards from the trailhead you will come to a junction where the 1.7-mile trail to the summit of Bald Mountain takes off to the right. The Notch Mountain Trail continues to the left along the southern slope of the peak for another 0.6 mile, and then turns northwest toward Notch Mountain.

After about 45 minutes the trail passes by the western side of Clegg Lake. Clegg is one of the smaller lakes you will see on this hike, but none can beat it for scenic beauty. Unlike many of the Uinta lakes, it was never dammed, and it is still in a pristine state. The setting is exquisite, with Bald Mountain to the east and Trial Peak to the west. On calm, clear days the reflections of these two peaks on the mirror smooth water of Clegg Lake are unforgettable—Trial Peak in the morning and Bald Mountain in the late afternoon.

Soon after leaving Clegg Lake the trail

see color photos, page 163

Bench Lake

crosses between Bald Mountain and Notch Mountain, leaving the Provo River Drainage and entering the Weber River Drainage. Within the next mile three more lakes will come into view along the eastern slopes of Notch Mountain: Dean Lake, Notch Lake, and Bench Lake. Of these, Notch Lake is the biggest and the most popular among fishermen, but I really can't say much for its scenic beauty. It has an active dam, and when the water level is low at the end of summer about half of the lake's surface area is replaced by lifeless, sun-bleached shoreline. Bench Lake, on the other hand, is a scenic gem with huge Engelmann spruce growing right to the water's edge.

The trail continues downhill from Bench Lake for another 1.5 miles, then crosses a small creek and begins a gentle uphill climb. Ten minutes later you should see the spur trail to Meadow Lake leaving on the right. The spur is marked by a small sign nailed to a spruce tree, but if you aren't paying at-

tention you can easily miss it. Meadow Lake is 0.4 mile off the main trail. It is the second largest off-road lake you will see on this hike, and it is a popular overnight stop among scout groups. Unfortunately, however, the lake has suffered from the same fate that has befallen so many other lakes in the High Uintas. It has an active dam on its north side, and the resulting fluctuations in water level often expose large ugly swathes of lifeless wasteland along its shores. But I am told that the fishing is good; Meadow Lake contains a large population of cutthroat trout.

The second half of this hike, from Meadow Lake to Trial Lake, is perhaps the most interesting. The trail meanders gently uphill for 2.0 miles, past Ibantik Lake and Lovenia Lake, then crosses through the Notch of Notch Mountain and drops down again into the Provo River watershed. There is a fine view of Lovenia Lake from the Notch, and to the south Wall Lake, the largest lake along the trail, glints through the forest.

Wall Lake was "under construction" when I last stood in the Notch in the summer of 1999. The sounds of heavy equipment drifted up from far below, and I could see from the denuded land on the south end of the lake that a major earth moving project was well underway. Although Wall Lake is no longer used for water storage, its ancient dam has for years been in need of repair. Many environmentalists suggested that the dam should be breached and the lake allowed to return to its natural size. The lake is very popular with fishermen, however,

and for that reason the Forest Service decided to reconstruct the dam and maintain the lake at its current size.

From the Notch, the trail descends across two narrow benches before coming to the southeast shore of Wall Lake. The route then follows the shore of the lake for 0.2 mile before coming to a junction near the dam where the trail to Lily Lakes departs. Bear left here for Trial Lake. Soon the lake will come into view, with the trail following closely along its western side. When you reach the south end of the lake you can walk across the dam to the parking area where your shuttle car is parked.

Lovenia Lake, as seen from the Notch

Clyde Lake

☆ ☆   **day hike**

Distance:	5.7 miles (loop)
Walking time:	3 hours
Elevations:	420 ft. gain/loss Lily Lakes Trailhead (start): 10,020 ft. Clyde Lake: 10,420 ft.
Trail:	Easy walk, but the trail can be confusing. In some places it seems briefly to disappear, and in other places there is more than one trail. A compass is useful.
Season:	Midsummer to mid-fall. Parts of the trail are usually covered with snow until late June.
Vicinity:	West of the High Uintas Wilderness Area, near Kamas
Maps:	Mirror Lake *(USGS)* High Uintas Wilderness Area *(Trails Illustrated, #711)*
Information:	http://www.utahtrails.com/clydelake.html *(Utah Trails)* http://www.fs.fed.us/wcnf/ *(Wasatch-Cache Nat. Forest)* phone: (435) 783-4338 *(Kamas Ranger District)*

To get to the trailhead drive east from Kamas on Highway 150 towards Mirror Lake. 6 miles from Kamas you will pass a Forest Service booth where you must purchase a recreation pass to hike in the area ($3.00/day for each vehicle). 26 miles from Kamas, or 6 miles before reaching Mirror Lake, there is a well marked road on the left leading to Trial Lake. Take this turn and follow the signs to Crystal Lake Trailhead, 1.2 miles from the highway. You will come to two junctions before the road reaches Crystal Lake Trailhead, but there are good signs marking the way at each junction. As you enter the trailhead parking area look for a large horse loading ramp made of logs on the right side of the road. The trail to Wall Lake and Clyde Lake begins at this ramp.

There are literally thousands of mountain lakes in and around the High Uintas. On the 55-square-mile Mirror Lake Quadrangle map alone there are 72 named lakes and several hundred unnamed ones. It is a fisherman's paradise, although most of the lakes are so high they are frozen much of the year. The area surrounding Clyde Lake is particularly well endowed with lakes. The loop trail described here, though only 5.7 miles long, passes by no fewer than fifteen of them.

Shortly after leaving the parking area the trail passes between the two Lily Lakes, each about 600 feet long and 300 feet wide, then continues northward along an almost level slope towards Wall Lake, one mile away. Because of the presence of an earthen dam on its southern side Wall Lake is one of the largest lakes in the area. It lies at an elevation of 10,140 feet, and measures about 0.5 mile by 0.3 mile.

see map, page 84

From Wall Lake the well-worn trail veers east and then north, passing tiny Hope Lake and several other unnamed lakes along the way. Just beyond Hope Lake the grade increases sharply, and the path climbs to a fine view point. Mount Watson (11,521 feet) lies 1.5 miles across the conifer forest to the west, on the opposite side of Wall Lake. The mountain seems to rise up from the lake in a continuous assent, but actually the grade is broken by a hidden plateau that lies about one-half mile down from the summit. This plateau is the locale of Clyde Lake, Watson Lake, and several other lakes that will be visited further along the trail.

From the view point the trail continues at a gradual assent for 0.5 miles, past another unnamed lake, before coming to the Clyde Lake trail junction. To complete the loop past Clyde and Watson Lakes and back to the trailhead, you must turn left here, but care is needed since the vague Clyde Lake trail can easily be missed. The junction occurs in the midst of a large, flat clearing in the forest about two hundred feet wide that runs along the base of Notch Mountain in an east-west direction. The most clearly defined path continues straight and soon starts climbing up into the Notch of Notch Mountain, only 0.2 miles away. The fainter Clyde Lake Trail turns abruptly to the left in the middle of the clearing and begins a gradual descent to Twin Lakes, 0.1 mile away. Don't worry if you have difficulty following the

trail; it gets better. Just walk due east along the base of Notch Mountain, neither climbing nor descending, and you should run right into the Twin Lakes.

The larger Twin Lake is about 500 feet in diameter, with the smaller Twin on the southern side about half that size. Although there is only a thin stretch of land between the two, the larger lake cannot be seen from its smaller twin, so if you run into the smaller lake first, turn north to find the larger one. The trail, more distinct now, runs around the northern shore of the larger Twin Lake. After leaving Twin

see color photo, page 162

Lakes the trail continues in a westerly direction for 0.2 mile before reaching the northeastern corner of Clyde Lake.

Clyde is a long narrow lake, about 500 feet wide and 0.3 mile long. At 10,420 feet above sea level, it is close to the highest point and roughly midway through the hike. If you want to do some fishing and have time for an overnight stay, there is a fine camping site on the northeastern corner of the lake.

Before leaving Clyde Lake, you should take a short side trip to the Three Divide Lakes, located in the saddle between West Notch Mountain and Mount Watson. There is no trail to these lakes, but they are very close to Clyde, and little climbing is involved. Simply turn north near the west end of Clyde Lake and walk away from the trail for about 300 feet. You should run right into Booker Lake, the first of the Three Divide Lakes. Turn west from Booker and you will soon see the other two. These lakes are all about 600 feet in diameter. They lie along an east-west line with only about 200 feet of land separating them from each other. The total distance from Clyde Lake to the last of the Three Divide Lakes is 0.3 mile.

From the southwestern corner of Clyde

Lake the trail turns southward along the base of Mount Watson to reach Watson Lake, 0.4 mile away. Watson Lake, which is about 500 feet in diameter, is the first of several small lakes that lie like a string of beads along the downhill path leading back to the Crystal Lake Trailhead. The path passes by Watson Lake, tiny Linear Lake, slightly larger Petit Lake, and finally Cliff Lake, all within a half mile of each other. Cliff Lake, about twice the size of Watson, is, in my opinion, the prettiest of the four. The route passes along the eastern shores of these lakes, so hikers coming down from Clyde Lake should bear to the left.

After leaving the southern corner of Cliff Lake the trail heads south into the woods again, loosing 240 feet of elevation and arriving at West Lily Lake after 0.2 mile. Here the path intersects the Crystal Lake Trail, and in order to return to the parking area you must turn left. If you are in the mood for one more lake, however, Crystal Lake is just a five minute walk to the right from the junction.

The Notch and Meadow Lake

As mentioned earlier, the Notch of Notch Mountain is only 0.2 mile from the point where the Clyde Lake Trail branches off the main trail. Before making the turn to Clyde Lake, some hikers may want to climb into the Notch. At an elevation of 10,580 feet, it is only 120 feet higher than the trail junction, and the view is well worth the climb. If you drop down on the other side of the Notch for another 0.2 mile you will come to Lovenia Lake, about 300 feet across, and beyond Lovenia the route passes Ibantic and Meadow Lakes. Meadow Lake, nearly as big as Wall Lake, is 2.5 miles from the Notch.

Mount Watson and Cliff Lake

Lake Country

☆ ☆   **day hike**

Distance:	8.0 miles (loop)
Walking time:	4³/₄ hours
Elevations:	690 ft. gain/loss
	Crystal Lake Trailhead (start): 10,020 ft.
	Island Lake: 10,160 ft.
	Duck Lake: 9,790 ft.
Trail:	Easy, well marked trail
Season:	Midsummer through mid-fall. The trail is generally covered with snow from mid-November through late June.
Vicinity:	Near Heber and the High Uintas Wilderness Area
Maps:	Mirror Lake, Erickson Basin *(USGS)*
	High Uintas Wilderness *(Trails Illustrated, #711)*
Information:	http://www.utahtrails.com/lakecountry.html *(Utah Trails)*
	http://www.fs.fed.us/wcnf/ *(Wasatch-Cache Nat. Forest)*
	phone: (435) 783-4338 *(Kamas Ranger District)*

Drive east of Salt Lake City on Highway 80 for 30 miles to Wanship and the junction with Highway 32. Then turn south on Highway 32 and drive for another 17 miles to Kamas. Turn left in the center of Kamas and drive east on Highway 150 (the Mirror Lake Highway). After 6 miles you will pass a Forest Service booth where you must purchase a recreation pass ($3.00/vehicle for *one day, or $6.00 for a week). 26 miles from Kamas there is a well-marked road on the left leading to Trial Lake. Take this turn and follow the signs for the next 1.2 miles to the Crystal Lake Trailhead. There are two trailheads at the end of the road. The one next to the packhorse loading ramp is* not *the one you want. The Crystal Lake Trailhead is 100 feet west of the loading ramp.*

Two miles west of Trial Lake, on the western side of the Uinta Mountains, lies a high alpine bench that the Forest Service is fond of calling Lake Country. The bench lies at the headwaters of the Weber River drainage (to the north) and the Provo River Drainage (to the south) and there are doz-ens of lakes in the area. Needless to say it is a favorite area for backcountry anglers, and you are likely to see many fishermen on this hike. Access into Lake Country is on the Smith Morehouse Trail which begins at the Crystal Lake Trailhead. The route described below is an easy day hike that

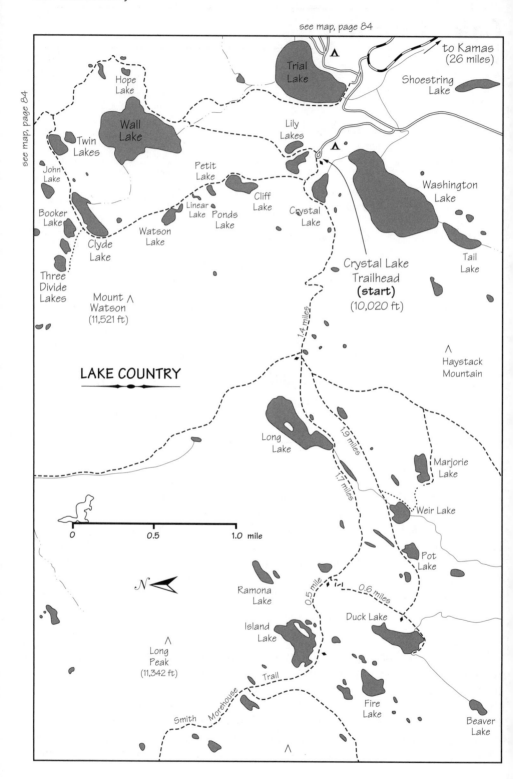

see map, page 84

to Kamas
(26 miles)

Shoestring
Lake

Trial
Lake

Hope
Lake

see map, page 84

Wall
Lake

Lily
Lakes

Twin
Lakes

John
Lake

Petit
Lake

Washington
Lake

Cliff
Lake

Booker
Lake

Linear
Lake

Ponds
Lake

Crystal
Lake

Watson
Lake

Clyde
Lake

Crystal Lake
Trailhead
(start)
(10,020 ft)

Tail
Lake

Three
Divide
Lakes

Mount ∧
Watson
(11,521 ft)

∧
Haystack
Mountain

1.4 miles

LAKE COUNTRY

1.9 miles

Long
Lake

Marjorie
Lake

1.7 miles

Weir Lake

0   0.5   1.0 mile

Pot
Lake

𝒩

Ramona
Lake

0.5 mile

0.6 miles

∧
Long
Peak
(11,342 ft)

Island
Lake

Duck
Lake

Morehouse   Trail

Fire
Lake

Smith

Beaver
Lake

∧

passes by three large lakes and a half-dozen smaller ones. For more adventurous backpackers interested in getting off the "beaten path" there are also several interesting off-trail lakes within a mile of the trail.

The trail begins by winding westward towards the north shore of Crystal Lake. For the first few hundred yards it follows what was once a road to the lake, but soon it narrows down to footpath size. After 0.2 mile you will see the trail to Cliff Lake and Clyde Lake branching off to the right, and shortly afterward the crystal blue water of Crystal Lake makes its appearance on the left. Few hikers bother to stop at Crystal Lake because it is so close to the trailhead, but it is one of the prettier lakes you will see on this hike. Although it is dammed its water level is not allowed to fluctuate; hence it is more pristine than many of the others, with grass and trees growing right to the water's edge.

Crystal Lake

After leaving Crystal Lake the trail climbs 250 feet to the top of a low pass between Haystack Mountain and Mount Watson, and then back down to the junction with North Fork Trail. Mount Watson is a particularly prominent landmark along this part of the walk. Its talus slopes rise gently to the top of a barren, dome-shaped summit a mile north and 1,300 feet above the trail.

When you reach the North Fork Trail junction, a half-hour from Crystal Lake, turn right towards Long Lake. This is the beginning of a loop through Lake Country that will take you past five named lakes and several smaller unnamed ones. Your return route will be along the North Fork Trail on your left. There is also a third trail near this junction that branches north towards the Middle Fork of the Weber River, but its departure point is unmarked and hard to find.

Another fifteen minutes will bring you to Long Lake, the largest of the lakes en-countered on this hike. The trail crosses the dam on the south side of the lake, and then turns left along the west side of the drainage below Long Lake. In the next mile you will pass by two more unnamed lakes before arriving at the junction where the Duck Lake Trail begins. Later you will have to turn south here to complete the Lake Country loop, but not before you have seen Island Lake. Like Crystal Lake, the water level in Island Lake does not fluctuate, and in my opinion it is the prettiest lake you will see on this hike.

To reach Island Lake just continue west on the Smith Morehouse Trail for another 0.5 miles. After gaining 200 feet in elevation the trail levels out on the south side of the lake. If you are

see color photo, page 164

looking for a place to spend the night, Island is a good choice. There are some good campsites on its west side, and this lake does not seem to be as heavily impacted as the other large lakes in the area. Beyond Island Lake there are no other major lakes on the Smith Morehouse Trail.

Shortly after leaving the Smith Morehouse Trail on the Duck Lake Trail, the path drops 150 feet to the north end of Duck Lake. Duck Lake is an active reservoir and there is usually a lot of bleached barren land exposed around the shoreline. Nevertheless, it is very popular among fishermen. Watch for a fork in the trail about midway along the east side of the lake, where you should bear left towards Weir Lake. There are no signs at the junction, but the trail is well trodden and easy to spot.

From Duck Lake the trail passes Pot Lake and two smaller unnamed lakes on its way to Weir Lake. As you leave Weir Lake you will pass another side trail marked by a sign that says "Route to Marjorie Lake".

This route heads generally in a southeasterly direction for 0.5 mile to Marjorie Lake. If you opt to take this route to Marjorie you can then complete the Lake Country loop by continuing east to the North Fork Trail and turning north.

I discourage you from visiting Marjorie Lake, however. It is too depressing to see what the dam builders and their bulldozers have done to what was once a lovely mountain pond. The southern shore of Marjorie now looks more like an unfinished highway construction project than a lake. The farmers in the Provo River watershed have secured a few more acre-feet of water storage capacity, but nature has paid the price.

From Weir Lake the trail continues westward for 1.0 mile to the North Fork Trail, where you must turn left to get back to the Smith Morehouse Trail. From there it is an easy 40-minute walk back to the Crystal Lake Trailhead.

Weir Lake

Fish Lake Loop

☆   day hike

Distance:	9.4 miles (loop)
Walking time:	6¹/₂ hours
Elevations:	2,400 ft. gain/loss
	Fish Lake Trailhead (start): 8,000 ft.
	Fish Lake: 10,180 ft.
	Ridge above Fish Lake: 10,400 ft.
Trail:	The first part of the trail is well used and easy to follow. The return portion of the trail from Fish Lake back to the road is sometimes vague, but the route is so well defined that a good trail is not really necessary.
Season:	Midsummer through mid-fall. The higher parts of the trail are usually covered with snow from mid-November until late June.
Vicinity:	40 miles east of Heber, near Oakley
Maps:	Whitney Reservoir *(USGS)*
	High Uintas Wilderness *(Trails Illustrated, #711)*
Information:	http://www.utahtrails.com/fishlake.html *(Utah Trails)*
	http://www.fs.fed.us/wcnf/ *(Wasatch-Cache Nat. Forest)*
	phone: (435) 783-4338 *(Kamas Ranger District)*

Drive east from Salt Lake City on Highway 80 for about 31 miles to Wanship and the junction with Highway 32. Turn south on Highway 32, towards Kamas, and drive for another 10 miles until you reach the farming community of Oakley. In the center of Oakley, just before you reach a Sinclair gas station you will see a large sign directing you to "Smith and Morehouse" and "Weber Can- *yon". Turn left here onto the Weber Canyon Road. After 12 miles the Weber Canyon Road forks and the pavement ends. Make a note of your odometer reading here, and continue driving straight ahead into the privately owned Thousand Peaks Ranch. From this point on you will see dozens of signs warning you not to leave the road. If you feel unwelcome, it is probably because you are. But, although the land is privately owned, the road itself is a public right-of-way that extends for 8.5 miles to the Forest Service boundary. 6.8 miles after entering the Thousand Peaks Ranch you will pass the entrance to the Holiday Park Subdivision. 0.2 miles later the road crosses Dry Fork Creek, and after another 0.2 miles you will see a small parking area on the left, next to a sign marking the trailhead.*

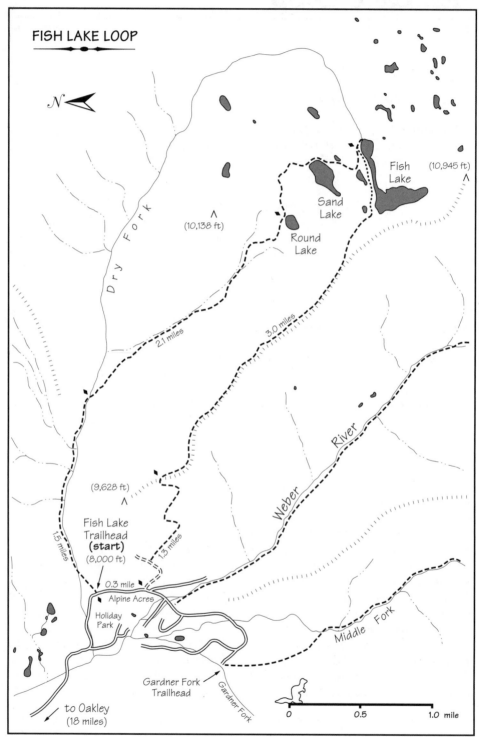

FISH LAKE LOOP

N

Dry Fork

∧ (10,138 ft)

Sand Lake

Round Lake

Fish Lake

(10,945 ft)

∧

2.1 miles

3.0 miles

Weber River

(9,628 ft)
∧

1.5 miles

Fish Lake Trailhead
(start)
(8,000 ft)

1.3 miles

0.3 mile

Alpine Acres

Holiday Park

Middle Fork

Gardner Fork Trailhead

Gardner Fork

to Oakley
(18 miles)

0   0.5   1.0 mile

see map, page 84

Fish Lake is a perfect example of why it is so imperative that we preserve the best of Utah's wild lands while we still can. Cut off from the High Uintas Wilderness Area by the Mirror Lake Highway, Fish Lake is located just above the beautiful Weber River Drainage on the western end of the Uintas. Conservationists have long pleaded that this region should be given wilderness protection too, but it is probably too late now for Fish Lake to be included. There are currently active housing developments within four miles of the lake, and the pressure to use the area's resources is unrelenting. Fish Lake is being used as a reservoir by the nearby inhabitants, and its shores are marred by the presence of dead trees, killed by fluctuating water levels. Also, ATV trails now climb the ridge east of the lake, and before too many more years they will almost certainly reach the lake itself.

Dry Fork

From the parking area the trail heads northeast through the aspen trees for 0.2 miles before reaching Dry Fork. In spite of the name, Dry Fork is seldom dry and must be forded (usually not a problem). The trail then climbs a few hundred feet above the north side of the creek for the next 1.3 miles, finally dropping back down to the stream in the middle of a small clearing for another crossing. Don't be confused at this point by the presence of another primitive trail that continues along the north side of Dry Fork. The trail up to the lakes lies on the south side of the creek.

After crossing Dry Fork, the trail leaves the water and begins a long slow ascent for the next 2.1 miles to Round Lake, the smallest of the three lakes you will pass on this hike. At 9,950 feet, Round Lake is 230 feet lower than Fish Lake and well below timberline. It is situated in a grassy meadow, surrounded by lodgepole pine and spruce, with a nice camping area on its northern shore.

see color photo, page 162

From Round Lake the trail climbs higher to Sand Lake (larger, but no grass around the sides), and finally, after 1.2 miles, to Fish Lake. Fish Lake is the source of the Dry Fork, and there is a small dam on its eastern side where the trail meets the lake. The flow through the dam is regulated to assure that there is always water running down the Dry Fork. The L-shaped lake is scenically situated at the base of a rocky ridge with one side of the L parallel to the ridge. The shores are also very rocky, but there are a few good camp sites on the northern side.

The trail seems to end at the dam, but if you proceed along the northern shore to the western end of the lake you will see another obvious trail starting up the ridge in a westerly direction from the corner of the L. The trail climbs 200 feet to the top of the ridge and then follows the crest back towards the road. The upper part of the trail is not well used and may occasionally seem to disappear. But don't be concerned if you have trouble following the trail. Just continue along the top of the ridge. Walking is very easy through the open forest, and as long as you stay on the ridge you can't really get lost. After 3.0 miles you will come to a saddle where the trail drops off the ridge's western side. Beyond the saddle the ridge heads abruptly upward to the top of a small peak. But the trail is very distinct as you approach the saddle, so you really don't have to worry about missing the route down.

The last 1.3 miles of trail, from the ridge to the road below, have been seriously degraded by ATVs driving up and down the mountain. The trail is occasionally completely obliterated by the ATV roads. About 0.5 miles before reaching the bottom you will encounter a steep, narrow gravel road which is part of the Alpine Acres Subdivision. Just follow this new road downhill until it reaches the main access road near the Weber River. When you reach the main road turn right and walk 0.3 miles back to your car.

Fish Lake

Nobletts Creek - Log Hollow

☆   **shuttle car or bicycle useful**
                                              day hike

Distance: 5.6 miles
                      (plus 1.1 miles by car, bicycle, or foot)

Walking time: 4 hours

Elevations: 1,620 ft. gain, 1,640 ft. loss
                      Nobletts Creek Trailhead (start): 7,460 ft.
                      Highest point: 9,080 ft.
                      Log Hollow Trailhead: 7,480 ft.

Trail: The trail is poorly maintained and often hard to follow. A
                      compass can be useful. There is no water along most of the trail,
                      but it is pleasantly shaded with conifers and aspen.

Season: Summer through mid-fall. The upper parts of the trail are usually
                      covered with snow from mid-November through mid-June.

Vicinity: Near Heber and Francis.

Maps: Soapstone Basin *(USGS)*
                      Wasatch Front *(Trails Illustrated, #709)*

Information: http://www.utahtrails.com/nobletts.html *(Utah Trails)*
                      http://www.fs.fed.us/r4/uinta/ *(Uinta National Forest)*
                      phone: (435) 654-0470 *(Heber Ranger District)*

From Francis take Highway 35 east through Woodland for 11 miles, where you will see a large sign on the right side of the road marking the boundary of Uinta National Forest. Just before you reach this sign there is an old jeep road leading into the forest from the left side of the road. This jeep road is where the hike will end, and your shuttle car or bicycle should be left here.

To get to Nobletts Creek, where the hike begins, continue driving on Highway 35 for another 1.1 miles past the Uinta National Forest sign. The trail starts on the north side of the creek, just before the road crosses the drainage, but unfortunately there is no sign to mark the trailhead. Don't be confused by a sign on the south side of the creek marking another more distinct trail to the Nobletts Creek Spring; this is not the trail you want for this hike.

This is a very pleasant hike through two small canyons on the edge of the Uinta National Forest. Both of the canyons are dry, although for a short distance the route follows the north side of the pretty Nobletts Creek. Unfortunately the Forest Service no longer maintains the trail and it is not heavily used; consequently it can be con-

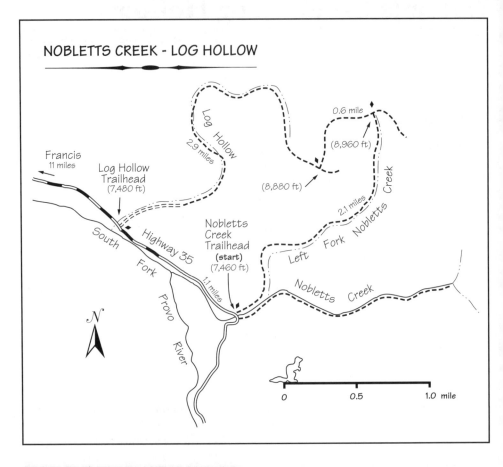

NOBLETTS CREEK - LOG HOLLOW

Log Hollow

0.6 mile

(8,960 ft)

Francis
11 miles

Log Hollow
Trailhead
(7,480 ft)

2.9 miles

(8,880 ft)

Nobletts
Creek
Trailhead
(start)
(7,460 ft)

2.1 miles

Left Fork Nobletts Creek

South Fork

Highway 35

1.1 miles

Nobletts Creek

Provo River

N

0   0.5   1.0 mile

Nobletts Creek

fusing in a few places. If you have some extra time before or after this hike, there is another better marked trail nearby that follows the south shore of Nobletts Creek for 1.5 miles to its source. That trail begins 200 feet further south, on the opposite side of Nobletts Creek.

From the road the track follows along the north side of Nobletts Creek for 0.3 mile to a point where the canyon forks. It then veers away from the stream and begins the long, gentle climb to the top of Left Fork Nobletts Canyon. After about 1.8 miles the canyon widens into a long grassy meadow where you will see an iron watering tank for sheep that are grazed in the area. (Tanks like this one are often full of dead birds that fly in to get a drink and drown trying to get out. If you want to help the birds, put something that floats, like a piece of wood, in the water so they will have a place to land when they come to get a drink.)

The meadow ends abruptly a short distance beyond the watering tank, and the trail intersects an old jeep trail. You should turn left at this point and follow the jeep trail in a westerly direction. After 0.3 mile the track swings to the south and begins descending again. This is the highest point on the hike. After another 0.3 mile you will enter a large grove of aspen, with a ground cover of tall green grass. You may find it difficult to follow the trail in the tall grass, but there are old blaze marks on the trees to help you.

Very soon you will run into the Log Hollow Trail, where you must make an abrupt right turn to complete the loop. Before starting down Log Hollow, however, I suggest that you turn left and go for about 300 yards to the east, where the trail dead-ends in a small clearing on the side of a knoll. Your reward is a terrific view of the South Fork Provo River Valley. Far below you can see Nobletts Creek where the hike began.

The remainder of the trail is easier to follow. After passing through two more meadows it slowly meanders downward through Log Hollow, finally coming to the end of an old jeep road about 2.3 miles from the top. Follow the jeep road for another 0.6 mile to Highway 35 where the hike ends.

Log Hollow

Row Bench

Distance: 5.2 miles
                   (plus 14.8 miles by car)

Walking time: 3¼ hours

Elevations: 960 ft. gain, 2,520 ft. loss
                   Row Bench Trailhead (start): 8,240 ft.
                   Highest point: 9,200 ft.
                   Center Canyon Trailhead: 6,720 ft.

Trail: Little used, but not too difficult to follow. Numerous sheep trails in the area can cause some confusion. A compass is useful.

Season: Summer through mid-fall. The road to Row Bench Trailhead may be closed from late November through May, and snow can be expected on the trail until mid-June.

Vicinity: Daniels Canyon, near Heber

Maps: Twin Peaks, Co-op Creek *(USGS)*
                   Wasatch Front *(Trails Illustrated, #709)*

Information: http://www.utahtrails.com/rowbench.html *(Utah Trails)*
                   http://www.fs.fed.us/r4/uinta/ *(Uinta National Forest)*
                   phone: (435) 654-0470 *(Heber Ranger District)*

Drive south from Heber on Highway 40 towards Strawberry Reservoir for 11 miles until you see a small sign on the left side of the road marking the turnout to Center Canyon. Turn left here on a small road that drops down to a parking area beside Daniels Creek. This parking area marks the end of the hike, and the shuttle car should be parked here.

To get to the beginning of the hike, return to Highway 40 from Center Canyon and drive south for 8.8 miles. You will come to a gravel road on the left side of the highway that heads north, through a wide, flat valley along the east side of the Strawberry River. Take this road (Forest Road #49) and drive north for 5.9 miles to Mill B Flat. There you will see a large livestock corral on the left side of the road. Park your car near the corral and walk about 200 yards farther down the road, across a cattle guard and a small bridge, where you will see a sign marking the Row Bench Trailhead.

The Row Bench Trail is a little used hiking trail that connects the upper part of Strawberry Valley to Daniels Canyon, southeast of Heber. Most of the walk is through

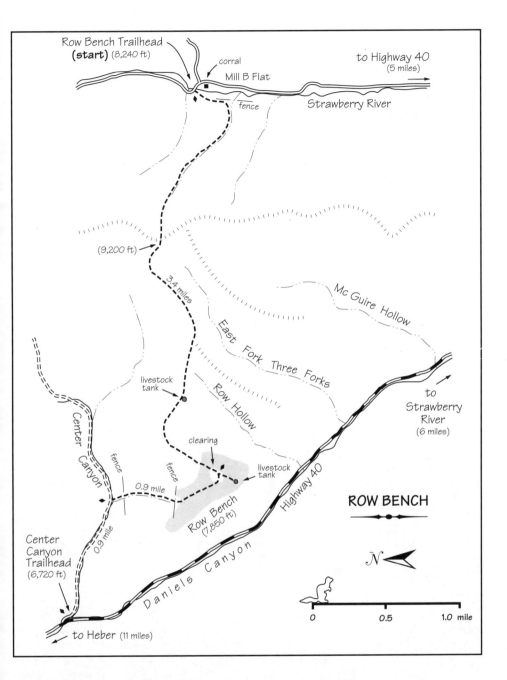

dense quaking aspen with some Douglas fir. It is very pretty—especially in September when the aspen are changing color. During the second half of the hike, as you begin to drop down from the ridge separating Straw-

berry Valley from Daniels Canyon, the forest opens up to some breathtaking views of Daniels Canyon and the mountains beyond. The area is open rangeland, so you may see some sheep. There is also a large population of deer in the area.

From Mill B Flat the trail rises gently in a southerly direction, up the side of Strawberry Valley, for about 0.2 mile before turning west to follow a dry wash towards the ridge above. You will see a barbed wire fence running below and parallel to the trail for about 0.1 mile before the path turns up the wash. After turning west, the trail climbs up the bottom

see color photo, page 164

of the dry wash for about 1.0 mile, then levels out near the top of the ridge above Strawberry Valley.

Soon after reaching this ridge, the trail crosses to a second ridge separating Center Creek and East Fork Three Forks. It then winds pleasantly along the crest for another 1.5 miles before descending abruptly onto Row Bench. Row Bench is a relatively flat plateau on the side of the mountain, running parallel to and about 900 feet above

the Daniels Canyon road. If you listen carefully you may hear the traffic on the road below at this point.

After you reach Row Bench the trail becomes somewhat confusing because sheep grazing on the bench have created other trails, and it is sometimes difficult to tell which trail is which. The correct trail continues in a southwesterly direction to a large clearing near the southern end of the bench, and then turns 90 degrees to a northwest heading. If you are on the correct trail you should see occasional blaze marks on some of the larger aspen trees. About 0.3 mile from the clearing the trail passes through a log fence and begins descending sharply through another small wash towards the bottom of Center Canyon. Finally, 0.5 mile after leaving the bench you will intersect a jeep road at the bottom of Center Canyon. Turn left and follow this jeep road for 0.9 mile, to Highway 40, where your shuttle car is parked.

Trail above Row Bench

Grandeur Peak

☆   **day hike**

Distance:	5.2 miles (round trip)
Walking time:	4 hours
Elevations:	2,340 ft. gain/loss Grandeur Peak Trailhead (start): 5,960 ft. Grandeur Peak: 8,299 ft.
Trail:	Well marked and well maintained
Season:	Summer through fall. The upper parts of the trail are usually covered with snow from late November through early June.
Vicinity:	On the east side of Salt Lake City
Maps:	Mount Aire, Sugar House *(USGS)* Wasatch Front *(Trails Illustrated, #709)*
Information:	http://www.utahtrails.com/grandeur.html *(Utah Trails)* http://www.fs.fed.us/wcnf/ *(Wasatch-Cache Nat. Forest)* phone: (801) 943-1794 *(Salt Lake Ranger District)*

Drive south of Salt Lake City on I-215 and turn east at the 3900 South exit. *After leaving the highway turn left at the first opportunity, drive one block north, and then east again onto 3800 South. 3800 South is the main road into Mill Creek Canyon. As you enter the canyon you will come to a toll booth where you will be charged an entrance fee of $2.00 per vehicle. Continue into the canyon for 2.3 miles beyond the toll booth, then turn left into the Church Fork Picnic Ground. The trailhead is on the north side of the picnic area, 0.3 mile from Mill Creek Canyon Road.*

There is only enough room for 8 cars at the trailhead, so unless you arrive early you may have to park on the main road outside the picnic ground. This will add an additional 0.6 miles round trip to the hike, but the walk up Church Fork is very pretty – even from the road. (Note: the road through the picnic ground is closed at 10:00 each night, so if you are planning a moonlight hike you had better park on the main road.)

Grandeur Peak is a favorite among residents of Salt Lake City simply because of its commanding position above the city. It is the last peak on the ridge separating Mill Creek Canyon from Parleys Canyon, and it seems to stand like a sentinel over South Salt Lake, watching every move in the city below. At 8,299 feet above sea level the peak

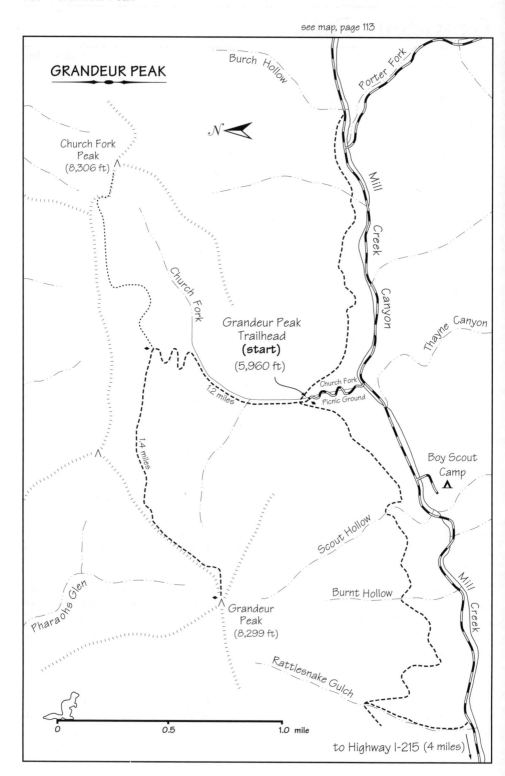

see map, page 113

GRANDEUR PEAK

Burch Hollow

Porter Fork

N

Church Fork
Peak
(8,306 ft)

Mill Creek Canyon

Church Fork

Thayne Canyon

Grandeur Peak
Trailhead
(start)
(5,960 ft)

1.2 miles

Church Fork
Picnic Ground

1.4 miles

Boy Scout
Camp

Scout Hollow

Pharaohs Glen

Burnt Hollow

Grandeur
Peak
(8,299 ft)

Mill Creek

Rattlesnake Gulch

0   0.5   1.0   mile

to Highway I-215 (4 miles)

is not particularly high, but from the ground it looks very imposing and many a resident of southeast Salt Lake has felt compelled to climb Grandeur just for the opportunity to view his neighborhood from the air.

The summit of Grandeur Peak is an especially fun place to be at sunset on a night with a full moon. As the sun sheds its last light on the valley the

see color photo, page 171

lights of the city slowly start to flicker on, until eventually the entire valley is aglow with the beacons of human activity. The moonlit descent down the upper portion of the trail is easy, but you will need a flashlight for the last 0.7 mile through the darker recesses of Church Fork Canyon.

For the first 0.7 miles the trail winds upward through the bottom of the heavily forested Church Fork Drainage. The trail is shaded by numerous bigtooth maples that turn fiery red in the Autumn, and the gurgling sounds of Church Fork are never far from the path. This pleasant part of the trail only lasts for 15-20 minutes though. Soon the small canyon veers east toward Church Fork Peak, and the trail begins a series of switchbacks up the left side of the canyon. As you leave the drainage the stately maple trees give way to a bushier cover of Gambel oak, as water becomes a more precious commodity.

After leaving Church Fork the trail climbs northward up the side of Mill Creek Ridge for another 0.4 miles, and then turns west for a more gradual assent to the top of the ridge. At the point where the trail finishes its last switchback and turns west toward Grandeur Peak you will see a more primitive trail departing on the right. This secondary, unmaintained trail leads to the top of Church Fork Peak, 1.2 miles away at the top of the Church Fork drainage.

Another 1.3 miles of relatively easy climbing will bring you to the top of the Mill Creek Ridge, and from there it is only 0.6 mile more to the summit of Grandeur. As you approach Grandeur Peak the entire Salt Lake Valley will open up under you. To the north are the high buildings surrounding Temple Square, and to the south are the more suburban towns of Murray and Midvale. Behind you is Church Fork Peak, with Mount Aire rising directly behind it. And further south the Twin Peaks, Lone Peak, and a dozen other peaks are prominently displayed above the Wasatch Front.

Salt Lake City, seen from Grandeur Peak

Mount Olympus

Mount Olympus Wilderness Area
day hike

Distance:	6.4 miles (round trip)
Walking time:	6 hours
Elevations:	4,200 ft. gain/loss Mount Olympus Trailhead (start): 4,830 ft. Mount Olympus: 9,026 ft.
Trail:	This is a very popular hike. The trail is well used and generally easy to follow. The last 0.1 mile below the summit, however, is very steep and rocky and some scrambling is necessary.
Season:	Summer through mid-fall. The upper parts of the trail are usually covered with snow from mid-November to early June.
Vicinity:	Near Murray and Salt Lake City
Maps:	Sugar House *(USGS)* Wasatch Front *(Trails Illustrated, #709)*
Information:	http://www.utahtrails.com/olympus.html *(Utah Trails)* http://www.fs.fed.us/wcnf/ *(Wasatch-Cache Nat. Forest)* phone: (801) 943-1794 *(Salt Lake Ranger District)*

This hike begins southeast of Salt Lake City, just east of I-215 on Wasatch Boulevard. If you are driving north on I-215 take the 3900 South exit to Wasatch Boulevard, then turn south and drive for 2.3 miles. If you are driving south on I-215 you will have to take the 4500 South exit to Wasatch Boulevard and then continue south for another 1.6 miles. Look for a paved parking lot on the east side of Wasatch and a sign that says "Mt. Olympus Trailhead".

Mount Olympus, the peak for which the Mount Olympus Wilderness Area was named, forms a very prominent part of the Murray skyline, and it has been a favorite hike of the nearby residents for almost as long as Murray has been a city. It is not unusual on weekends to see fifty hikers relaxing together on the rocky summit.

The climb described here leads to the south summit of Mount Olympus, but there is also a north summit. The two are about 300 yards apart, separated by the upper reaches of Tolcats Canyon. The south summit is higher than the north summit by 67 feet. It is also the only one with a good trail leading to it, and the one most frequently visited by hikers. The north face of the north summit, however, is a favorite among more serious mountain climbers. Although it looks foreboding, there is actually a route

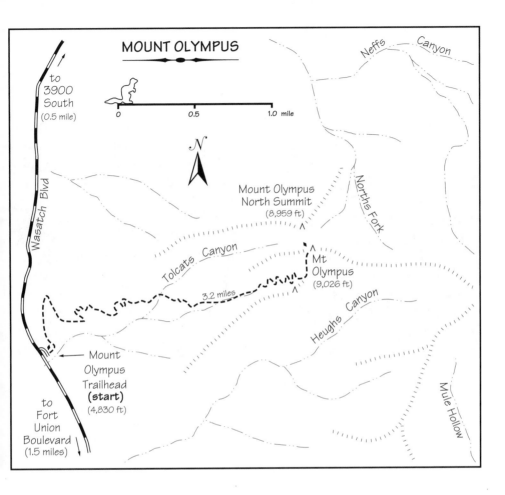

up the north face which requires little or no technical rock climbing skill. (See *Hiking the Wasatch*, by John Veranth.[2])

As you start up the trail to Mount Olympus you can look down and be thankful that in 1984, after a long and difficult fight by concerned citizens, most of it was included in the Mount Olympus Wilderness Area. The first half mile of the trail, however, crosses private land, and there is a real danger that some day it will be obliterated by real estate developers. Hopefully when this land is developed public access to the trail will be preserved.

Initially this is a desert hike. The trail winds upward from the parking area on Wasatch Boulevard through the dry grass lands that dominate the foothills, finally coming to the first juniper trees after a climb of about 500 feet. Then, as the trail enters Tolcats Canyon, the dominant vegetation turns to Gambel oak. The path crosses the bottom of Tolcats Canyon 1.7 miles from the trailhead, but, except in the spring, there is seldom water in the canyon.

Continuing upward along the south side of Tolcats Canyon, the trail never stops climbing until it reaches a small saddle 0.2

[2] John Veranth, *Hiking the Wasatch*, Wasatch Publishers, Salt Lake City, 1991.

Looking north from the summit of Mount Olympus

mile from the peak. As you approach the saddle the conditions change dramatically. A very pretty grove of Douglas fir occupies the ridge, and, for the first time since beginning the hike, you are on level ground. The presence of a few campsites indicates that hikers sometimes spend the night here, although there is no water.

From the saddle the trail turns directly north and soon encounters the rocky base of the summit. From here you must ascend the last 500 feet in scarcely more than 0.1 mile, scrambling up the Precambrian quartzite that caps most of the mountains around Big Cottonwood Canyon. You will occasionally need both hands, but if you stick to the trail the danger of injury from a fall is not great. Pay attention to the route. There is basically only one easy way up this side of Mount Olympus, and if you take a wrong

turn you will soon be confronted with a much more difficult climb. If that happens just stop and look around, and you will probably find the trail just a few feet away. The greatest danger is from falling rocks, so as you climb be careful not to dislodge loose rocks onto other climbers below.

The summit is little more than a giant's rock pile of jagged boulders, but the views are great. Much of Salt Lake City lies below, and the full expanse of the Wasatch Mountains stretches

see color photo, page 171

to the east. Lone Peak, Twin Peaks, and Dromedary Peak are clearly visible to the south, across the Cottonwood Canyons. To the north the summit drops off sharply into the upper reaches of Tolcats Canyon, beyond which, less than 300 yards away, is the north summit of Mount Olympus.

Gobblers Knob - Alexander Basin

☆ ☆ ☆ ☆

Mount Olympus Wilderness Area
shuttle car or bicycle useful
day hike

Distance: 7.0 miles (loop)
(plus 3.4 miles by car or bicycle)

Walking time: 6¼ hours

Elevations: 4,030 ft. gain, 3,110 ft. loss
Bowman Trailhead (start): 6,220 ft.
Baker Pass: 9,340 ft.
Gobblers Knob: 10,246 ft.
Alexander Basin Trailhead: 7,140 ft.

Trail: The trail to the top of Gobblers Knob is mostly well maintained and easy to follow, but for 0.7 mile, from Gobblers Knob down into the upper part of Alexander Basin, there is no trail. The descent is very steep and rocky but not technically difficult.

Season: Midsummer to mid-fall. Alexander Basin is usually filled with snow each year until July. Also, the road to the Alexander Basin Trailhead is closed each year until June 1.

Vicinity: Mill Creek Canyon, 10 miles east of Salt Lake City

Maps: Mount Aire *(USGS)*
Wasatch Front *(Trails Illustrated, #709)*

Information: http://www.utahtrails.com/gobblers.html *(Utah Trails)*
http://www.fs.fed.us/wcnf/ *(Wasatch-Cache Nat. Forest)*
phone: (801) 943-1794 *(Salt Lake Ranger District)*

Drive south of Salt Lake City on I-215 and turn east at the 3900 South exit. After leaving the highway turn left at the first opportunity, drive one block north, and then east again onto 3800 South. 3800 South is the main road into Mill Creek Canyon. As you enter the canyon you will come to a toll booth where you will be charged an entrance fee of $2.00 per vehicle. Continue into *the canyon for 3.9 miles beyond the toll booth, then turn right into the Terrace Campground. The Bowman Trailhead is near a parking area in the back of the campground, 0.2 miles from the main road. This is where the hike begins.*

To get to the Alexander Basin Trailhead, where the hike ends, return to the Mill Creek Canyon Road and drive 3.2 miles further up-canyon. Just beyond "The Firs" summer homes area you will see a small sign marking the Alexander Basin Trailhead on the right.

Note: Before June 1 of each year a locked gate on the Mill Creek Canyon Road prevents

cars from driving the last 2.4 miles to the Alexander Basin Trailhead. The Forest Service closes the gate ostensibly because of winter snow conditions, but I suspect there are other reasons as well. The snow in Mill Creek Canyon is usually gone well before June 1.

The relative ease with which Gobblers Knob can be climbed makes it one of the most popular summit destinations in the Wasatch Mountains. It is the highest point on the ridge separating Mill Creek Canyon from Big Cottonwood Canyon, and the view from the top is exceptional. It lies on the boundary of the Mount Olympus Wilderness Area just above the north-facing bowl of picturesque Alexander Basin. Gobblers Knob's proximity to Alexander Basin is in large part why it is such a delightful place; but, regrettably, it was also this proximity that prevented it, in 1984, from being wholly included in the Mount Olympus Wilderness Area. As a result, there is now a very real possibility that some day the view from the peak will be marred by the presence of ski lifts on its northern slopes.

Alexander Basin is one of those alpine gems for which the future is very uncertain. A fierce political battle was fought in the early 1980s over the boundaries of the proposed Mount Olympus Wilderness Area. Protection of Alexander Basin was a high priority among Utah's environmentalists, but since the basin is used by helicopter skiers they were opposed by the state's skiing industry. In the end the skiers won, and the scenic glacial cirque was excluded. The boundaries of the Mount Olympus Wilderness Area are now distorted by a huge gouge on the eastern side where Alexander Basin lies. Not only is the basin still used by helicopter skiers, but, even worse, it could easily become part of a future ski resort in upper Mill Creek Canyon. Proposals for such a resort have already been submitted to the Forest Service.

For the first 1.1 miles the trail to Gobblers Knob follows Bowman Fork, a small,

pleasantly shaded creek that originates north of the peak. All too soon, however, the path leaves the water and begins a series of switchbacks up through a stand of large conifers to the top of White Fir Pass, 600 feet above Bowman Fork. Once you reach the top of he pass the forest becomes less dense, and the trail settles down to a more gradual climb. Soon you will see Mount Raymond looming through the quaking aspen, and shortly after that you will see a trail to Alexander Basin departing on the left. Continuing upward towards Gobblers Knob, the next point of interest is Baker Spring.

Baker Spring was once the site of an old mining camp. There was a cabin here until the 1980s, but unfortunately it burned down

Looking North from Baker Pass

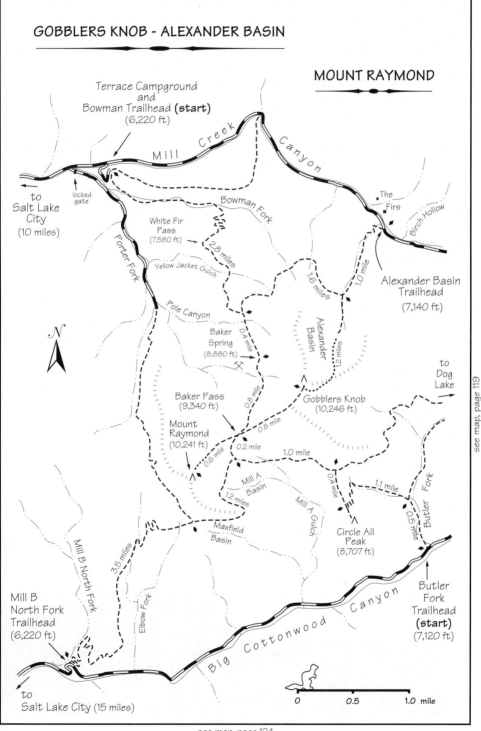

GOBBLERS KNOB - ALEXANDER BASIN

MOUNT RAYMOND

Terrace Campground
and
Bowman Trailhead **(start)**
(6,220 ft)

Mill Creek Canyon

to
Salt Lake
City
(10 miles)

locked
gate

Bowman Fork

The
Firs

Birch Hollow

White Fir
Pass
(7,580 ft)

2.8 miles

Porter Fork

Yellow Jacket Gulch

1.6 miles

1.0 mile

Alexander Basin
Trailhead
(7,140 ft)

Pole Canyon

Baker
Spring
(8,880 ft)

0.4 mile

Alexander
Basin

1.2 miles

to
Dog
Lake

Baker Pass
(9,340 ft)

0.8 mile

Gobblers Knob
(10,246 ft)

Mount
Raymond
(10,241 ft)

0.8 mile

0.2 mile

1.0 mile

0.6 mile

Mill A
Basin

1.2 miles

0.4 mile

Mill A Gulch

1.1 mile

Butler Fork

0.5 mile

Maxfield
Basin

Circle All
Peak
(8,707 ft)

Mill B North Fork

3.5 miles

Elbow Fork

Mill B
North Fork
Trailhead
(6,220 ft)

Butler
Fork
Trailhead
(start)
(7,120 ft)

Big Cottonwood Canyon

to
Salt Lake City (15 miles)

0   0.5   1.0 mile

see map, page 119

see map, page 124

and now there is no trace left of it. If you look around, however, you will see remnants of the mining activity. Baker Mine is about 300 yards south of the spring, and there are remains of a smaller mine just above the trail. Gobblers Knob is said to have gotten its name from the noise made by a flock of turkeys that were once kept by miners living in the area.

Beyond Baker Spring the scenery continues to become more and more inspiring. As you pass the 9,000 foot level the forest opens up to some fine views of Gobblers Knob, Mount Raymond, and the Great Salt Lake. When you reach the summit of Baker Pass, 0.8 mile later, you will be greeted by a panorama of the Twin Peaks Wilderness Area south of Big Cottonwood Canyon. To the right and to the left are Mount Raymond and Gobblers Knob, both rising about 900 feet above the saddle. Also at the crest of the pass you will see two other trails taking off in either direction along the ridge to the two nearby summits. You should turn east here for the climb to the top of Gobblers Knob. (See page 115 for a description of the trail up Mount Raymond.)

The trail up Gobblers Knob is not maintained, but it is well used and easy to follow. Except for the fact that it is all uphill, it is a fairly easy walk. The only downside is that there are several false summits along the route, and it is discouraging to see another heart-pounding climb in front of you after reaching what you thought was the top. Nevertheless, 45 min-

see color photo, page 172

utes of determined walking should get you to the top. The views are similar to the views from Baker Pass, but from this vantage point you can look down on Mount Raymond (5 feet lower).

Alexander Basin is the large bowl immediately northeast of Gobblers Knob. There is no trail from the top of the Knob into Alexander Basin, but it is not too difficult to drop off the summit and pick your way down through the basin to the trail below. The best way is to circle around the south side of Gobblers Knob to a saddle that lies about 400 yards east of the summit. The slope is very steep, but it is not too difficult to walk or slide down the north side of the saddle into Alexander Basin. Try to stay on the east side of the bowl as you make your descent, and after you have lost about 800 feet you will run into the trail coming up from Alexander Basin Trailhead. From there it is an easy 1.3 miles of downhill walking to the Mill Creek Canyon Road.

Summit of Gobblers Knob

Mount Raymond

 ☆ ☆ ☆ ☆

Mount Olympus Wilderness Area
shuttle car or bicycle useful
day hike

Distance: 9.3 miles
(plus 3.9 miles by car or bicycle)

Walking time: 7 hours

Elevations: 3,120 ft. gain, 4,020 ft. loss
Butler Fork Trailhead (start): 7,120 ft.
Baker Pass: 9,340 ft.
Mount Raymond: 10,241 ft.
Mill B North Fork Trailhead: 6,220 ft.

Trail: The trail is generally well used and easy to follow, except for the last two hundred yards below the summit of Mount Raymond. Here the path vanishes, and some scrambling is needed for the final ascent up a rocky ridge to the top.

Season: Midsummer to mid-fall. The higher parts of the trail are usually covered with snow each year until late June.

Vicinity: Big Cottonwood Canyon, east of Salt Lake City

Maps: Mount Aire *(USGS)*
Wasatch Front *(Trails Illustrated, #709)*

Information: http://www.utahtrails.com/raymond.html *(Utah Trails)*
http://www.fs.fed.us/wcnf/ *(Wasatch-Cache Nat. Forest)*
phone: (801) 943-1794 *(Salt Lake Ranger District)*

Drive south from Salt Lake City on I-215 and take the 6200 South exit. After exiting turn left, under the highway overpass, and drive southeast for about 1.8 miles. The road soon becomes Wasatch Boulevard, and shortly afterward you will come to a stop light at Fort Union Boulevard. Turn left on Fort Union and proceed into Big Cottonwood Canyon. About 4.3 miles up the canyon the *road enters a big "S" curve. Half way through the "S" there is a turn to the right into a parking lot at the Mill B North Fork Trailhead. This is where the hike ends, and where you should leave your shuttle car or bicycle.*

To get to the Butler Fork Trailhead, where the hike begins, continue up Big Cottonwood Canyon for another 3.9 miles. There you will see a smaller parking area on the left side of the road next to a sign marking the trailhead.

Mount Raymond is slightly lower than   its popular neighbor, Gobblers Knob, but it is more fun to climb. The angular peak rises from the apex of three weathered limestone ridges that come together at roughly equal angles on the eastern side of the Mount Olympus Wilderness Area. The assent route described here follows one of the ridges up from Baker Pass. It is an easy walk most of the way, but the last few hundred yards involve just enough scrambling to make the climb interesting. At the top you will be treated to an exhilarating view of Dromedary Peak and Twin Peaks on the other side of Big Cottonwood Canyon and Gobblers Knob east of Baker Pass.

see map,
page 113

This hike begins in Butler Fork, one of the prettiest areas in Big Cottonwood Canyon. The path meanders along the fork through the aspen and Douglas fir for about 0.5 miles, and then turns left onto another trail that follows a side canyon to the ridge east of the Mill A Basin. A Forest Service sign clearly marks the trail junction where you should bear left. From Butler Fork the trail climbs steadily to the west, beginning a series of switchbacks just before it reaches the ridge. Then, when you finally reach the ridge above Butler Fork the trail abruptly becomes flat again, and makes a sudden turn along the ridge to the north.

Once you reach the ridge, stop for a moment and look both ways. The main trail heads north to begin the long traverse around Mill A Basin, but you should see another fainter trail going back to the south. This is the trail to Circle All Peak. The trail to Circle All Peak is only 0.2 mile long with an elevation gain of 150 feet, so it would be a shame to miss it. The ten minute walk to the top will reward you with a nice view of Big Cottonwood Canyon, and also of your destination, Mount Raymond.

Continuing north on the main trail again, after 0.4 mile of level walking you will come to another trail junction. The right fork leads to Dog Lake, but to get to Baker Pass and Mount Raymond you must turn left. Again, the junction is clearly marked with a Forest Service sign. The next 1.2 miles across Mill A Basin to the top of Baker Pass is one of the most pleasant parts of the hike. The forest is more open here, with only an occasional grove of quaking aspen blocking the view, and Mount Raymond is clearly in sight. As you walk, study the ridge that runs from the west side of Bakers Pass to Mount Raymond. This will be your route to the summit. From the trail you can see the outcroppings of limestone on the ridge near the summit where you will have to do some scrambling to reach the top. Ten minutes before you reach Baker Pass you will see a smaller trail leading off to the left. This is the Mill B North Fork Trail that you will take on your way down. The trail to Baker Pass turns upward at this junction, reaching Baker Pass 0.2 mile later.

From Baker Pass it is a short but steep

Mt. Raymond, seen from Gobblers Knob

climb to the top of Mount Raymond. You still have about 900 feet of elevation to gain at this point. Two smaller trails branch off the main trail at the top of the pass, one leading to Gobblers see color photos, page 172 Knob and one leading to Mount Raymond. Turn left here for Mount Raymond. (See page 111 for a discussion of the trail to Gobblers Knob.)

The trail to Mount Raymond climbs steadily up the grassy ridge for 0.5 miles, but then seems to disappear at the base of a badly fractured knife-edge ridge of quartzite. Proceed straight up the crest of the ridge. Although you will need both hands, the climb along the knife-edge is not nearly as bad as it looks. Furthermore, this is the worst part of the climb. Beyond the knife-edge there is more minor scrambling, with bits and pieces of the trail visible. It is easiest if you stay right on the crest of the ridge. Within another ten to fifteen minutes you should be at the top.

While you are at the top be sure to study the route from Baker Pass back down on the Mill B North Fork Trail. The first part of the trail is clearly visible south of the peak. Also, you might want to study the ridge connecting Baker Pass to Gobblers Knob, just in case you want to do that hike on another day.

When you are ready to return retrace your steps to the point about 0.2 mile below Baker Pass where you earlier passed the Mill B North Fork Trail junction. Turn right here and continue walking in a southerly direction. The Mill B North Fork Trail winds around the south side of Mount Raymond for 1.2 miles, then comes to another junction with the Porter Fork Trail. Bear to the left at this point, towards Big Cottonwood Canyon. For the next 3.5 miles the trail meanders down the south slope of Mount Raymond, cutting through two small canyons and a grove of huge Douglas Fir trees before reaching the Mill B North Fork Trailhead. Finally, if you have time and energy left, you might want to double back up the bottom of Mill B North Fork Canyon to see Hidden Falls before you leave. It is only 0.1 mile from the trailhead.

Mount Raymond, seen from Mill A Basin

Dog Lake

Distance: 5.2 miles
(plus 0.8 mile by car, bicycle, or foot)

Walking time: 3³/₄ hours

Elevations: 1,680 ft. gain, 1,540 ft. loss
Butler Fork Trailhead (start): 7,120 ft.
Dog Lake: 8,740 ft.
Mill D Trailhead: 7,260 ft.

Trail: Popular, well maintained trail

Season: Summer through mid-fall. The higher parts of the trail are usually covered with snow until early June.

Vicinity: Big Cottonwood Canyon, near Salt Lake City

Maps: Mount Aire *(USGS)*
Wasatch Front *(Trails Illustrated, #709)*

Information: http://www.utahtrails.com/doglake.html *(Utah Trails)*
http://www.fs.fed.us/wcnf/ *(Wasatch-Cache Nat. Forest)*
phone: (801) 943-1794 *(Salt Lake Ranger District)*

Drive south from Salt Lake City on I-215 and take the 6200 South exit. Turn east on 6200 South (which soon becomes Wasatch Boulevard) and drive for two miles to the stop light at Fort Union Boulevard. Turn left on Fort Union, note your odometer reading, and proceed into Big Cottonwood Canyon. You will see the Mill D Trailhead and parking area on the left side of the road 9.1 miles up the canyon. This trailhead marks the end of the hike.

To get to Butler Fork Trailhead, where the hike begins, drive a short distance from Mill D Trailhead back down Big Cottonwood Canyon toward Salt Lake City. After 0.8 mile you will see another parking area on the north side of the road and a small sign marking the Butler Fork Trailhead.

The prettiest part of the Dog Lake loop is probably the first two miles of the hike along Butler Fork. Butler Fork meanders northward through a narrow canyon filled with dense groves of quaking aspen, eventually emerging into a more open forest of Engelmann spruce and Douglas fir along the ridge above Mill Creek Canyon. Although Dog Lake itself lies outside the wilderness boundary, Butler Fork is part of the Mount Olympus Wilder-

see color photos,
page 172

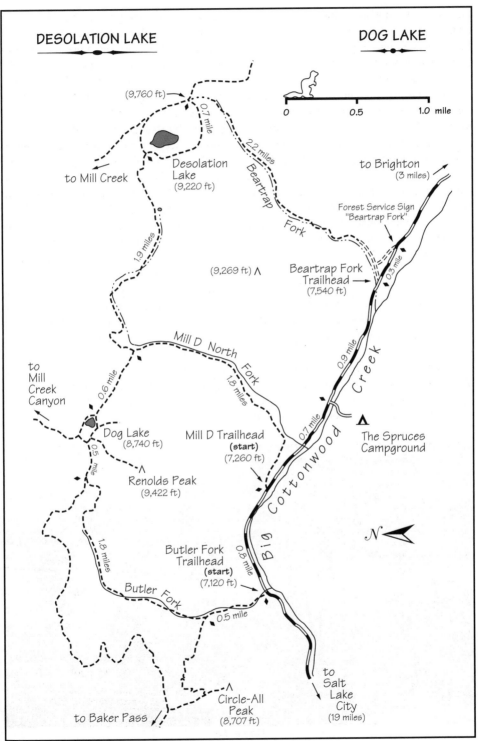

DESOLATION LAKE

DOG LAKE

(9,760 ft)

0.7 mile

2.2 miles

Beartrap Fork

to Brighton
(3 miles)

Forest Service Sign
"Beartrap Fork"

Desolation
Lake
(9,220 ft)

to Mill Creek

0   0.5   1.0 mile

1.9 miles

(9,269 ft) ∧

Beartrap Fork
Trailhead
(7,540 ft)

0.3 mile

Mill D North Fork

0.9 mile

to
Mill
Creek
Canyon

1.8 miles

0.9 mile

Dog Lake
(8,740 ft)

Mill D Trailhead
(start)
(7,260 ft)

0.7 mile

The Spruces
Campground

0.5 mile

∧
Renolds Peak
(9,422 ft)

Big Cottonwood Creek

N

1.8 miles

Butler Fork
Trailhead
(start)
(7,120 ft)

0.8 mile

Butler Fork

0.5 mile

to
Salt
Lake
City
(19 miles)

to Baker Pass

∧
Circle-All
Peak
(8,707 ft)

see map, page 113

ness Area. It is not uncommon to see moose along this part of the trail. Look for their hoof tracks along the path—similar to deer tracks, but two to three times larger.

Dog Lake is located in a shallow, heavily forested basin just south of the ridge that separates Mill Creek Canyon from Big Cottonwood Canyon. It is aptly named, since it is very popular among hikers with dogs. If you want to take a dog to Dog Lake, however, you will have to use the Big Water Trail which begins in Mill Creek Canyon. The Big Cottonwood Creek watershed area is a source of culinary water for Salt Lake City; hence dogs are prohibited along the route described here.

About 0.5 mile from the Butler Fork Trailhead you will encounter a fork in the trail with the better used left fork leading to Mill A Basin. Take the right fork for Dog Lake. The trail climbs steadily for another 1.8 miles, finally coming to another fork about 1,680 feet above the trailhead at the top of the ridge. Again, bear right along the crest of the ridge. As you near Dog Lake, about 0.5 mile further

east along the ridge, you may be confused by a number of trails that branch off to the north and south. Pay attention to the map, and remember that Dog Lake is just a short way below the ridge on the south side. If you start climbing abruptly to the south you are probably headed for Renolds Peak. If you start descending abruptly to the north you are probably headed down into Mill Creek Canyon. Look for Dog Lake just a few hundred feet after the trail begins descending to the south.

From the southeast corner of Dog Lake a well used mountain bike trail descends for 0.6 mile to another trail junction. Here you will see a sign directing you to either Desolation Lake (left) or Mill D Trailhead (right). Take the right fork to the Mill D Trailhead. There are a lot more hikers on this side of the loop than along Butler Fork. There are also some summer homes along the east side of Mill D North Fork, and you may catch glimpses of a lower trail that follows the east side of the creek. Finally, you should arrive at Big Cottonwood Canyon and the Mill D Trailhead about an hour after leaving Dog Lake.

Dog Lake

Desolation Lake

☆ ☆

shuttle car or bicycle useful
day hike

Distance:	6.6 miles
	(plus 1.6 miles by car, bicycle, or foot)
Walking time:	5 hours
Elevations:	2,500 ft. gain, 2,220 ft. loss
	Mill D Trailhead (start): 7,260 ft.
	Desolation Lake: 9,220 ft.
	Desolation Lake Overlook: 9,760 ft.
	Beartrap Fork Trailhead: 7,540 ft.
Trail:	Most of the trail is well maintained and easy to follow, but some parts of the Beartrap Fork section can be confusing.
Season:	Summer through mid-fall. The higher parts of the trail are usually covered with snow until early June.
Vicinity:	Big Cottonwood Canyon, near Salt Lake City
Maps:	Mount Aire, Park City West *(USGS)*
	Wasatch Front *(Trails Illustrated, #709)*
Information:	http://www.utahtrails.com/desolation.html *(Utah Trails)*
	http://www.fs.fed.us/wcnf/ *(Wasatch-Cache Nat. Forest)*
	phone: (801) 943-1794 *(Salt Lake Ranger District)*

Drive south from Salt Lake City on I-215 and take the 6200 South exit. Turn east on 6200 South (which soon becomes Wasatch Boulevard) and drive for two miles to the stop light at Fort Union Boulevard. Turn left on Fort Union Boulevard, note your odometer reading, and proceed into Big Cottonwood Canyon. You will see the Mill D Trailhead and parking area on the left side of the road 9.1 miles up the canyon. This trailhead marks the beginning of the hike.

To get to Beartrap Fork Trailhead, where the hike ends, continue up the canyon for another 1.6 miles until you see a locked gate on the left side of the road with the words "Beartrap Fork Gate No. 1" painted on it. This is where the hike will end, and this is where you should leave your shuttle car or bicycle. Don't be confused by a forest service sign 0.3 miles further up the highway that says "Beartrap Fork". If you park your shuttle at the forest service sign you will have that much farther to walk along the road.

Desolation Lake is a popular destination for mountain bikers, so you are bound to see a few of them on this hike. But don't expect all of them to be riding—there is a 2,000-foot elevation gain from the trailhead to the lake, and riding a bike uphill is much harder than walking.

The lake itself is located at the bottom of what, at first glance, looks like an old volcanic crater. The 550-foot-deep crater is actually a large bowl that was scooped out at the head of Mill D North Fork Canyon by a glacier during the last ice age. The view from the crater rim can be quite spectacular, especially in early September when the aspen trees on the northwest side of the lake are displaying their fall colors. On weekends one can often see fifteen or twenty mountain bikers parked on the trail above the lake, pausing to enjoy the view before their long downhill ride back to Big Cottonwood Canyon.

see map,
page 119

From Mill D Trailhead the trail winds up through the aspens along the north side of Mill D North Fork for 1.8 miles to the intersection with Desolation Trail. If you want to see Dog Lake before continuing on, bear left here for 0.6 mile. Otherwise, turn right for Desolation Lake. Up to this point the hike has been an almost unbroken uphill climb. There is still more uphill walking to come, but for the last 1.9 miles before Desolation Lake there is also a fair amount of level ground. It is a beautiful walk, through occasional meadows with fine views of the surrounding peaks. Finally, with almost no warning, the trail runs into the lake.

see color photos,
pages 172, 173

To reach the rim above Desolation Lake, bikers normally take the better used trail that goes up the northern side of the crater. But if you want to connect with Beartrap Fork, as I suggest, you should bear right and go up the lesser used path that climbs the crater's southern flank. Once you have negotiated the 550-foot climb to the top, follow the south rim trail around in an easterly direction until it meets the trail coming from the north. At the point where the trails meet, above the southeastern side of the lake, you will see Beartrap Fork Canyon directly below you to the south. This is the route that will take you back to the highway in Big Cottonwood Canyon.

Unfortunately, the first few hundred feet of the Beartrap Fork Trail are so vague you probably won't believe you are on a trail at all. But don't worry, the track soon becomes evident. As you descend from the top of the ridge into Beartrap Fork you will first see an occasional cairn. Then you will see faint trample marks in the grass, and by the time you reach the trees, 100 yards from the rim, you will be on a proper hiking trail. Initially the trail tends to follow the right side of the creek bed, which is on the left side of the canyon.

There are few switchbacks on the Beartrap Fork Trail, and for the first mile the path is quite steep. But soon the canyon floor levels out in a dense grove of quaking aspen, where you will begin to appreciate the beauty of the little used route. Finally, about 0.5 mile from the highway, the trail turns into a jeep road. Some confusion may occur as you near the end, because the jeep road is intersected by other primitive roads. Just remember to always take the road that heads downhill, and you should intersect the highway exactly at the point where you parked your shuttle.

Mountain biking on Desolation Trail

Lake Blanche

☆ ☆ ☆

Distance:	5.6 miles (round trip)
Walking time:	4½ hours
Elevations:	2,580 ft. gain/loss Lake Blanche Trailhead (start): 6,320 ft. Lake Blanche: 8,900 ft.
Trail:	Popular, well maintained trail
Season:	Summer through mid-fall. Snow can be expected on the upper parts of the trail from mid-November through mid-June.
Vicinity:	Big Cottonwood Canyon, near Salt Lake City
Maps:	Mount Aire, Dromedary Peak *(USGS)* Wasatch Front *(Trails Illustrated, #709)*
Information:	http://www.utahtrails.com/blanche.html *(Utah Trails)* http://www.fs.fed.us/wcnf/ *(Wasatch-Cache Nat. Forest)* phone: (801) 943-1794 *(Salt Lake Ranger District)*

Drive south from Salt Lake City on I-215 and take the 6200 South exit. After exiting turn left, under the highway overpass, and drive southeast for about 1.8 miles. The road soon becomes Wasatch Boulevard, and shortly afterward you will come to a stop light at Fort Union Boulevard. Turn left on Fort Union and proceed into Big Cottonwood Canyon. About 4.3 miles up the canyon the *road enters a big "S" curve. Just as the "S" begins you will notice a smaller road branching off to the right. Take this road for 0.2 mile and look for the Lake Blanche Trailhead near a Forest Service toilet on the right.*

Lake Blanche is one of the most popular hikes in the Salt Lake City area, not only because the walk is relatively short and the trailhead easy to get to, but because of the scenic beauty and the geologic attractions within the Lake Blanche Basin. Blanche and its two sister lakes, Florence and Lillian, sit in a high alpine basin that was dug out by a glacier during the last ice age. Long straight scratch marks and deep polished grooves, etched out by the glacier, are still clearly visible on the stone surrounding the lakes. Picturesque Sundial Peak (10,320 ft.), which the Wasatch Mountain Club uses as its emblem, rises abruptly from the south shore of Lake Blanche, and Dromedary Peak (11,170 ft.) is only a mile to the southwest. Blanche, its two sister lakes, Dromedary Peak, and the Sundial are all part of Utah's 11,300-acre Twin Peaks Wilderness Area.

see map, page 113

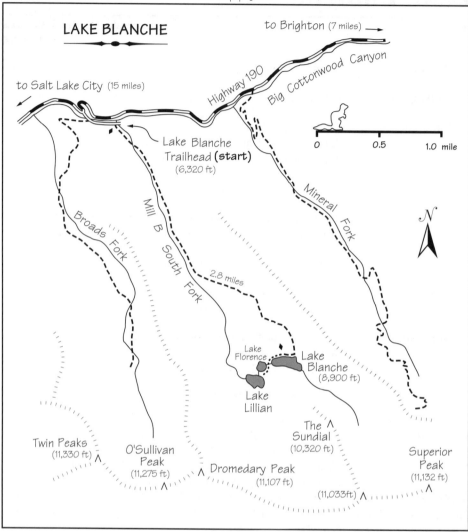

LAKE BLANCHE

to Brighton (7 miles) ➝

to Salt Lake City (15 miles)

Highway 190

Big Cottonwood Canyon

Lake Blanche
Trailhead (start)
(6,320 ft)

0   0.5   1.0 mile

Broads Fork

Mill B South Fork

Mineral Fork

N

2.8 miles

Lake
Florence

Lake
Blanche
(8,900 ft)

Lake
Lillian

The
Sundial
(10,320 ft)

Twin Peaks
(11,330 ft)

O'Sullivan
Peak
(11,275 ft)

Dromedary Peak
(11,107 ft)

(11,033 ft)

Superior
Peak
(11,132 ft)

From the trailhead the path begins climbing immediately, and continues to climb at a fairly steady grade of about a thousand feet per mile all the way to the lake. The trail crosses Mill B South Fork once, after 0.3 mile, and then stays on the east side of the canyon for the rest of the hike. About half way to the lake the trail leaves the stream and veers to the east in order to avoid some cliffs at the head of the canyon. Also at about this time you will leave the quaking aspen and enter into a conifer forest.

As you climb towards the lake you will see frequent evidence of winter and spring avalanches, and in at least one area a rock slide has obliterated the trail. When you reach this part of the path just proceed across the slide area and look for the trail continuing on the other side. Such gaps in the track are never very long, but they do serve to warn hikers of the potential dangers of hiking the Wasatch in the early spring.

When you are near the top you will begin to see the Sundial rising behind the pass at the head of the canyon. The trail gets steeper here, but you can take heart in the fact that you are almost at the end. Lake Blanche is just on the other side of the pass. As you approach the lake be sure to look for the long scratches in the polished red rock, scraped out by the glacier that carved Lake Blanche Basin in the last million years.

Glacier scratches at Lake Blanche

Most hikers don't bother to visit Lake Florence and Lake Lillian. The two smaller lakes can't actually be seen from Lake Blanche, but they are only a short walk away and shouldn't be missed. Walk to the old dam at the west end of Blanche and you will be able to look down on Florence and Lillian, about 120 feet lower and 200 yards away. The view of the Sundial isn't quite as spectacular from Florence and Lillian, but if you enjoy solitude either one is a much more peaceful place to eat your lunch than Blanche. Also you are more likely to see deer and other wildlife there.

Sundial Peak, across a frozen Lake Blanche

Red Pine Lake

☆ ☆   **Lone Peak Wilderness Area**
                                              day hike

Distance:	7.0 miles (round trip)
Walking time:	5 hours
Elevations:	2,040 ft. gain/loss
	White Pine Trailhead (start): 7,580 ft.
	Red Pine Lake: 9,620 ft.
Trail:	Popular, well maintained trail
Season:	Summer through mid-fall. The upper parts of the trail are usually covered with snow from late November through late June.
Vicinity:	Little Cottonwood Canyon, near Salt Lake City
Maps:	Dromedary Peak *(USGS)*
	Wasatch Front *(Trails Illustrated, #709)*
Information:	http://www.utahtrails.com/redpine.html *(Utah Trails)*
	http://www.fs.fed.us/wcnf/ *(Wasatch-Cache Nat. Forest)*
	phone: (801) 943-1794 *(Salt Lake Ranger District)*

Drive south from Salt Lake City on I-215 and take the 6200 South exit. After exiting turn left, under the highway overpass, and drive southeast onto Wasatch Boulevard. The road soon passes the entrance to Big Cottonwood Canyon at Fort Union Boulevard and, after another four miles, arrives at the entrance to Little Cottonwood Canyon. Here you should turn left toward the *Snowbird and Alta skiing areas. Five miles up from the mouth of Little Cottonwood Canyon, or 1.2 miles past the Tanner Flats Campground, you will come to a paved parking lot on the right side of the highway where you will find the White Pine Trailhead. This is also the trailhead for Red Pine Lake.*

Located in the heart of Utah's Lone Peak Wilderness Area, Red Pine Lake definitely ranks among the prettiest of the Wasatch Mountains' high alpine lakes. It is a popular day or overnight hike and you are bound to meet many other trekkers along the way. But if you are looking for more solitude there are also several possible side trips off the main trail that receive far fewer visitors.

see color photos, page 174

From the parking area the trail winds down a short distance to Little Cottonwood Creek, which it crosses on a wooden foot bridge, and then proceeds at a gentle up-

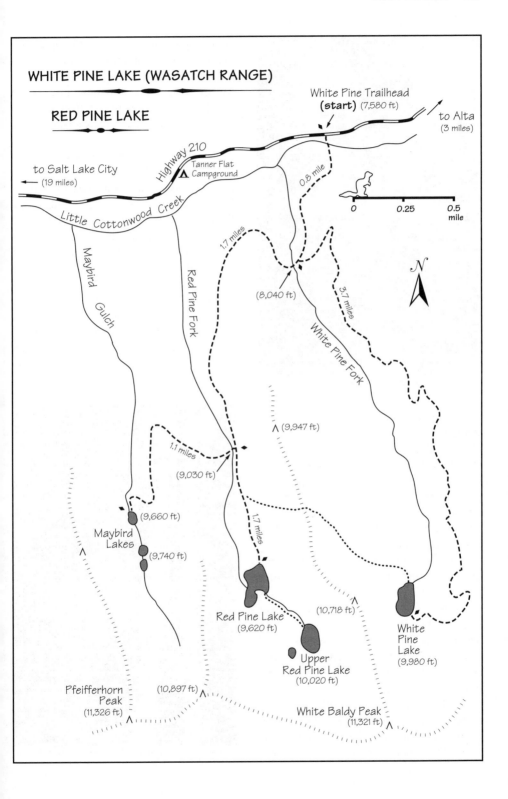

WHITE PINE LAKE (WASATCH RANGE)

RED PINE LAKE

White Pine Trailhead
(start) (7,580 ft)

to Alta
(3 miles)

Highway 210

Tanner Flat
Campground

to Salt Lake City
(19 miles)

Little Cottonwood Creek

0.8 mile

0   0.25   0.5
                          mile

Maybird Gulch

Red Pine Fork

1.7 miles

(8,040 ft)

3.7 miles

White Pine Fork

N

∧ (9,947 ft)

1.1 miles

(9,030 ft)

(9,660 ft)

Maybird
Lakes

(9,740 ft)

1.7 miles

Red Pine Lake
(9,620 ft)

(10,718 ft)

White
Pine
Lake
(9,980 ft)

Upper
Red Pine Lake
(10,020 ft)

Pfeifferhorn
Peak
(11,326 ft)

(10,897 ft) ∧

∧ White Baldy Peak
(11,321 ft) ∧

Red Pine Lake Trail

cipitously on the right, opening up a panorama of Little Cottonwood Canyon. Tiny cars can be seen meandering up from the canyon mouth on a gray thread of asphalt two thousand feet below, but after a few hundred feet the trail ducks back again into the trees and the brief contact with civilization is lost. The grade then becomes somewhat steeper as the path climbs deeper into Red Pine Canyon. Finally, at an elevation of 9,030 feet and a distance of 2.5 miles from the trailhead, the trail reaches the creek in the bottom Red Pine Canyon. At this point there is another junction in the trail, with the path to Maybird Lakes crossing Red Pine creek on the right. Red Pine Lake hikers should continue straight ahead on the east side of the creek, but not before pausing to appreciate the beauty of this spot. The forest now has turned from aspen to conifer, and there is an abundance of wildflowers

ward slope along the east side of White Pine Canyon. The first part of the trail is actually an old jeep road that was once used by miners in the upper part of the White Pine Canyon. The mining activity long ago proved uneconomical, however, and today few signs of this piece of Little Cottonwood's history are evident. Vehicles are no longer allowed on the trail.

About a mile from the parking lot the trail breaks out of the aspen trees to meet the water at White Pine Fork, and at this point the Red Pine Lake trail branches off to the right. Red Pine hikers must cross another foot bridge to follow a smaller westward trail. The elevation at this junction is about 8,040 feet, or 460 feet higher than the trailhead parking lot.

Half a mile farther the path rounds the ridge separating Red Pine Canyon from White Pine Canyon and again bends to the south. At one point the terrain drops off pre-

Aspen Trees along Red Pine Lake Trail

Red Pine Lake

self is about 600 feet across, with a smaller bay protruding on the south end where the forest comes right to the water's edge.

Upper Red Pine Lake

Southeast of Red Pine Lake, 0.4 mile distant and 400 feet higher in elevation, lies Upper Red Pine Lake. There is no established trail to Upper Red Pine, and very little vegetation exists around the lake. The setting, however, is spectacularly wild and rugged. The lake, which is about the same size as its lower twin, lies directly beneath the dramatic ridgeline. The best way to get there is along a small stream which comes down from the upper lake to the southeast side of Lower Red Pine. The route involves some scrambling over boulders but is not technically difficult.

Maybird Lakes

As mentioned earlier, the trail to Maybird Lakes leaves the Red Pine Trail about 2.5 miles from the highway, or about one mile down from Red Pine Lake. The Maybird Trail branches to the west, crossing Red Pine Fork on a narrow wooden bridge just after Red Pine Trail first meets the creek. It then follows a fairly level route for about 0.5 mile in a westerly direction before turning south again for the assent through Maybird Gulch to the three tiny Maybird Lakes.

The first lake is about 1.3 miles from the Red Pine trail junction at an elevation of 9,660 feet, and the second and third lakes are situated a quarter of a mile further up the gulch. The lakes are all small, only 100 to 150 feet across, and the trees surrounding them are stunted. The gulch is filled with the breakdown of the nearby cliffs, and there is not enough soil to support a more luxuriant forest. But the lack of vegetation does afford a fine view of Pfeifferhorn Peak, a popular summit that cannot be seen from the Red Pine Lakes.

along the grassy river bank – perfect for a short break.

Large patches of snow often lie across the last mile of the trail, sometimes until late July. This section of the canyon is well shaded on all sides except the north and the snow seems to last forever. The path also gets noticeably steeper near the top of the canyon, but finally, at an elevation of 9,600 feet, it abruptly levels off. The lake is a five or ten minute walk to the left from the top of the canyon.

The setting of Red Pine Lake is exquisite. The rugged crest that separates Little Cottonwood and American Fork Canyons, as well as the Wasatch and Uinta National Forests, lies just beyond the lake. White Baldy Peak (11,321 ft.) juts out prominently just a mile to the southeast, and to the north, across Little Cottonwood Canyon, Dromedary Peak (11,107 ft.) and Superior Peak (11,132 ft.) are clearly visible. The lake it-

White Pine Lake, Wasatch Range

☆   day hike

Distance:	9.0 (round trip)
Walking time:	6¹/₂ hours
Elevations:	2,540 ft. gain/loss White Pine Trailhead (start): 7,580 ft. White Pine Lake: 9,980 ft.
Trail:	Well maintained, easy to follow trail
Season:	Summer through mid-fall. Upper parts of trail are usually covered with snow from mid-November through mid-June.
Vicinity:	Little Cottonwood Canyon, near Salt Lake City
Maps:	Dromedary Peak *(USGS)* Wasatch Front *(Trails Illustrated, #709)*
Information:	http://www.utahtrails.com/whitepine.html *(Utah Trails)* http://www.fs.fed.us/wcnf/ *(Wasatch-Cache Nat. Forest)* phone: (801) 943-1794 *(Salt Lake Ranger District)*

Drive south from Salt Lake City on I-215 and take the 6200 South exit. After exiting turn left, under the highway overpass, and drive southeast onto Wasatch Boulevard. The road soon passes the entrance to Big Cottonwood Canyon at Fort Union Boulevard and, after another four miles, arrives at the entrance to Little Cottonwood Canyon. Here you should turn left toward the Snowbird and Alta skiing areas. Five miles up from the mouth of Little Cottonwood Canyon, or 1.2 miles past the Tanner Flats Campground, you will come to a paved parking lot on the right side of the highway, where you will find the White Pine Trailhead.

Like Alexander Basin, ten miles to the north, the area around White Pine Lake has long been the subject of intense controversy between Utah's environmentalists and ski resort owners. The original boundaries of Lone Peak Wilderness Area, created in 1977, were meant to include White Pine Lake, but lobbyists representing the nearby Snowbird Ski Resort succeeded in having White Pine Canyon excluded. Snowbird's Gad Valley ski lifts are only one mile from White Pine Fork, yet in spite of the nearness of civilization the pristine alpine lake still has that wild feeling of remoteness. What a shame it would be to open it up to commercial activity.

The trail to White Pine Lake actually follows an old jeep road that was built during the first part of this century to service small-

see map, page 127

claim mines in the canyon. The mining activity proved uneconomical, however, and it has been many years since the road was used. Now the Forest Service no longer allows motor vehicles in the area, and the vegetation has been so successful in reclaiming the track that few hikers will recognize that they are following an old road. Because the trail was originally a road it is not as steep as it would probably otherwise be. But, by the same token, the winding route is much longer than necessary.

From the parking area the White Pine Trail first crosses Little Cottonwood Creek on a small wooden foot bridge, and then begins its long gentle assent up White Pine Canyon. After 0.8 mile it breaks out of the quaking aspen to meet White Pine Fork, and then abruptly swerves again to the east away from the water. Near the water's edge the path splits, with the trail to Red Pine Lake departing to the right. If you cross the creek you are on the wrong trail.

see color photos, pages 174, 175

After a long switchback the trail again turns south and continues its meandering course towards the lake. The path never returns to the stream again, but it passes through several very attractive meadows. If you have sharp eyes you may spot the tailings of a few abandoned mines along the way, but time and nature have already healed most of the canyon's scars and the forgotten mines are no longer obvious.

As you approach the end of the trail the route makes a few large switchbacks up the east side of White Pine Cirque, just below the Red Baldy-White Baldy ridge, and then traverses westward along the talus slopes. Finally, the trail drops 120 feet into a small basin on the west side of the cirque, wherein is located the lake. White Pine Lake is about 300 feet wide and 600 feet long, about the same size as Red Pine Lake. The altitude is too high for lush vegetation, but there are some fair-sized spruce trees near the water's edge and a few good camping sites on the south shore. The elevation of the lake is just short of 10,000 feet.

Traversing to Red Pine Lake

Some experienced trekkers might want to add a little off-trail adventure to this hike by crossing the ridge that separates White Pine Lake from Red Pine Lake and returning to the trailhead via the Red Pine Trail (page 126). The traverse is not technically difficult, but be prepared for some scrambling across the bolder-strewn ridge. There is no established trail between the two lakes.

Begin by following the contour of the land from the northern shore of White Pine Lake in a general westerly direction for 0.5 mile to the crest of the ridge. From there Red Pine Lake is visible below, and it is just a matter of picking your way down the slope to intersect the Red Pine Trail a short distance north of the lake. The traverse can also be done in the opposite direction, but it is less tiring to start from White Pine Lake which is about 360 feet higher than Red Pine.

White Pine Lake Trail

Lake Mary - Grizzly Gulch

☆ ☆ ☆ ☆
shuttle car or bicycle useful
day hike

Distance:	6.4 miles (plus 2.5 miles by car or bicycle)
Walking time:	4¼ hours
Elevations:	1,370 ft. gain, 2,030 ft. loss

Elevations: 1,370 ft. gain, 2,030 ft. loss

Catherine Pass Trailhead (start):	9,400 ft.
Catherine Pass:	10,220 ft.
Lake Mary:	9,520 ft.
Twin Lakes Pass Trailhead:	8,740 ft.

Trail: Easy to follow, but numerous jeep roads and ski runs in the area create some confusion.

Season: Midsummer through mid-fall. The higher parts of the trail are usually covered with snow until July.

Vicinity: Alta ski area, above Salt Lake City in Little Cottonwood Canyon

Maps: Brighton, Dromedary Peak *(USGS)*
Wasatch Front *(Trails Illustrated, #709)*

Information: http://www.utahtrails.com/lakemary.html *(Utah Trails)*
http://www.fs.fed.us/wcnf/ *(Wasatch-Cache Nat. Forest)*
phone: (801) 943-1794 *(Salt Lake Ranger District)*

Drive south from Salt Lake City on I-215 and take the 6200 South exit. After exiting turn left, under the highway overpass, and drive southeast onto Wasatch Boulevard. The road soon passes the entrance to Big Cottonwood Canyon at Fort Union Boulevard and, after another four miles, arrives at the entrance to Little Cottonwood Canyon. Here you should turn left toward the *Snowbird and Alta skiing areas. Eight miles up Little Cottonwood Canyon you will enter the town of Alta, and after another 0.5 mile the pavement ends. Just before the pavement ends you will see a large parking lot on the right side of the highway overlooking two ski lifts that run up the side of Albion Basin. On the left side of the highway, directly across from the parking lot, a small sign marks the trail that leads up Grizzly Gulch to Twin Lakes Pass. This is where your hike will end, and where you should leave your shuttle car.*

To get to Catherine Pass Trailhead, where the hike begins, continue up the highway for another 2.5 miles towards the Albion Basin Campground. About 0.2 mile before reaching the campground you will come to a short, 100-yard-long road departing on the left. Catherine Pass Trailhead, also called Lake Mary Trailhead, is at the end of this road.

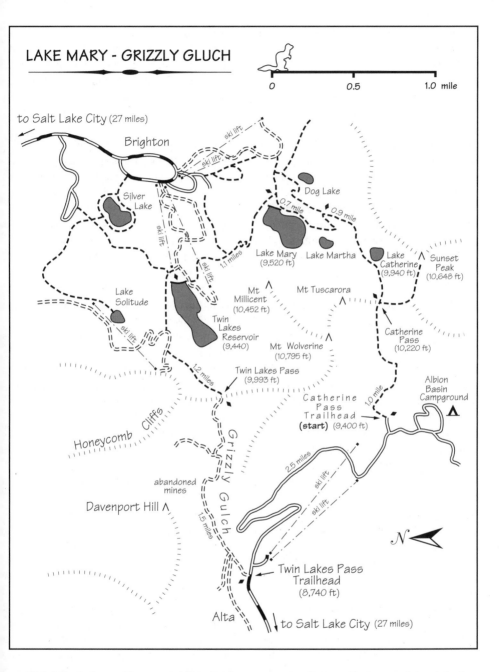

This hike is located between the ends of Big and Little Cottonwood Canyons, in the midst of the Brighton and Alta ski areas. It is a very pretty area, with many alpine lakes and green meadows, but unfortunately the presence of so much commercial activity has inevitably degraded the area's hiking potential. Especially around Brighton, at the end of Big Cottonwood Canyon, the mountains have been extensively bulldozed to fill the ever growing need for more ski runs and their associated service roads.

Grizzly Gulch, the return leg of this hike, is an open museum of the mining activity in Utah at the turn of this century. There are dozens of abandoned mines in the steep canyon, along with old boilers and pipes, and other relics of days gone by. Like most history lessons, this one also contains a message for the present. Looking at the heaps of mine tailings that now fill Grizzly Gulch, one can't help but wonder what the once pristine canyon was like before man's arrival, and how many other beautiful areas are being destroyed, even now, by unregulated mining activity.

From Catherine Pass Trailhead the trail immediately starts up a series of switchbacks. It continues to climb for about 820 feet, finally reaching the summit of Catherine Pass after a distance of 1.0 mile. Catherine Pass, with Catherine Lake immediately below it, is the most impressive viewpoint on this hike. The trail forks here, with the main trail dropping down to Catherine Lake on the left. If you enjoy panoramic views, however, you might want to turn right and climb to the top of Sunset Peak before continuing. Sunset Peak is the highest point on the ridge above Catherine Lake. The trail to the summit is 0.6 mile long (1.2 miles round trip), and involves an additional climb of 430 feet.

After passing Catherine Lake the next point of interest is Lake Martha, a small but very pretty lake at the base of the cliffs below Mount Tuscarora. Finally, only a few minutes beyond Lake Martha is Lake Mary. Lake Mary, actually a reservoir, is quite large (about 1,500 by 800 feet) and deep. It is also very scenic when full. But since it is used as part of Salt Lake City's water supply its size varies considerably, and when the water level is low its shores have an ugly barren look. After the trail passes Lake Mary Dam it starts descending towards Brighton.

Watch carefully here for another trail that leads off to the left, just below the dam, and climbs back up to the north side of the lake. This trail, called the Granite Lakes Trail, goes to Twin Lakes Reservoir.

You should follow the Granite Lakes Trail for 1.1 miles until it arrives at Twin Lakes Reservoir, crossing under the Millicent Ski Lift along the way. When you reach Twin Lakes Dam you must once again walk below and around the dam to the north side of the lake, where you will find the trail that goes to Twin Lakes Pass. For a short distance below the dam you will be on the a jeep road that was built from Brighton to service the dam.

Once you are on the north side of the Twin Lakes Reservoir start following a trail that climbs in a westerly direction, roughly parallel with the lake shore. Follow this trail until it intersects a ski run, then continue climbing on the ski run for another 0.2 mile or so, until you see the trail departing again on the left. When this trail leaves the ski run it climbs steeply for a few hundred feet to the top of the ridge, from where you can see the Twin Lakes Reservoir again far below. From there

| see color photos, |
| pages 175, 176 |

the trail traverses across the top of the Wolverine Cirque to Twin Lakes Pass, about 0.4 mile away.

To get from Twin Lakes Pass to Alta, where your shuttle car is parked, you must descend on the trail through Grizzly Gulch. This part of the trail is actually an old wagon road that was originally built by miners working the canyon at the turn of the century. It is very rocky and, in places, very steep. Judging from the remnants of all the mine shafts that scar the canyon bottom, there must have been a thriving community here. Grizzly Gulch may soon become the sight of still more construction activity; it is now the location of another proposed ski lift from Alta to the top of the Wolverine Cirque.

Mount Timpanogos

 ☆ ☆ ☆ ☆ ☆

Mount Timpanogos Wilderness Area
shuttle car or bicycle required
overnight hike

Distance: 17.3 miles
(plus 5.3 miles by car or bicycle)

Walking time: day 1: 8¹/₂ hours
day 2: 6¹/₂ hours

Elevations: 5,730 ft. gain, 5,280 ft. loss

Aspen Grove Trailhead (start):	6,910 ft.
Emerald Lake:	10,380 ft.
Mount Timpanogos:	11,749 ft.
Timpooneke Trailhead:	7,360 ft.

Trail: Popular, well maintained trail

Season: Midsummer through mid-fall. The higher parts of the trail are usually covered with snow from mid-November until July.

Vicinity: Near Sundance Ski Resort, above Provo and Orem

Maps: Timpanogos Cave, Aspen Grove *(USGS)*
Uinta National Forest *(Trails Illustrated, #701)*

Information: http://www.utahtrails.com/timpanogos.html *(Utah Trails)*
http://www.fs.fed.us/r4/uinta/ *(Uinta National Forest)*
phone: (801) 785-3563 *(Pleasant Grove Ranger District)*

Drive north through Provo on Highway 189 (University Avenue), or east through Orem on Highway 52 (800 North), until you reach the mouth of Provo Canyon. Continue east into the canyon on Highway 189 for 6.8 miles to the junction with Highway 92. Turn north here and drive for another 4.9 miles, past the Sundance Ski Resort, until you see a Forest Service sign on the left marking the Theater in the Pines Picnic Area. The Aspen Grove Trailhead, where the hike begins, is located just west of the parking area. (Note: Just before you reach the picnic area you will pass a Forest Service booth where you must purchase a $3.00/day recreation pass to park and hike in the area.)

To get to the Timpooneke Trailhead, where the hike ends, continue north on Highway 92 for another 5 miles to the entrance of Timpooneke Campground. Turn into the campground and drive for another 0.3 miles until you see the Timpooneke Trailhead and parking area on the left.

Mount Timpanogos has, for most of this century, been the most popular mountain climbing destination in Utah. The majestic mountain, second highest in the Wasatch

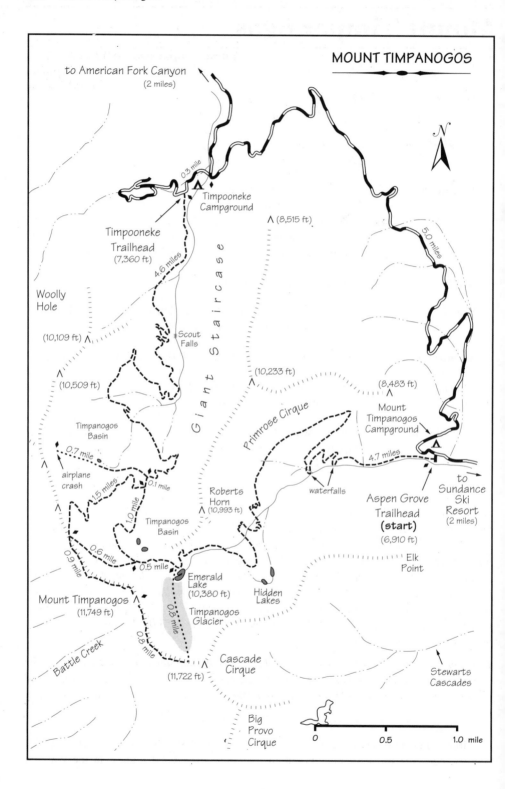

MOUNT TIMPANOGOS

to American Fork Canyon
(2 miles)

N

0.3 mile

Timpooneke
Campground

∧ (8,515 ft)

5.0 miles

Timpooneke
Trailhead
(7,360 ft)

4.6 miles

G i a n t   S t a i r c a s e

Woolly
Hole

(10,109 ft) ∧

Scout
Falls

(10,509 ft)

∧ (10,233 ft)

(8,483 ft)
∧

Mount
Timpanogos
Campground

Timpanogos
Basin

Primrose Cirque

0.7 mile

∧

airplane
crash

1.5 mile

0.1 mile

1.0 mile

∧

Roberts
Horn
∧ (10,993 ft)

4.7 miles

waterfalls

Aspen Grove
Trailhead
(start)
(6,910 ft)

to
Sundance
Ski
Resort
(2 miles)

Timpanogos
Basin

0.6 mile

0.9 mile

0.5 mile

Emerald
Lake
(10,380 ft)

Hidden
Lakes

Elk
Point

Mount Timpanogos ∧
(11,749 ft)

0.8 mile

Timpanogos
Glacier

Battle Creek

0.8 mile

(11,722 ft) ∧

Cascade
Cirque

Stewarts
Cascades

Big
Provo
Cirque

0   0.5   1.0 mile

Timpanogos Trail, Upper Primrose Cirque

Range, seems to have everything—an alpine lake just below the summit, a small glacier, waterfalls along the trail, and high alpine meadows that in late summer are filled with wildflowers. A herd of mountain goats can frequently be seen at the higher elevations, and history buffs can visit the remains of an old World War Two bomber that crashed north of the summit in the winter of 1955.

Timpanogos was popularized early this century by a local folk hero named Eugene "Timp" Roberts. Roberts was raised in Provo, and in the early 1900s he worked as the athletic director at Brigham Young University. As a young man he enjoyed exploring the mountains along the Wasatch Front, and while he was working at the university he began taking small groups of students up Mount Timpanogos. (In those days the trail began in Provo Canyon, and getting to the summit and back was a three-day trip.) The

excursions gradually grew in popularity, and by 1913 Roberts' hikes to the top of Timpanogos had become a university tradition.

Soon other enthusiasts from outside the university were clamoring to join the outings, and the annual event took on a life of its own. All-night parties were held in Aspen Grove, commemorative badges were handed out on the summit, special walking sticks were presented to dignitaries, sandwiches were sold at Emerald Lake, buses were chartered to carry hikers to the trailhead, and people showed up by the thousands. The event continued for the next 59 years.

In 1961 over 2,000 people reached the summit in a single day, and the Forest Service began to worry openly about the impact that so many hikers were having on the environment. In 1970 over 7,000 people participated in the "Timp Hike" with 3,500 of them reaching the summit. The pressure of so many hikers on the mountain in one day proved to be an unmitigated environmental disaster, and reluctantly the Forest Service ended the popular event.

Although the Timp Hike is no longer an organized annual event the mountain is still very popular, and thousands of people continue to climb to its summit every summer. Now, however, the trails are much better maintained and the number of visitors is more evenly distributed throughout the summer. Also the trails are now patrolled during summer weekends and holidays by a volunteer organization known as the Timpanogos Emergency Responce Team (TERT). The primary purpose of the TERT volunteers is to provide emergency medical assistance, but they also help protect the mountain by reporting illegal fires and other environmentally destructive activities to the Forest Service.

Day 1 (7.5 miles)
From the Aspen Grove Trailhead the

route heads west along a small unnamed creek that drains Primrose Cirque. Initially the grade is very gradual, but that soon changes. After 0.9 mile the trail reaches the base of a small water-fall, where it makes an abrupt right turn

see color photos, pages 176,177

and begins climbing through a series of switchbacks. In another 0.5 mile the path passes a second waterfall, and then enters a long switchback as it continues its assent up the north side of the cirque.

Finally, after a distance of 3.8 miles and an elevation gain of 2,930 feet from the trailhead, the well-worn path reaches the top of Primrose Cirque and passes into a flat open area south of Roberts Horn. If you got off to a late start you will see a delightful camping spot in a small grove of Engelmann spruce at the edge of the meadow; the site is about 100 yards south of the main trail at the end of a short spur. From this point it is another 1.0 miles to Emerald Lake, the first

major attraction of this hike.

Emerald Lake is one of the gems that make the Timpanogos hike so special. The tiny lake lies just on the edge of timberline at an elevation of 10,380 feet. To the south is Roberts Horn, and to the west, only 550 horizontal yards away, is the summit of Mount Timpanogos. The lake is frozen most of the year, but even when it is not covered with ice its temperature hovers near freezing. It is fed by a permanent snowfield that descends from the summit ridge to the south end of the lake. Although this snowfield is hardly a glacier it has been affectionately referred to as the Timpanogos Glacier at least since 1916.

The small valley around Emerald Lake also seems to be a favorite late-summer hangout for the mountain goats that live in the wilderness area, so be sure to look for them while you are there. The shaggy, majestic creatures have thrived since their introduction in 1981. Occasionally they ven-

Emerald Lake and the Timpanogos Glacier

ture to within a hundred feet of campers by the lake, but more often you will need a pair of binoculars to study them in detail.

Many backpackers camp at Emerald Lake on their way up Mount Timpanogos, especially if they plan to return to the Aspen Grove Trailhead. If you didn't bring a tent it is possible to sleep in a stone shelter that was built there in 1959 during the days of the Timp Hike. You will probably be more comfortable in a tent, though, as the stone shelter is very dark and dingy inside and has a cold cement floor. If you plan to finish the hike at the Timpooneke Trailhead, as I describe, I suggest you continue for another 1.8 miles into the Timpanogos Basin before making camp.

From Emerald Lake the trail continues west for 0.5 mile, and then loses 200 feet as it contours around the southwest side of Timpanogos Basin. 1.5 miles after leaving the lake you will come to a junction where the summit trail takes off to the left. Bear right at the summit trail junction, and within 200 yards you should see another trail leaving on the left near a sign that says "toilet". Turn left here and walk west into the upper part of Timpanogos Basin. You will pass the Forest Service toilet after 100 yards, and another 150 yards will bring you to an excellent camping area with running water nearby.

If you have time after making camp you will probably want to see the remains of the bomber that crashed in the back of Timpanogos Basin in 1955. It is only 0.5 mile from your campsite; in fact if you know what to look for you can see it from your camp. Look west, high into the back of the basin, and find the long line of cliffs that begin about 200 feet below the summit ridge. Just below the cliffs is a steep bench, and for a few hundred yards on the south side of the basin the bench is covered with talus from the cliffs above. The airplane crash is near the middle

Airplane crash in Timpanogos Basin

of this talus slope, about 400 feet above the bottom of the basin. It is an easy climb up to the crash. You should head in a direction that is almost exactly magnetic west of the Forest Service toilet.

The airplane that crashed was a World War Two B-25. Both engines are still intact, as are the main landing gear and some sections of the wings and tail. The airplane did not ignite on impact, although the Forest Service later burned the wreckage in an attempt to dispose of it. You may notice a peculiar chemical smell near the crash site; perhaps it is a remnant of the aviation fuel that was dumped on the ground when the plane crashed.

Day 2 (9.8 miles)

In order to climb to the top of Mount Timpanogos you must backtrack to the summit trail, which departs from the main trail

Emerald Lake, as seen from the summit

0.1 mile south of the Timpanogos Basin trail. You will be coming back the same way, so you can leave your backpack in Timpanogos Basin and retrieve it on the way down.

The summit trail immediately starts winding upward toward a saddle on the ridge north of the peak. The saddle is about 900 feet higher than the basin and well above timberline, so be ready for some marvelous views. Provo, Orem, and Utah Lake are prominently displayed below the west side of the ridge, while Timpanogos Peak holds a commanding position above the ridge 0.6 mile to the south.

The trail crosses the ridge and goes into a series of short, rocky switchbacks on the west side of the mountain, then, after a half-hour, ends at the small metal shelter that marks the summit. The steel structure was originally built by surveyors who, before the days of aerial mapping, used the peak as a triangulation point for their measurements.

Mount Timpanogos is situated directly on the geological boundary that separates the Rocky Mountain Province from the Great Basin Province. To the east, as far as the eye can see, is nothing but mountains; while to the west the Great Basin Desert stretches endlessly across western Utah, Nevada, and into California. Three other wilderness areas lie to the north within twenty miles of Timpanogos, and many other popular peaks such as Lone Peak and Twin Peaks are clearly visible. Mount Nebo, the highest mountain in the Wasatch Range, is 35 miles to the south.

The 4.6-mile walk down from Timpanogos Basin to the Timpooneke Trailhead provides another interesting lesson in geology. The route descends through a steep, glaciated valley that looses about 3,000 feet over a distance of two miles, but the grade is far from uniform. The valley descends over a series of five flat benches that are collectively known as the "Giant Staircase". It is interesting to speculate as how these stair steps were formed. The structural characteristics of the various horizontal layers of rock that make up the mountain are undoubtedly an important factor; the Timpanogos massif is composed primarily of limestone, quartzite, and sandstone, and I noticed that the tops of at least two of the benches are made up of smooth, unfractured limestone. Another factor could be that the valley was not carved by a single glacier, but by several glaciers of varying sizes and thicknesses. Over the past 2.5 million years the mountain has been subjected to the forces of glaciation on at least five different occasions.

A one-day hike

If you are planning this hike as a one-day outing I suggest you begin at the Aspen Grove Trailhead and return the same way, mostly because this route will give you the opportunity to visit Emerald Lake. The total distance to the summit and back from Aspen Grove is 13.4 miles and the elevation gain is 4,840 feet.

There is a shortcut trail near Emerald Lake that allows hikers to climb to the summit ridge without walking all the way into Timpanogos Basin. The shorter trail leaves the main trail 0.5 mile west of the lake near the bottom of a talus slope. You may have trouble finding the trail, since the talus is very unstable and subject to occasional landslides. If the shortcut trail has been obliterated just angle up the side of the slope in a northwesterly direction for a few hundred yards until you run into the well-marked summit trail just below the top of the ridge.

The normal return to Emerald Lake is along the same trails used for the assent; however more adventurous hikers might want to attempt an alternative route down the Timpanogos Glacier. A faint trail continues along the ridge for another 0.6 mile

beyond the summit of Mount Timpanogos to the top of the glacier that feeds the lake. It is only a fifteen-minute slide from the ridge to the lake, but be aware that under some conditions the descent down the glacier can be dangerous. Many injuries have been sustained by people sliding into rocks on the glacier, especially late in the summer when buried boulders are often exposed by the melting snow. There have also been cases of people breaking legs after falling through snow bridges, and even falling into the freezing lake at the bottom of the glacier. In my opinion, however, the degree of danger is not great for a person with some experience on snow and some common sense. The grade is very steep for the first few hundred feet, but after that one can easily walk down the snow. An ice axe is useful but thousands of hikers make the descent every summer without one. A short, strong stick can also be a great help in steering and braking on the snow, but don't expect to find any sticks above Emerald Lake.

Upper Timpanogos Basin (July)

Santaquin Peak

☆ ☆   **day hike**

Distance:	11.4 miles (round trip)
Walking time:	8 hours
Elevations:	3,195 ft. gain/loss Loafer Mountain Trailhead (start): 7,490 ft. Santaquin Peak: 10,685 ft.
Trail:	Well used and easy to follow
Season:	Summer through mid-fall. The upper parts of the trail are usually covered with snow from mid-November through late June.
Vicinity:	Near Spanish Fork and Payson
Maps:	Payson Lakes, Birdseye *(USGS)* Uinta National Forest *(Trails Illustrated, #701)*
Information:	http://www.utahtrails.com/santaquin.html *(Utah Trails)* http://www.fs.fed.us/r4/uinta/ *(Uinta National Forest)* phone: (801) 798-3571 *(Spanish Fork Ranger District)*

Leave I-15 at exit 254 and drive one mile south into the town of Payson. Once you are in Payson make your way to the corner of 100 North and 600 East and turn south onto 600 East. This is the beginning of the Mount Nebo Scenic Loop Drive. 12.2 miles from the beginning of the scenic loop drive, or 0.1 mile before reaching the turnoff to Payson Lakes, you will see a small parking area on the left next to a sign marking the Loafer Mountain Trailhead.

Although many peaks along the Wasatch Front are considerably higher than Santaquin Peak, few of the area's hikes are more scenic than this one. The trail is especially beautiful in the fall, as it passes through numerous groves of maple and aspen on its way to Loafer Ridge. Although the elevation gain is over 3,000 feet, the gain is fairly well distributed along the 5.7 mile length of the hike; hence the climb is not excessively strenuous. You should carry a pair of binoculars to the top, since there is a lot to see. Splendid views of Mount Nebo and the Payson Lakes can be seen to the south, while Mount Timpanogos and Utah Lake provide a backdrop for Provo, Payson, and other nearby towns in the north.

From the trailhead the path winds through the woods for 1.1 miles, gaining about 350 feet in elevation before coming to a trail sign and junction near an old coral.

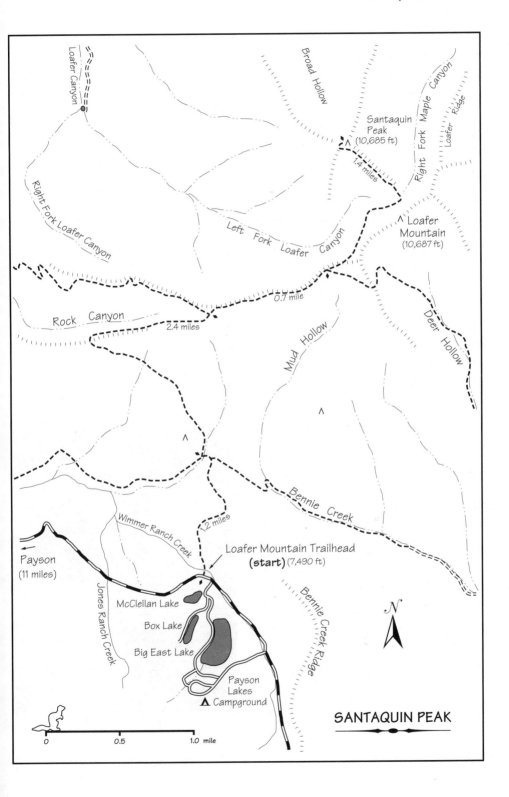

Loafer Canyon

Broad Hollow

Right Fork Maple Canyon

Loafer Ridge

Santaquin Peak (10,685 ft)

1.4 miles

Right Fork Loafer Canyon

Left Fork Loafer Canyon

Loafer Mountain (10,687 ft)

0.7 mile

Rock Canyon

2.4 miles

Mud Hollow

Deer Hollow

Bennie Creek

.2 miles

Wimmer Ranch Creek

Loafer Mountain Trailhead **(start)** (7,490 ft)

Payson (11 miles)

Jones Ranch Creek

McClellan Lake

Box Lake

Big East Lake

Bennie Creek Ridge

N

Payson Lakes Campground

0   0.5   1.0 mile

SANTAQUIN PEAK

Turn left here in order to stay on the Loafer Mountain Trail. (You will be on the Loafer Mountain Trail for the first 4.3 miles of this hike.) The trail continues east for only 0.1 mile before coming to another junction where you must turn right. Again there is a forest service sign at the junction. You should stay on the Loafer Mountain Trail, No. 98.

The trail now settles down to a long, gradual climb of 2,000 feet over the next 2.4 miles to the top of the Loafer Mountain Ridge. Once you reach the ridge you will be out of the trees and you can start enjoying the views. Payson Lakes are directly below you, and Mount

see color photos, pages 177, 178

Nebo (11,928 ft.) is the pyramid-shaped peak above the horizon 12 miles to the south. Santaquin Peak, your destination, will also come into view in front of you as you climb onto the ridge. Santaquin is the most prominent peak on the left.

After another 0.7 mile the ridge reaches a shallow saddle, where a faint trail branches off to the right. The lesser used trail is the continuation of the Loafer Mountain Trail, which swings to the east at this point and eventually descends down the mountain through Deer Hollow. To reach Santaquin Peak you must bear left at this saddle, staying on the better trail. There shouldn't be any confusion because the other trail is so vague you might not even see it. Furthermore, you goal, Santaquin Peak, is directly in front of you now and it is quite obvious which direction you should go.

Before continuing, pause for a moment at the saddle to study the two peaks in front of you, Santaquin on the left and Loafer on the right. They are about 0.7 mile apart and are separated by a deep notch. From this prospective Santaquin appears to be the higher of the two, but it is actually slightly lower. Nevertheless, Santaquin is a much more interesting climb. Loafer is not really a peak at all, but rather just the highest point on a long, unappealing ridge. Also, it is hard to see Utah Valley from Loafer Peak because the view is obstructed by Santaquin. But if you insist on scaling the higher of the two peaks it isn't too difficult to make your way from the saddle up the ridge to the top of Loafer. The climb will require about 880 feet of elevation gain. There is no trail but there are no serious obstacles either, and the route is quite straightforward

The trail from the saddle to the top of Santaquin Peak contours around the west side of the Loafer Mountain Ridge until it reaches the bottom of the notch separating the two peaks. It then ascends toward the top of Santaquin, traversing around the south side of the summit and reaching the peak 0.6 mile later. The elevation gain from the bottom of the notch is about 430 feet.

Santaquin Peak

Mount Nebo

 ☆ ☆

Distance:	13.2 miles (round trip)
Walking time:	day 1: 5 hours day 2: 7 hours
Elevations:	5,400 ft. gain/loss Nebo Bench Trailhead (start): 6,480 ft. Suggested campsite: 9,440 ft. Mt. Nebo (south summit): 11,877 ft. Mt. Nebo (north summit): 11,928 ft.
Trail:	The trail is generally easy to follow, however it is very steep in places and has no reliable water.
Season:	Midsummer through mid-fall. The upper parts of the trail are usually covered with snow from mid-November until July.
Vicinity:	Mount Nebo Wilderness Area, near Nephi
Maps:	Nebo Basin, Mona *(USGS)* Uinta National Forest *(Trails Illustrated, #701)*
Information:	http://www.utahtrails.com/nebo.html *(Utah Trails)* http://www.fs.fed.us/r4/uinta/ *(Uinta National Forest)* phone: (801) 798-3571 *(Spanish Fork Ranger District)*

Take Exit 225 off I-15 near Nephi and proceed east on Highway 132 towards Moroni. After you have driven 5.0 miles from I-15 you will see a sign directing you to the Mount Nebo Scenic Loop Road on the left. Turn here and drive north for 3.3 miles until you see another paved road on the left going to Ponderosa Campground. Turn left again and drive for 1.3 miles, past Ponderosa Campground, until you see a small parking area on the left where there is a trail register and a sign marking the Nebo Bench Trailhead.

Mount Nebo, the centerpiece of the Mount Nebo Wilderness Area, is the highest peak in the Wasatch Mountains. As one might expect, the views from its summits are spectacular, but it is also one of the most strenuous hikes in this book. The trail to the southern summit climbs 5,400 feet, over a mile of elevation gain, in only 6.6 miles of trail, and, to make matters worse, there is no reliable source of water along the way. Most people who climb Nebo reach only the southern summit (11,877 ft.), where the trail stops, but the northern summit (11,928 ft.) is actually the highest point. The two lie about a

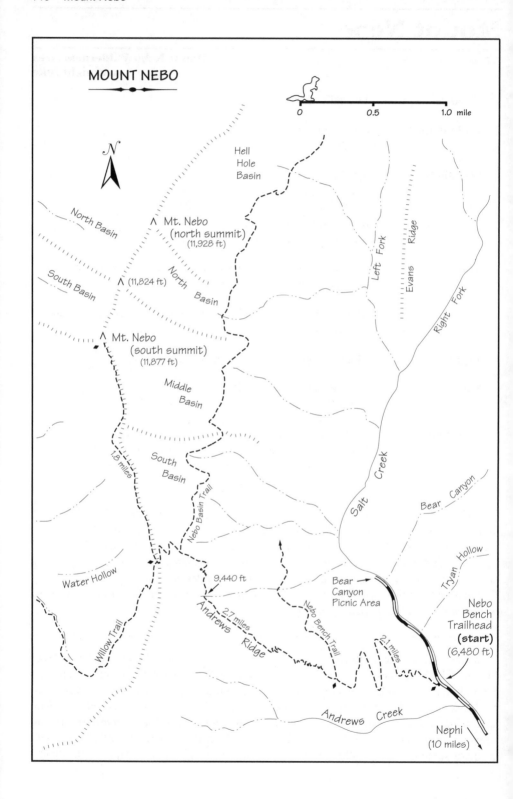

MOUNT NEBO

N

0   0.5   1.0 mile

Hell Hole Basin

North Basin

South Basin

∧ Mt. Nebo (north summit) (11,928 ft)

∧ (11,824 ft)

North Basin

∧ Mt. Nebo (south summit) (11,877 ft)

Middle Basin

South Basin

1.8 miles

Nebo Basin Trail

Water Hollow

Willow Trail

9,440 ft

2.7 miles

Andrews Ridge

Nebo Bench Trail

2.1 miles

Left Fork

Evans Ridge

Right Fork

Salt Creek

Bear Canyon

Tryan Hollow

Bear Canyon Picnic Area

Nebo Bench Trailhead **(start)** (6,480 ft)

Andrews Creek

Nephi (10 miles)

Andrews Ridge, below Mount Nebo

mile apart on a long knife-edge summit ridge, with a third, slightly lower peak between them.

Many hikers climb Mount Nebo's southern summit as a day hike, and a few hardy souls even manage to ascend the northern summit in one day. But it is a very strenuous climb, and if you enjoy the mountains I suggest an overnighter might be more appropriate. There are several good campsites along the way, and the extra day will give you time to really appreciate the rugged alpine wilderness.

Day 1 (3.8 miles)

From the trailhead the Nebo Bench Trail begins by ascending in a westerly direction through the dense conifer forest. Then, after about 0.5 mile, it swings to the north to begin the first of four wide, altitude-gaining switchbacks up to Andrews Ridge. This section of the trail appears to have been improved and relocated in the early 1990s,

probably for the benefit of the many pack horses that use the Nebo Bench Trail. After 2.0 miles the trail finally breaks out of the forest into a relatively clear area of wildflowers, sage brush, and scattered shrub oak. This clearing represents the beginning of Andrews Ridge, up which the Nebo Peak Trail runs for the next 1.5 miles.

The Nebo Peak Trail departs from the Nebo Bench Trail just above the point where it first reaches Andrews Ridge. Watch carefully as you leave the clearing, and after about 200 yards you should see a smaller trail leaving the main trail on the left. The Peak Trail is unmarked and, worse, it is obscured by a dense undergrowth of Gamble oak, but if you are attentive, you should be able to spot it. The main trail continues climbing gradually in a northerly direction, while the trail to Nebo Peak rises more steeply to the west.

Beyond the trail junction the Nebo Peak Trail makes its way westward along Andrews Ridge for a distance of 1.4 miles before finally dropping off the north side of the ridge. I suggest you establish a camp here at the top of the ridge. At this point you are 3.1 miles from the south summit of Mount Nebo, and the elevation is 9,450 feet. There are also some nice camp sites on the summit ridge, 1,100 feet higher, but you will sleep much better at the lower altitude. Furthermore, carrying a backpack above 10,000 is very tiring.

Day 2 (9.4 miles)

From the top of Andrews Ridge the trail bears north for 0.9 mile, crossing into South Nebo Basin, and then turns west again for the climb up to the top of the summit ridge. Don't be confused by another less well used trail that continues north across South Nebo Basin. This is the old route of the Nebo Bench Trail. Finally, 1.3 miles after leaving Andrews Ridge the trail reaches a shallow saddle in the summit ridge. An old wooden sign indicates that this is also the point where Willow Creek Trail reaches the ridge. The Willow Creek Trail is another route to the top of Mount Nebo that begins east of the town of Mona.

The next 1.3 miles along the summit ridge, towards the base of Mount Nebo's south peak, is probably the most pleasant part of the hike. The views are outstanding. On the west side of the ridge is the farming community of Mona, surrounded by fields of grain and alfalfa, with I-15 snaking past on its way up the Utah Valley. To the east, as far as the eye can see, are mountains and forests—Uinta National Forest, Manti-La Sal National Forest, and beyond that, Ashley National Forest. But most spectacular of all is the view to the north along the summit ridge. The three peaks of Mount Nebo, each one more rugged than the last, cling tenuously to the knife-edge ridge of uplifted limestone as they reach for the open sky above. Even in mid-July the ridge is often accented with patches of white snow, and the prevailing west winds frequently pile the snow into long graceful cornices along the eastern side. The trail avoids the cornices by staying slightly below the western side of the ridge.

see color photo, page 178

Just before reaching the south summit the trail crosses a small flat bench, then it climbs the last 500 feet to the top. The trail ends at the south summit, and this is as far as most people go. The north summit, 0.9 mile further on, is 51 feet higher, but getting there and back adds at least two more hours to the hike. The route is not technically difficult, but some hand-over-hand scrambling is required and there are a few places where a fall could be disastrous. The north summit is particularly dangerous in bad weather. Do not attempt to reach it unless you have plenty of time and the weather is good.

Mount Nebo, North Peak, as seen from South Peak

Fish Creek

☆

Distance:	9.9 miles (plus 38 miles by car)
Walking time:	5¹/₂ hours
Elevations:	1,080 ft. loss Upper Fish Creek Trailhead (start): 8,780 ft. Lower Fish Creek Trailhead: 7,700 ft.
Trail:	This trail has been designated as a National Recreation Trail. It is a gentle, downhill walk along a small mountain stream, usually well maintained and easy to follow.
Season:	Summer through mid-fall. The road to the upper trailhead is generally closed each year from the end of November until mid-June, and the upper reaches of the trail are very muddy until the end of June.
Vicinity:	Fifty miles southeast of Spanish Fork, near Scofield
Maps:	C Canyon, Scofield Reservoir *(USGS)*
Information:	http://www.utahtrails.com/fishcreek.html *(Utah Trails)* http://www.fs.fed.us/r4/mantilasal/ *(Manti-LaSal Nat. Forest)* phone: (435) 637-2817 *(Price Ranger District)*

Turn off I-15 at exit 261 (near Spanish Fork) and drive east toward Price for 44 miles until you reach the junction with Highway 96. Turn right here and drive south for another 16.7 miles to the town of Scofield. On the west side of Scofield you will find a small paved road that heads north along the west side of the Scofield Reservoir. Drive north on this road. After 3.6 miles the pave- *ment ends, and 0.3 miles farther the road splits. Bear to the left here, away from the lake, and within 1.6 miles you will arrive at Fish Creek Campground where the lower Fish Creek Trailhead is located. This is where the hike ends, and where you should leave your shuttle car.*

To get to the upper trailhead, where the hike begins, drive back to Scofield and continue south on Highway 96. After three miles you will encounter a junction where Highway 264 begins. You should bear to the right here onto Highway 264. Finally, 18.5 miles from Scofield, you will come to a stop sign at the junction where Highway 264 meets Highway 31. Two hundred yards before you reach the stop sign you will see a gravel road, North Skyline Drive, leaving on the right. Turn onto North Skyline (forest road 150) and continue for 13.7 miles, until you see a small forest service sign that says "Fish Creek Trail". The actual

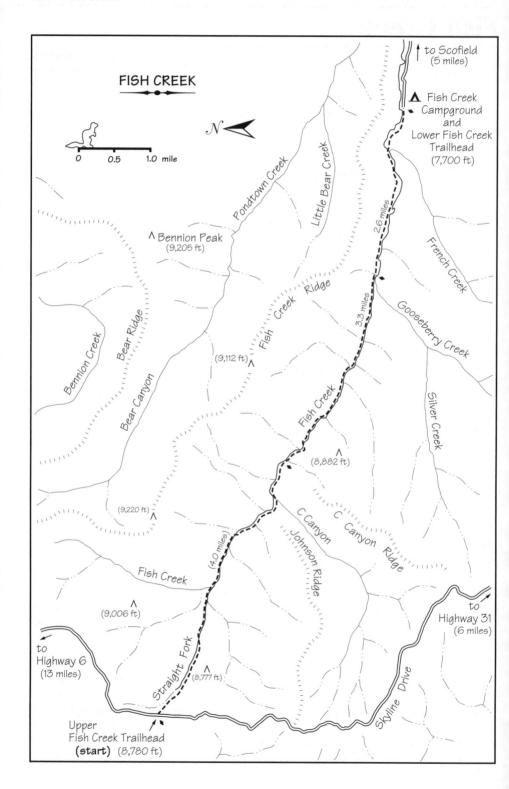

FISH CREEK

0   0.5   1.0 mile

N

to Scofield
(5 miles)

Fish Creek
Campground
and
Lower Fish Creek
Trailhead
(7,700 ft)

Pondtown Creek

Little Bear Creek

French Creek

Λ Bennion Peak
(9,205 ft)

2.6 miles

Gooseberry Creek

Bear Ridge

Fish Creek Ridge

3.3 miles

Bennion Creek

(9,112 ft) Λ

Fish Creek

Silver Creek

Bear Canyon

(8,882 ft) Λ

(9,220 ft) Λ

C Canyon

C Canyon Ridge

Fish Creek

(4.0 miles)

Johnson Ridge

(9,006 ft) Λ

to
Highway 31
(6 miles)

to
Highway 6
(13 miles)

Straight Fork

(8,777 ft) Λ

Skyline Drive

Upper
Fish Creek Trailhead
(start) (8,780 ft)

trailhead is about 200 yards down a jeep road that begins near this sign.

Note: You can get back to Highway 6 by continuing north on Skyline Drive for another 14.7 miles beyond the trailhead.

Fish Creek runs down a wide, gently sloping canyon from a point near Skyline Drive to the Scofield Reservoir. The canyon is popular with hunters because of the abundance of deer and elk in the area. Deer are everywhere, but the elk seem to prefer grazing in the large, open meadows high above the south bank of the creek. Take along a pair of binoculars and stop occasionally to scan these grassy meadows. If you are attentive you are almost certain to see at least a few of the magnificent animals.

The creek runs from west to east, and you will notice a tremendous difference in vegetation between [see color photo, page 179] the north and south facing sides of the canyon. The north facing side is covered with aspens and conifers, interspaced with lush green meadows. The south facing side, on the other hand, is sage brush country with scarcely a tree to be found. Unfortunately the trail spends most of its time on the shadeless south facing side of the canyon.

From Upper Fish Creek Trailhead the path winds down Straight Fork a distance of 1.9 miles before reaching the confluence with Fish Creek. Occasionally you may see other faint trails coming into the canyon, including one where Straight Fork joins Fish Creek. If you are confused just take the path that follows closest to the creek; the route never strays far from the bottom of the valley. Over the length of the hike the path crosses the creek four times, but for the most part it stays on the north side of the streambed.

After walking 4.0 miles you will encounter the first of three Forest Service signs: a sign marking the bottom of C Canyon Ridge. C Canyon Ridge is also a popular access route into Fish Creek Canyon, and it was once possible to get to within a mile of the creek on a jeep road that follows the ridge. For several reasons, however, including the fact that Fish Creek is an important part of Scofield Reservoir's watershed area, the road is now closed.

As you continue down the canyon the volume of water in Fish Creek gradually increases, but for most of its length the stream isn't deep enough for good fishing. There would be more fish if the canyon's beaver population could make more permanent ponds in the streambed. The trail passes by numerous beaver dams, but virtually all of them have been breached. The dams rarely survive the spring floods. Only after Gooseberry Creek joins Fish Creek, 2.6 miles above the campground, does fishing really become feasible.

At French Creek, 0.7 miles from the end, the trail finally crosses to the shady south side of the canyon. Then, fifteen minutes later, it emerges from the forest at the lower trailhead in Fish Creek Campground.

Fish Creek Trail

Candland Mountain Loop

☆ ☆ ☆

shuttle car or bike required
day hike

Distance:	9.1 miles (plus 4.4 miles by car or bicycle)
Walking time:	6¼ hours
Elevations:	2,125 ft. gain, 2,505 ft. loss
	Mill Canyon Trailhead (start): 8,080 ft.
	Candland Mountain: 10,205 ft.
	Left Fork Huntington Creek Trailhead: 7,700 ft.
Trail:	Most of the trail is well maintained and easy to follow, but there are a few confusing junctions. The last 4.2 miles are along a designated National Recreation Trail.
Season:	Summer through mid-fall. Upper parts of trail are usually covered with snow from mid-November through mid-June.
Vicinity:	Huntington Canyon, near Price
Maps:	Candland Mountain *(USGS)*
Information:	http://www.utahtrails.com/candland.html *(Utah Trails)* http://www.fs.fed.us/r4/mantilasal/ *(Manti-LaSal Nat. Forest)* phone: (435) 637-2817 *(Price Ranger District)*

Drive south from Price on Highway 10 for 20 miles to the town of Huntington. At Huntington turn north on Highway 31 towards Huntington Canyon and Cleveland Reservoir. After 18 miles you will see a sign marking the turnoff to the Forks of Huntington Campground on your left. The Left Fork Huntington Creek Trailhead is at the back of Forks of Huntington Campground, 0.3 mile from the highway. This trailhead marks the end of the hike, and a shuttle car or bicycle should be left here.

To get to the Mill Canyon Trailhead, where the hike begins, return to Highway 31 and note the mileage on your odometer at the entrance to the Forks of Huntington Campground. Drive north for exactly 4.1 miles and you will see a small meadow on the west side of the road at the mouth of Mill Canyon. You will find a parking area beside the stream on the shoulder of the highway at the north end of the meadow, and if you look carefully across the stream you will see a small sign marking the beginning of Mill Canyon Trail. If you can't find the sign, don't worry. Just proceed across the meadow towards the mouth of the small canyon and within a few hundred feet you should stumble onto the trail.

The Candland Mountain Loop offers a fine combination of mountain and canyon hiking, with just enough elevation gain to let you know that you have been on a hike and not just a Sunday afternoon stroll. The final 4.2 miles of the hike are down the Left Fork Huntington Creek, an exceptionally pretty stream, on a designated National Recreation Trail.

see color photo, page 179

From the mouth of Mill Canyon the trail begins its assent almost immediately, gaining about a thousand feet per mile for the next 2.1 miles. When you reach the top of the ridge you will intersect an old pack trail that starts farther north and follows the long summit ridge of Candland Mountain. You could continue straight across the pack trail at this point, but if you do so you will miss the marvelous views along the ridge. Instead, turn left and follow the pack trail along the ridge in a southerly direction.

After a five-minute climb up the old

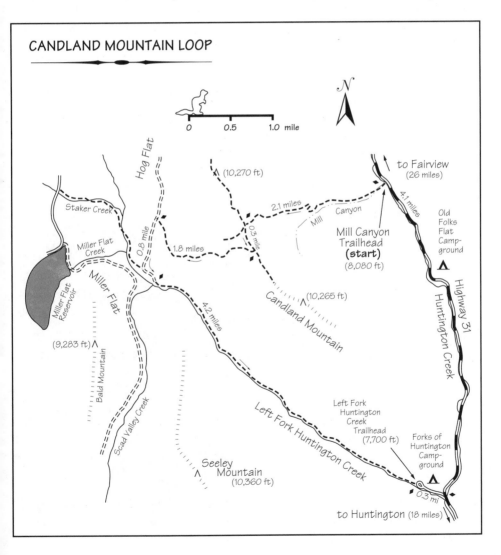

CANDLAND MOUNTAIN LOOP

Left Fork Huntington Creek Trailhead

Candland Mountain pack trail you will reach a local summit (10,205 ft.) where the forest opens up in the west for a wonderful view of Miller Flat and Hog Flat below. Bald Mountain is clearly visible along the western boundary of Miller Flat, and Seeley Peak lies about 2.5 miles to the south. In between Candland Mountain and Seeley Peak is the 2,000-foot-deep Left Fork Huntington Canyon, which will be your return route. The two mountains were once connected, before the erosive powers of the Left Fork Huntington Creek carved the deep gouge between them millions of years ago. Continuing southward on the pack trail for 10 minutes more will bring you to another junction where a trail drops off to the right. You should leave the ridge at this point and begin your descent to Hog Flat.

After walking 1.8 miles and dropping 1,600 feet below Candland Mountain ridge, the trail intersects a jeep road. Turn left and walk along the jeep road for another 0.8 mile to the mouth of Left Fork Huntington Canyon, where the road comes to a dead end. At the end of the road the Left Fork Huntington Creek enters an abrupt break in the mountains, and within just a few hundred feet the terrain changes completely from a sage-covered flat to a tree-lined canyon. This canyon will be your route through the mountains back to Highway 31—a much easier

walk that the climb over Candland Mountain was!

All that remains of the hike now is to walk down Left Fork Huntington Creek to the Forks of Huntington Campground, 4.2 miles distant. This part of the hike has been officially designated as a National Recreation Trail, and it is very pretty. Huge conifers grow right to the water's edge on the south side of the stream, with bands of quaking aspen higher up the canyon walls. There are several excellent camping areas farther downstream where many people stay to take advantage of the fishing. Note the difference in vegetation between the north and south facing sides of the canyon. The forest is much more alpine in nature on the heavily shaded north-facing side, while sage brush and other semi-arid plants grow on the sunny south-facing side. The trail runs along the sunny side of the canyon, where there are fewer obstacles to impede its progress.

Left Fork Huntington Creek

San Rafael River Gorge

☆ ☆ ☆ ☆

shuttle car required
overnight hike

Distance: 16.6 miles
             (plus 18.3 miles by car)

Walking time: day 1: 4 hours
                 day 2: 5 hours

Elevations: 160 ft. loss
             Fuller Bottom (start):   5,250 ft.
             San Rafael Campground: 5,090 ft.

Trail: There is a good horse trail most of the way along the river. The trail crosses the river fifteen times, so be sure to wear wettable shoes.

Season: Summer, fall. The most important factor to consider in planning this hike is the amount of water in the San Rafael River. The water level is highest in the spring, between early May and mid-June, and fording the river with a backpack may be difficult or impossible at that time. Before driving to the trailhead I strongly suggest that you call the Bureau of Land Management in Price at (435) 636-3600, and ask them about the river's flow rate. If it is higher that 120 cfs (cubic feet per second) you may have difficulty. When the flow rate reaches 180 cfs the deepest ford will be about 3 feet. If the rate is greater than 150 cfs you might want to consider floating down the river in a small rubber raft or canoe. Floating the San Rafael can be a delightful experience.

Vicinity: Near Price

Maps: Sids Mountain, Bottleneck Peak *(USGS)*

Information: http://www.utahtrails.com/sanrafael.html *(Utah Trails)*
             http://www.blm.gov/utah/price/information.htm *(BLM, Price)*
             phone: (435) 636-3600 *(BLM, Price Field Office)*

Take Exit 241 off Highway 6 in Price, and drive south on Highway 10 towards Castledale. After you have driven 11.4 miles you will come to the junction with Highway 155. Turn left here and follow the signs to Cleveland. Continue driving south through Cleveland until you come to a T junction 1.5 miles from the town center. Turn east here and begin following the signs to Buckhorn Wash and San Rafael Campground. There are many roads in this area, but the junctions are all clearly marked with BLM signs. It is 26.4 miles from Cleveland to the bottom of Buck-

horn Wash where the San Rafael Campground is located. Only the first two miles are paved.

You can also get to the San Rafael Campground from Interstate Highway 70. Take exit 129, 31 miles west of Green River and follow the signs north for 20 miles to the bottom of Buckhorn Wash.

San Rafael Campground is where this hike ends and where you should leave your shuttle car. To get to Fuller Bottom where the hike begins drive back up Buckhorn Wash towards Cleveland for 12.3 miles until you come to a 4-way junction, then turn left towards the Wedge Overlook. Just 0.5 mile from the 4-way junction you will see a smaller dirt road departing on the right for Fuller Bottom. This road deadends after 5.4 miles at the San Rafael River in Fuller Bottom, where the hike begins. The road is sandy in places, but with care an ordinary car can usually make it.

This hike provides an opportunity to follow a small desert river along a meandering course that cuts directly through one of Utah's most interesting geologic formations: the San Rafael Swell. The San Rafael Swell is a huge elliptical-shaped bubble in the Colorado Plateau that formed some 65 million years ago during a time of great mountain building activity in the American West (known to geologists as the Laramide Orogeny event). The uplift, or anticline, is some 70 miles long and 35 miles wide, with the San Rafael River flowing through its northern half. About half way between Fuller Bottom and Buckhorn Wash the river flows through a particularly scenic section of the gorge known as the

see color photo, page 180

Little Grand Canyon. Here the canyon walls rise abruptly over a thousand feet above the river as it meanders around a fin-like obstacle below the Wedge Plateau.

In addition to the hike through the San Rafael River Gorge there are several other points of interest in this area that you may want to see before or after your hike. The Cleveland Lloyd Dinosaur Quarry is located at the end of a gravel road about ten miles east of Cleveland. This is one of the world's most prolific dinosaur fossil sources, having yielded more than 30 complete dinosaur skeletons since excavations first began in

1929. Also one of the best prehistoric Indian pictograph panels in Utah is located beside the road in Buckhorn Wash 4 miles above the San Rafael Campground. Finally, if time permits you should drive to the Wedge Overlook, 6.2 miles off the road to Fuller Bottom. The Wedge Overlook offers a fine view of the San Rafael Gorge from a vantage point directly above the Little Grand Canyon.

Day 1 (7.2 miles)

The best way to begin this hike is to cross the river at Fuller Bottom and follow a jeep road downstream along the south shore for the first 20 minutes. But before you start find yourself a strong stick at least 7 or 8 feet long to help with the river crossings. As you walk place the stick on the river bottom, tilted at a 45 degree angle on the downstream side, and use it like a third leg. The extra support is a tremendous help, especially if the current is strong.

After 0.8 mile the road will come back to the water again before veering away to the south, and here you must abandon it and try to follow the cow trails. The wide valley floor is covered with tamarisk trees for a short distance and getting through them can be a problem with a big backpack. But don't be discouraged. As the canyon narrows they become less abundant, and within

San Rafael River

another half mile the multitude of cow trails converge into a single good trail.

About 2.0 miles from the Fuller Bottom Trailhead the trail crosses again to the north side of the river. This is the second of 15 fords that will be necessary between Fuller Bottom and Cane Wash, so don't discard your stick yet. About ten minutes after the river crossing the trail passes below a small petroglyph panel at the base of the cliffs on the left. Watch carefully as it is easy to miss. Then, after another ten minutes, another river crossing.

The next item of interest is easy to spot: the Sorrel Mule Mine. It is situated about 60 feet above the west side of the river, at the top of a large pile of yellowish tailings just 200 yards below the third river ford. A close look at the area will reveal the rotting timbers of an old log cabin near the mine as well as dozens of rusted tin cans. Copper was briefly extracted from the Sorrel Mule Mine in 1898. Amazingly, the small shaft

penetrates some 2000 feet into the mountain.

A mile below the Sorrel Mule Mine you will cross Salt Wash, a wide, sandy bottomed dry wash that enters the San Rafael River Gorge from the south, and 3.1 miles farther you will come to Virgin Spring Canyon. Virgin Spring Canyon is easily the prettiest side canyon in the gorge. It is one of the few canyons that isn't heavily grazed by cattle, and there is a reliable spring not too far from its entrance. It is an excellent place to make camp for the night and, if time permits do a little exploring. Unfortunately the trail is on the wrong side of the gorge as it passes the mouth of Virgin Spring Canyon, but the river is an easy ford at this point.

Day 2 (9.4 miles)

Before leaving Virgin Spring Canyon take some time to check out the pictographs. The Virgin Spring pictograph panel is located about a quarter of a mile from the mouth of the canyon on its west side. It is

see map, page 159

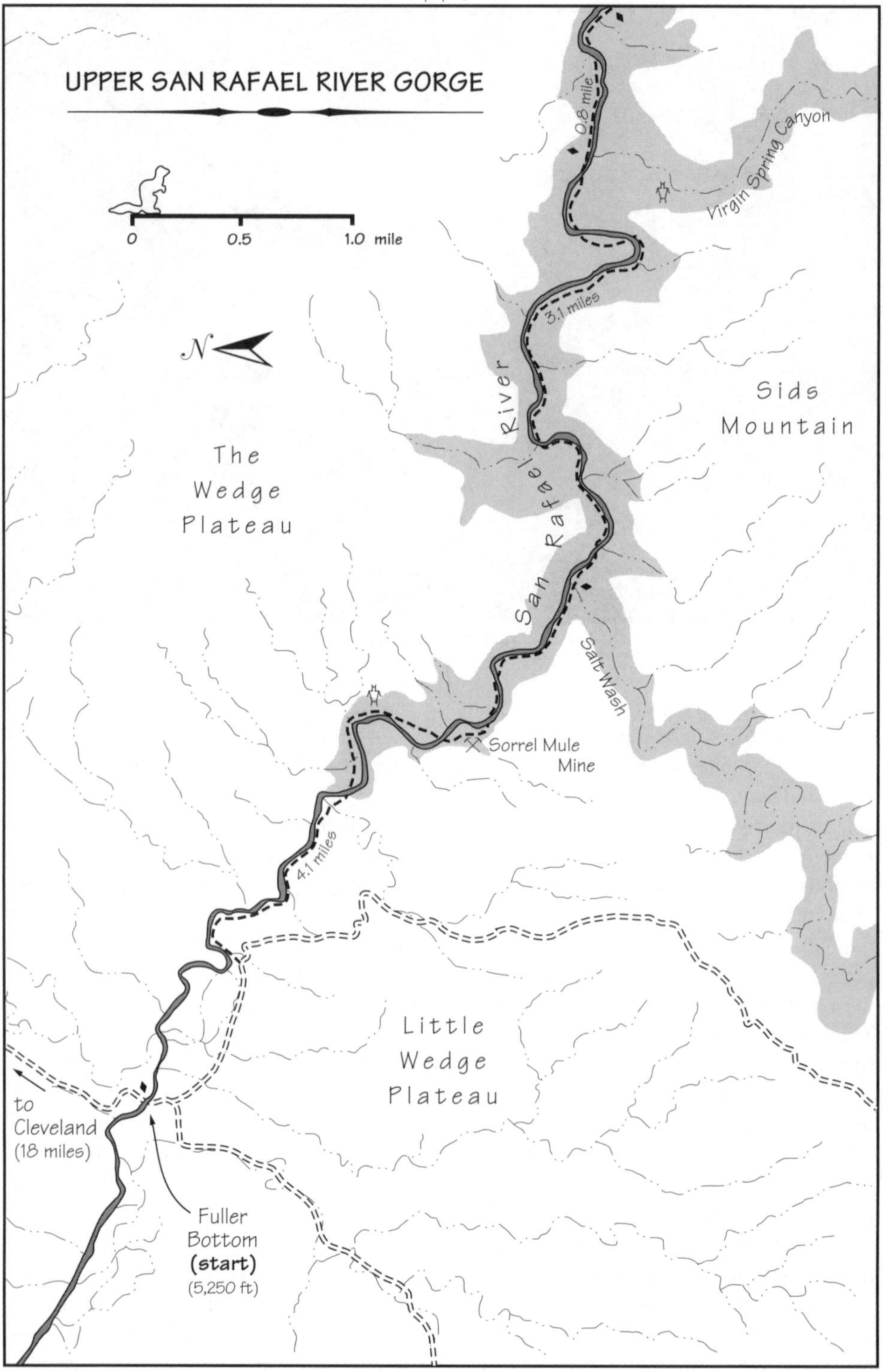

UPPER SAN RAFAEL RIVER GORGE

0   0.5   1.0 mile

N

0.8 mile

Virgin Spring Canyon

3.1 miles

Sids
Mountain

The
Wedge
Plateau

San Rafael River

Salt Wash

✕ Sorrel Mule
Mine

4.1 miles

Little
Wedge
Plateau

to
Cleveland
(18 miles)

Fuller
Bottom
(start)
(5,250 ft)

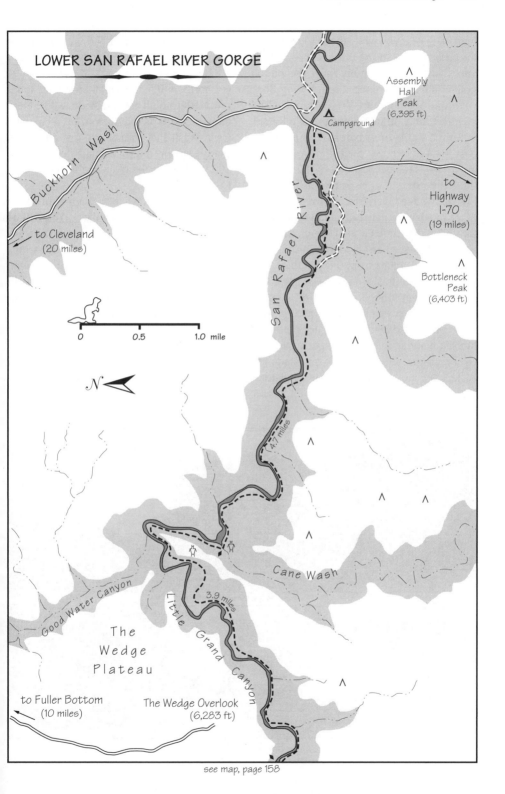

LOWER SAN RAFAEL RIVER GORGE

Buckhorn Wash

Assembly
Hall
Peak
(6,395 ft)

Campground

to Cleveland
(20 miles)

to
Highway
I-70
(19 miles)

San Rafael River

Bottleneck
Peak
(6,403 ft)

0   0.5   1.0 mile

N

4.7 miles

Cane Wash

Good Water Canyon

3.9 miles

The
Wedge
Plateau

Little Grand Canyon

to Fuller Bottom
(10 miles)

The Wedge Overlook
(6,283 ft)

see map, page 158

high on the canyon wall, about 15 feet from the ground. The spring is located about 150 yards further up-canyon from the pictographs at the head of the Virgin Spring Box.

From the mouth of Virgin Spring Canyon the trail continues down the San Rafael River for a mile or so before coming to the next point of interest, the Little Grand Canyon. This is the deepest part of the gorge, a three-mile stretch of river that lies just below the Wedge Overlook. There is also another interesting panel of pictographs near the end of the Little Grand Canyon that you may want to see before continuing.

About 3.0 miles from the mouth of Virgin Spring Canyon the river swings north in order to get around a large fin-like protrusion in the streambed. The pictographs lie on the west side of this fin, just below its highest point and above the spot where the river meanders closest to its base. Look for a clearly visible window in the sandstone fin high above the trail. The pictograph panel is to the right of the window at the bottom of the Wingate Sandstone cliffs.

Beyond the pictographs the trail continues north for 0.5 mile and then swings south toward the mouth of Cane Wash, where there are still more pictographs to be seen. The Cane Wash Pictographs are just above the sandy canyon floor in a small alcove, about 100 yards from the river on the east side of Cane Wash.

From Cane Wash to the campground the trail is well used by day hikers. You will be on the south side of the river for the remainder of the hike; hence no more crossings are necessary. After about 3 more miles the valley widens and the vegetation is again dominated by tamarisk trees. 1.5 miles from the end you will encounter another jeep road which you can take if you prefer, although the trail along the river is more interesting. The jeep road joins Buckhorn Wash Road 0.4 mile south of the San Rafael Campground.

San Rafael River

Top: *Naomi Peak Trail (page 25)*
Bottom Left: *White Pine Lake Trail, Bear River Range (page 27)*
Bottom Right: *Coldwater Canyon Trail, below Wellsville Ridge (page 31)*

Top: *Ogden Peak (page 34)*
Bottom Left: *Clyde Lake Trail (page 89)*
Bottom Right: *Round Lake (page 97)*

162

Top: *Clegg Lake (page 85)*
Bottom: *Trial Lake (page 85)*

Top: *Center Canyon, Row Bench Trail (page 104)*
Bottom: *Island Lake (page 93)*

Top Left: *Ryder Lake (page 58)*
Top Right: *Stillwater Creek (page 58)*
Bottom: *Amethyst Lake (page 60)*

Top: *Looking south from Bald Mountain Ridge (page 55)*
Bottom: *The Red Castle above Lower Red Castle Lake (page 55)*

Top: *Looking south from the summit of Kings Peak (page 46)*
Bottom: *Flat Top Mountain, as seen from the Kings Peak Trail (page 46)*

Top: *Unnamed lake, East Basin (page 68)*
Bottom: *East Basin Pass (page 68)*

Top: *Faxon Lake, upper Naturalist Basin (page 80)*
Bottom Left: *Grandaddy Basin (page 74)*
Bottom Right: *Grandaddy Basin, near Rainbow Lake (page 74)*

Top: *Looking north from the summit of Deseret Peak (page 37)*
Bottom Left: *Green River, below Flaming Gorge Dam (page 40)*
Bottom Right: *Red Canyon (page 40)*

Top: *Looking west from the summit of Mount Olympus (page 110)*
Bottom Left: *Jones Hole (page 43)*
Bottom Right: *Grandeur Peak (page 107)*

Top Left: *Butler Fork (pages 117, 118)*
Top Right: *Mount Raymond, as seen from Gobblers Knob (pages 114,117)*
Bottom: *Mill D North Fork (pages 118, 122)*

Top: *Mill Creek Ridge (Mount Raymond in background) (page 122)*
Bottom: *Desolation Lake (page 122)*

Top: *Trail junction between White Pine Lake and Red Pine Lake Trails (pages 126, 131)*
Bottom: *Winter trail to Red Pine Lake (page 126)*

Top: *Twin Lakes, seen from Twin Lakes Pass (page 134)*
Bottom: *White Pine Lake (Wasatch Mountains) (page 131)*

Top: *Catherine Pass (page 134)*
Bottom: *Mount Timpanogos Trail, east of Emerld Lake (page 138)*

Top: *Looking northwest from the peak of Mount Timpanogos (page 138)*
Bottom Left: *Unnamed waterfall below Emerald Lake, Mount Timpanogos Trail (page 138)*
Bottom Right: *Looking north from the summit of Santaquin Peak (page 144)*

Top: *Approaching the south summit of Mount Nebo (page 148)*
Bottom: *Loafer Mountain Trail (page 144)*

Top Left: *Fish Creek (page 151)*
Top Right: *Lower Black Box of the San Rafael River, near Sulfur Spring (page 206)*
Bottom: *Left Fork Huntington Creek (page 153)*

Top: *Landscape Arch, Arches National Park (page 209)*
Bottom: *San Rafael River Gorge (page 156)*

Top: *Negro Bill Canyon (page 214)*
Bottom: *Fisher Towers Trail (page 218)*

Top: *Looking northeast from Mount Tukuhnikivatz at Mount Mellenthin (page 222)*
Bottom Left: *Lower Courthouse Wash (page 210)*
Bottom Right: *San Rafael Swell, between Bell and Little Wild Horse Canyons (page 225)*

Top: *Jumbled debris in the center of Upheaval Crater (page 233)*
Bottom Left: *Little Wildhorse Canyon narrows (page 225)*
Bottom Right: *The Maze, near Chimney Rock Trailhead (page 254)*

Top: *Murphy Wash trail junction (page 237)*
Bottom: *Indian pictographs in Horseshoe Canyon (page 228)*

184

Top: *Chesler Park (page 243)*
Bottom: *Chesler Canyon (page 243)*

Top: *Lost Canyon Trail (page 250)*
Bottom: *The Land of the Standing Rocks (page 258)*

Top: *The Chocolate Drops, as seen from the bottom of the Maze (pages 254, 258)*
Bottom: *Looking east across the Colorado River Gorge into the Needles District of Canyonlands National Park (page 259)*

Top: *Dark Canyon, seen from the top of the Sundance Trail (page 265)*
Bottom Left: *Dark Canyon, near the junction with Lost Canyon (page 265)*
Bottom Right: *Anasazi artifacts in Mule Canyon (page 299)*

Top: *Kachina Natural Bridge (page 268)*
Bottom: *Split Level Ruin, Grand Gulch (page 274)*

Top: *Anasazi Ruin in Grand Gulch (page 276)*
Bottom Left: *Grand Gulch, near Pollys Canyon (pages 276, 285)*
Bottom Right: *Grand Gulch, near Collins Canyon (page 276)*

Top: *Anasazi Granary in lower Fish Creek Canyon (page 297)*
Bottom: *Chimney Rock Canyon Trail (page 306)*

Top: *Fremont River Valley, as seen from the Cohab Canyon Trail (page 303)*
Bottom: *Upper Muley Twist Canyon, from the top of the Waterpocket Fold (page 310)*

Top: *Lower Muley Twist Canyon (page 314)*
Bottom Left: *The Pine Creek Box (page 318)*
Bottom Right: *Lower Calf Creek Falls (page 321)*

Top: *Death Hollow, as seen from the Boulder Mail Trail (page 332)*
Bottom: *The Escalante River (pages 326, 332)*

Top: *Coyote Natural Bridge (page 339)*
Bottom Left: *Death Hollow (pages 326, 332)*
Bottom Right: *Lower Coyote Gulch (page 339)*

Top: *Lower Hackberry Canyon (page 350)*
Bottom Left: *Jacob Hamblin Natural Arch (page 339)*
Bottom Right: *Round Valley Draw (page 350)*

Top: *Whipple Valley (page 396)*
Bottom Left: *Lower Willow Gulch, near Lake Powell (page 344)*
Bottom Right: *Buckskin Gulch (page 354)*

Top: *Fairyland Loop Trail (page 363)*
Bottom Left: *Queens Garden Trail (page 361)*
Bottom Right: *Riggs Spring Trail (page 364)*

198

Top: *The West Rim of Zion Canyon, seem from Cable Mountain (pages 380, 383)*
Bottom Left: *Cedar Breaks (page 369)*
Bottom Right: *The Zion Narrows (page 373)*

Top: *Hop Valley (page 388)*
Bottom Left: *Upper North Fork Virgin River (page 373)*
Bottom Right: *Middle Fork Taylor Creek (page 392)*

Lower Black Box of the San Rafael

4WD vehicle useful
3-day hike

Distance:	16.3 miles (round trip)
Walking time:	day 1: 2¹/₂ hours day 2: 7 hours day 3: 3 hours
Elevations:	1,250 ft. loss/gain 2WD car park (start): 5,550 ft. Beginning of Lower Black Box: 4,400 ft. Sulphur Spring: 4,300 ft.
Trail:	There is no trail through the Lower Black Box. In many places the canyon floor is filled with water and swimming or floating is necessary. In other places it is necessary to scramble over rock falls. Do not attempt this hike without adequate preparation.
Season:	Midsummer to mid-fall. The success of this hike requires good weather, warm temperatures, and low river flow rates; consequently there are only a few weeks during the year when it should be attempted. The best all around time is usually between early July and mid-August. Some important points: (1) Always make sure you have a good weather forecast before entering into the Black Box, but be especially careful during the rainy season in late summer and early fall. (2) Water temperatures in the Black Box are too cold for travel in the winter or early spring. (3) There is generally too much water flowing in the San Rafael River to attempt the Black Box in late spring or early summer. Whatever date you chose, be sure to call the Bureau of Land Management in Price at (435) 636-3600, and ask them about the river's flow rate. If it is higher that about 30 cfs (cubic feet per second) don't go.
Vicinity:	Near Green River
Maps:	Spotted Wolf Canyon *(USGS)*
Information:	http://www.utahtrails.com/blackbox.html *(Utah Trails)* http://www.blm.gov/utah/price/information.htm *(BLM, Price)* phone: (435) 636-3600 *(BLM, Price Field Office)*

Drive west of Green River on I-70 for 31 miles and take Exit 129. After you have left I-70

drive east along the gravel frontage road on the north side of the highway
towards Buckhorn Wash. The frontage road parallels the highway for 3.3
miles and then veers to the north. After you have driven 5.8 miles on this road
you will come to a sign marking a smaller road on the right that leads to
Sinkhole Flat and Jackass Benches. Make a note of your odometer reading
and turn east onto this road. After 1.8 miles you will come to a junction where you must bear
left. At 4.5 miles you will encounter the road to Sulphur Springs. Again, turn left. At 7.5
miles you will see the road to Drowned Hole Draw on your left; bear right here. At 9.1
miles, another junction; bear left towards Swaseys Leap. At 10.3 miles you will come to a
small pullout. This is about as far as you can go on this road with a 2WD vehicle. Unless
you have a 4WD park here and walk the last 5.0 miles to Swaseys Leap and the San Rafael
River. Note: There are about 50 head of wild burros living on Jackass Benches, the area
where the car park is located. Be observant and you might have the opportunity to see some
of them.

The Lower Black Box is a deep, narrow canyon of the San Rafael River located on the eastern edge of the San Rafael Swell. This hike involves floating 3.7 miles down the river through the Lower Black Box, and then walking back 2.6 miles along the eastern side of the gorge to the starting point. The trip is an exciting one with a lot to see, but it requires careful planning and it isn't suitable for everyone.

First, the trip through the Lower Black Box shouldn't be attempted by anyone who doesn't know how to swim. It is also important that everyone in the group have an inflated inner tube to float through the long, deep pools. I have done this trip with a small rubber raft, but I don't recommend it. There are a number of places in the canyon where scrambling is necessary to get around rock falls, and getting a rubber raft across these obstacles is difficult.

Second, don't try to carry anything more than your inner tube, a small floatable day pack, and a walking stick when you go through the Black Box. Both of your hands must be free when you are scrambling over the rock falls and fighting your way through the canyon narrows. You should include a 30-foot length of rope in your pack for emer-

gency use and for lowering down backpacks. As for clothing, shorts, a shirt, and wettable boots are best. You will be walking over submerged rocks much of the time, so be sure you have good footwear. Also, forget

Lower Black Box of the San Rafael River

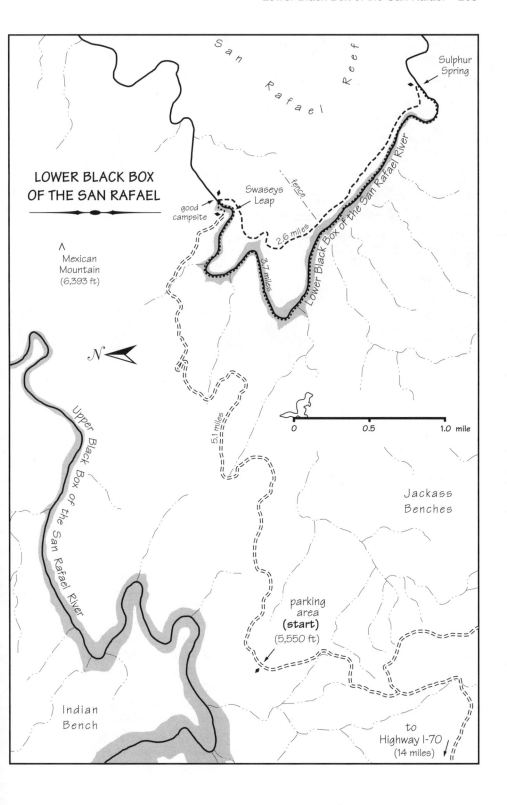

LOWER BLACK BOX
OF THE SAN RAFAEL

San Rafael Reef

Sulphur Spring

Swaseys Leap

good campsite

fence

2.6 miles

3.7 miles

Lower Black Box of the San Rafael River

⋀
Mexican
Mountain
(6,393 ft)

N

5.1 miles

0   0.5   1.0 mile

Upper Black Box of the San Rafael River

Jackass
Benches

parking
area
(start)
(5,550 ft)

Indian
Bench

to
Highway I-70
(14 miles)

Northern end of the Lower Black Box

about trying to keep your things dry. Every-thing you take with you will be soaking wet when you finish with this trip.

Third, timing is important. Once you enter the Black Box it is difficult to turn around. It isn't the sort of place you want to get caught in after dark, so be sure to allow plenty of time for the trip. The season is also important. You don't want to do this trip unless the weather is good, the tempera-ture is warm, and there isn't too much water in the canyon.

Day 1 (5.0 miles)

From the car parking area to the San Rafael River and the Lower Black Box is only a 2.5 hour walk, but since it is best to get an early start when you go through the Box you should plan on going only as far as the river on the first day. There are several good campsites on the river just above the entrance to the Lower Black Box.

From the 2WD parking area just continue walking east along the jeep road towards Swaseys Leap. The road ends after 5.0 miles at a view point above the river overlooking Swaseys Leap. If you have a 4WD vehicle you can shorten the walk by driving another 2.5 miles down the road. In the past it was possible to drive a 4WD vehicle all the way to the river, but the area is now part of the Mexican Mountain Wilderness Study Area and the last 2.5 miles of the road have been closed by the BLM.

From the view point at the end of the road it is an easy fifteen-minute scramble down the last 280 feet to the river. The best route is down a small rock-filled drainage on the north side of the view point. Once you reach the river you will find a good campsite about a hundred yards upstream near the tamarisk trees.

Swaseys Leap is the name given to the narrowest part of the canyon just below the overlook point. According to local legend a cowboy named Sid Swasey once won a bet from his brother, Joe, by jumping the ten-foot gap on his horse. A few years later, probably just after the turn of the century, two sheep ranchers named Paul Hanson and Hyrum Seeley built a log bridge across Swaseys Leap for the purpose of getting their sheep across the flooded river. Amazingly, a few logs of that bridge are still in place today.

Day 2 (6.3 miles)

Getting through the Lower Black Box and back is the goal of the second day. Going through the Box can be an exciting and interesting experience, but, once again, make sure you are prepared and that the weather is good before you start out. Although the Lower Black Box is only 3.7 miles long, you should allow 7 hours for the round trip, including 2 hours for the walk back from the bottom of the Box.

The first point of interest is Swaseys

Swaseys Leap

Leap. You will float under it just a few minutes after leaving your campsite. Looking up at the last remaining logs of Hansen's bridge, fifty feet above the river, you will probably wonder how many sheep he lost trying to get them across.

The first few hundred yards of the journey through the Box is a very pleasant float, but soon after passing under Swaseys Leap you will begin to encounter a series of obstacles. There are about six or eight places in the upper half of the canyon where large rock falls will force you to climb out of the stream to scramble over the sandstone boulders. Although the conditions change from year to year, the rock falls are generally not difficult to get around—just tiring and time consuming. But be sure you have a rope in case you encounter something unexpected. Usually you will be back in the water again floating comfortably on your inner tube after ten minutes of scrambling.

In many areas it is possible to walk on a sandy bank near the canyon wall, but if the ground is too wet you will soon discover that quicksand is a problem. It is usually easier to stay in the water.

After the first two miles the canyon starts

Lower Black Box of the San Rafael River

getting easier to negotiate, and soon you will pass the last serious rock fall. The last rock fall is located in the middle of a long straight section of river that runs almost due southeast for a full mile. As you near the end of this straight section of river you will begin to see water seeping out of the porous sandstone of the canyon walls. The seeps become more and more prodigious as you progress downstream. Also, you will notice that the height of the canyon walls is decreasing.

Eventually the river makes a sharp bend to the southwest, and then bends lazily around again to a northeasterly course. Pay attention to where the sun is. If it is shining in your face when you look downstream and if it is about the middle of the day, then the river has turned south and you are near the end of your float. When the river's course swings to the northeast start looking for a large spring that flows down the right bank. This is Sulphur Spring, and it isn't hard to see why it is called that. You can smell the sulphur and see the twigs and branches on the south side of the river encased in a yellowish crust. Needless to say, this water is not drinkable.

When you reach Sulphur Spring it is time to climb back out of the water and begin your trek back to camp along the east side of the San Rafael. Soon you should see a hiker-made trail that follows the bench above the river. The walk is

see color photo, page 179

an easy one with only a little up and down, the scenery is excellent, and the warm desert sun is welcome. There are also a number of impressive views down into the Lower Black Box on the way back. Stopping occasionally to enjoy the scenery, you should get back to your camp near Swaseys Leap after about two hours.

Day 3 (5.0 miles)

All that remains of the hike now is the 5.0 mile walk back to your car. It will take about 3 hours if you parked at the 2WD area, or less if drove a 4WD vehicle down to the wilderness study area boundary.

The San Rafael Reef, above the Lower Black Box of the San Rafael River

Devils Garden

☆ ☆ ☆ ☆ ☆

Arches National Park
day hike

Distance:	7.6 miles (including side trips to all points of interest)
Walking time:	4¹/₄ hours
Elevations:	280 ft. gain/loss
	Devils Garden Trailhead (start): 5,180 ft.
	Landscape Arch: 5,320 ft.
	Dark Angel: 5,460 ft.
Trail:	Generally easy, well used trail
Season:	Spring, summer, fall, winter. The trail is quite hot in summer, so carry plenty of water.
Vicinity:	Arches National Park, near Moab
Maps:	Mollie Hogans, Klondike Bluffs *(USGS)*
	Arches National Park *(Trails Illusrated, #211)*
Information:	http://www.utahtrails.com/devils.html *(Utah Trails)*
	http://www.nps.gov/arch/home.htm *(Arches National Park)*
	phone: (435) 259-8161 *(Visitor Center)*

Drive north from the Arches National Park Visitor Center along the scenic park road for a distance of 19 miles. Devils Garden Trailhead is at the end of the road, just beyond the campground.   (Note: If you plan to stay at the campground you had better arrive early. It is very popular.)

If the strange and wonderful rock formations of Southern Utah interest you, you will love this hike. Devils Garden contains eight of the best known sandstone arches in Arches National Park, including Landscape Arch, the park's longest span. The area is a particularly good place to study the life cycle of natural arches. You will see many spans of different ages as you wander through the jumbled canyons of stone. On the return portion of the loop you will pass through a giant maze of long vertical sandstone fins, all parallel to one another with narrow canyons between. These fins are the raw materials from which future arches are being made. In another million years, when all of the present arches are gone, there will be many new ones in these canyons to replace them. Some of the new arches might even be more spectacular than the present ones. Although we mortals are allowed only a fleeting glimpse of her current display, Nature is continually modifying and replacing her artwork.

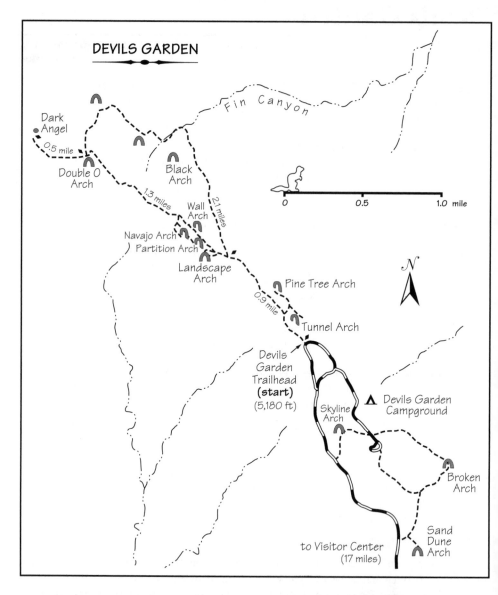

From the trailhead the path goes for only 0.3 mile before another spur trail leaves on the right to Pine Tree Arch and Tunnel Arch. Both Pine Tree and Tunnel are very young arches with relatively small openings surrounded by large masses of rock. They are not as impressive as some of the other arches, but as a prelude to the next arch—one of oldest—you should take the time to see them. The side trip to these two arches will extend your hike by about 0.6 mile.

Continuing northward on the main trail for another 0.6 mile will bring you to another junction. You will be returning on the path to the right, so for now bear left for a short distance to the Landscape Arch. For most people, Landscape Arch is the high point of the Devils Garden hike.

This arch is so improbably long and slender its span seems to defy the laws of physics. The slender ribbon of stone extends for some 300 feet from base to base, and rises 105 feet above the sandy desert floor. Because of its size it is difficult to photograph Landscape Arch. But if you want to try plan to be there in the morning, and make sure you bring along a wide angle lens.

Landscape is a very old arch, definitely in the last stages of its existence, but how much longer it will endure is anybody's guess. Maybe another century, maybe several, but certainly not more that a thousand years. In years past it

see color photo, page 180

was possible to walk through the opening on a short spur trail; however that is now deemed too dangerous. The spur was closed in 1996 after a large piece of sandstone broke away and fell to the ground below.

From Landscape the trail continues northward, past Wall Arch, to another short spur trail leading to Navajo and Partition Arches. Navajo Arch, on the western edge of Devils Garden, is the larger of the two. A detour to these two arches will add about 0.7 mile onto your hike.

The main trail ends at Double O Arch, 2.2 miles from the trailhead, but from there another spur trail continues on for fifteen minutes to the base of the Dark Angel. Dark

Angel is an impressive sandstone monolith, about 150 feet high, that stands prominently on the edge of a long narrow bench overlooking Salt Valley. It also commands a nice view of the Klondike Bluffs on the western edge of the national park.

When you are ready to return, you should turn north from Double O Arch, and take the loop trail that goes back through Fin Canyon. This trail is what the Park Service calls a "primitive trail". It is not as well developed as the main Devils Garden Trail, but it is quite easy to follow and, in my opinion, it is the most interesting part of the hike. The trail wonders through an intriguing collection of thin stone fins, all aligned in a northwest-southeast direction. The fins were formed millions of years ago when the ground rose beneath a solid block of sandstone, causing it to fracture and separate into long, parallel vertical sheets. The existence of these large fins is the primary reason why so many arches have been formed in Arches National Park.

After spending about a mile in Fin Canyon, the trail breaks out on the eastern side of Devils Garden and eventually meets the main trail again just east of Landscape Arch. From the junction it is an easy 0.9 mile walk back the trailhead.

Sandstone sculptures of Devils Garden

Lower Courthouse Wash

☆

Distance: 6.2 miles
(plus 6.7 miles by car or bicycle)

Walking time: 3¹/₂ hours

Elevations: 120 ft. loss
Courthouse Wash Trailhead (start): 4,120 ft.
Highway 191: 4,000 ft.

Trail: No trail, but very easy walking along bottom of a sandy wash.
Some wading is necessary, so wear wettable shoes.

Season: Spring, summer, fall, winter.

Vicinity: Arches National Park, near Moab

Maps: The Windows Section, Moab *(USGS)*
Arches National Park *(Trails Illustrated, #211)*

Information: http://www.utahtrails.com/courthouse.html *(Utah Trails)*
http://www.nps.gov/arch/home.htm *(Arches National Park)*
phone: (435) 259-8161 *(Visitor Center)*

*Drive north from the Visitor Center along the road into Arches National Park
for a distance of 4.6 miles to the point where the road crosses Courthouse
Wash. The wash is clearly marked by a road sign. There is a small parking
area about 100 yards beyond the wash on the west side of the road. The hike
begins in the wash on the east side of the bridge.*

*Before beginning the hike you will have to leave a shuttle car or bicycle where Courthouse
Wash crosses Highway 191. Drive east on Highway 191, toward Moab, for a distance of 1.8
miles from the entrance of Arches National Park. Here, just before the highway crosses
Courthouse Wash, you will see a small Park Service parking lot on the left where you can
leave your shuttle.*

Courthouse Wash is a short, but very
pretty canyon near the entrance to Arches
National Park. You
won't see any arches
in Courthouse but it
is, nevertheless, a pleasant half-day walk.
The canyon almost always has at least some
water in it; consequently it is filled with cottonwoods and willows. The easiest place to
walk is usually in the stream bed, so you
should wear sneakers or other shoes suitable
for wading. There are deer and raccoon
tracks in the canyon, but the animal you are
sure to see a lot of is frogs.

see color photo,
page 182

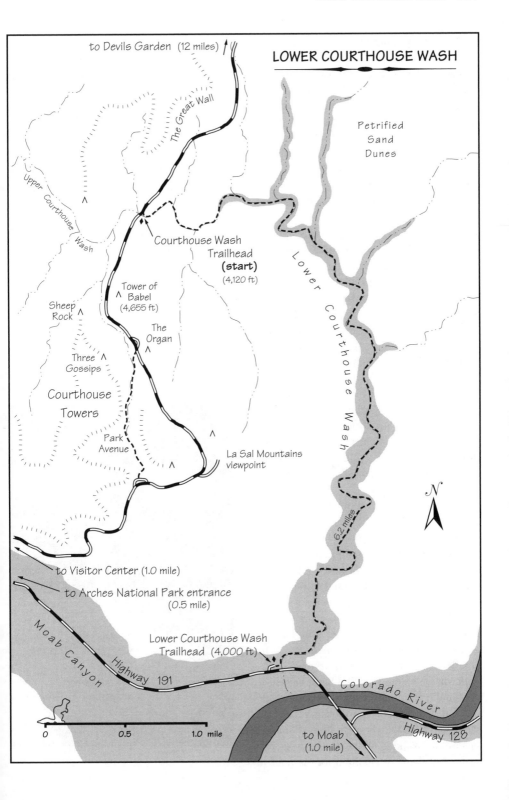

LOWER COURTHOUSE WASH

to Devils Garden (12 miles)

The Great Wall

Petrified
Sand
Dunes

Upper Courthouse Wash

Courthouse Wash
Trailhead
(start)
(4,120 ft)

Lower Courthouse Wash

Tower of
Babel
(4,655 ft)

Sheep
Rock

The
Organ

Three
Gossips

Courthouse

Towers

Park
Avenue

La Sal Mountains
viewpoint

6.2 miles

N

to Visitor Center (1.0 mile)

to Arches National Park entrance
(0.5 mile)

Moab Canyon

Highway 191

Lower Courthouse Wash
Trailhead (4,000 ft)

Colorado River

to Moab
(1.0 mile)

Highway 128

0   0.5   1.0 mile

Before dropping into lower Courthouse Wash to begin your hike, pause for a while to study the red sandstone towers that rise from the surrounding valley. These photogenic formations are all part of the Entrada Sandstone geologic formation that dominates most of Arches National Park. The Courthouse Towers, after which Courthouse Wash was named, are located about a mile south of the trailhead.

Underneath the Entrada Sandstone Formation lies the Navajo Sandstone, a thick layer of light-colored rock that is very prominent in the canyons of Southern Utah. Navajo Sandstone is generally much whiter than the reddish Entrada Sandstone, and it tends to erode into deep narrow canyons and smooth-walled cliffs with little fracturing. Entrada Sandstone, on the other hand, has an interesting tendency to erode into unlikely looking pillars and arches of the kind that have made Arches National Park famous. This hike begins very close to the boundary that separates the Entrada Sandstone from the older Navajo Sandstone. At first the canyon is very shallow, but as you proceed downstream the gorge cuts deeper into the Navajo Sandstone and the canyon walls soon become much higher.

You will be following the bottom of Courthouse Wash all the way to the point where Highway 191 crosses it, 0.2 mile before it reaches the Colorado River. The canyon starts out in a general easterly direction, then gradually swings around to the south. Four smaller side canyons join the wash before it reaches the Colorado, all coming in from the northeast, but in each case it is obvious which canyon is the main one. The smaller canyons all lead to an area in the park known as the Petrified Sand Dunes.

Sand, of course, is a by-product of the erosion that carved Courthouse Wash, and the floor of the canyon is filled with a thick layer of it. Walking on the dry, loose sand is tiring, but there is usually a lot of water in the streambed and it is easier to walk in or along the edge of water. Many people take their shoes off and walk barefoot most of the way.

Upper Courthouse Wash

If you want a longer walk you can begin your hike farther north on Highway 191 at the top of upper Courthouse Wash. The upper part of the wash begins on the east side of Highway 191, 5.7 miles north of the park entrance or about 0.2 mile south of the road leading to Dead Horse Point. This route first passes through a narrow canyon in the Entrada Sandstone, and then, after about 2.5 miles, emerges into a wide valley at the bottom of the Entrada. There is usually water in the streambed after the first 2.3 miles. Finally, after 7.8 miles, the wash reaches the national park road, where the hike through lower Courthouse Wash begins.

Lower Courthouse Wash

Negro Bill Canyon

☆   **day hike**

Distance:	4.5 miles (round trip)
Walking time:	2³/₄ hours
Elevations:	400 ft. gain/loss Negro Bill Canyon Trailhead (start): 3,980 ft. Morning Glory Natural Bridge: 4,380 ft.
Trail:	Moderately popular, easy to follow trail
Season:	Spring, summer, fall, winter. There is occasionally snow in the canyon during the winter months.
Vicinity:	Near Moab and Arches National Park
Maps:	Moab *(USGS)* Arches National Park *(Trails Illustrated, #211)*
Information:	http://www.utahtrails.com/negrobill.html *(Utah Trails)* http://www.blm.gov/utah/moab/ *(BLM, Moab)* phone: (435) 259-6111 *(BLM, Moab Field Office)*

Drive north from Moab for two miles on Highway 191, then turn east on Highway 128 and continue along the south shore of the Colorado River. 3.1 miles after turning onto Highway 128 You will see a dirt parking area on the right side of the road at the mouth of Negro Bill Canyon. A small sign at the back of the parking area marks the beginning of the trail.

Negro Bill Canyon was named after William Granstaff, a black prospector and rancher who grazed his cattle here during the late 1800s. It is a lovely canyon, cut into the Navajo Sandstone by a small, perennial stream that begins about six miles from the southern shore of the Colorado River. The trail winds along the stream through an oasis of cottonwood and willow trees, cut off from the desert above by towering sandstone cliffs. Like all good hikes, this one also has a reward at the end. Morning Glory Natural Bridge spans the head of one of Negro Bill's side canyons at the end of the trail. According to Bureau of Land Management statistics, Morning Glory is the sixth largest natural bridge in the United States. It's span is 243 feet.

In 1979 Negro Bill Canyon gained a great deal of notoriety over an action of the so called "Sagebrush Rebellion". The Bureau of Land Management, wanting to study the canyon as a possible wilderness area, placed a barrier at its entrance to keep out recreational vehicles. This infuriated a group of local anti-wilderness activists who, with the

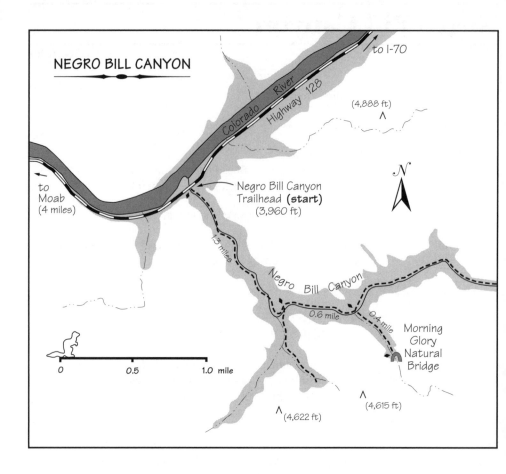

help of the Grand County commissioners, bulldozed down the barrier. The county commissioners then publicly declared that the county, not the federal government, owned the canyon, and when another barrier was erected it was again bulldozed down. The conflict was resolved only after a lawsuit was filed against Grand County in the U.S. district court.

Today the canyon is still a wilderness study area, and may some day become part of a Negro Bill Wilderness Area. Many residents of Grand County are still against the idea, but fortunately tempers are no longer as hot as they once were. Four-wheel-drive vehicles are not now using the canyon and, although there are still some visible signs of

the old jeep roads, most of the mess has now been cleaned up. With each passing year the old, unsightly scars are becoming less noticeable.

From the mouth of Negro Bill Canyon the trail begins by winding its way up the left side of the stream, and then crosses the water four or five times. You may have to get your feet wet at some of the cross- see color photo, page 181 ings, especially during the spring runoff. Wildlife is abundant along the canyon floor, and you can often see hawks soaring over the pink sandstone cliffs searching for prey. After 1.2 miles you will see a second large canyon intersecting

Negro Bill on the right. Another less-used trail heads into this canyon which you can follow if you feel like exploring. This is not the canyon containing Morning Glory Natural Bridge; however it does contain some nice campsites and picnic spots.

Continuing along the main trail for another 0.6 mile will bring you to the next major side canyon, again intersecting Negro Bill Canyon from the right. Here the path splits again, but this time the main trail turns right, into the side canyon, and proceeds southward toward Morning Glory Natural Bridge. The bridge is at the extreme end of the canyon, 0.4 mile from the junction.

Morning Glory Bridge is unique because it was carved at the base of a waterfall, rather than across an open stream as most natural bridges are. The space between the bridge and the cliff over which the water once plunged is extremely narrow, only about 15 feet wide, but the span of the bridge is awesome. What a spectacle the waterfall behind the sandstone bridge must have been when the water was flowing in full force. Water seldom flows in the dry river bed now, but there is a small permanent spring near the base of the bridge's eastern leg.

Negro Bill Canyon

Fisher Towers

☆ ☆ ☆   **day hike**

Distance: 4.2 miles (round trip)

Walking time: 2¹/₂ hours

Elevations: 650 ft. gain/loss
                       Fisher Towers Trailhead (start): 4,740 ft.
                       Viewpoint: 5,390 ft.

Trail: Popular, easy to follow trail

Season: Spring, summer, fall, winter. There may be some snow on the
                       trail during the winter months. This area is very hot in the
                       summer months and there is no water, so be sure to carry some.

Vicinity: Near Moab

Maps: Fisher Towers *(USGS)*

Information: http://www.utahtrails.com/fishertowers.html *(Utah Trails)*
                       http://www.blm.gov/utah/moab/ *(BLM, Moab)*
                       phone: (435) 259-6111 *(BLM, Moab Field Office)*

Drive north from Moab for two miles on Highway 191, then turn east on High-
way 128 and continue along the south shore of the Colorado River. Exactly 21
miles after turning onto Highway 128 (just a few feet from milepost 21) you
will see a gravel road leaving to the right with a small sign that says "Fisher
Towers". (Do not confuse this road with the road to Fisher Valley Ranch
nearer milepost 20.) Turn here and drive for 2.1 miles to the small Fisher Towers picnic
area, where the trail starts.

Few of natures geologic creations are more bizarre to look at than Utah's Fisher Towers. About a dozen of the strange monoliths stand near the Colorado River east of Moab, grouped together like petrified skyscrapers from some prehistoric city. The brick-red sandstone skyscrapers rise abruptly from the desert floor, while a network of gullies and canyons form the city's avenues and boulevards below. The residents of this weird metropolis are an endless collection of goblins and gargoyles frozen in the canyon walls beneath the towers.

The Fisher Towers have long been objects of fascination among rock climbers, and on holidays and weekends you are likely to see a few of the human spiders here. The trail passes by the bases of a half dozen of the sandstone monoliths, including the 900-foot Titan, and finally ends on the crest of a ridge commanding a spectacular view of the Towers. If you are interested in photograph-

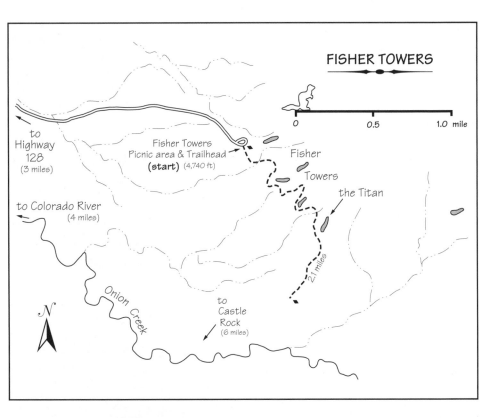

FISHER TOWERS

| 0 | 0.5 | 1.0 mile |

to Highway 128 (3 miles)

Fisher Towers Picnic area & Trailhead **(start)** (4,740 ft)

Fisher Towers

the Titan

to Colorado River (4 miles)

2.1 miles

Onion Creek

to Castle Rock (6 miles)

N

Fisher Towers

ing them try to be at the viewpoint about half an hour before sunset, when the low western sun inflames the spires' reddish hue and striates them with deep shadows.

The Titan, largest of the Fisher Towers, remained unclimbed until the 1960s when a team of three Colorado climbers, sponsored by the National Geographic Society, made an assent to the top. On his impressions at the top of the 900-foot pinnacle, team member Huntley Ingalls wrote:

> *It was a strange, awesomely isolated place, a flat, rough area of bare orange sandstone about 70 feet long and 40 feet wide. Its boundary was the free air. It overhung the body of the tower below it, which plunged in rippling bulges and converging fluted ribs to the distant desert floor.*[3]

From the campground the trail first drops down to cross a small dry wash, and then winds its way back to the Towers. For the next two miles it proceeds

see color photo, page 181

in a general southerly direction along the tower bases, meandering in and out of a succession of arroyos, but never straying far from the Towers. The entire length of the trail is decorated with an enormous variety of rock art, sculpted by the wind and the rain from the soft red sandstone, and it is in large part this spectacle that makes the hike so delightful.

The last major tower on the route is the Titan, which the trail passes after about 1.5 miles. After passing the Titan the path veers southwest onto a long ridge from which you will be rewarded with a majestic view of the Towers. The most common assent route up the Titan is on the south side, the side nearest to the viewpoint.

The ridge at the end of the trail also offers

Climbing the Titan

a fine view of Castle Rock and the Priest and Nuns, about six miles to the southwest. Confusingly, there is also another formation which the USGS Fisher Tower map calls Titan Tower about 1.2 miles northeast of the viewpoint. The tower that most locals know as the Titan, however, and the one scaled by the National Geographic team is the one near the trail.

---

[3] Huntley Ingalls, *We Climbed Utah's Skyscraper Rock*, National Geographic Magazine, November, 1962. (with permission)

Mount Tukuhnikivatz

Distance:	4.8 miles (round trip)
Walking time:	4½ hours
Elevations:	2,362 ft. gain/loss La Sal Pass (start): 10,120 ft. Mount Tukuhnikivatz: 12,482 ft.
Trail:	There is a vague hiker-made trail most of the way to the top of Tukuhnikivatz, but don't worry if you never see it. It is fairly easy to trace the route up the mountain. The terrain is fairly open with few obstacles to impede your progress, but the climb is very steep.
Season:	Midsummer through mid-fall. The road to La Sal Pass is usually closed from mid-November until the end of June.
Vicinity:	Near Moab
Maps:	Mount Tukuhnikivatz, Mount Peale *(USGS)*
Information:	http://www.utahtrails.com/tukuhnikivatz.html *(Utah Trails)* http://www.fs.fed.us/r4/mantilasal/ *(Manti-LaSal Nat. Forest)* phone: (435) 259-7155 *(Moab Ranger District)*

Drive south from Moab on Highway 191 for 23 miles to the La Sal Junction. Turn left here and drive east on Highway 46 for another 9 miles to the town of La Sal. Continue past La Sal for 3.7 miles to the Canopy Gap Road, a gravel road, where you must turn left. Another 2.0 miles will bring you to San Juan County Road 123 (La Sal Pass Road), where you must again turn left. After *driving 2.1 miles on Road 123 you will come to La Sal Creek. This small creek has to be forded, but under normal conditions most cars shouldn't have a problem getting across. The creek is only 10 feet wide and seldom more than 10 inches deep. It can be a problem, however, after a heavy rain. Continuing on Road 123 beyond the creek for 5.3 miles will bring you to the top of La Sal Pass and the trailhead. You will know you have reached La Sal Pass when you see a sign identifying Mount Peale near a short log fence on the right side of the road 0.3 mile beyond the turnoff to Medicine Lake.*

Anyone who has visited Canyonlands or Arches National Parks in the early summer has probably gazed admiringly at the snow capped peaks of the La Sal Mountains. The sight of snow seems oddly out of place in the midst of the desert heat, but snow is usu-

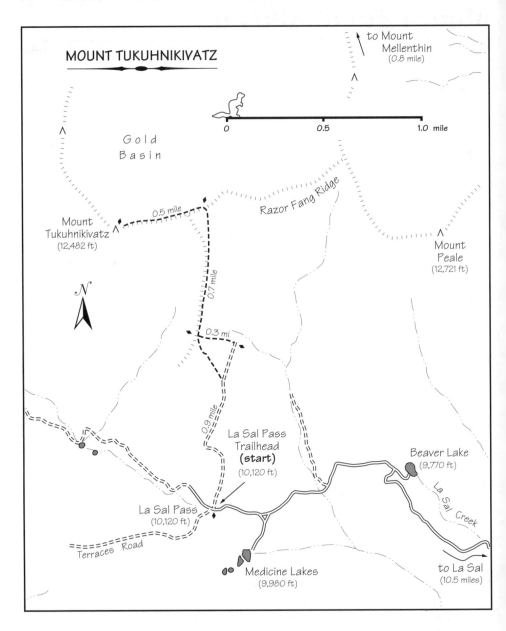

MOUNT TUKUHNIKIVATZ

to Mount
Mellenthin
(0.8 mile)

0   0.5   1.0 mile

Gold
Basin

Razor Fang Ridge

0.5 mile

Mount
Tukuhnikivatz
(12,482 ft)

Mount
Peale
(12,721 ft)

0.7 mile

N

0.3 mi

0.9 mile

La Sal Pass
Trailhead
(start)
(10,120 ft)

Beaver Lake
(9,770 ft)

La Sal Creek

La Sal Pass
(10,120 ft)

Terraces Road

Medicine Lakes
(9,980 ft)

to La Sal
(10.5 miles)

ally visible on the higher summits of the La
Sals well into July. Tradition has it that the
mountains were named by Silvestre Valez
de Escalante, the Spanish missionary and explorer, who saw them during his expedition
through Utah in 1776. He called them the
Sierra La Sal, or "Salt Mountains" because
he deemed it so unlikely that they could be

covered with snow so late in the summer.

As small and isolated as the La Sal Range
is, it is actually the second highest mountain range in Utah. Only northern Utah's
Uinta Mountains are higher. The highest
point in the La Sals is Mount Peale (12,721
feet), but the most celebrated peak is the one
with the most unpronounceable name:

Mount Tukuhnikivatz, as seen from the La Sal Pass Trailhead

Mount Tukuhnikivatz. Tukuhnikivatz is prominently situated on the western side of the La Sals and can be easily seen from the desert canyon country around Moab (see photograph, page 247). The exquisite red rock wilderness of Canyonlands and Arches is laid out in a vast panorama below the peak, and the resulting view from the top of Tukuhnikivatz on a clear sunny day is extraordinary. The mountain's tantalizing name is supposed to mean "The Place where the Sun Sets Last" in the language of the Ute Indians.

Before you begin the hike, pause to look northward from the parking area at the top of La Sal Pass. Mount Peale is the broad peak on your right, and Tukuhnikivatz is the slightly lower but more pointed peak on the left. The two peaks are connected by a long summit ridge that runs in an east-west direction for about two miles. From the top of Tukuhnikivatz the ridge drops down at a 30 degree angle into a small saddle about 500 feet below the summit of the mountain, and it is from that saddle that your final assent

will be made. The best way to reach the summit ridge is to climb upward along the broad crest of the secondary north-south ridge that begins about a half mile from the trailhead and ends at the saddle near the peak.

You will start by walking northward through the open meadow in front of the parking area along an old jeep road. After a few hundred yards the jeep road bends to the left and then heads north again through a grove of spruce trees. The road stays in the trees for 0.2 mile and then emerges once more into another meadow. At this point you are at the foot of the secondary ridge which you must climb in order to reach the summit ridge. There is a vague trail leaving the jeep road and heading into the trees at the foot of the ridge, but the trail is difficult to find. Instead of wasting time looking for it just continue walking northward along the jeep road. The road follows the eastern side of the ridge for another 0.4 mile before it ends. When the road ends simply turn west and start climbing until you reach the crest of the ridge. The crest of the ridge is about

Descending along the east face of Mount Tukuhnikivatz

500 feet above the road at this point. It is a tiring climb, but at least there are no trees to hinder your progress.

When you reach the top of the secondary ridge you will find a trail that climbs along its crest to the summit ridge above. The route is very steep, but there are few obstacles. The trail finally reaches the Peale-Tukuhnikivatz summit ridge about 0.5 mile east of Mount Tukuhnikivatz, where once again you will be on relatively level ground. What a relief! The elevation is just over 12,000 feet, and the ground is covered with the grasses, mosses, and wild flowers of the Arctic-Alpine Tundra life zone. This area is part of the Mount **see color photo, page 182** Peale Research Natural Area, an area that was established in the 1980s to protect several species of endangered plants that occupy the above-treeline slopes of the La Sals. Try to tread gently across the tundra–especially if you are in a large group.

The route to the top of Mount Tukuhnikivatz from the summit ridge is quite obvious. Walking westward the grade soon increases, and the pleasant carpet of plant life is replaced by a tortuous field of broken stones. There is no trail – just a lung busting climb up the last few hundred feet to the top of the talus covered peak.

From the top a large swath of some of the most interesting terrain in Utah is clearly visible. To the north, in Arches National Park, the Courthouse Towers rise dramatically from the desert floor like tombstones in a cemetery for giants. The Behind the Rocks area west of Moab is also clearly discernible, and the Colorado River Gorge that separates the Needles District from the rest of Canyonlands National Park meanders darkly through the maze of canyons, buttes, and mesas, patiently looking for Lake Powell. In the words of Edward Abbey:

All around the peaks of the Sierra La Sal lies the desert, a sea of burnt rock, arid tablelands, barren and desolate canyons. The canyon country is revealed from this magnificent height as on a map and I can imagine, if not read, the names on the land.[4]

---

[4]   Edward Abbey, *Desert Solitaire, a Season in the Wilderness*, Simon & Schuster, New York, 1968. (with permission)

Little Wild Horse Canyon

☆ ☆ ☆   **day hike**

Distance:	9.4 miles (loop)
Walking time:	5¹/₂ hours
Elevations:	730 ft. gain/loss Little Wild Horse Canyon Trailhead (start): 4,940 ft. San Rafael Swell: 5,670 ft.
Trail:	There is no developed trail for this hike, but the route is very easy to follow. The middle 1.6 miles of the hike is along an old jeep road, and the rest is along the bottoms of two dry desert slot canyons. It is an easy walk, but carry plenty of water.
Season:	Spring, summer, fall, winter. Do not enter the canyons when rain threatens. Also, the road to the trailhead may occasionally be impassable after periods of heavy rainfall.
Vicinity:	Near Hanksville and Goblin Valley State Park
Maps:	Little Wild Horse Mesa *(USGS)*
Information:	http://www.utahtrails.com/littlehorse.html *(Utah Trails)* http://www.blm.gov/utah/price/information.htm *(BLM, Price)* phone: (435) 636-3600 *(BLM, Price Field Office)*

Drive south of I-70 on Highway 24 towards Hanksville for 24 miles, where you will see a paved road leaving on the right for Goblin Valley State Park. Take this road and follow the signs towards Goblin Valley. Two miles before you reach the state park (11 miles from Highway 24) you will come to a well marked junction where the road to Wild Horse Mesa begins. Turn right here and drive another 5.3 miles to the trailhead and parking area.

This dry, desert canyon hike follows the bottoms of two narrow slot canyons as they cut their way through the southeastern side of the San Rafael Reef. The hike begins by following Bell Canyon from the south to the north side of the reef, then returns through Little Wild Horse Canyon to the starting point. Both canyons have some impressive narrows, but the narrows in the last half of Little Wild Horse Canyon are especially noteworthy. In one section the canyon meanders along for well over a mile with the distance between the sides rarely exceeding five feet. Walking down Little Wild Horse Canyon often feels more like exploring a cave that hiking in the desert. Children seem to get a particular thrill out of walking in the narrow passages, and this relatively easy hike is a good one for a family outing.

From the car parking area, the trail follows Little Wild Horse Wash northward towards the San Rafael Reef. After 0.4 mile you will see a small sign on the left side of the wash indicating that you have entered the Crack Canyon Wilderness Study Area, and a few hundred yards farther the flat streambed is interrupted by a small dry waterfall. The easiest way around this obstacle is to climb slightly up the left side of the canyon and drop back to the bottom a short distance later near the confluence of Bell and Little Wild Horse Canyons. When you reach the confluence bear left into Bell

Canyon.

The next section of the hike is an easy walk up the flat, sandy bottom of Bell Canyon. The canyon is quite narrow at first, but it steadily widens, finally breaking out of the San Rafael Reef and onto the San Rafael Swell some 1.9 miles later. Immediately after the canyon exits the San Rafael Reef you should see a jeep road crossing the sandy streambed. You will have to turn right onto the primitive road to reach Little Wild Horse Canyon, but first I suggest you turn left and walk for 0.4 mile to the site of the old Cistern Mine. The Cistern is an abandoned uranium mine that was developed in the 1950s or early 1960s. There are a number of interesting artifacts in the area,

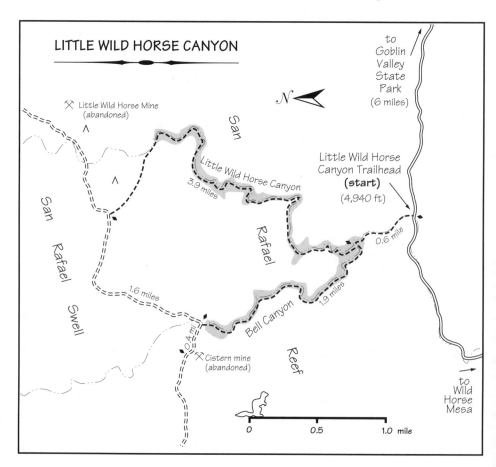

including a cabin that is still standing and the remains of an old truck. Whoever lived in the cabin must have had children, because there are also a few toys scattered around.

The road from the mouth of Bell Canyon to Little Wild Horse Canyon winds lazily eastward along the base of the San Rafael Reef, climbing about 370 feet before dropping down see color photos, pages 182, 183 again. After 1.6 miles it crosses a small wash that is a tributary of Little Wild Horse. Turn off the road at this point, and follow the smaller wash for 0.6 miles until it reaches the mouth of Little Wild Horse Canyon.

Little Wild Horse looks much like the northern end of Bell Canyon for the first 0.5 mile, but then the canyon suddenly drops down under a boulder and into its first section of narrows. This is an introduction to the long stretch of extremely tight narrows that begins about half way down Little Wild Horse. As mentioned before, it is more like walking through a cave than a canyon. There may be water in a few places in the narrows if it has rained recently, but usually you won't have any trouble getting through with dry feet. There is no permanent water in either of the canyons, and the rainwater seems to drain out quite quickly. Needless to say, however, the canyons are no place to be if a storm threatens. The water can come up to the danger level as quickly as it goes down, and once inside the narrows there is no place to escape a flood.

After 3.3 miles Little Wild Horse Canyon emerges again at the confluence with Bell Canyon, and from there it is an easy matter to retrace your steps 0.6 mile back to the road.

Little Wild Horse Canyon narrows

Horseshoe Canyon

☆ ☆

Distance:	7.4 miles (round trip)
Walking time:	4¼ hours
Elevations:	540 ft. gain/loss Horseshoe Canyon Trailhead (start): 5,340 ft. Great Gallery pictograph panel: 4,800 ft.
Trail:	The descent into the canyon is made on a slickrock trail with rock cairns. Inside the canyon a vague trail winds along the bottom of the sandy wash. There is intermittent water in the canyon, but it is usually stagnant.
Season:	Spring, summer, fall, winter. The canyon is quite hot in midsummer, so carry plenty of water.
Vicinity:	Horseshoe Canyon Detached Unit of Canyonlands National Park, near Hanksville
Maps:	Sugarloaf Butte *(USGS)* Canyonlands Maze District *(Trails Illustrated, #246)*
Information:	http://www.utahtrails.com/horseshoe.html *(Utah Trails)* http://www.nps.gov/cany/home.htm *(Canyonlands Nat. Park)* phone: (435) 259-2652 *(Hans Flat Ranger Station)*

Drive south from I-70 on Highway 24 for 25 miles. 0.6 miles beyond the turnoff to Goblin Valley State Park you will see a well marked gravel road leaving the east side of the highway for Roost Flats and Hans Flat Ranger Station. Turn left at this point. After 24.2 miles you will come to a signed fork in the road with the right fork leading to Hans Flat Ranger Station and the left fork to Horse- *shoe Canyon. Again you should turn left, toward Horseshoe Canyon. Another 5.1 miles will bring you to a smaller road, departing on the right, with a sign that says "Horseshoe Canyon Foot Trail". Follow this road for 1.8 miles to the trailhead.*

Horseshoe Canyon contains what is probably the finest display of prehistoric Indian rock art in the United States. The famous Great Gallery, largest of several Horseshoe Canyon sites, is 200 feet long, 15 feet high, and contains dozens of intriguing red, brown, and white pictographs. The paintings are at least 2,000 years old, and possibly as old as 8,000 years. Rock art is notoriously difficult to date accurately, but from the style we can be reasonably certain that the work was done by the so called Archaic People who

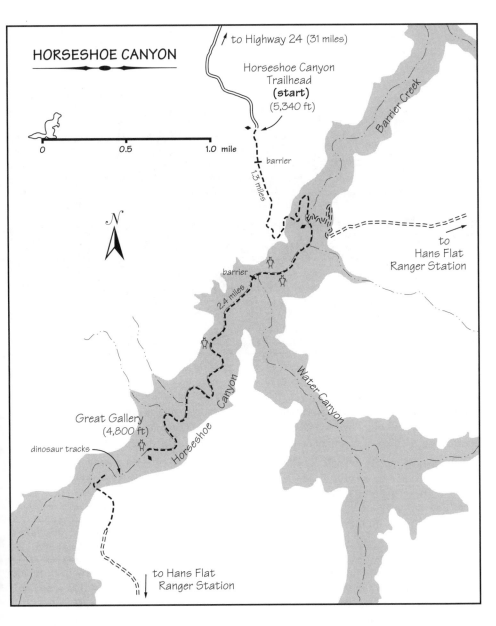

HORSESHOE CANYON

to Highway 24 (31 miles)

Horseshoe Canyon Trailhead
(start)
(5,340 ft)

0   0.5   1.0 mile

barrier

1.3 miles

to
Hans Flat
Ranger Station

barrier

2.4 miles

Barrier Creek

Water Canyon

Great Gallery
(4,800 ft)

dinosaur tracks

Horseshoe Canyon

to Hans Flat
Ranger Station

lived in the area before the arrival of the Anasazi and Fremont Indian cultures. Archaic clay figurines that closely mimic the pictographs have been found about nine miles away in Spur Fork, a tributary of Horseshoe Canyon, and the figurines have been dated to about 4700 B.C.

For years archaeologists have struggled to interpret the strange anthromorphs that are depicted in the Great Gallery. In addition to many smaller figures, the huge panel contains about twenty life size human shapes, all of which have a strange mummy-like appearance. They lack arms or legs, and often have huge insect-like eyes and bucket-shaped heads. Most intriguing of all is the

Horseshoe Canyon

figure known as the "Holy Ghost". This seven-foot-high painting stands out among the others because of its size and its ethereal appearance. Perhaps it was intended to portray a revered ancestor, or a mythical deity.

From the car parking area, the trail proceeds into the canyon along an old jeep road originally built by an oil exploration company. A barrier has been erected across the trail about 0.2 mile from the car park to keep recreational vehicles out, and another barrier has been placed 0.5 mile farther down to keep cattle out of the canyon. The trail finally reaches the canyon bottom 1.3 miles from the trailhead, then turns south along Barrier Creek. There is seldom running water in Barrier Creek, but the canyon is rarely completely dry either.

As you drop into the canyon you can see another jeep road descending from the opposite rim. This primitive road meets the trail at the canyon bottom, and for a while you will be walking on it. The road ends 0.6 mile upstream, just beyond the intersection of Water Canyon, where the Park Service has erected another barrier to keep vehicles out of upper Horseshoe Canyon.

As you approach Water Canyon be sure to watch for the first two pictograph sites, one on each side of the canyon. The trail passes right by them. These sites, like the other two that you see color photo, page 184 will see later, were painted by the Archaic People between 2,000 and 8,000 years ago. The third site is situated in a huge alcove on the west side of the stream, about 0.6 mile up-canyon from the first two. Unfortunately the alcove site has sustained substantial damage, both natural and man-caused, and it is not as impressive as the others.

Finally, 1.3 miles from the alcove site, or 3.7 miles from the beginning of the trail, you will come to the Great Gallery. This display of rock art has been called the Louvre of the

Southwest, and, indeed, it is a phenomenal relic of the past. Dozens of intricate human and animal figures decorate the panel, mostly in red, with some brown and white. The pigments were made from finely ground minerals, and then mixed with a liquid base, perhaps animal tallow or vegetable juices, to form a crude paint. After thousands of years all traces of the base have disappeared, but the mineral coloring still adheres to the rock and the paintings remain preserved in astonishing detail.

If you have sharp eyes, and if you are willing to walk just a little further, this hike will reward you with another unexpected bonus. About 0.2 mile upstream from the Great Gallery, Barrier Creek flows over a small slab of flat sandstone that appears harder and darker than the surrounding stone. Look carefully at the dark, flat surface near the west side of the creek, and you will see the tracks of a three-toed dinosaur that passed this way between 50 and 100 million years ago. The imprints are about ten inches in diameter, and there are at least three of them, spaced about four feet apart.

The "Holy Ghost", Great Gallery pictograph panel, Horseshoe Canyon

Upheaval Dome

☆ ☆

Canyonlands National Park
day hike

Distance: 8.0 miles (loop)

Walking time: 6 hours

Elevations: 1,460 ft. loss/gain
Upheaval Dome Trailhead (start): 5,680 ft.
Upheaval Canyon: 4,220 ft.

Trail: This is one of the most popular trails in Canyonlands National Park. It is very steep and rocky but well marked with rock cairns and easy to follow.

Season: Spring, summer, fall, winter. Canyonlands is very hot in the summertime and receives some snow in the winter. The best seasons for this hike are spring and fall.

Vicinity: Canyonlands Island in the Sky District, near Moab

Maps: Upheaval Dome *(USGS)*
Canyonlands Needles and Island Districts *(Trails Illustrated, #210)*

Information: http://www.utahtrails.com/upheaval.html *(Utah Trails)*
http://www.nps.gov/cany/home.htm *(Canyonlands Nat. Park)*
phone: (435) 259-7164 *(Canyonlands Nat. Park, Moab)*

Drive south of I-70 on Highway 191 for 20 miles until you see a paved road leaving on the right for Dead Horse Point and Canyonlands National Park. Turn here and drive for 21 miles to the Island in the Sky Visitor Center. Continuing past the visitor center for another 6.4 miles will bring you to another well marked junction where you must turn right. This road ends after 4.9 miles at the Upheaval Dome picnic area and trailhead.

Upheaval Dome is one of the most interesting geologic formations in Utah. At first glance the unusual circular structure appears to be a large crater, but geologically it more closely resembles an ancient dome. The strange formation consists of a huge circular pit, about a mile in diameter and 1,100 feet deep, surrounded by concentric rings of uplifted rock that were originally several

thousand feet under the ground.

What kind of natural force could account for such a structure? Volcanic forces often cause both uplifting and cratering, but it is highly unlikely that Upheaval Dome was created by a volcano. There is no evidence of volcanism anywhere in the area, and none of the rock in or around the dome is volcanic. A meteorite could have produced the

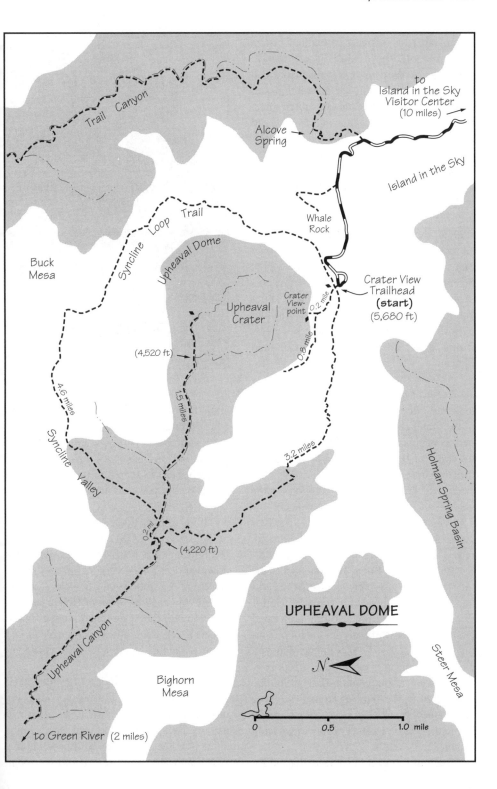

Trail Canyon

to
Island in the Sky
Visitor Center
(10 miles)

Alcove
Spring

Island in the Sky

Whale
Rock

Syncline Loop Trail

Upheaval Dome

Buck
Mesa

Upheaval
Crater

Crater
View-
point

0.2 mile

Crater View
Trailhead
(start)
(5,680 ft)

(4,520 ft)

0.8 mile

4.6 miles

1.5 miles

3.2 miles

Syncline Valley

Holman Spring Basin

0.2 mi

(4,220 ft)

UPHEAVAL DOME

Upheaval Canyon

Bighorn
Mesa

N

Steer Mesa

to Green River (2 miles)

0   0.5   1.0 mile

crater, but it is difficult to explain how a meteorite could have caused the extensive uplifting. A third theory is that Upheaval Dome is the remanent of an ancient salt dome that was pushed up by subterranean forces millions of years ago and then eroded to its present form. But this theory doesn't adequately account for the crater at the top of the dome.

In the past the salt dome theory had the widest following among geologists. However new research, including a microscopic study of the sand grains at the bottom of the crater, suggests that Upheaval Dome may indeed have been formed by a meteorite. Scientists now hypothesize that the meteorite that struck Upheaval Dome was about one-third of a mile in diameter, and fell about 60 million years ago—long before the formation of the Green River or the Colorado Plateau.

Trail into Upheaval Crater

A short trail leads from the parking area to several nice viewpoints on the south side of the crater rim. Be sure to take this walk before beginning your longer hike around the crater on the Syncline Loop Trail. From the rim a magnificent panoramic view of the crater will give you an appreciation for the geology of Upheaval Dome as well as show you where the hike will take you. The best viewpoint is the first one you will come to, only a quarter mile from the parking lot.

The Syncline Loop Trail intersects the viewpoint trail just a few feet from the parking area. This is the trail you will use for your eight-mile hike around Upheaval Dome. You can walk around the loop in either direction, but I recommend that you circle the crater in a clockwise direction by turning west at the junction (left, if you are coming from the parking area). Walking around the loop in a clockwise direction will insure that the best scenery is always in front of you.

The trail stays on fairly level ground for about 0.8 mile as it skirts along the southern edge of the crater, but soon it begins a downward plunge that will eventually take you to the bottom of Upheaval Canyon. The trail is steep, but the scenic rewards are ample. Occasionally you can catch a glimpse of the Green River peering up through the twists and folds of the canyons below. Finally, after a descent of 1,000 feet, the trail reaches the bottom of a wash and then continues downward at a more gradual grade until it arrives at the bottom of Upheaval Canyon. When you reach the floor of Upheaval Canyon you will find a sign marking the trail to Green River, three miles away. You should turn right at this junction to stay on the Syncline Loop Trail.

A short walk upcanyon from the Green River Trail junction will bring you to the mouth of Syncline Valley, where you can usually find water. The trail then climbs about 100 feet to the top of a bench above Upheaval Canyon where you will see a sign marking the beginning of the spur trail that leads into the center of Upheaval Crater. You may want to make a side trip at this point; the trail into the crater is about 1.5 miles, one way. Inside the crater you will find a massive jumble of de-

see color photo,
page 183

bris, including great piles of gray pulverized sand that was once a part of the White Rim geologic formation. It is this debris that has provided the strongest evidence to support the theory that Upheaval Dome was formed by a meteorite impact.

From the junction with the Upheaval Crater Trail the Syncline Loop Trail continues north into Syncline Valley. Again, there is usually water along this part of the hike, sometimes in large pools. After less than a mile the lower part of Syncline Valley ends in a box canyon, and the trail begins following a steep and rocky route up the valley's north side. Some scrambling may be necessary at this point, but once you reach the upper valley the trail again turns into a pleasant walk. There isn't usually as much water in the upper part of Syncline Valley as in the lower part, but it is still a green oasis in the desert canyon country. The path meanders for about a mile through the tamaracks and cottonwood trees, and then suddenly exits to the south through a large, unexpected break in the canyon wall. Hidden as it is from the outside world, Syncline Valley is the kind of place that would have made a perfect hideout for a band of outlaws at the turn of the century.

Once you have climbed out of Syncline Valley through the narrow slot in the canyon wall you are back on top of the Island in the Sky. From there it is a relatively easy walk of about two miles through the juniper forest back to the trailhead and parking area.

Upheaval Crater

Murphy Trail

☆ ☆   **Canyonlands National Park**
day hike

Distance:	9.0 miles (loop)
Walking time:	6 hours
Elevations:	1,390 ft. loss/gain
	Murphy Trailhead (start): 6,190 ft.
	Murphy Hogback: 5,200 ft.
	Murphy Wash: 4,800 ft.
Trail:	Good trail most of the way, but very steep and rocky for a half mile at the beginning and end.
Season:	Spring, summer, fall, winter. Canyonlands is very hot in the summertime and receives some snow in the winter. The best seasons for this hike are spring and fall.
Vicinity:	Canyonlands Island in the Sky District, near Moab
Maps:	Monument Basin, Turks Head *(USGS)*
	Canyonlands Needles and Island Districts *(Trails Illustrated, #210)*
Information:	http://www.utahtrails.com/murphy.html *(Utah Trails)*
	http://www.nps.gov/cany/home.htm *(Canyonlands Nat. Park)*
	phone: (435) 259-7164 *(Canyonlands Nat. Park, Moab)*

Drive south of I-70 on Highway 191 for 20 miles until you see a paved road leaving on the right for Dead Horse Point and Canyonlands National Park. Turn here and drive for 21 miles to the Island in the Sky Visitor Center. Continuing past the visitor center for another 6.4 miles will bring you to another well marked junction, where you must turn left towards Grand View Point. 2.5 *miles from the last junction you will see a well marked dirt road leading off to the right towards Murphy Point. The trailhead is 0.5 mile from the pavement on this dirt road.*

Hiking the Murphy Trail is an excellent way to gain an appreciation for the wild beauty and expanse of Canyonlands National Park. It is also a good way to sample some of the history of Canyonlands. The trail was built during World War One by the Murphy brothers, who grazed cattle in the area from 1917 until about 1920. The area on and be-

low the Island in the Sky Mesa was used extensively for winter grazing by local cattle ranchers during the first half of this century, and many remnants of their occupation can still be seen.

The Island in the Sky district was also an active exploration area for uranium prospectors during the 1950s. Uranium ore is

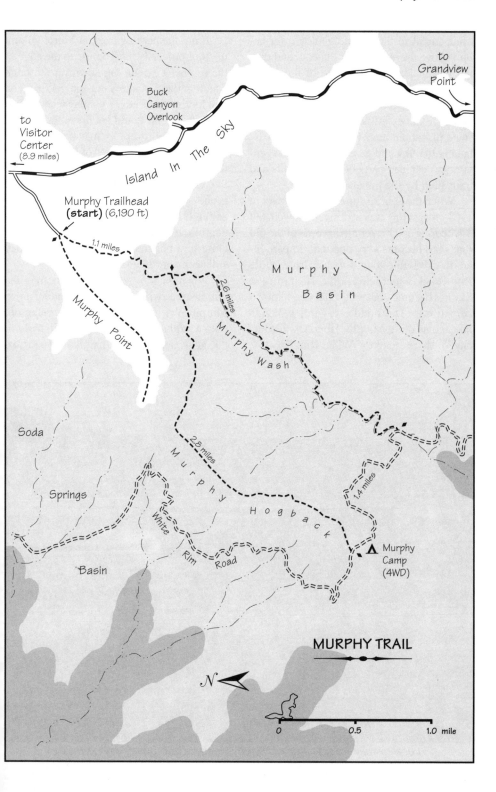

to
Grandview
Point

Buck
Canyon
Overlook

to
Visitor
Center
(8.9 miles)

Island In The Sky

Murphy Trailhead
(start) (6,190 ft)

1.1 miles

Murphy Point

M u r p h y
B a s i n

2.6 miles

Murphy Wash

Soda

2.8 miles

M u r p h y

1.4 miles

Springs

White

H o g b a c k

Rim

Road

Murphy
Camp
(4WD)

Basin

MURPHY TRAIL

N

0   0.5   1.0 mile

often found in the Chinle geologic formation above the White Rim Plateau, and during the nuclear energy craze of the 1950s prospectors came from all over the country to try their luck in Canyonlands. There are no active mines in the area now, but if you stand just about anywhere on the rim of Island in the Sky and gaze down into the canyon you can see parts of the old roads and trails built by the miners.

When the area became a national park in 1964 prospecting was no longer allowed, but 4-wheeling and bicycling on some of the old roads has become very popular. In particular, the 100-mile-long 4-wheel drive White Rim Road, which circles the Island in the Sky has become one of the parks best known attractions. The middle 1.4 miles of this hike, connecting Murphy Hogback to Murphy Wash, is along the White Rim Road.

From the parking area on Murphy Point the trail proceeds for 0.6 mile to the edge of the rim before plunging downward through a fault in the Wingate Sandstone. When you first look over the edge you may wonder how on earth anyone could get down there. But, miraculously, there is a way. The trail switchbacks down a series of ledges near the top, then finds a debris-scattered slope for the rest of the route. Near the bottom there is one exciting part where the Murphy brothers built a wooden bridge across a ten-foot gap in the trail. The logs in the bridge are close to a hundred years old now, but they still seem sturdy enough.

When the trail reaches the bottom of the cliff it splits, with the left fork heading down Murphy Wash and the right fork going out onto Murphy Hogback. If it is still early in the day I suggest you turn right here and take

Looking west from the top of Murphy Hogback into Soda Springs Basin

the Murphy Hogback Trail, but if it is near noon you should go down Murphy Wash first. The reason for this is that the most beautiful part of the hike is along the Hogback, and you should save this portion for when the sun is lower in the sky. If the sun is directly overhead the geology of the shadowless canyons is not as interesting. From a practical point of view it doesn't really matter which fork you take. The trails are joined at the other end by the White Rim Road, and the loop can be walked in either direction. I will assume here, however, that you choose to proceed via the Hogback trail.

see color photo, page 184

The views from Murphy Hogback are so impressive that, upon reaching the White Rim Road, many hikers choose to return the same way. The Soda Springs Basin lies below you on the northwest side, with the photogenic towers of the Organ Rock Formation reaching up along the shores of the Green River. The river makes a huge meander into the basin, circling around another famous formation known as the Turks Head. And farther to the south, across the hidden recesses of the Colorado River, are the pinnacles of the Canyonlands Needles District. It is an immense 360 degree panorama. Many of the same features can more easily be seen from the viewpoints above the rim, but it is not quite the same up there. Down on the Hogback you get the feeling that you are more than just an observer. You are somehow a part of it all.

Once you reach the White Rim Road turn left and walk southeast along the road for 1.4 miles until you see a sign marking the beginning of the Murphy Wash Trail. Murphy Wash is interesting in a less dramatic way. The sandy wash is more protected and receives more water that the exposed Hogback; hence the plant life is quite different there. Soon after leaving the road you will pass by a small spring which, as the animal tracks attest, attracts a good deal of canyon wildlife. As you near the top of the wash you will pass by an old corral, one of many left by the ranchers who worked the area. Finally, 2.6 miles after leaving White Rim Road, the trail climbs out of Murphy Wash and rejoins the original trail for the climb back to the rim.

White Rim Road on Murphy Hogback

Confluence Overlook

☆

Canyonlands National Park
day hike

Distance:	10.4 miles (round trip)
Walking time:	6 hours
Elevations:	220 ft. gain/loss
	Big Spring Canyon Trailhead (start): 4,940 ft.
	Big Spring Canyon: 4,820 ft.
	Overlook point: 4,920 ft.
Trail:	Easy, well marked trail
Season:	Summer, spring, winter and fall. This hike is very hot in the summer and cold in the winter. The best times are during the spring and fall.
Vicinity:	Canyonlands National Park, Needles District, near Moab
Maps:	The Loop, Spanish Bottom *(USGS)*
	Canyonlands Needles and Island Districts *(Trails Illustrated, #210)*
Information:	http://www.utahtrails.com/confluence.html *(Utah Trails)*
	http://www.nps.gov/cany/home.htm *(Canyonlands Nat. Park)*
	phone: (435) 259-7164 *(Canyonlands Nat. Park, Moab)*

Drive south of Moab on Highway 191 for 40 miles until you see a paved road on the right leading to the Needles District of Canyonlands National Park. (Don't confuse this road with the road to the Needles Overlook, 7 miles closer to Moab.) Turn right, towards Canyonlands National Park and drive for another 35 miles to the Visitor Center. Continue past the Visitor Center on the paved Scenic Drive Road for 6.5 miles. The road finally ends at a small parking area on the rim of Big Spring Canyon where the hike begins.

Canyonlands, the largest of Utah's five national parks, is neatly split into thirds by the intersection of the Green and the Colorado Rivers. Both rivers have carved thousand-foot-deep canyons through the high surrounding desert, and the view of their confluence at the center of the park is one of Canyonlands' most impressive sights.

Both of the famous rivers have now been largely tamed by a series of dams built over the last sixty years, but from this prospective one can still see the same wild scene that John Wesley Powell saw during his historical voyage down the Green and Colorado Rivers in 1869. In July of that year, while his party was camped on the north side of the confluence, Powell and one of his men climbed above the rivers to a point just south of the

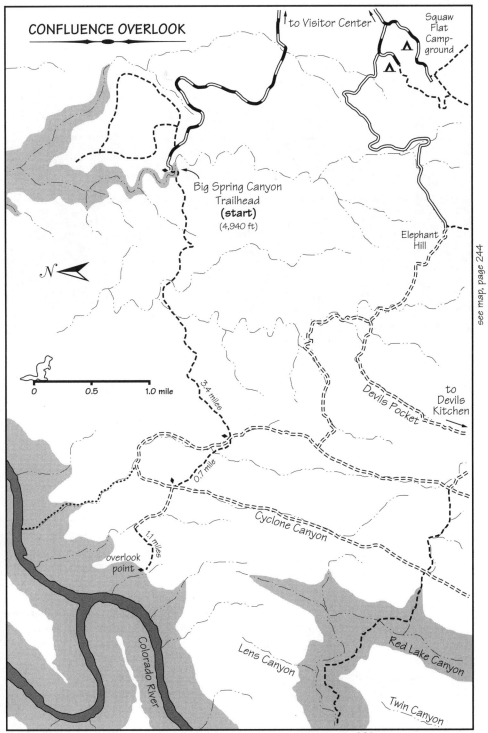

CONFLUENCE OVERLOOK

to Visitor Center

Squaw Flat Camp-ground

Big Spring Canyon Trailhead
(start)
(4,940 ft)

Elephant Hill

N

0   0.5   1.0 mile

3.4 miles

Devils Pocket

to Devils Kitchen

0.7 mile

Cyclone Canyon

1.1 miles

overlook point

Colorado River

Lens Canyon

Red Lake Canyon

Twin Canyon

see map, page 244

see map, page 260

Elephant Canyon from the Confluence Overlook Trail

present day overlook trail. In the following passage, first printed in Scribner's Monthly in 1875, Powell describes what he saw:

From the north-west came the Green in a narrow, winding gorge. From the north-east came the Grand [Colorado] through a canyon that seemed, from where we stood, bottomless.... Wherever we looked there was a wilderness of rocks – deep gorges where the rivers are lost below cliffs, and towers, and pinnacles, and ten thousand strangely carved forms in every direction, and beyond them mountains blending with the clouds.[5]

From the trailhead the trail immediately drops into Big Spring Canyon, and then climbs up the other side. This is really the only strenuous part of the route, but it doesn't last long. Big Spring Canyon is only 120 feet deep at this point. After leaving Big Spring Canyon the trail meanders pleasantly across the open desert for another 3.1 miles before crossing a jeep road at the northern end of another shallow canyon called Devils Lane. After another 0.7 mile the trail crosses the road again as the road doubles back into Cyclone Canyon. At the point where the trail meets the jeep road the second time you will see another spur road branching off to the west. The trail continues down this road.

After walking west on the spur road for 0.6 miles you will come to a dead end, where there is a small outhouse and a parking area for jeeps. A Park Service sign points the way to the trail that will lead you the last 0.5 mile to the overlook point.

The Colorado River

After seeing the rivers from the overlook

---

[5] John Wesley Powell, *The Canyons of the Colorado*, reprinted by Outbooks, Golden, Colorado, 1981.

point, many hikers feel a great urge to descend into the canyon to the shore of the Colorado. There are at least two ways to do this. Three if you include Powell's route below the overlook point, but I would hardly recommend his route. It is quite exposed and requires some rock climbing skills. (Amazingly, Powell did it with only one arm! He had lost his right arm 7 years earlier in the Civil War.)

The easiest way to get to the Colorado River is on the Lower Red Lake Canyon Trail, which descends from Cyclone Canyon 3.5 miles south of the overlook. To get there retrace your steps back to the place where the trail leaves the road in Cyclone Canyon. Then turn south and walk along the Cyclone Canyon jeep road for a distance of 2.4 miles until you see a sign marking the Lower Red Lake Canyon Trailhead on the west side of the road. It is 4.0 miles from Cyclone Canyon to the Colorado River along this trail. It is also possible to walk upstream along the Colorado River from the mouth of Lower Red Lake Canyon to the confluence, a distance of 3.6 miles.

If you want to hike to the Colorado via the Lower Red Lake Canyon Trail you had better pack for at least two days. However, if you have a four-wheel-drive vehicle you can easily visit the Colorado River and the confluence overlook in one day. A well-used jeep road from Elephant Hill to Cyclone Canyon will give you access to both the Lower Red Lake Canyon Trail and the Overlook Trail, allowing you to see everything with only about nine miles of hiking. (See page 242 for an explanation of how to get to Elephant Hill.)

The other way to reach the Colorado River involves a side trip of 2.0 miles each way from the confluence overlook trail. If you elect to follow this route, walk back to Cyclone Canyon and turn north at the point where the trail leaves the jeep road. Follow the Cyclone Canyon jeep road north for 0.5 mile. The road starts out heading almost due north, and then swings around to the east. Just after the turn to the east you will see the beginning of a drainage that heads off in a northwesterly direction towards the river. You can follow this drainage all the way to the Colorado River. The route involves about 1.5 miles of off-trail hiking, but many hikers have gone before you and the way is clearly marked by cairns. The route becomes very steep as you approach the river and some scrambling is necessary, but the danger is minimal if you are careful to follow the cairns. Once you reach the Colorado it is another 0.9 mile walk downstream to the confluence itself.

Confluence of the Green and Colorado Rivers

Chesler Park

☆ ☆ ☆ ☆ ☆

Canyonlands National Park
overnight hike

Distance: 17.0 miles (loop)

Walking time: day 1: 6³/₄ hours
day 2: 6 hours

Elevations: 1,400 ft. gain/loss
Elephant Hill Trailhead (start): 5,120 ft.
Chesler Park: 5,600 ft.
Druid Arch: 5,740 ft.

Trail: This is almost entirely a slickrock trail, with stone cairns marking the way. The terrain is very rugged and you will be continually climbing over and around obstacles; hence the trail seems longer than it really is.

Season: Spring, early summer, and fall. This is one hike you probably won't want to do in July or August. There is very little water or shade, and daytime summer temperatures are nearly always over 100 °F. Winter hikes are possible, but the high desert is often cold at night.

Vicinity: Canyonlands National Park, Needles District, near Moab

Maps: Druid Arch, The Loop (USGS)
Canyonlands Needles and Island Districts (Trails Illustrated, #210)

Information: http://www.utahtrails.com/chesler.html (Utah Trails)
http://www.nps.gov/cany/home.htm (Canyonlands Nat. Park)
phone: (435) 259-7164 (Canyonlands Nat. Park, Moab)

Drive south of Moab on Highway 191 for 40 miles until you see a paved road on the right leading to the Needles District of Canyonlands National Park. (Don't confuse this road with the road to the Needles Overlook, 7 miles closer to Moab.) Turn right, towards Canyonlands National Park and drive for another 35 miles to the Visitor Center. You will have to stop there to obtain an *overnight backcountry permit. From the Visitor Center just follow the signs to Elephant Hill where you will see the trailhead and parking area. The distance is 6.0 miles, with the last 3.0 miles unpaved.*

Note: A fee of $10.00 is charged for hiking permits. A single permit will cover everyone in your group, but the maximum group size is seven people. Most important, only 5 groups are allowed to camp each night in Chesler Park. The permits are issued at the Visitor Center on a first come-first served basis, but if you don't have an advance reservation you probably *won't be able to get a permit. You can obtain a campsite reservation by fax or by mail, but you must contact the park at least two weeks before your intended stay. For more detailed information on how to make reservations call (435) 259-4351 between 8:00 a.m. and 12:30 p.m., Monday through Friday.*

If you can stand the high desert temperatures, the Needles District of Canyonlands is a hiker's paradise. The needles themselves are the main attraction. Carved by the wind and the rain from the multicolored Cedar Mesa Sandstone, they present a startling array of spires and pinnacles that rise from the slickrock like a forest of sandstone trees. Some parts of the trail wind torturously through the stone towers and canyons, forcing hikers to negotiate one obstacle after another.

Deep inside the rugged needles country lies an unexpected refuge of gentle grassland. This is Chesler Park—a flat, circular-shaped meadow about a mile in diameter, almost completely surrounded by the sandstone needles. There are three designated camping areas on the perimeter of the meadow, and one could hardly ask for a more beautiful place to spend a night or two. There are also several other interesting things to see within an easy walk of Chesler Park, including an impressive natural arch and a small Anasazi Indian ruin. The one drawback that prevents Chesler from being a perfect hiking destination is the unavailability of water. The nearest reliable spring is two miles away in Elephant Canyon, so you will have to carry most of your water with you.

see color photos, page 185

Day 1 (9.1 miles)

The route from Elephant Hill Trailhead to Chesler Park is only about 3.3 miles long, depending on which camp site you use. The trail is almost entirely across slickrock, marked by stone cairns. There is a great deal of up and down, and this makes the distance seem greater than it actually is. There are three junctions with intersecting trails along the way, but the route is clearly marked with signs at each junction so there shouldn't be any confusion as to which way to turn. After 2.8 miles the trail emerges from behind a row of needles to give you your first view of the northern side of Chesler.

Once you reach Chesler Park you should decide where you are going to camp so you can shed your packs. The Park Service allows camping in three places along the eastern edge of the meadow, but, in my opinion, the southern camp sites have the most to offer. To reach this area continue south from the last trail junction, along the eastern side of the park, until you meet another trail coming in from Elephant Canyon. Turn right here, onto the Joint Trail, and soon you will pass by the southern side of a rocky island in the center of the park. The camping area (marked by signs) is along the southwestern side of the island. The western side of this rock island was also a camping area for cowboys who ran cattle in Chesler Park from the late 1800s until the early 1960s. You can still see the remains of their camp just north of the backpackers camping area.

After you have established a camp site, leave your backpacks behind and check out the Joint Trail. Continue walking west from the camping area along the main trail for about 0.8 mile, where you will find a long, narrow flight of stone stairs that lead down into a dark, slender crack in the sandstone. The trail continues through the bottom of the three-foot crack, called a "joint" by old-timers, for some 300 yards before emerging

see map, page 239

CHESLER PARK

to
Elephant
Hill

Elephant
Hill
Trailhead
(start)
(5,120 ft)

to
Visitor
Center
(6 miles)

to Lower
Red Lake
Canyon

N

Elephant
Hill

Soda
Spring

Devils Lane

Devils
Kitchen
Camp

Devils Pocket

Elephant Canyon

1.3 miles

0.6 mile

0.7 mile

to
Squaw Flat
Campground

0.2 mile

1.4 mile

see map page 249

0.5 mile

0.9 mile

Chesler Park
(5,600 ft)

camp site

1.0 mile

to
Squaw
Flat
Camp-
ground

0.5 mile

historic
cowboy camp

camp site

1.0 mile

0.7 mile

1.7 mile

Joint Trail

Elephant Canyon

1.8 miles

Chesler Canyon

Virginia
Park

0   0.5   1.0 mile

Druid Arch

once again at the top of the slickrock. The Chesler Park hike is full of surprises, but for many the joint is the most exciting part of the trip.

Soon after emerging from the joint you will cross the dry streambed of Chesler Canyon and meet a jeep trail coming down from Elephant Hill. You will have to walk north along the jeep trail for a short distance to reconnect with the Chesler Park Trail and complete the loop back to your camp site. The sides of Chesler Canyon, through which the sandy road winds, are lined with hundreds of stone needles. Like giant terrestrial pin cushions, even the hills surrounding the canyon are packed with clusters of needles. After 0.7 mile on the jeep road you will see another sign marking the departure of the trail to Chesler Park. Turn right here and then right again at the next trail junction. Finally, 1.9 mile from the road you will again arrive at the northeast corner of Chesler Park.

Day 2 (7.9 miles)

After breaking camp you should leave Chesler via the southeast exit to Elephant Canyon. About 0.2 mile before you arrive at Elephant Canyon you will have the opportunity to see an Anasazi Indian ruin. The ruin is a few hundred feet below the trail, in the bottom of a small canyon on the north side. You can't see the ruin from the trail itself, but just above the site there is a place where previous hikers have left the main path to walk to a viewpoint only 15 feet away that looks directly down onto it.

There is another trail junction in the bottom of Elephant Canyon. The northern path leads back to Elephant Hill where your car is parked. But before going back you should take off your backpacks and make a side trip to Druid Arch, 1.8 miles south of the junction at the head of Elephant Canyon. You will probably see a few scattered water holes in the creek bed as you make your way up the canyon. This is one of the few places

The Joint Trail, Chesler Park

Druid Natural Arch

in the area where you can usually obtain water—a useful thing to know if you plan to spend more than one night in Chesler Park.

Druid Arch itself is extremely impressive. It stands high on the mesa top above Elephant Canyon, with nothing but blue sky behind it. The appearance of the huge arch reminds many people of Stonehenge in southern England, hence its name. (The Druids are the people who built Stonehenge.) In her book, *Desert Quartet*, Terry Tempest Williams shares with us her first impression of Druid Arch:

Red Rock. Blue sky. This arch is structured metamorphosis. Once a finlike tower, it has been perforated by a massive cave-in, responsible now for the keyholes where wind enters and turns. What has been opened, removed, eroded away, is as compelling to me as what remains. Druid Arch—inorganic mat-ter—rock rising from the desert floor as a creation of time, weathered, broken, and beautiful.[6]

The best time to see Druid Arch is in the morning. The trail ends at a magnificent viewpoint high on the east side of Elephant Canyon where, on most days, the arch is bathed in the morning sunlight.

From the Chesler Park trail junction, where you left your backpacks, the trail back to Elephant Hill continues down the bottom of Elephant Canyon for another 1.4 miles before reaching the trail used on the first day to reach Chesler Park. From that junction it is another 1.9 miles back to the Elephant Hill Trailhead.

Alternative Routes

As the map suggests, there are many alternative routes for this hike. In my opinion it would be a shame to visit the area

---

[6] Terry Tempest Williams and Mary Frank, *Desert Quartet,* Pantheon Books, New York, 1995. (with permission)

without (1) spending at least one night in Chesler Park, (2) experiencing the Joint Trail, and (3) seeing Druid Arch; and the route I have suggested will allow you to do those things with a minimum amount of walking. If you have the time, however, I suggest you begin your hike at the Squaw Flat Campground rather than Elephant Hill, and spend two nights in Chesler Park (see map on page 249). Doing so will add 2.1 miles to the outbound distance, and 2.7 miles (via Big Spring Canyon) to the return distance. The section of trail between Elephant Canyon and Big Spring Canyon is particularly interesting, with another cave-like crack to walk through and two strategically placed ladders to negotiate.

Virginia Park

If you fancy yourself an explorer, I will leave you with a final thought. Chesler Park isn't the only desert Shangrila in Canyon-lands. Only a mile southeast of Chesler there lies another smaller, but equally beautiful grassy meadow: Virginia Park. Virginia Park is so well protected by a surrounding wall of sandstone that its isolation is nearly complete, and for that reason it is considered to be a very special place by the Park Service. It is one of the few places on the Colorado Plateau that was never grazed by cattle or sheep, and, consequently, its plant life is still in a nearly pristine state. For botanists and ecologists Virginia Park has great scientific value and the Park Service is striving to maintain it in its original state; hence it has been closed to hikers. There is no marked trail leading to it, but possible routes into the park exist from Elephant Canyon and Chesler Canyon. If you succeed in finding your way to Virginia Park, please do not defile it in any way. Be especially careful not to damage the cryptogamic plant life that exists in the park's dry, undisturbed soil.

La Sal Mountains, as seen from the Chesler Park Trail

Lost Canyon

Distance:	9.0 miles (loop)
Walking time:	5¼ hours
Elevations:	360 ft. gain/loss
	Squaw Flat Trailhead (start): 5,120 ft.
	Lost Canyon: 5,100 ft.
	Highest point: 5,460 ft.
Trail:	Well marked trail through the bottoms of two desert canyons. Some wading may be necessary in wet years.
Season:	Summer, spring, winter and fall. This hike is very hot in the summer and cold in the winter. The best times are during the spring and fall.
Vicinity:	Canyonlands National Park, Needles District, near Moab
Maps:	Druid Arch, The Loop *(USGS)*
	Canyonlands Needles and Island Districts *(Trails Illustrated, #210)*
Information:	http://www.utahtrails.com/lost.html *(Utah Trails)*
	http://www.nps.gov/cany/home.htm *(Canyonlands Nat. Park)*
	phone: (435) 259-7164 *(Canyonlands Nat. Park, Moab)*

Drive south of Moab on Highway 191 for 40 miles until you see a paved road on the right leading to the Needles District of Canyonlands National Park. (Don't confuse this road with the road to the Needles Overlook, 7 miles closer to Moab.) Turn right, towards Canyonlands National Park and drive for another 35 miles to the Visitor Center. From the Visitor Center just follow the signs to Squaw Flat Campground, Section A. In the back of the campground you will see a parking area and a sign marking the Squaw Flat Trailhead.

This loop hike passes through two sandstone canyons near Squaw Flat Campground in the Needles District of Canyonlands National Park. The parallel canyons are only about a half mile apart, but they are very different in character. Squaw Canyon is dry and generally uninteresting, while Lost Canyon is deeper and has a surprising amount of water and vegetation.

Because of its water, Lost Canyon was well known to the cowboys who lived and worked in Canyonlands during the first half of this century. Even when other sources of water had given way to the dry summer heat, their livestock could always depend on finding a pool or two of the life-giving liquid in

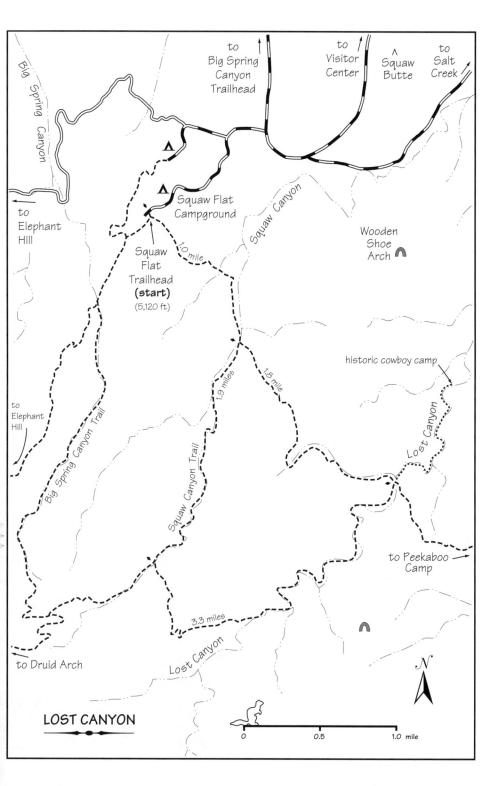

to
Big Spring
Canyon
Trailhead

to
Visitor
Center

Squaw
Butte

to
Salt
Creek

Big Spring Canyon

to
Elephant
Hill

Squaw
Flat
Campground

Squaw Canyon

Wooden
Shoe
Arch

Squaw
Flat
Trailhead
(start)
(5,120 ft)

.10 mile

to
Elephant
Hill

Big Spring Canyon Trail

Squaw Canyon Trail

1.9 miles

1.8 mile

historic cowboy camp

Lost Canyon

to Peekaboo
Camp

to Druid Arch

3.3 miles

Lost Canyon

Lost Canyon

LOST CANYON

N

0   0.5   1.0   mile

the green recesses of Lost Canyon. Today, one of the most interesting attractions of the canyon is an old cowboy camp that was used by cattlemen during the 1920s. The historic site still contains an old table, some pots and pans, old bottles and cans, and other implements. The camp is not hard to find, but it requires a 2.4 mile detour downstream from the main trail.

After leaving Squaw Flat Campground the trail proceeds southward for about 200 feet, then splits. Turn left at the fork, following the sign to Lost Canyon and Squaw Canyon. The path winds across the flat desert country for another mile before reaching a trail junction in Squaw Canyon Wash, where the loop through the two canyons begins. It doesn't make much difference which direction you take around the loop, but I will describe a clockwise direction here.

After passing Squaw Canyon Wash the trail continues for about 1.0 mile before dropping into the mouth of a small, unnamed canyon. It then winds along the sandy bottom of the small canyon for another 0.8 mile, finally intersecting a large wash. A Park Service sign at this point will tell you that you have reached Lost Canyon. The trail up Lost Canyon turns right at the sign and heads south.

see color photo, page 186

Before following the trail up Lost Canyon you should consider a side trip to the cowboy camp historic site described earlier. This option will add 2.4 miles to the length of the hike. The cowboy camp is downstream (left) from the Lost Canyon trail junction, so to get there you will have to leave the trail at the junction. Although there is no trail the route is not difficult; just turn north and follow the sandy bottom of the Lost Canyon streambed for 35-40 minutes (1.2 miles). You will come to a large pool of water with a sandstone alcove, partially hidden by trees, just a few feet above the left shore. The historic camp is in that alcove.

What tales the walls of the sheltered camp would tell if they could talk. We can only image the interesting characters that must have gathered here in days past, and the yarns they must have exchanged to pass the lonely nights. Over the years a collection of artifacts accumulated in the cowboys' home away from home, and today, three-fourths of a century later, these simple treasures offer a priceless window through which visitors can view the past. Enjoy their presence, but please don't be tempted to remove anything. These treasures are far more interesting in the context of the camp than they would be in your drawer at home. Also, refrain from the urge to add your name to the signatures the old cowboys scratched onto the walls of the alcove. These cowboyglyphs indicate that the camp was occupied at least as early as 1920, but it was probably used much earlier than that.

Back on the trail, the path continues from the Lost Canyon trail junction up Lost Canyon for a distance of 2.0 miles before climbing out the north side of the canyon onto the ridge above. From there the route drops back down to the bottom of Squaw Canyon and proceeds for another 1.9 miles to the beginning of the loop. From there it is an easy 1.0 mile walk back to the Squaw Flat Trailhead.

Lost Canyon Trail

The Maze

☆ ☆ ☆

Canyonlands National Park
4WD vehicle required
overnight hike

Distance: 12.9 miles (loop)

Walking time: day 1: 5¹/₄ hours
day 2: 3¹/₄ hours

Elevations: 1,560 ft. loss/gain
Chimney Rock Trailhead (start): 5,460 ft.
Harvest Scene Pictographs: 4,580 ft.
Maze Overlook: 5,160 ft.

Trail: That portion of the trail in the sandy bottom of the Maze is unmarked, but the route is not difficult to find. The slickrock part of the trail above the Maze is marked with cairns. Some scrambling is necessary to reach the Maze Overlook, and a 20-foot length of rope is useful in raising and lowering backpacks.

Season: Spring, early summer, and fall. This hike is very hot in the summer and cold in the winter. The best times are during the spring and fall. The road to the trailhead may be impassable, even with a 4WD, after a heavy snow or rain.

Vicinity: Canyonlands National Park, Maze District, near Hite

Maps: Spanish Bottom, Elaterite Basin *(USGS)*
Canyonlands Maze District *(Trails Illustrated, #246)*

Information: http://www.utahtrails.com/maze.html *(Utah Trails)*
http://www.nps.gov/cany/home.htm *(Canyonlands Nat. Park)*
phone: (435) 259-2652 *(Hans Flat Ranger Station)*

Nearly all of the trailheads in this book can be reached with an ordinary car.
The Chimney Rock Trailhead, however, is an exception; you must have a 4WD high clearance vehicle to reach this trailhead. Also, your vehicle should have a short wheel base. Full sized pickup trucks will have trouble getting around some of the turns and through some of the washes on the Chimney Rock Road. There are several ways to reach Chimney Rock Trailhead, but all require 4WD vehicles. The route described here is the most feasible way, but it will still take you 7 hours of off-highway driving to get there! Be sure to carry plenty of fuel and water, and be prepared for unexpected emergencies.

Before you start be sure to obtain a backcountry camping permit from the Park Service. You can do this over the telephone by calling the Hans Flat Ranger Station at (435) 259-2652. Have a credit card ready; the cost is $10.00 per group for off-road camping. There are

restrictions on the number of campers allowed in the Maze each day so, if possible, it is wise to get your permit in advance, especially during the peak spring and fall seasons. For more information on how to make advance reservations call the park headquarters in Moab at (435) 259-4351 between 8:00 a.m. and 12:30 p.m., Monday through Friday. Advance reservations must be made at least two weeks before the time of your visit.

To get to Chimney Rock Trailhead, first drive south from Hanksville on Highway 95 for 45 miles until you come to a bridge crossing the Dirty Devil River. 1.2 miles south of this bridge you will see a graded dirt road departing on the left. This is the road to the Maze. If you are coming from the other direction this road will be 1.0 mile north of the bridge across Lake Powell. The trailhead is 48 miles from Highway 95 by way of this road. The first 34 miles can be driven by almost any high clearance vehicle, but you will need a 4WD for the last 14 miles. The route is fairly straightforward, although there are a few forks where other less distinct roads join the main road. In these cases just stick to the better traveled route. Thirty miles from the highway, in a meadow called Waterhole Flat, you will come to a four way junction. Turn right here and follow the signs to the Doll House and Standing Rocks. Finally, 3.5 miles before reaching the Doll House, you will see a sign marking the Chimney Rock Trailhead and parking area.

The Maze District of Canyonlands National Park, separated from the rest of the park by the Green and Colorado Rivers, is one of the most rugged and remote desert areas in the United States. As described above, just getting there requires seven bone rattling hours of driving across a narrow unimproved road, the last fourteen miles of which cannot be completed without a 4WD vehicle. To their credit, the National Park Service intends to preserve the remoteness, and there are no plans to improve the access roads. Indeed, there could hardly be a more appropriate preamble to an experience in the Maze than the long journey across the open desert required to reach it; the rugged canyon country's isolation definitely adds to its appeal.

The Maze, which actually occupies only a small part the Canyonlands Maze District, includes about thirty square miles of land, etched and sliced apart by five major canyons and dozens of smaller side canyons. How could such a small piece of land be carved into so many canyons? From the plateaus above it looks like a labyrinth with the top removed. A convoluted work of art, tenaciously sculpted by ten million years of rainwater searching for a way to the Colorado River.

This loop hike affords fine views of the Maze from the upper plateaus, as well as the experience of walking through one of the canyons below. In addition, the route passes by the Harvest Scene Pictograph Panel, a fine example of Indian rock art produced by the Archaic Culture more than 2000 years ago. Many hikers complete the basic loop in one day, but spending an extra night in the canyons will allow you to include a side trip to the Maze Overlook, the best single place to see the Maze from above. Also, it would be a shame not to spend part of a day exploring a few side canyons before climbing back to the trailhead.

Day 1 (8.4 miles)

There are four cairned trails leaving from the Chimney Rock parking area. The first trail on the left, bearing around the west side of Chimney Rock, leads to the bottom of Pictograph Fork. When you return to the trail-

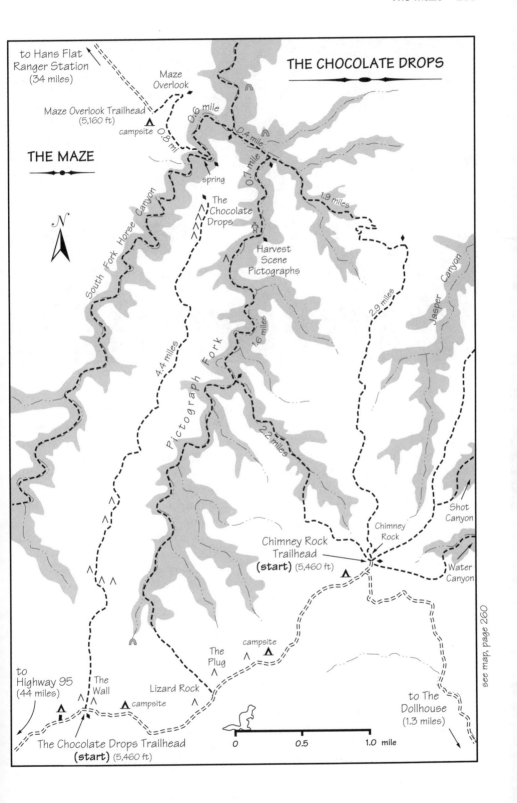

to Hans Flat
Ranger Station
(34 miles)

Maze
Overlook

THE CHOCOLATE DROPS

Maze Overlook Trailhead
(5,160 ft)

0.6 mile

campsite 0.8 mi

0.4 mile

THE MAZE

0.7 mile

spring

The
Chocolate
Drops

1.9 miles

Harvest
Scene
Pictographs

South Fork Horse Canyon

Jasper Canyon

N

2.9 miles

4.4 miles

1.6 miles

Pictograph Fork

2.2 miles

Shot
Canyon

Chimney Rock Trailhead
(start) (5,460 ft)

Chimney
Rock

Water
Canyon

see map, page 260

The
Plug

campsite

to Highway 95
(44 miles)

The
Wall

Lizard Rock

campsite

to The
Dollhouse
(1.3 miles)

The Chocolate Drops Trailhead
(start) (5,460 ft)

0   0.5   1.0 mile

Climbing to the Maze Overlook (note the "mushroom" formation on the right)

head at the end of the loop you will be on this trail. The second trail from the left passes by the east side of Chimney Rock and heads north across the plateau above Pictograph Fork. The hike starts on this trail. (The third and forth trails from the left lead to Jasper Ridge and Water Canyon, respectively.)

As you walk northward across the slickrock from Chimney Rock you will see Petes Mesa directly in front of you. The large butte behind Petes Mesa is Ekker Butte. If you loose track of the cairns just stay high on the ridge as you continue towards Petes Mesa. When you get to within a half mile of the mesa, however, be sure to watch more carefully for the cairns so you will not miss the turn when the trail begins its descent down into the Maze. Also, be on the lookout for mountain sheep in this area. They are often sighted on the plateau near Petes Mesa.

Once you reach the bottom of the Maze

you will be on the sandy floor of a small side canyon leading in a northwesterly direction. Soon you should see three large red rocks that look like a cluster of giant mushrooms growing out of the edge of the rim about a mile down the canyon. This rock formation lies just below the Maze Overlook.

Within fifteen minutes after you spot the mushroom rocks you will pass by another major canyon entering the drainage from the south. This is Pictograph Fork, the canyon containing the famous Harvest Scene Pictograph Panel. There are several other smaller side canyons in the area, but Pictograph Fork is the largest one. It is nearly 200 yards wide at the junction, *see color photos, pages 183, 187* with a 150-foot-wide span of slickrock in the center of the stream bed. Also the Chocolate Drops formation is clearly visible from the canyon mouth. This junction is a very pleasant place to stop for the night. There are several good campsites in the area and it is also a good base from which to take a side trip to the Maze Overlook.

Maze Overlook

If you got off to a late start you may want to wait and see the Maze Overlook in the morning. But if you plan to take photographs it is best to be there in the afternoon when the sun is in the west. Plan on about two hours for the walk from the mouth of Pictograph Fork to the overlook and back.

From the mouth of Pictograph Fork continue walking northwest along the floor of the Maze towards the mushroom formation. After 0.4 mile the drainage ends at South Fork Horse Canyon. Turn left here and walk south for another 0.6 mile to a point where a break in the canyon wall provides access to the rim above. The cairned trail up to the rim begins on the end of a long toe of sandstone that protrudes into South Fork from the west rim. Look for the cairns marking the canyon exit point. Also, there is a spring in the canyon at the end of the toe, and there is usually a large pool of water in the stream bed at the point where the route starts up.

The trail from the bottom of South Fork to the Maze Overlook is an exciting one, with some scrambling required. If you are carrying a backpack you should have a 20-foot length of rope with you to pull your pack up some of the pitches. If you exercise reasonable care the route is not dangerous, but there is just enough scrambling to make it fun. The trail heads straight up to a ledge just below the White Rim Formation, then turns north and traverses around the stone mushrooms to a break in the White Rim. From there it is an easy climb out to the top.

The view from the overlook point is one of the grandest views in Canyonlands National Park. The loneliness and serenity of this point, with the tortuous jumble of

South Fork Horse Canyon, seen from the Maze Overlook

nature's handiwork in the canyons below is enough to inspire even the weariest of hikers . How and why could such a vista have been created? The complexity of the panorama astounds.

Given enough time, one must conclude that almost anything is possible. It has taken the forces of nature ten million years to produce this scene. They began by washing away thousands of vertical feet of sedimentary rock that had been deposited during an earlier era to get down to the 250-million-year-old Cedar Mesa Sandstone, from which the Maze was sculpted. The excavation is ongoing, and is still not complete. Here and there one can see remnants of younger rock that still has not been entirely removed: Chimney Rock, the Chocolate Drops, Lizard Rock, the Standing Rocks. Everything else has already been washed down and swept away by the relentless Colorado River. Presently the Maze itself is slowly being etched and chiseled away by the rain and the sun and washed to the sea by the river. The dramatic scene we see now represents only a brief interlude in the long evolution of the Colorado Plateau.

Day 2 (4.5 miles)

From the mouth of Pictograph Fork it is 0.7 miles up the dry canyon to the Harvest Scene Pictograph Panel. The panel is located at the bottom of the cliffs, about ten feet above the west side of the stream bed. You will find it about three hundred yards before you come to a thumb-shaped pillar of sandstone in the bottom of the canyon.

No reliable method has yet been developed for dating Indian rock art, but most archeologist believe that the Harvest Scene was painted by the Archaic People who lived in Utah from 8,000 to 2,000 years ago. These are the same people who produced the famous Great Gallery pictographs 18 miles to the north in Horseshoe Canyon (see page 229). The Archaic People, who predated the better known Anasazi, left few other remnants of their ancient culture for us to study; hence archeologist have long struggled to interpret their art. But deciphering the paintings has proven just as difficult as dating them, and we still know little about what they mean. In this panel, one of the figures appears to be holding a sheaf of rice grass; hence the name Harvest Scene.

Continuing up the canyon from the Harvest Scene for another 1.6 miles will bring you to another junction with a major side canyon. The trail splits at this point. If you bear right you will be continuing up Pictograph Fork on a little used trail that finally ends near the east end of Lizard Rock. Most hikers, however, turn left at this junction and follow the cairns up an easier route to the rim that finally ends at the Chimney Rock Trailhead.

Harvest Scene Pictograph Panel

The Chocolate Drops

Canyonlands National Park
4WD vehicle required
day hike

Distance:	8.8 miles (round trip)
Walking time:	5 hours
Elevations:	540 ft. loss/gain Chocolate Drops Trailhead (start): 5,460 ft. Chocolate Drops: 5,080 ft.
Trail:	This is a slickrock trail, well marked by stone cairns.
Season:	Spring, early summer, and fall. This hike is very hot in the summer and cold in the winter. The best times are during the spring and fall. The road to the trailhead may be impassable, even with a 4WD, after a heavy snow or rain.
Vicinity:	Canyonlands National Park, Maze District, near Hite
Maps:	Spanish Bottom, Elaterite Basin *(USGS)* Canyonlands Maze District *(Trails Illustrated, #246)*
Information:	http://www.utahtrails.com/chocolate.html *(Utah Trails)* http://www.nps.gov/cany/home.htm *(Canyonlands Nat. Park)* phone: (435) 259-2652 *(Hans Flat Ranger Station)*

See page 251 (The Maze) for a detailed description on how to reach the Chimney Rock Trailhead.

From the parking area at Chimney Rock Trailhead, drive back towards the highway for a distance of 3.0 miles, past Lizard Rock and the Wall, to another monolith on the north side of the road about 200 yards west of the Wall. As the road passes this monolith you will see a small parking area on the north side of the road. This parking area marks the beginning of the Chocolate Drops trail.

What shall we name those four unnamed formations standing erect above this end of The Maze? From our vantage point they are the most striking landmarks.... In a far-fetched way they resemble tombstones, or altars, or chim- *ney stacks, or stone tablets set on end.[7]*

When Edward Abbey first wrote these words he was standing on the Maze Overlook (page 255) looking at what we now call the Chocolate Drops. The Maze has since

---

[7] Edward Abbey, *Desert Solitaire, a Season in the Wilderness*, Simon & Schuster, New York, 1968. (with permission)

been protected as a part of Canyonlands National Park, and consequently it is still possible to share the feeling of wonderment that Abbey must have experienced forty years ago.

The Chocolate Drops formation consists of four vertical rectangular shaped columns of Organ Shale that rise almost 200 feet above the ridge separating South Fork Horse Canyon from Pictograph Fork Canyon. They are one of the most prominent landmarks in the Maze and can be seen from miles around. The trail described here also passes by a half dozen other pillars of Organ Shale on its way to the Chocolate Drops. These formations are all part of an area known as the Land of Standing Rocks.

see map, page 253

Follow the cairns from the parking area around the east side of the large monolith beside the road, then on towards the other spires farther out on the plateau. All of these formations are the unlikely remains of a 200-foot-thick layer of Organ Shale that once covered Canyonlands. By now, however, the unrelenting forces of erosion have almost completely removed the crumbling rock from the area, and only a few pinnacles of red shale still remain. After about thirty minutes the trail passes by the next group of Organ Shale formations, including one particularly picturesque mound that is topped by an enormous balanced rock. So precarious is the capstone that it is hard to pass beneath it without unconsciously walking a little faster.

see color photos, pages 186, 187

From the balanced rock to the first Chocolate Drop is about three miles. The route is well marked with cairns and not difficult to follow. It is generally an easy walk across level ground, however at one point some minor scrambling is necessary to get to the bottom of a low spot on the ridge. If you look to the right when you reach this point you will find an easy way down the slickrock to the bottom of the incline (about 50 feet lower), and beyond this point there are no additional obstacles.

As you walk northward along the ridge you can frequently peer into the bottom of Pictograph Fork on your right. At one point you can look directly down at the Harvest Scene Pictograph Panel (page 256). From the trail the panel is almost three-fourths of a mile away, however—too far to recognize any of the pictographs. When you finally reach the last Chocolate Drop on the end of the plateau you will also have a clear view of the trail down from the Maze Overlook.

The Chocolate Drops

Green & Colorado River Overlook

Canyonlands National Park
4WD vehicle required
day hike

Distance:	8.9 miles (round trip)
Walking time:	5 hours
Elevations:	300 ft. loss/gain
	Green & Colorado River Trailhead (start): 5,100 ft.
	Overlook point: 5,000 ft.
Trail:	Easy, well marked
Season:	Spring, early summer, and fall. This hike is very hot in the summer and cold in the winter. The best times are during the spring and fall. The road to the trailhead may be impassable, even with a 4WD, after a heavy snow or rain.
Vicinity:	Canyonlands National Park, Maze District, near Hite
Maps:	Spanish Bottom *(USGS)*
	Canyonlands Maze District *(Trails Illustrated, #246)*
Information:	http://www.utahtrails.com/colorado.html *(Utah Trails)*
	http://www.nps.gov/cany/home.htm *(Canyonlands Nat. Park)*
	phone: (435) 259-2652 *(Hans Flat Ranger Station)*

See page 213 (The Maze) for a detailed description on how to reach the Chimney Rock Trailhead.

Continue driving east from the parking area at Chimney Rock Trailhead for 3.8 miles. Near the end of the road, just in front of the Doll House rock formation the road crosses a small wash where a sign marks the trailhead.

For colorful desert scenery it is hard to beat this popular hike. The normally light colored Cedar Mesa Sandstone has a rich red layer running through it in this area, which makes it much more colorful than the same formation in the nearby Maze. Beginning with the impressive Doll House, at the beginning of the trail, the rock formations along this hike are truly magnificent. They are particularly pretty in the late afternoon when the sunlight tends to enhance the red bands in the sandstone.

From the trailhead the trail winds northward, through clusters of sandstone formations similar to

> see color photo,
> page 187

those found on the other side of the Colorado in the Needles District of Canyonlands. Within 0.8 mile you will see the small Bee-

see map, page 239

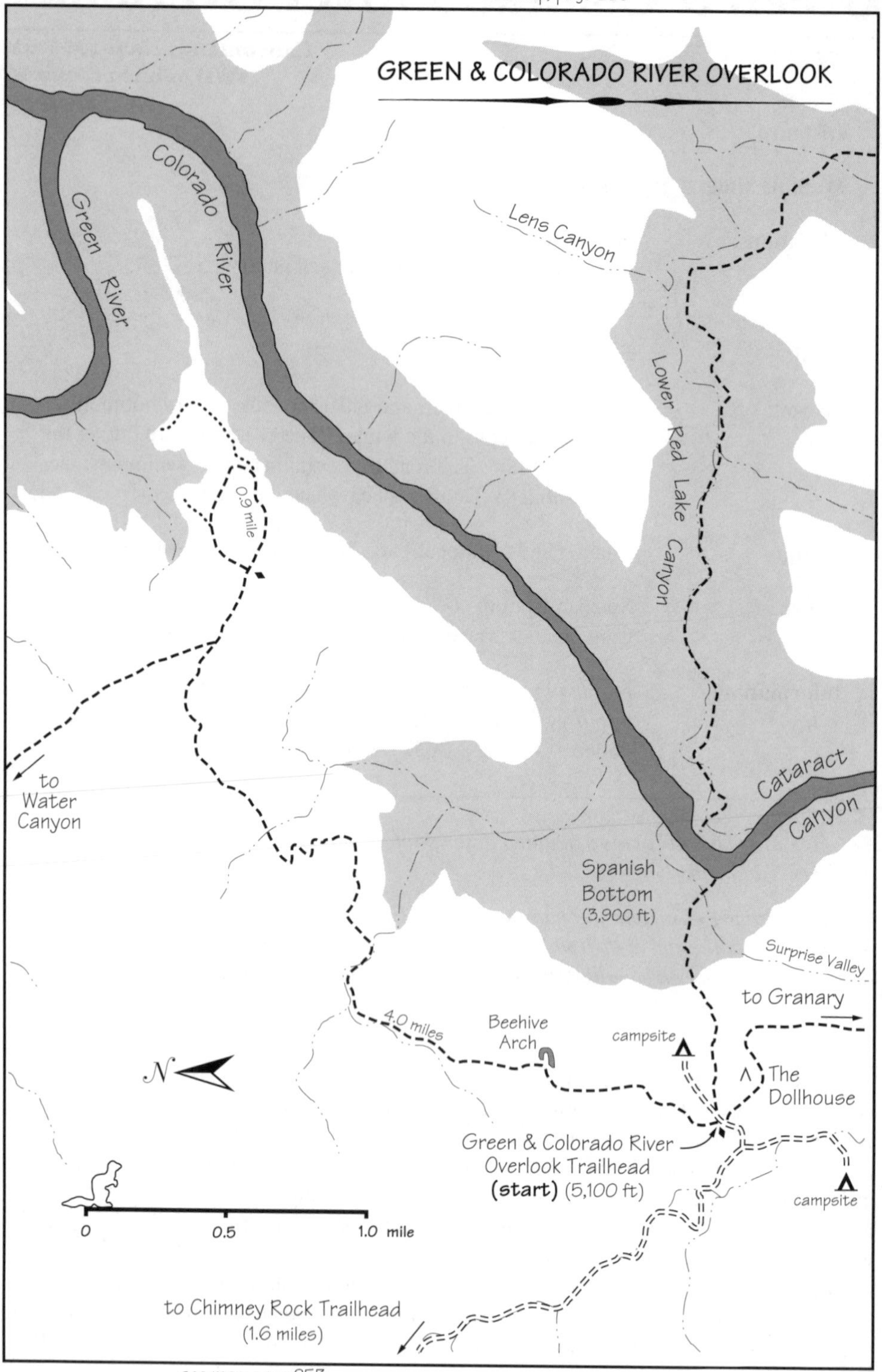

GREEN & COLORADO RIVER OVERLOOK

see map, page 239

Green River

Colorado River

Colorado River

Lens Canyon

Lower Red Lake Canyon

0.9 mile

Cataract Canyon

see map, page 253

to Water Canyon

Spanish Bottom (3,900 ft)

Surprise Valley

to Granary

4.0 miles

Beehive Arch

campsite

The Dollhouse

N

Green & Colorado River Overlook Trailhead (start) (5,100 ft)

campsite

0   0.5   1.0 mile

to Chimney Rock Trailhead (1.6 miles)

see map, page 253

Green & Colorado River Overlook Trail

ters a large open meadow, similar to Chesler Park in the Needles District. In the center of this meadow you will encounter another trail coming in from the northwest. This trail leads to Water and Shot Canyons, and ultimately back to the Chimney Rock Trailhead.

Continue east and soon the overlook trail splits into a 0.9 mile loop that goes past the overlook points. If you bear right here for another 0.4 mile you will arrive at the western rim of the Colorado River Gorge. The river is only about 400 yards away at this point, at the bottom of a nearly vertical wall. From there the path bends around to the west again, passing by a fine view of the Green River. You might want to do a little off-trail hiking before you leave this loop in order to achieve better views of the rivers. Soon after the trail leaves the Green River viewpoint it drops back into the meadow to complete the loop. From that point back to the trailhead is 4.0 miles.

hive Arch on your left. The trail winds down the slope a little ways and then back, passing right beside it.

About a mile beyond the arch start watching for pieces of flint scattered on the ground, particularly at the base of the sandstone cliffs on the left side of the trail. This glassy stone was brought here by prehistoric Indians from other locations in the park. Look carefully at the smaller pieces and you will see that most of them are actually flakes that have been chipped from larger stones. These flakes are especially prevalent in a few alcoves along the trail where prehistoric Indians must have worked, chipping the hard rock into points, scrapers, and other tools.

Halfway to the overlook point the trail skirts past the head of a large canyon. Although you can't see it from this perspective the Colorado River is below you, over a thousand feet down at the northern end of Cataract Canyon in an area called Spanish Bottom.

A mile beyond the canyon the trail en-

Green River

Dark Canyon

☆ ☆ ☆   overnight hike

Distance:	16.0 miles (with side trips)
Walking time:	day 1: 5 hours day 2: 5 hours
Elevations:	2,000 ft. loss/gain Sundance Trailhead (start): 5,600 ft. Dark Canyon Creek: 4,000 ft. Lake Powell: 3,600 ft.
Trail:	The Sundance Trail into Dark Canyon is a slickrock trail, well marked by rock cairns. From the rim of the canyon to the bottom is a very steep descent, but little or no scrambling is necessary. Some scrambling is necessary to reach Lake Powell, but the route is not technically difficult.
Season:	Spring, summer, fall. The unpaved road to the trailhead is normally closed during the winter and after heavy rains.
Vicinity:	Near the Hite Marina on Lake Powell
Maps:	Indian Head Pass, Bowdie Canyon West *(USGS)* Manti-LaSal National Forest *(Trails Illustrated, #703)*
Information:	http://www.utahtrails.com/dark.html *(Utah Trails)* http://www.blm.gov/utah/monticello/ *(BLM, Monticello)* phone: (435) 587-2141 *(BLM, Monticello Field Office)*

Drive south on Highway 95 from Hanksville until you arrive at the Hite Marina turnoff, just south of the Colorado River. Continue following the highway south and 0.2 mile beyond the Hite turnoff, near milepost 49, you will come to a gravel road leaving the left side of the highway. This is the Horse Tanks Road (San Juan County Road 208a). Make a note of your odometer reading *and turn east onto the Horse Tanks Road. After 4.1 miles you will come to a junction; bear left here. At 7.3 miles you will pass Road 209a on your left; continue straight. At 7.7 miles you will see another road coming in from the right; again, continue straight. At 8.6 miles you will come to another junction where you must turn left. At 9.3 miles you will see another road taking off on the left; continue straight. At 10.9 miles you will see a smaller road on the left marked with two large stone monuments; turn left here. This road ends after 0.2 mile at a cattle tank. The Sundance Trail begins at the parking area near the tank.*

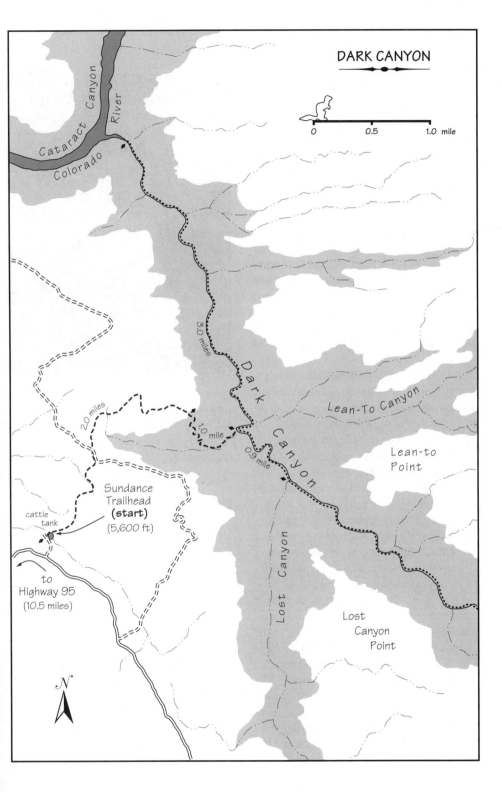

DARK CANYON

0   0.5   1.0 mile

Cataract Canyon

Colorado River

3.0 miles

Dark Canyon

Lean-To Canyon

Lean-to Point

2.0 miles

1.0 mile

0.9 mile

Sundance Trailhead **(start)** (5,600 ft)

cattle tank

Lost Canyon

to Highway 95 (10.5 miles)

Lost Canyon Point

N

One can hardly visit this remarkable canyon without wondering about the dozens of other similar tributaries of Glen Canyon that were flooded by Lake Powell in 1964. Dark Canyon is more than 200 river miles upstream from Glen Canyon Dam, and consequently it was spared most of the destruction of the lower canyons. What were the other canyons like before they were filled with water? What geological, biological, and archeological treasures did we loose? And what gems of natural beauty are now gone forever? A few of the canyons were photographed and studied before the man-made flood occurred, but many of them had never been visited by more than a few hundred people before they were erased from our maps and replaced with jagged blue lines. We cannot know how much we have lost, but if Dark Canyon is any clue the loss was substantial.

The hike described here touches only a few miles of Dark Canyon—the section just above Lake Powell. In my opinion, however, this is the most beautiful part of the canyon. There is a reliable stream here, and the greenery contrasts sharply with the pink sandstone and shale in the canyon walls. Near the bottom of the canyon is a fascinating layer of Honaker Trail Limestone that is chock full of well preserved 300-million-year-old fossils. Beneath that the picturesque creek flows for several miles across a layer of smooth limestone, adorned with a series of idyllic swimming holes and water slides.

Dark Canyon is over thirty miles long, and there are many other hiking opportunities along its length. The upper part of the canyon is part of the Manti-La Sal National Forest, and since 1984 it has been protected as the Dark Canyon Wilderness Area. The lower part, unfortunately, is on BLM land and is not within the boundaries of the wilderness area. Another interesting hike through Dark Canyon begins in the wilder-

Dark Canyon

ness area at Woodenshoe Canyon, near Natural Bridges National Monument, and exits 31 miles later on the Sundance Trail described here. Unfortunately, however, the two trailheads are 63 miles apart.

Day 1 (8.0 miles)

The Sundance Trail is not really a trail at all, but rather a well marked route into Dark Canyon. From the car parking area just walk across the earthen dam below the cattle tank and look for the first rock cairn on your left. After you have spotted the first cairn you should have no trouble following the rest. The trail meanders northward across the slickrock for about a mile before you begin to notice the presence of a deep side canyon on your right. It then skirts around the northern edge of this side canyon, bearing east for another mile until it reaches the rim of Dark Canyon. It will take you about an hour to walk from the trailhead to the canyon rim.

The view from the rim of Dark Canyon is awesome. The canyon is 1,280 feet deep at this point, and the sensation is not unlike the feeling one gets when looking into the Grand Canyon: a feeling of grandeur, a feeling of immensity, and most of all a feeling of personal insignificance. It is also abundantly clear from this vantage point that the climb down is going to be a steep one. The canyon bottom is only 1750 horizontal feet from the rim, and 1280 vertical feet. If the trail had no switchbacks it would have to descend at an angle of nearly 40 degrees. Of course there are switchbacks, and the route down is about a mile long. Nevertheless it is a knee breaker, especially if you are carrying a heavy pack.

see color photos, page 188

After the trail leaves the rim it drops slightly and then traverses west a short distance to a place where an ancient landslide has made it possible to get below the cliffs of the Cedar Mesa Sandstone. It then follows the rubble slope down, all the way to the bottom of the small side canyon, and finally emerges from a sandy wash to meet Dark Canyon Creek.

Once you reach the creek the next order of business is choosing a suitable campsite. There are a few nice sites in the area where you first meet the water, and more sites upstream over the next mile. Beyond the confluence with Lost Canyon, however, there are fewer campsites. After a camp is established you will probably want to do some exploring. As discussed below, there is plenty to see both up and down canyon.

Day 2 (8.0 miles)

Plan on 2$^1/_2$ hours to climb back up the Sundance Trail and walk to your car. But before you leave be sure to take some time to look around. Many people spend four or five days enjoying the quiet beauty of Dark Canyon, but you should be able to see most of the highlights on a two-day trip.

Dark Canyon, above Lost Canyon

Side trips

The Sundance Trail meets Dark Canyon Creek in a section where three major canyons come together, so there are many opportunities for exploration in the area. Lean-to Canyon joins Dark Canyon 0.2 mile downstream from where the trail ends, and the junction with Lost Canyon is 0.9 mile upstream. Both of these side canyons are dry; hence few visitors bother to go very far into them. But if what you are looking for is solitude they might be just your thing.

The bottom of Dark Canyon above the confluence with Lost Canyon is particularly interesting. Here the creek flows over long stretches of hard, blue-gray limestone which has strange intrusions of chert imbedded in it. Occasionally another layer of limestone is also exposed just above the intruded layer that is a treasure-trove of marine fossils. Youngs Canyon, a beautiful canyon with a stream and a waterfall at its mouth, is about 6.0 miles upstream from the Sundance Trail. The creek in the bottom of Dark Canyon ends about a mile above Youngs Canyon, so if you plan to continue beyond that point you will have to carry your own water.

The most popular side trip in lower Dark Canyon is the hike downstream to Lake Powell. The round trip from the Sundance Trail requires only about 3 hours, but some minor scrambling is necessary. For the first half hour it is an easy walk along the bottom of Dark Canyon. Several stream crossings are necessary, but there are no serious obstacles to impede the way. After about a half hour, however, you will encounter a series of pouroffs in the canyon that are increasingly difficult to get around. When you reach a point where you can no longer stay in the bottom of the canyon you will have to scramble up to a ledge about 15 feet above the right (east) side of the streambed. If you can't find a way up, just backtrack a ways until you see an easy way to climb to the ledge.

Once you reach the ledge you will see a fairly distinct trail that continues downstream above the creek. This trail continues for the next mile, climbing as high as 150 feet above the water. Finally you will come to a point where another large side canyon comes into Dark Canyon from the east, and it is here that the trail again descends to the canyon floor. Once the trail gets back to the floor of Dark Canyon just continue downstream for another 1.1 miles. After a half hour the stream becomes stagnant and the bottom of the canyon is covered with a thick, gooey mud that gets deeper and deeper as you proceed. This is the beginning of the lake. Unless the lake level is low, the last mile of Dark Canyon will be flooded, making it impossible to get to Cataract Canyon and the Colorado River without a boat.

Dark Canyon, below Lean-to Canyon

Natural Bridges Loop

☆ ☆ ☆ ☆

Natural Bridges National Monument
day hike

Distance:	8.6 miles (loop)
Walking time:	5 hours
Elevations:	490 ft. gain/loss
	Sipapu Bridge Trailhead (start): 6,200 ft.
	Kachina Bridge: 5,710 ft.
	Owachomo Bridge: 5,920 ft.
Trail:	The trail is mostly well maintained and easy to follow, although it can be confusing in a few places—especially near Kachina Bridge. There are signs at all of the major trail junctions.
Season:	Spring, summer, winter, fall. The canyon is quite hot in mid-summer. Expect some rain in late summer.
Vicinity:	Natural Bridges National Monument, near Blanding
Maps:	Moss Back Butte *(USGS)*
	Manti-LaSal National Forest *(Trails Illustrated, #703)*
Information:	http://www.utahtrails.com/bridges.html *(Utah Trails)*
	http://www.nps.gov/nabr/ *(Natural Bridges Nat. Monument)*
	phone: (435) 692-1234 *(Visitor Center)*

Drive east from the Natural Bridges National Monument Visitor Center on Bridge View Drive. After about 2.5 miles you will see Sipapu Bridge Overlook on your right. Continue for another 0.5 mile to the Sipapu Bridge Trailhead and parking area.

The highlights of this hike are the three enormous natural bridges for which Natural Bridges National Monument was named: Sipapu, Kachina, and Owachomo Bridge. The canyon-bottom trail passes under all three, while offering views of at least two other less-spectacular arches further up the side of the canyon walls. Also of interest are a number of Indian ruins within the canyon. The present-day park was used extensively by the prehistoric Anasazi Indians who lived here until about 1300 A.D.

From the Sipapu Bridge Trailhead the trail immediately drops 440 feet in 0.6 mile to the creek bed under Sipapu Bridge. The trail is quite steep in places; the park service has even constructed stairs to help in the descent. But don't be discouraged by the grade. Once you reach the bottom the trail is almost entirely on the canyon floor.

A short side trail branches off to the left

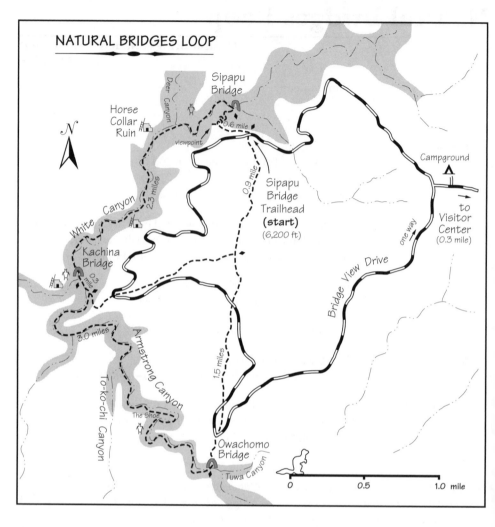

about half way down for a magnificent view of the bridge. This is probably the best photo opportunity you will have of Sipapu, the largest bridge in the monument. With a span of 268 feet and a height of 220 feet, it is only 10 feet shorter and 89 feet lower than Rainbow Natural Bridge, the largest natural bridge in the world.

From Sipapu the trail winds down the floor of picturesque White Canyon for another 2.3 miles to Kachina Bridge. Watch for Indian ruins along this part of the trail. The well known Horse Collar Ruin is on the south side of White Canyon just below the confluence with Deer Canyon, about 0.8 mile below Sipapu. There are other ruins as well, including a small granary just above the south side of the trail about 1.9 miles below Sipapu. Finally, you will see Kachina Bridge looming over the trail. Only slightly smaller than Sipapu, Kachina spans 204 feet and is 210 feet tall. It is, however, a much younger, bulkier bridge, fully 93 feet thick at its crown. Kachina Bridge will still be standing many thousands of years from now.

Don't miss the petroglyphs near Kachina

see color photo, page 189

Bridge. There are dozens of them on the rock face just a hundred feet south of the bridge on the west side of the canyon. Kachina Bridge got its name from these petroglyphs, which remind some observers of the art that decorates Hopi Kachina dolls. There are also the remains of two ancient granaries in the same area.

From Kachina Bridge it is very easy to take a wrong turn and get off the trail (as I did the first time I walked this loop). Do not bear right into White Canyon. Rather, follow the main path which bears left from Kachina Natural Bridge and goes up towards the canyon rim. After about 0.3 mile you will see a well marked junction in the trail with a sign directing you to Owachomo Bridge. At this point you are no longer in White Canyon; you have made the transition into Armstrong Canyon.

Owachomo Bridge is 3.0 miles down Armstrong Canyon from the trail junction near Kachina Bridge. This part of the trail is not as popular, and you are not likely to see other hikers until you reach Owachomo. There are not as many ruins of the Anasazi culture here, but at one point you can see quite an interesting collection of well preserved petroglyphs just above the right side of the trail. You are also much more likely to see deer and other wildlife during this part of the hike.

Finally, as the trail passes under Owachomo, you will immediately recognize it as the oldest of the three bridges. Owachomo spans 180 feet, is 106 feet high, and is only 9 feet thick at its crown. It is a very shallow arch and gives the appearance that it could fall at any time. Its life span is, of course, impossible to predict, but it will probably not remain intact for more than a few more centuries.

From Owachomo it is a short walk to the canyon rim, from where another trail leads 2.2 miles through the pinyon-juniper forest, back to the Sipapu Bridge Trailhead where the hike began.

Owachomo Natural Bridge

Grand Gulch - Bullet Canyon

☆ ☆ ☆ ☆   **shuttle car or bicycle required**
                                                        3-day hike

Distance: 22.8 miles
                       (plus 8.3 miles by car or bicycle)

Walking time: day 1: 4^1/$_4$ hours
                       day 2: 4 hours
                       day 3: 5^1/$_4$ hours

Elevations: 1,080 ft. loss, 1,040 ft. gain
                       Kane Gulch Trailhead (start): 6,440 ft.
                       Bullet Canyon confluence: 5,360 ft.
                       Bullet Canyon Trailhead: 6,400 ft.

Trail: Parts of the trail are primitive and unmaintained, but the route is
                       well marked and generally easy to follow. Getting out of Bullet
                       Canyon can be tricky—especially with a heavy backpack.
                       Inexperienced climbers may find a 20-foot length of rope useful
                       for hauling packs up the slickrock in a few places.

Season: Spring through early summer, fall. Water can be a problem in
                       Grand Gulch after June. Much of the canyon contains running
                       water in early spring, but the water soon dries up as the weather
                       becomes hotter. By mid-June there are only occasional pools
                       left, and by mid-July most of them have dried up. There is
                       usually enough rain in late August and September to refill the
                       pools and make hiking feasible again in the fall.

Vicinity: Near Mexican Hat and Natural Bridges National Monument

Maps: Kane Gulch, Cedar Mesa North, Pollys Pasture *(USGS)*
                       Grand Gulch Plateau *(Trails Illustrated, #706)*

Information: http://www.utahtrails.com/grand.html *(Utah Trails)*
                       http://www.blm.gov/utah/monticello/ *(BLM, Monticello)*
                       phone: (435) 587-2141 *(BLM, Monticello Field Office)*

---

*Drive south from the junction of Highway 261 and Highway 95 (near Natural
Bridges National Monument) towards the town of Mexican Hat. 3.9 miles
from the junction you will arrive at Kane Gulch Ranger Station where the hike
begins.*

*To get to Bullet Canyon Trailhead where the hike ends continue south from
Kane Gulch Ranger Station on Highway 261. After driving 7.2 miles you will see a clearly
marked graded road on the right. Turn here and drive the last 1.2 miles to the Trailhead.*

Note: The BLM asks that all hikers in the Grand Gulch area register at the trailheads and obtain permits before entering the canyons. Day hikers will be charged $2.00 for the permit, and backpackers will be charged $5.00/person for a maximum of 7 days. Advance reservations are necessary for overnight hikers entering the canyons between March 1 to June 15, and can be obtained by telephone from the BLM office in Monticello at (435) 587-1532. The cost is $8.00/person.

Grand Gulch is the premier area in Utah to see the ruins of the prehistoric Anasazi Indians. Their culture flourished in the canyon between 700 and 2000 years ago, and today dozens of cliff dwellings and other stone and mud structures remain to remind us of their occupancy. The most obvious ruins are from the so called Pueblo III culture of the thirteenth century, but more subtle remnants of the earlier Basketmaker culture that existed in the canyon from 200 to 700 A.D. are also present if one knows where to look.

By 1300 the Anasazi had deserted Grand Gulch and the surrounding canyons and moved southeast into the Rio Grande Valley of New Mexico. Precisely why they left is not known for certain, but drought, depletion of natural resources, and pressure from other nomadic Indians probably all played a role. For the past seven hundred years the Anasazi homes have stood in silence, clinging to the high canyon walls and causing the occasional canyon visitor to stare in wonder.

The first known white men to see Grand Gulch were the Mormons, who crossed Cedar Mesa in 1880. Soon afterward a series of amateur archaeologists begin to arrive in search of pots and other artifacts from the ruins. Between 1890 and 1897 at least nine expeditions entered Grand Gulch to dig for artifacts. The most famous of these was lead by Richard Wetherill, a rancher from southern Colorado who sold many Anasazi arti-

Turkey Pen Ruin, Grand Gulch

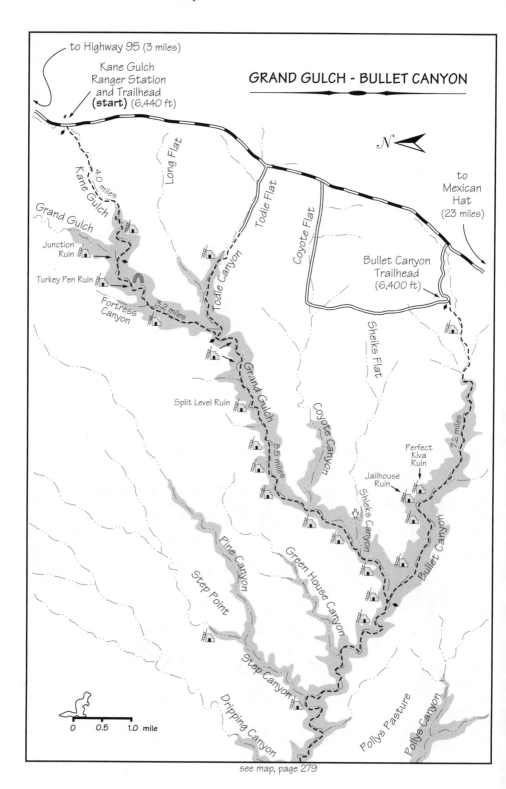

to Highway 95 (3 miles)

Kane Gulch
Ranger Station
and Trailhead
(start) (6,440 ft)

GRAND GULCH - BULLET CANYON

Long Flat

Kane Gulch

4.0 miles

Grand Gulch

Junction
Ruin

Turkey Pen Ruin

Fortress
Canyon

3.2 miles

Todie Canyon

Todie Flat

Coyote Flat

N

to
Mexican
Hat
(23 miles)

Bullet Canyon
Trailhead
(6,400 ft)

Sheiks Flat

Grand Gulch

Split Level Ruin

8.5 miles

Coyote Canyon

Perfect
Kiva
Ruin

Jailhouse
Ruin

7.2 miles

Shieks Canyon

Bullet Canyon

Pine Canyon

Step Point

Green House Canyon

Step Canyon

Dripping Canyon

Pollys Pasture

Pollys Canyon

0   0.5   1.0 mile

see map, page 279

facts to the American Museum of Natural History in New York. Wetherill carved his name into the sandstone at several of the sites he excavated.

Needless to say, these early explorers did tremendous harm to the archeological record in Grand Gulch. Now, of course, it is against the law to remove artifacts from the canyons or to deface the ruins in any way. Please do not carry out pottery shards, corn cobs, flint flakes, or any other artifacts you may find laying on the ground. Also, do not climb on the ruins, and try to stay off the middens as much as possible. If everyone cooperates the wondrous Anasazi ruins of Grand Gulch will be there for many more years to come, and our children will have the opportunity to enjoy them as much as we do.

Day 1 (7.2 miles)

From the top of Kane Gulch the trail meanders gently downward for 3.8 miles before reaching the bottom of Grand Gulch. You should see your first ruin high on the southern wall of the Cedar Mesa Sandstone, about an hour into the hike. This ruin is unusual in that it is on the north-facing rather than the south-facing side of the canyon. The Indians generally preferred to build their dwellings on the south-facing side where they received more winter sun.

Upon reaching the bottom of Grand Gulch you can't miss seeing the extensive Junction Ruin slightly upstream from the confluence. This area contains many fine camping sites under the cottonwood trees, and if you got a late start you may want to consider spending the night here.

Junction is one of the largest ruins in the canyon. It must have been home to many dozens of Indians when they lived in the canyon, and the number of stone buildings is impressive. It is also located near the stream bed and is quite accessible. Unfortunately, the midden in front of the ruin has been extensively excavated by amateur ar-

Kane Gulch

chaeologists and pot hunters over the years. As a result of all the digging, thousands of pottery shards, corn cobs and flints are now scattered about the ground's surface in front of the ruin. Enjoy the patterns and designs on them, but, again, please leave them where you find them so others can enjoy them too.

Turkey Pen Ruin, another large accessible site, is only 0.7 mile below Junction Ruin, and fifteen minutes later, if you have sharp eyes, you will see another less accessible ruin in an alcove above the cottonwood trees. Finally, 2.5 miles below Turkey Pen Ruin, you will arrive at the mouth of Todie Canyon, where I suggest you make camp.

Day 2 (8.4 miles)

From Todie Canyon to Bullet Canyon, the suggested camp site for the second day, you will scarcely be able to walk a half hour without seeing a ruin of some sort. By my count there are at least eleven distinct ruins sites in the 8.4 miles between the two Canyons. Sometimes they consist of only a small granary or two, and at other times they will include the remains of fifteen or twenty buildings. The first ruin is only a five minute walk from the mouth of Todie. Stay on the right side of the can- | see color photo, page 189 | yon as you walk downstream, and you will see it just as the stream bed swings around to the northeast.

The most impressive ruin in this section of the Grand Gulch is Split Level Ruin, so named because it includes a structure with two adjoining rooms, one higher than the other. Also notice, at this as well as other ruin sites, the presence of many *kivas*. The *kivas* are the low, round shaped structures, with a bench built into the wall and a fire pit near one side. The present-day Hopi Indians have similar structures in their pueblos, which leads many anthropologists to believe that they are modern descendants of the Anasazis.

As the trail approaches Bullet Canyon you will see the wide, flat-bottomed canyon opening up on the left. The trail forks at Bullet Spring. There are no signs, however, so take care not to miss the turn. There are several excellent campsites within three hundred feet of the spring as you proceed into Bullet Canyon.

If you have time after pitching camp in Bullet Canyon you may want to spend an hour backtracking to Shieks Canyon (1.4 miles upstream from Bullet in Grand Gulch). There is an excellent panel of pictographs in the back of Shieks Canyon, 15 minutes from its mouth. There is also an interesting ruin on the canyon wall immediately above the Bullet Canyon camping area, just a few hundred yards up Bullet Canyon from Grand Gulch.

Day 3 (7.2 miles)

Most hikers complete the loop on the third day, walking up Bullet Canyon to the trailhead above the rim. There are at least five ruins to be seen in Bullet Canyon on the way up, but the most interesting one is Jail House Ruin, 2.4 miles from the canyon mouth. You will know you have arrived at Jailhouse Ruin when you see its unique pictograph consisting of two large white circles. The circles can be seen all the way across the canyon, but archaeologists have no idea what they were meant to represent. The ruin was named Jailhouse because of a small barred hole in the wall of one of its structures. The nearby Perfect Kiva Ruin is also interesting. It contains an extraordinarily well preserved *kiva* with a wooded ladder leading down into its interior. There are no restrictions against entering the *kiva*, but please take care not to damage it in any way.

As you proceed further up the canyon it soon narrows and becomes much more rocky. There are no ruins in upper Bullet Canyon, at least none that I have seen. The canyon bottom is completely unsuitable for farming here, so if the Indians did build any dwellings they would most likely be near the top of the rim. As you approach the top of the rim you will be walking on slickrock part of the time, and there are some areas where a bit of scrambling will be necessary. A short piece of rope is useful for lifting backpacks in one or two places, so that you can climb unencumbered. Be sure to watch for rock cairns in the places where the canyon splits.

About ten minutes before you reach the top of the rim look up on the north side at a square masonry tower that was built by the Anasazis on the very edge of the rim. Why would the Indians build a dwelling in such an exposed place? Perhaps it was a watch tower or a monitoring station to keep track of who was descending into the gulch. The parking area is about a quarter mile beyond the square tower ruin.

Grand Gulch - Collins Canyon

☆ ☆ ☆ ☆

4-day hike

Distance:	29.9 miles (plus 35 miles by car)
Walking time:	day 1: 4 hours day 2: 4 hours day 3: 3$^1/_2$ hours day 4: 5$^1/_4$ hours
Elevations:	1,680 ft. loss, 370 ft. gain

Bullet Canyon Trailhead (start):	6,400 ft.
Bullet Canyon confluence:	5,360 ft.
Collins Canyon confluence:	4,720 ft.
Collins Spring Trailhead:	5,090 ft.

Trail: There are good trails down both Bullet Canyon and Collins Canyon. There is a primitive trail through most of Grand Gulch, but often it is easiest just to walk in the streambed.

Season: Spring through early summer, fall. Water can be a problem in Grand Gulch after June. Much of the canyon contains running water in early spring, but the water soon dries up as the weather becomes hotter. By mid-June there are only occasional pools left, and by mid-July most of them have dried up. There is usually enough rain in late August and September to refill the pools and make hiking feasible again in the fall.

Vicinity: Near Mexican Hat and Natural Bridges National Monument

Maps: Cedar Mesa North, Pollys Pasture, Red House Spring *(USGS)* Grand Gulch Plateau *(Trails Illustrated, #706)*

Information: http://www.utahtrails.com/collins.html *(Utah Trails)* http://www.blm.gov/utah/monticello/ *(BLM, Monticello)* phone: (435) 587-2141 *(BLM, Monticello Field Office)*

Drive south from the junction of Highway 261 and Highway 95 (near Natural Bridges National Monument) towards the town of Mexican Hat. 3.9 miles from the junction you will arrive at Kane Gulch Ranger Station, where you can buy maps of the area and get the latest information on water and trail conditions in the canyon. Continue south on Highway 261 for another 7.2 miles from the Kane Gulch Ranger Station until you see a sign that says "Bullet Canyon Trailhead, 2 miles". Turn right here onto a graded dirt road and drive another 1.2 miles to the trailhead.

In order to get to the Collins Spring Trailhead, where the hike ends, you must return to the junction of Highway 261 and Highway 95 and drive west for 9.5 miles to Highway 276. Turn south on Highway 276 and continue for another 6.8 miles until you see a sign that says "Collins Spring Trailhead, 6 miles". Turn left here and follow a graded gravel road for 6.6 miles to the trailhead. 2.5 miles after leaving the pavement you will encounter a fork in the road where you should bear right. The last two miles of the road are quite rough in a few places, but with care most cars should be able to make it.

Note: The BLM asks that all hikers in the Grand Gulch area register at the trailheads and obtain permits before entering the canyons. Day hikers will be charged $2.00 for the permit, and backpackers will be charged $5.00/person for a maximum of 7 days. Advance reservations are necessary for overnight hikers entering the canyons between March 1 to June 15, and can be obtained by telephone from the BLM office in Monticello at (435) 587-1532. The cost is $8.00/person.

The Grand Gulch and its side canyons offer a number of interesting routes for extended backpacking in southeastern Utah. Personally, I have found the lower part of Grand Gulch, between Bullet Canyon and Collins Canyon, to be especially appealing. This portion of the Gulch is wilder and receives far fewer visitors than the section above Bullet Canyon, yet it contains many points of interest. Of course, the main attraction is the canyon's Anasazi Indian ruins. When I did this hike in 1999 I spotted no fewer than twenty cliff dwelling and pictograph sites, and I am certain many more could be found—especially if one takes the time to walk into some of the side canyons along the way.

The total distance of the hike described here, from Bullet Canyon Trailhead to Collins Spring Trailhead, is 29.9 miles. However Grand Gulch can also be accessed from the Government Trail (see page 284), which lies about halfway between Bullet and Collins Spring; hence it is possible to break the trip up into two shorter hikes. If you were to exit at Government Trailhead the total walking distance would be 21.4 miles, with a 12.6 mile shuttle. Alternatively, the distance from Government Trailhead to Collins Spring Trailhead is 15.4 miles and requires a 45.4-mile shuttle.

see color photos, page 190

Grand Gulch ends at the San Juan River, 15.7 miles below Collins Canyon, and every year some ambitious backpackers hike the entire length of the canyon. This trip requires considerable planning, however, as the lower end of the Gulch is accessible only by boat. Furthermore, finding drinking water can be serious problem below Collins Canyon. This must have been the case during the time of the Anasazi as well, since there are far fewer Indian ruins in that sec-

Anasazi ruin near Deer Canyon

tion of Grand Gulch.

Day 1 (7.2 miles)

From the trailhead the trail meanders along the north rim of Bullet Canyon for 0.2 mile before suddenly turning south to descend into the upper reaches of the canyon. After loosing 120 feet of elevation, the path turns west again to follow the dry streambed downward through an open forest of pinion pine and juniper. Soon you will see your first Indian ruin, a small stone tower that stands above the canyon on the edge of the north rim. It is clearly visible from the trail 0.5 mile below the point where the path first drops into Bullet Canyon. Its location seems to indicate that the 10-foot-square tower was some kind of an observation post built by the Anasazis to keep track of who was going in and out of the canyon.

You won't see any other ruins in Bullet Canyon for the next 3.8 miles, but there are several excellent ones in the lower part of the drainage. The next one you will encounter is called the Perfect Kiva Ruin, and it is one of the few that have been given a name. Look for a place where a small side canyon comes in from the right, directly opposite an unusually steep cliff on the left. The trail splits in this area, and if you bear left you will miss the Perfect Kiva Ruin. Bear right along a trail that goes toward the small side canyon on the north side of Bullet. As you approach the side canyon you will notice a large, shaded south-facing alcove about one-third of the way up from the canyon floor on your left. Look closely and you will see a low square structure in the back of the alcove that appears darker than the surrounding rock. This structure was built by the Anasazi and is part of the ruin.

It is an easy climb of about 100 feet from the trail to the bottom of the alcove in which the Perfect Kiva Ruin is located. Your reward will be the remains of at least six rooms

plus an intact underground *kiva* with a wooden ladder leading into it. It is rare to find a *kiva* in such good condition; hence seeing this one is a real treat. The round subterranean rooms were common in the Anasazi culture, but they all contained fire pits and most of them eventually succumbed to accidental fires. There are many of them in the Cedar Mesa area, but I only know of one other one, in Slickhorn Canyon, that has survived relatively undamaged.

Jailhouse Ruin is located just 0.2 mile further down-canyon from Perfect Kiva. Continue along the trail, staying close to the north side of Bullet Canyon, and within five minutes you should see two large white circles on your right near the base of the cliff. The circles are part of a pictograph panel above the Jailhouse Ruin.

Several unusual features make Jailhouse Ruin a particular interesting one. It provides an excellent example of the "wattle and daub" method of construction occasionally used by the Anasazis. With this technique

Trail down upper Bullet Canyon

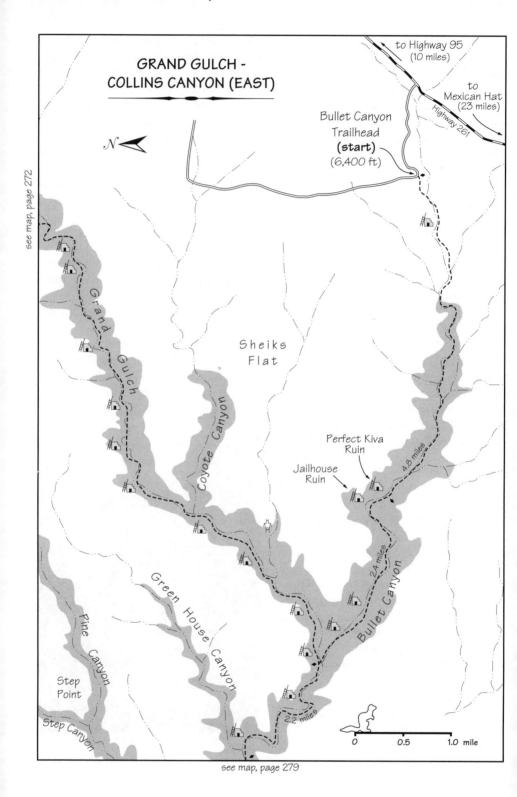

GRAND GULCH -
COLLINS CANYON (EAST)

to Highway 95
(10 miles)

to
Mexican Hat
(23 miles)

Highway 261

Bullet Canyon
Trailhead
(start)
(6,400 ft)

N

see map, page 272

Grand Gulch

Sheiks
Flat

Coyote Canyon

Perfect Kiva
Ruin

Jailhouse
Ruin

4.8 miles

2.4 miles

Bullet Canyon

Green House Canyon

Pine Canyon

Step
Point

Step Canyon

2.2 miles

0   0.5   1.0 mile

see map, page 279

see map, page 278

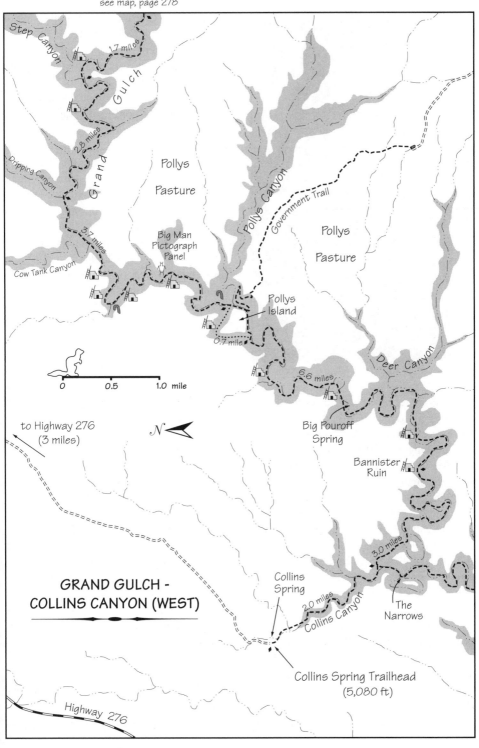

Step Canyon

1.7 miles

Grand Gulch

2.8 miles

Dripping Canyon

Grand

Pollys
Pasture

Pollys Canyon

Government Trail

Pollys
Pasture

3.7 miles

Cow Tank Canyon

Big Man
Pictograph
Panel

Pollys
Island

0.7 mile

Deer Canyon

6.6 miles

0   0.5   1.0 mile

to Highway 276
(3 miles)

N

Big Pouroff
Spring

Bannister
Ruin

3.0 miles

GRAND GULCH -
COLLINS CANYON (WEST)

Collins
Spring

2.0 miles

Collins Canyon

The
Narrows

Collins Spring Trailhead
(5,080 ft)

Highway 276

Anasazi ruin near Step Canyon

the wall is first framed with sticks and twigs, and then plastered with mud. One of the windows even contains a few exposed wattle sticks, giving it the appearance of a jail cell. Another interesting feature is the presence of a very small room that opens directly into the living area; it looks as if this room might have been a granary, or a "kitchen pantry".

You will pass by two more ruins in the next 2.4 miles between the Jailhouse Ruin and Grand Gulch—both of them are clearly visible from the trail on the north side of the canyon. Unless you got a very early start you will probably want to make camp when you reach Grand Gulch; there is an excellent campsite at the confluence with a reliable spring in the streambed of Bullet Canyon.

Day 2 (7.6 miles)

Most Grand Gulch hikers exit the can-

yon either at Kane Gulch or Bullet Canyon, so as you continue downstream from the mouth of Bullet you will probably see few if any other hikers. Yet, in my opinion, this is the most interesting part of the entire Grand Gulch. The next Indian ruin is 0.3 miles below the confluence, again on the right side of the canyon.

There is another fine campsite at the mouth of Greenhouse Canyon, 2.1 miles from the Bullet Canyon confluence, with good water availability. Greenhouse Canyon Spring lies about 300 yards upcanyon from Grand Gulch, but there is usually a nice pool of water at the canyon junction as well. There is also a small Indian ruin 100 feet above the junction, on the north side of the main canyon. This is a very pleasant place to stop, if only for a lunch break.

Many of the ruins in Grand Gulch are located in areas where side canyons meet the main canyon. Just before the trail reaches the junction with Step Canyon, 1.8 miles downstream from Greenhouse Canyon, it passes below a ledge that contains three more interesting ruins. One of them is a two-story structure about 10 feet square by 12 feet high. It is still largely intact, and it is possible to enter the bottom room and look through a hole in the ceiling into the second story.

2.8 miles beyond Step Canyon the trail passes the mouth of Dripping Canyon and, after another 0.5 mile, Cow Tank Canyon. There is usually water in this area, and if it is late you might want to start looking for a place to camp. Both Cow Tank and Dripping Canyons have reliable springs about 0.8 miles up from the main canyon, but except in late summer there are usually intermittent pools in Grand Gulch itself. It is seldom necessary to walk far to find water.

If the spring runoff has finished and it doesn't look like rain you might want to consider camping right in the streambed. There is an excellent place to do this 0.4 mile down

Grand Gulch near Polly's Island (May)

canyon from Cow Tank. Ten minutes after leaving the side canyon you will come to a sharp bend where the Gulch briefly turns north and then makes a hairpin curve back to the south. The northern canyon wall forms a sheer cliff, and if you look up you will see dozens of small red and white pictographs along a ledge about 50 feet from the bottom. The canyon floor is quite flat here, and you can lie on your sleeping bag and contemplate the dozens of handprints and strange bucket-shaped pictographs above you. Many Anasazis undoubtedly slept in this very spot, and as you gaze at their art you can almost hear the prehistoric Indian children laughing and playing on the ledge. There is also a deep, shaded pool nearby that usually retains water for most of the summer.

Day 3 (6.4 miles)

    0.7 miles down-canyon from your stre-

ambed campsite you can see a large natural arch high on the right side of the canyon. There are also two Indian ruins in the area— one about 300 yards upcanyon from the arch, on the same side of the canyon, and one about the same distance down-canyon on the opposite side. Arches must have held a mystical attraction for the ancient Anasazi, because they frequently chose to live near them. In some cases they even selected building sites that were greatly inferior, just so they could live in the vicinity of a natural arch.

    Fifteen minutes after passing the natural arch you should start looking for the Big Man Pictograph Panel high on the left side of the canyon. (See photo on page 287.) The panel is located at the bottom of a 200-foot sheer cliff, facing west and framed by two long streaks of black desert varnish that flow down from the canyon rim. The bottom of the cliff is about 150 feet above the canyon floor, but if you are observant you can just see the Big Man's head peering down from behind the juniper trees at the foot of the precipice.

    If you look carefully you will find a primitive hiker-made trail leading up from the streambed to the Big Man Pictograph Panel. There are also two more small Anasazi granaries hidden in the trees on the right side of the canyon within the next 0.4 mile below the pictographs.

    The next major point of interest is Polly's Island, a 25-acre mesa that has been detached from the canyon rim by a dry meander in the streambed. Walk down-canyon from the Big Man Pictograph Panel for 1.4 miles and look for another natural bridge near the rim on the left side. Polly's Island is situated on the northwest side of the canyon, just beyond the natural bridge and opposite the confluence with Polly's Canyon. This is also where the Government Trail enters Grand Gulch and, as mentioned earlier, it is possible to exit the canyon and end the hike at this point. (See page 284.) The Government Trail leaves Grand Gulch 0.2 mile below Polly's Canyon.

An interesting diversion on this hike is to leave the main canyon and walk the long way around Polly's Island. The route is easy, and it will only add 0.3 mile onto the total distance. Watch for a secondary trail that leaves the streambed just below the natural arch, and climbs up the sandy embankment in a westerly direction. Soon the trail breaks out of the undergrowth and proceeds around the back side of the island, across an open meadow of sagebrush and cactus. A million years ago this was the main channel of the Grand Gulch. But this section of the canyon has long since been bypassed, and is now filled with 30 feet of sand and other debris deposited over the centuries by the wind.

Look for an interesting Indian ruin op-

Grand Gulch (July)

posite Polly's Island on the north east side of the rincon (see photo on page 15). The people who lived here had a fabulous view from their veranda, with the cliffs of Polly's Island rising above the meadow in front of them. I wonder if they grew corn in the flat meadow below their home? I wonder if any of them tried to find a way to the top of the Island, and if they were successful?

In my opinion, the most interesting Anasazi ruins you will see on this hike are at a site 1.4 miles down-canyon from Polly's Island. These ruins are all situated along a ledge about 300 yards long and 60 feet above the ground. The canyon runs due west at this point, and the ledge is on the south facing side of the canyon. One fork of the path runs along the north side of the canyon directly under the ruins, but they are also easy to spot if you happen to be walking in the streambed. The ledge is easily accessible from the east side, but only two of the ruins can be reached without some rock climbing skill. Unfortunately the best ruins are hard to get to, but even seeing them from the ground is a real treat. One of them is a multi-dwelling structure with four exterior doors in near pristine condition. But the most striking building is a round cylindrical-shaped structure, about ten feet high, with a small door near the bottom.

There is an excellent campsite near the cliffs on the opposite side of the canyon from these ruins, so if you want to spend more time studying them this might be a good place to stop. Otherwise, I suggest you continue on for another 1.3 miles and establish a camp at Big Pouroff Spring. Be sure to keep an eye out for additional cliff dwellings as you walk; you should see at least two more small sites along the way.

You can't miss Big Pouroff; it is located right in the middle of the streambed, and when water is flowing in the Gulch it plunges over the 20-foot drop into a perpetual pool below. There is also a seep near the bottom of the pouroff, so even when the streambed is dry it is rare to find the pool completely empty. There is plenty of flat ground in the vicinity for a camp, but there are no trees near the pouroff so if you want shade you will have to camp away from the spring.

Day 4 (8.7 miles)

From Big Pouroff Spring to Bannister Ruin is 3.7 miles. There are at least four smaller ruins along the way, but Bannister is the last major point of interest on this hike. This unusual cliff dwelling is a multi-room structure where several families must have lived. A large part of it is fashioned with the wattle and daub method, and it is in excellent condition. Unfortunately it lies on the opposite side of the canyon from the trail and it would be hard to reach even with a ladder. Most hikers are content to view it at a distance from the trail.

After Bannister Ruin the trail improves significantly. It is only 5.0 miles to the Collins Spring Trailhead, and many hikers visit Bannister as a day hike. This part of the trail is also frequently used by horseback riders. There is a spring 0.3 mile below Bannister Ruin, but beyond that you will notice a significant decrease in the amount of available water in the canyon as you continue. Also, Bannister is the last obvious Anasazi site that you will see.

From Bannister Ruin to the mouth of Collins Canyon is 3.0 miles, and it is another 2.0 miles up Collins Canyon to the trailhead. But if you have enough energy left when you reach the mouth of Collins Canyon you may want to make a 0.3-mile side trip to the Narrows before starting up. This slender section of the canyon was formed when the Grand Gulch long ago abandoned another one of its meanders to form a dry rincon in the streambed. The Narrows is the short section of canyon at the head of the rincon. The streambed here is about 12 feet wide at its narrowest point, and the walls on each side are about 50 feet high. The total length of the Narrows, however, is only about 30 feet.

Finally, I should tell you how to find the spring at Collins Spring Trailhead—after 4 days on the trail you will probably appreciate knowing where it is! If you look down into Collins Canyon from the trailhead you can see that the actual drainage reaches the rim about two hundred feet east of where the trail comes up. Walk to the west side of the parking area and drop down 60 feet to the bottom of the Collins Canyon drainage, then turn south and walk down the bottom of the streambed. After 100 feet you will come to a pouroff in the center of the drainage with an alcove under it. Collins Spring is hidden in the back of the alcove.

Bannister ruin

Big Man Pictographs

☆ ☆ ☆   **day hike**

Distance:	10.6 miles (round trip)
Walking time:	6¹/₄ hours
Elevations:	620 ft. loss/gain car parking area (start): 5,670 ft. Government Trailhead: 5,370 ft. Grand Gulch: 5,050 ft.
Trail:	The first 2.8 miles of trail is actually an old jeep road that has been closed to vehicles by the BLM. The 0.8 mile section of trail that descends from the canyon rim into Grand Gulch is a good trail, probably built by CCC workers in the 1930s. The remainder of the route is an easy walk through the bottom of Grand Gulch.
Season:	Spring, summer, fall. Spring or fall are the ideal times for this hike. The canyon is very hot in the summer and cold in the winter. The road to the car parking area is unpaved for the last 9 miles and may be impassable in wet weather.
Vicinity:	Near Mexican Hat and Natural Bridges National Monument
Maps:	Pollys Pasture *(USGS)* Grand Gulch Plateau *(Trails Illustrated, #706)*
Information:	http://www.utahtrails.com/bigman.html *(Utah Trails)* http://www.blm.gov/utah/monticello/ *(BLM, Monticello)* phone: (435) 587-2141 *(BLM, Monticello Field Office)*

Drive south from the junction of Highway 261 and Highway 95 (near Natural Bridges National Monument) towards the town of Mexican Hat. After 3.9 miles you will arrive at the Kane Gulch Ranger Station where you can buy maps, if you wish, and get more information. Continuing south from the ranger station for another 9.6 miles will bring you to a junction where two dirt roads *join the paved highway. The road on the left is marked with a sign that says "Cigarette Spring". Turn right, onto the unmarked road opposite the Cigarette Spring road, and continue for 7.5 miles. You will encounter major forks in the road in at least two places; in each case you should bear to the right.*

After you have driven 7.5 miles from the paved highway you will see a smaller dirt road branching off on the right with a sign that says "Government Trail". Turn here and drive the *last 1.5 miles to the parking area beside a small cattle pond. The last 1.5 miles of road is very rocky, but with care most cars can make it. If it is too rough for your car just pull over to the side and walk the remaining distance to the pond. There is a trail register near the pond and a sign directing you to the Government Trail. There is also a fee collection box where day hikers are requested to deposit $2.00 for a permit to enter Grand Gulch.*

Before you begin this hike, pause to examine the small pond near the car parking area. The pond is an oasis in the middle of a largely waterless tableland. Although it was constructed originally by local ranchers for the purpose of watering their cattle, it has since become a haven for birds, deer, and coyotes. If you arrived too late in the day to begin your hike, the pond is a delightful place to spend the night. One starry, spring evening while I was camped there I was treated to an unforgettable outdoor performance by a local orchestra of very talented frogs and birds. The concert began at dusk with a few bass frogs tuning up their instruments, and as the night wore on they were joined by a variety of birds and insects and even an occasional coyote yipping from a nearby hill. By about 10:00 p.m. the musicians all seemed to be doing their utmost to outdo each other, and although none of them could be seen I am sure they could be heard at least a mile away.

Years ago it was possible to drive a jeep from the cattle pond all the way to the rim of Grand Gulch, where the Government Trail begins. The Grand Gulch is now designated as a Primitive Area, however, and the road beyond the pond is closed to all vehicles. Getting to Government Trail today requires a 2.8 mile walk along the former jeep road. The walk can be hot in the summer, but it is not without a measure of scenery. The road parallels Pollys Canyon, across a flat, open forest of juniper and pinion pine and lots of sagebrush. It is ideal rabbit country and, consequently, supports a large population of coyotes. After an hour's walk the road suddenly arrives at the canyon rim, where a weathered wooden sign identifies the Government Trail.

The view from the rim into Grand Gulch is magnificent. Polly's Island, a huge piece of the mesa separated from the canyon walls by a dry meander in the streambed, rises directly to the east, while up and down the Gulch the bright green canyon floor borders the pink, convoluted walls of Cedar Mesa Sandstone. Government Trail is only 0.8 mile long, and is the easiest of any of the five trails leading into Grand Gulch. It was probably built in the 1930s by the CCC workers to provide a way for ranchers to get cattle in and out of the canyon. The trail reaches the canyon floor at the base of Polly's Island, 0.2 mile south of the confluence with Polly's Canyon.

see color photo, page 190

Once on the canyon floor it is an easy walk up the flat streambed of Grand Gulch to the Big Man Pictograph Panel. The Gulch is particularly pretty in this section, and there are numerous nice places to camp if you are so inclined. If you are observant you should be able to spot a small natural arch high on the east wall of the Gulch near the confluence with Polly's Canyon, and there are at least two Anasazi ruins on the canyon's west side as you approach Big Man.

The Big Man Panel is about 200 feet above the canyon floor and it is not visible from the trail, so it is easy to miss if you are not paying attention to the map. About 1.2 miles upstream from Polly's Canyon you will see another large side canyon coming into

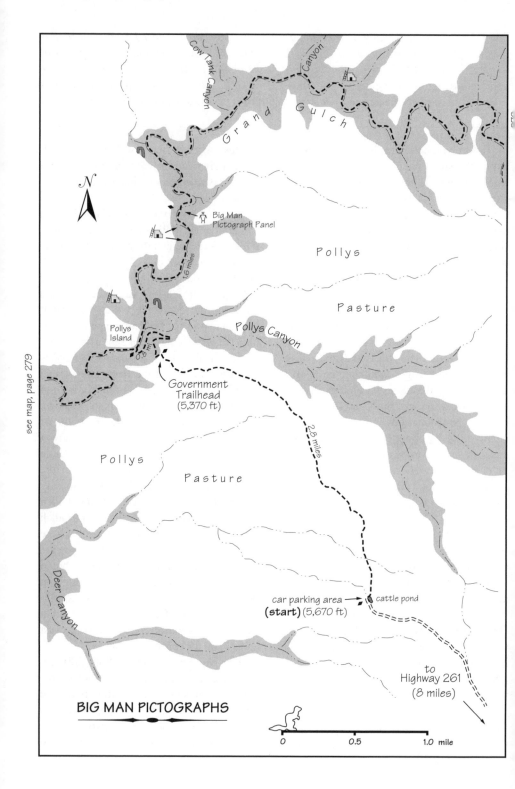

Cow Tank Canyon

Canyon

G r a n d   G u l c h

N

Big Man
Pictograph Panel

1.6 miles

P o l l y s

Pollys
Island

Pollys Canyon

P a s t u r e

0.9 mi.

Government
Trailhead
(5,370 ft)

2.8 miles

see map, page 279

P o l l y s

P a s t u r e

Deer Canyon

car parking area
(start) (5,670 ft)

cattle pond

to
Highway 261
(8 miles)

BIG MAN PICTOGRAPHS

0   0.5   1.0 mile

Big Man Pictograph Panel

Grand Gulch from the east. Beyond this point the streambed swings around to the west to get around a bulge in the canyon's eastern wall. The Big Man Pictograph Panel is located precisely at the apex of this bulge, where the streambed straightens out again and then swings back to the east. If you watch carefully as you walk this section of the trail you should see footprints where other hikers have left the trail to climb up to the pictographs. The main trail follows the east side of the streambed in this area. If you see the trail crossing back to the west side it means you have gone too far.

When you see the pictograph panel it will become obvious why it was named Big Man. The central focus of the art is two life size human figures, one of which appears to be a woman and the other obviously a man. There is also a pictograph of a woman carrying a baby. But for me the most interesting part of the artwork is the signature handprints of the artists. Many pictographs of the Southwest include such handprints. The Big Man

Pictographs were probably made by the Anasazi people who resided in Grand Gulch between 200 and 1300 A.D., but they could have been made much earlier than that. Archeologists have long been frustrated by the fact that no method now exists for accurately dating such art.

Handprints, Big Man Pictograph Panel

Slickhorn Canyon

☆ ☆ ☆ **shuttle car or bicycle required**
day hike

Distance:	10.1 miles (loop) (plus 4.5 miles by car or bicycle)
Walking time:	7 hours
Elevations:	860 ft. loss, 950 ft. gain First Fork Trailhead (start): 6,080 ft. Trail Canyon confluence: 5,220 ft. Trail Canyon Trailhead: 6,170 ft.
Trail:	The trail is very primitive, unmaintained, and poorly marked. Also, there are a few sections near the beginning and end that are steep and rocky. Because of the difficulty of carrying a backpack down the rocky terrain, I recommend you do this one as a long day hike rather than an overnighter.
Season:	Spring, summer, fall. Spring or fall are the ideal times for this hike. The canyons are very hot in the summer and cold in the winter. The road to the trailheads is unpaved and may be impassable in wet weather, but it is usually okay for most cars.
Vicinity:	Near Mexican Hat and Natural Bridges National Monument
Maps:	Pollys Pasture, Slickhorn Canyon East *(USGS)* Grand Gulch Plateau *(Trails Illustrated, #706)*
Information:	http://www.utahtrails.com/slickhorn.html *(Utah Trails)* http://www.blm.gov/utah/monticello/ *(BLM, Monticello)* phone: (435) 587-2141 *(BLM, Monticello Field Office)*

Drive south from the junction of Highway 261 and Highway 95 (near Natural *Bridges National Monument) towards the town of Mexican Hat. 3.9 miles from the junction you will arrive at the Kane Gulch Ranger Station where you can buy maps, if you wish, and get more information. Continuing south from the ranger station for another 9.6 miles will bring you to a junction where two dirt roads join the paved highway. The road on the left is marked with a sign that says "Cigarette Spring". Turn right onto the unmarked road to go to the Slickhorn Canyon trailheads. Soon you will encounter an unlocked gate and a trail register, where day hikers are requested to deposit $2.00 for a permit to enter Slickhorn Canyon.*

2.6 miles after leaving the highway the road forks, with the right fork leading to Grand Gulch, and the left fork leading to Slickhorn Canyon. Make a note of your odometer reading at this junction and turn left (south). After 1.7 miles you will see the road to the First Fork

Trailhead leaving on the right. (This 0.4 mile road ends at the top of First Fork, where the hike starts.) After 4.5 miles you will pass by the top of Third Fork Canyon, down which another trail leads to Slickhorn Canyon. After 5.8 miles you will come to a corral in the middle of a large meadow on your right. This corral marks the entrance to Trail Canyon, where the hike ends, and you should leave your shuttle car or bicycle here.

Slickhorn Canyon offers an alternative for those who are interested in the Anasazi Ruins of Cedar Mesa but want more solitude than Grand Gulch can offer. The ruins are not as extensive as those in Grand Gulch, but Slickhorn does have one bonus: an almost perfectly preserved *kiva* with the original roof still completely intact. The BLM has even provided a replica of an Anasazi ladder to give hikers access to the subterranean room through the opening in the roof. Also, the Slickhorn ruins do not appear to have been ravaged by Richard Wetherill and the other pot hunters of the late 1800s who excavated so many of the Grand Gulch ruins. Perhaps they didn't know about Slickhorn Canyon.

Like the Grand Gulch, Slickhorn Canyon runs in a southeasterly direction from the edge of Cedar Mesa to the San Juan River. There are a number of side canyons which join the main canyon from the east side, and it is through three of these side canyons, First Fork, Third Fork, and Trail Canyon, that most hikers find access to Slickhorn. The hike described here is a loop between First Fork and Trail Canyon.

From the parking area at the top of First Fork, begin by walking down the bottom of the drainage in a southwesterly direction. There are no signs and no maintained trail,

Slickhorn Canyon, above Second Fork

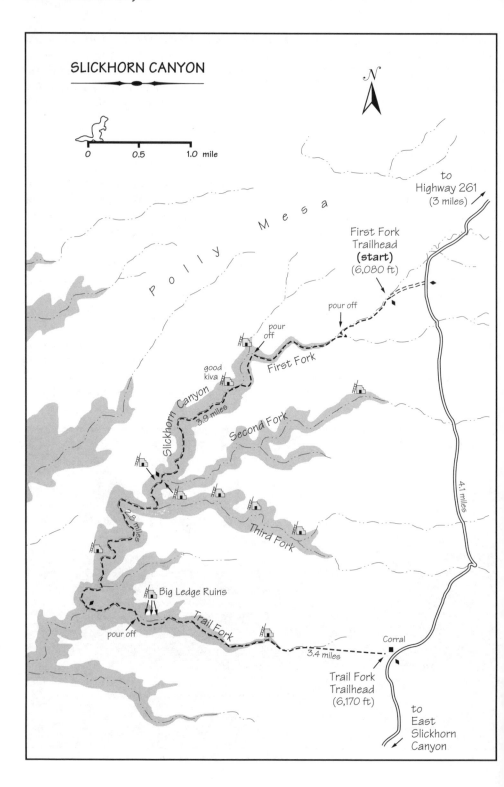

SLICKHORN CANYON

N

0   0.5   1.0 mile

P o l l y   M e s a

to Highway 261 (3 miles)

First Fork Trailhead **(start)** (6,080 ft)

pour off

pour off

First Fork

good kiva

Slickhorn Canyon

3.9 miles

Second Fork

4.1 miles

2.9 miles

Third Fork

Big Ledge Ruins

pour off

Trail Fork

3.4 miles

Corral

Trail Fork Trailhead (6,170 ft)

to East Slickhorn Canyon

but enough hikers use this route that a primitive trail is beginning to form. After a fifteen minute walk you will come to a small pouroff that you can easily get around by detouring a short distance into a shallow side canyon on the left. Another mile down canyon will bring you to a much larger pouroff that cannot be dealt with so easily. This time you will have to climb up the south side of the canyon to a bench just below the top of the mesa that you can follow around the obstacle. Many hikers before you have taken this route, so look for the cairns they have left behind to guide you.

While you are on the bench be sure to look into the back of the short side canyon on the opposite side of First Fork; there is a small ruin near the top of the canyon wall. Also, take note of a large sandstone monolith that stands on the opposite side of the main canyon, about 500 yards downstream from the pour off. This monolith is approximately opposite the point where the trail again descends to the canyon floor, so be sure to watch for cairns.

The monolith will also help you find your second ruin. Look carefully at the opposite canyon wall about 200 yards downstream from the monolith and you will see a large alcove about half way up the side of the canyon wall. The ruin is in the back of this alcove. Once you reach the canyon floor, walk downstream for five or ten minutes until you see a faint trail leading up to the right. This is the way to the alcove. The ruin is not visible from the bottom, and there are very few cairns marking the assent (perhaps removed by rangers?), so it is easy to miss. Some scrambling is necessary, but the climb is not difficult. You will certainly want to spend some time checking out this ruin because it contains an extraordinarily well preserved *kiva*.

The Anasazi *kivas* are of special interest to anthropologists who study Indian cultures

Balancing rock, Slickhorn Canyon

of the Southwest. Every Anasazi community seems to have had one of them, and the basic architecture has endured for centuries. *Kiva*-like structures have been around for at least 1300 years, and they still exist today in a few modern Indian cultures. The *kiva* in First Fork, though 700 years old, is almost identical to a modern Hopi *kiva*. Notice, for instance, the small hole in the center of the floor. Similar holes appear in the seventh century pithouse *kivas* of Mesa Verde, as well as in present-day Hopi *kivas*. The Hopis, who call the hole a *sipapu*, or spirit hole, believe it is an entrance to the underworld. They believe that their ancestors entered and exited our world through a *sipapu*.

Below the *kiva* ruin the trail becomes much less rocky, and after 1.6 miles it opens up into a large, sandy meadow where it meets another canyon coming in from the left (Second Fork). There are two other ruins near

Anasazi granary, Slickhorn Canyon

is another pour off which must be detoured. If you see the pour off you have probably missed the way, and you will have to backtrack a short distance downstream to find a faint trail that climbs about 100 feet up the south side of the canyon in order to get around the obstacle. Again, the way is marked by small cairns. As you pass above the pour off look across to the other side of the canyon at three small ruins perched precariously on a long, narrow ledge. These are the Big Ledge Ruins. Two of them look particularly interesting because they are build primarily of juniper logs rather than stone. What a chore it must have been to chop down all of those logs with stone tools and haul them to the high canyon ledge.

After the Big Ledge Ruins the trail again becomes very rocky as it climbs upward toward the mesa top. Occasional minor scrambling may be necessary, and if you are carrying a bulky backpack you will wish you weren't. Finally, after two miles, the trail breaks over the top of the rim into a large flat meadow of sagebrush. Continue walking eastward across the meadow and soon you will spot the corral where your shuttle car or bicycle is parked.

the canyon floor at this confluence. The one on the west side of the canyon, a small granary, is particularly well preserved. 0.4 miles further downstream will bring you to the confluence with Third Fork. If you are interested in shortening your hike you can return to the top of the mesa through Third Fork. Doing this will shorten the hike by 2.0 trail miles and 1.3 road miles.

From the confluence with Third Fork, it is 2.4 miles of easy walking to Trail Canyon. Along the way you will pass at least one other ruin site on the west side of Slickhorn Canyon, and one other major side canyon coming in from the east. There are no signs, so be sure you turn into Trail Canyon and not the one before or after it. Just remember that Trail Canyon will be the fourth major side canyon you encounter coming into Slickhorn Canyon from the east.

About 0.6 miles up Trail Canyon there

Pottery shards, Slickhorn Canyon

Owl and Fish Creek Canyons

☆ ☆ ☆   **overnight hike**

Distance: 16.1 miles (loop)

Walking time: day 1: 6 hours
                       day 2: 5 hours

Elevations: 1,340 ft. loss/gain
                       Owl and Fish Creek Trailhead (start):   6,180 ft.
                       Owl and Fish Creek Confluence: 4,840 ft.

Trail: The trail is primitive and unmaintained, but it is well marked
                       with rock cairns and easy to follow. Getting in and out of the
                       canyons can be tricky—especially with a heavy pack. A twenty-
                       foot piece of rope is useful for lowering backpacks down one
                       small ledge at the top of Fish Creek Canyon.

Season: Spring, summer, fall. Spring or fall are the ideal times for this
                       hike. The canyons are very hot in the summer and cold in the
                       winter. The road to the trailhead is unpaved for the last five miles
                       and may be impassable in wet weather, but it is usually okay for
                       most cars.

Vicinity: Near Mexican Hat and Natural Bridges National Monument

Maps: Snow Flat Spring Cave, Bluff NW *(USGS)*
                       Grand Gulch Plateau *(Trails Illustrated, #706)*

Information: http://www.utahtrails.com/owl.html *(Utah Trails)*
                       http://www.blm.gov/utah/monticello/ *(BLM, Monticello)*
                       phone: (435) 587-2141 *(BLM, Monticello Field Office)*

---

*Drive south from the junction of Highway 261 and Highway 95 (near Natural
Bridges National Monument) towards the town of Mexican Hat. After 3.9 miles
you will pass the Kane Gulch Ranger Station, a good place to obtain more
information about the trail and buy a map. Continue south from the ranger
station on Highway 261 for another 1.1 miles and you will see a graded road
leaving the pavement on the left. Turn here and drive another 5.3 miles to the Owl and Fish
Creek Trailhead and parking area.*

*Note: The BLM asks that all hikers register at the trailhead and obtain permits before
entering the canyons. Backpackers will be charged $5.00/person for a maximum of 7 days.
Advance reservations are necessary for overnight hikers entering the canyons between March
1 to June 15, and can be obtained by telephone from the BLM office in Monticello at (435)
587-1532. The cost is $8.00/person.*

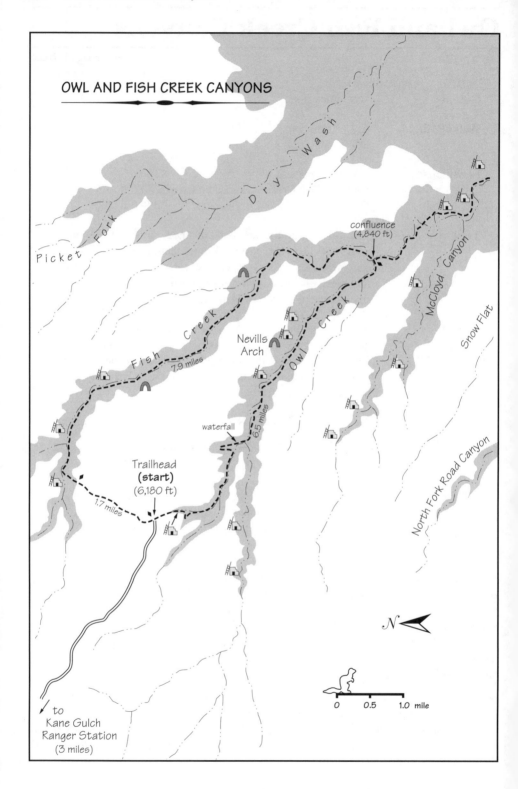

OWL AND FISH CREEK CANYONS

Dry Wash

Picket Fork

confluence
(4,840 ft)

McCloyd Canyon

Snow Flat

Fish Creek

7.9 miles

Nevills Arch

Owl Creek

waterfall

6.5 miles

Trailhead
(start)
(6,180 ft)

1.7 miles

North Fork Road Canyon

N

0   0.5   1.0 mile

to
Kane Gulch
Ranger Station
(3 miles)

Ruins of an Anasazi kiva near the trailhead in Owl Creek Canyon

Southeastern Utah has one of the largest concentrations of Anasazi Indian ruins in the United States, and the area around Owl Creek and Fish Creek is one of the best places to see them. Most of the ruins in these two canyons are, unfortunately, located high on the cliffs in inaccessible alcoves. They are not generally obvious to the casual observer, and many hikers complete the loop having seen only one or two ruins. There is one excellent site, however, which is right on the trail in Owl Creek Canyon, so everyone can be assured of seeing at least one ruin site.

You will have better luck in finding the Anasazi ruins if you know where to look. First, bear in mind that these canyons are cold in the wintertime, and the inhabitants preferred to build their homes where they could get as much winter sunshine as possible. That means on the south-facing, or north side of the canyon. Rarely will you see a ruin on the south side of a canyon. Second, the Indians tended to live as close as

possible to the land they were farming; consequently there are more ruins in those areas where the canyon bottom is wide and flat. In places where the canyon bottom is too narrow or rocky the Indians farmed above the rim, and in those locations the ruins will be nearer to the top. When looking for cliff dwellings it helps to have a small pair of lightweight binoculars. I spotted seven ruin sites the first time I walked this loop, but two or three of them would have been impossible to identify without binoculars.

Indian ruins are not the only attraction this hike has. There is also plenty of interesting scenery—especially in Owl Creek Canyon. The reddish colored Cedar Mesa Sandstone has been carved into an eye-catching display of pinnacles and spires, and at least three natural arches. Nevills Arch, about half way up Owl Creek Canyon, is particularly impressive. There are also a number of fine camp sites in both canyons—particularly near the confluence.

The loop can be walked in either direction. The ranger station recommends that hikers go down Owl Creek Canyon first, primarily because the trail down from the rim of Fish Creek Canyon is rather steep and rocky, and it is easier to climb out of that canyon with a pack than to climb into it. Personally, however, I feel it is better to begin at the top of Fish Creek and exit through Owl Creek Canyon. The trail along Fish Creek is sometimes vague, and when coming out of that canyon it is easy to miss the turn where the route leaves the streambed. Also there is more to see in Owl Creek Canyon, and I like to save the best for last.

Day 1 (9.6 miles)

From the parking area walk north on a well-trodden path for 1.7 miles to the edge of Fish Creek Canyon. The canyon rim, incidentally, is a good place to camp if you are getting off to a late start. Before dropping below the rim look carefully along the bottom of the cliffs on the opposite side of Fish Creek Canyon, and if you have sharp eyes you may spot your first ruin. The remains of a small, square, stone dwelling with a door on the right side are located there. The structure is quite far away, and with the unaided eye it is difficult to positively identify it as man-made. But with binoculars you will be able to see the telltale pattern of brick work and the log beams that once supported the roof.

Shortly after leaving the rim the trail comes to a ten-foot ledge that can be troublesome getting down with a backpack. The best way to negotiate this obstacle, especially if you are hiking alone, is to lower your pack to the bottom with a short piece of rope before climbing down. The remainder of the trail down to the canyon floor is quite steep and rocky, but well marked with stone cairns. Take care not to twist an ankle. Once you reach the canyon floor the walking is much easier.

There are not as many Indian ruins in up-

per Fish Creek Canyon as their are along Owl Creek; hence the 7.9 mile walk down Fish Creek to the confluence with Owl Creek is rather uneventful. I was only able to see one other cliff dwelling along this section of the hike. The canyon is quite rugged, however, and there is some interesting scenery. There are also at least two unnamed natural arches in upper Fish Creek Canyon, but unless you watch the canyon walls carefully you may not see both of them. As you approach the confluence the canyon widens, the juniper forest thins out, and more cottonwood trees can be seen. The best camp sites are in the immediate vicinity of the confluence.

If you have time after pitching camp you may want to leave your pack behind and continue down into lower Fish Creek Canyon for a few miles. The canyon floor is wide and flat in this area and the walking is fast and easy along a good trail. There are a lot of ruins along lower Fish Creek, some of them quite well preserved and easy to get to. This area was probably extensively

Owl Creek Canyon

farmed by the Anasazis.

The first ruin in lower Fish Creek Canyon is located just above the confluence with McCloyd Canyon, about a half-hour walk from Owl Creek. Look to the left as the trail crosses a grassy meadow under a large, partially fallen cottonwood tree. It is not too difficult to climb up to this ruin, and a few pottery shards are still *see color photo, page 191* visible near it. Please don't remove anything, however. Such artifacts have far more meaning if they are seen in the wild where their original owners left them than they could ever have in your private collection. There are several other ruins in lower Fish Creek Canyon, and also in McCloyd Canyon; you may want to spend an extra day in the area to examine them.

Day 2 (6.5 miles)

Today will be spent climbing out of Owl Creek Canyon. The first half of the trail is flat and easy, through an area that was undoubtedly farmed by the Anasazis. Again, the canyon walls have been carved into an impressive array of columns and monoliths that stand like sentinels above the canyon. The most impressive geologic formation, however, is Nevills Arch, located 2.0 miles above the confluence. This huge arch, high on the canyon's north side, would be impressive in any setting, but seeing it in the wilderness of Owl Creek Canyon is especially memorable. There are at least three Anasazi cliff dwellings within a half-mile of the arch, and its presence surely played an important role in their lives. It is a pity that today we know nothing of what the arch meant to the canyon people, or even what they called it.

Soon after Nevills Arch the canyon narrows, and the trail passes several small waterfalls as it slowly winds its way upward. There is usually not enough water in Owl Creek to present much of a spectacle at the falls, but they generally have at least a little water flowing over them. Two of the falls have fine swimming holes at the bottom— clear pools of water that have probably been a child's delight for a thousand years. The last fall, located about 2.1 miles from the arch, effectively blocks the canyon floor, forcing the trail to make a 0.4 mile detour into a side canyon to get around it.

Finally, about 0.1 mile below the canyon rim, the trail passes a hidden cliff dwelling with an exceptionally well preserved *Kiva* as its centerpiece. Many of the juniper beams that once supported the structure's round roof are still in place, and its cylindrical walls are almost entirely intact. This ruin has been exceptionally well preserved because it is located in a deep alcove, well sheltered from the wind and the rain. It must have been bitter cold here in the winter, however, as little sun ever reaches the alcove. Perhaps the Indians had their winter living quarters elsewhere, and used this site primarily for grain storage and religious activities.

From this last Anasazi ruin a crude, cairn marked trail climbs straight up the slickrock drainage to the rim above. Once you climb out of the canyon, continue following the cairns in a northerly direction for another 0.3 mile to reach the parking lot where the hike ends.

Nevills Arch, Owl Creek Canyon

Mule Canyon

☆☆☆   **overnight hike**

Distance:	10.0 miles (round trip)
Walking time:	day 1: 2 hours day 2: 3¹/₂ hours
Elevations:	420 ft. gain/loss Mule Canyon Trailhead (start): 5,980 ft. Camp site: 6,180 ft. Upper Mule Canyon: 6,400 ft.
Trail:	There is an unmaintained trail throughout most of Mule Canyon. In some places it may be hard to follow, but if you loose it just follow the canyon bottom. There is very little scrambling and the brush is minimal. You should wear wettable footwear, however, as it is frequently necessary to cross the stream bed.
Season:	Spring, summer, fall. The canyon is quite hot in midsummer and cold in winter. The ideal times for this hike are spring and fall.
Vicinity:	Near Blanding and Natural Bridges National Monument
Maps:	Hotel Rock, South Long Point *(USGS)* Grand Gulch Plateau *(Trails Illustrated, #706)*
Information:	http://www.utahtrails.com/mule.html *(Utah Trails)* http://www.blm.gov/utah/monticello/ *(BLM, Monticello)* phone: (435) 587-2141 *(BLM, Monticello Field Office)*

Drive east on Highway 95 from the entrance to Natural Bridges National Monument, checking your odometer as you pass the junction with Highway 261. After 9.1 miles (0.5 miles beyond the turnoff to Mule Canyon Indian Ruins) you will see a gravel road on the north side of the highway leading to Texas Flat. Turn left here and drive for 0.3 miles to the point where the Texas Flat *road crosses Mule Canyon. You should see a sign marking the trailhead below the left side of the road as you climb up the northeast side of the canyon.*

Note: The BLM asks that all hikers register at the trailhead before entering Mule Canyon. Backpackers will be charged $5.00/person for a permit; for day hikers the cost is $2.00. Advance reservations are necessary for overnight hikers from March 1 to June 15, and can be obtained by telephone from the BLM office in Monticello at (435) 587-1532.

This hike could easily be done in one day   instead of two, but there is so much to see

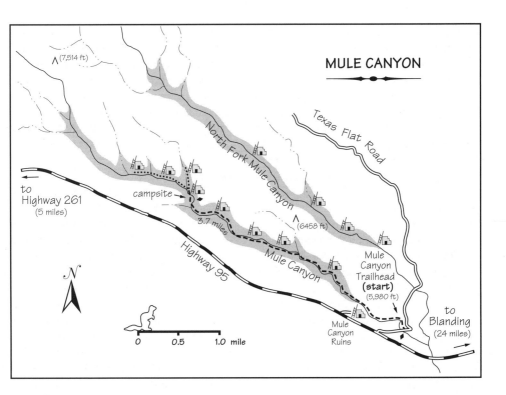

you will want to take your time and make many stops along the way. The main attractions are the Anasazi Indian ruins that can be seen under the cliffs on the north side of the canyon.

The Anasazis occupied this area for about 550 years between 750 and 1300 A.D. They were a peaceful people who farmed the canyon lands throughout the four corners area, and, judging from the number of archeological sites they left behind, their population was substantial. In the last half of the thirteenth century the Anasazi people began to leave places like Mule Canyon, and by 1300 their communities had been completely abandoned. Why? A long drought that plagued the southwest between 1276 and 1299 was undoubtedly a major factor. Some archeologist believe another factor was the southern migration of Navajos and other nomadic tribes that came into the region at about that time.

The ruins you will see in Mule Canyon are between seven and nine hundred years old. They are not part of any national park, monument, or wilderness area, and they have never been excavated or restored in any way. The opportunity to discover these ruins in this wild setting, with no rangers around telling you how to behave, is what makes Mule Canyon such an exciting place. But with that freedom comes great responsibility. The ruins are a precious national treasure and should be treated as such. View them with awe, but please do not deface them in any way, and do not steal any of the pottery shards or other artifacts you may find around them. Help preserve them so that others may also experience the magic of the canyon.

see color photo, page 188

Day 1 (5.0 miles)

At the point where the trail enters Mule

Canyon, the rim is only about 60 feet above the creek bed. The surrounding pinion-juniper forest is typical of the environment where Indian ruins are often found, but initially no ruins are evident. As you walk up the canyon it will begin to deepen, and you will notice occasional alcoves that have been eroded under the sandstone cliffs. These alcoves are the kinds of places often chosen by the Anasazis for their homes. Pay particular attention to the north side of the canyon as you proceed. The ancient Indians preferred to live on the north side because it receives more sun during the winter.

Finally, after walking about 1.3 miles, you should see your first ruin. It is only about 100 feet from the trail on the north side, but it is partially hidden by the trees and easy to miss. This ruin consists of about 5 rooms, some of which are very well preserved. From this point on, if you are observant, you should see at least one or two ruins for every mile of the trail.

As you continue up the canyon you will notice the forest gradually changing from pinion and juniper to ponderosa pine. A good place to camp is at a junction, about 3.7 miles from the trailhead, where two small side canyons meet Mule Canyon and the canyon floor becomes much wider. Here the forest is primarily ponderosa pine and the canyon floor is open and flat. Also, there is a nice ruin to explore about 200 feet above the creek bed on the north side.

Day 2 (5.0 miles)

Using your camp site as a base, you will want to explore further up Mule Canyon, and also check some of its small side canyons before heading back. I saw a total of eight ruin sites in Mule Canyon, four of which were above the camp site, but with some determination I am sure many more can be found. Be sure to check out the three short side canyons above the camp site coming into Mule Canyon from the north. Mule Canyon itself continues for about three miles beyond the camping area before arriving at the top of the rim, but don't expect to find too many ruins in the last mile. The higher reaches of the canyon were probably too cold for permanent Indian settlements.

Anasazi Ruins in Mule Canyon

Cohab Canyon - Cassidy Arch

☆ ☆

Capitol Reef National Park
shuttle car or bicycle useful
day hike

Distance: 7.0 miles
(plus 3.6 miles by car or bicycle)

Walking time: 4¹/₂ hours

Elevations: 1,040 ft. gain, 1,060 ft. loss

Cohab Canyon Trailhead (start):	5,420 ft.
Highest point:	6,460 ft.
Grand Wash Trailhead:	5,400 ft.

Trail: Popular, well maintained trail

Season: Spring, summer, fall, winter. There is snow on some parts of the trail during the winter months. During the summer months the trail is very hot, with temperatures often exceeding 100 degrees F. There is no water along the way so be sure to carry plenty.

Vicinity: Capitol Reef National Park, near Fruita

Maps: Fruita *(USGS)*
Fish Lake/Capitol Reef Nat. Park *(Trails Illustrated, #213)*

Information: http://www.utahtrails.com/cohab.html *(Utah Trails)*
http://www.nps.gov/care/ *(Capitol Reef National Park)*
phone: (435) 425-3791 *(Visitor Center)*

Drive south of the Capital Reef National Park Visitor Center for a distance of 3.4 miles to the turnout into Grand Wash. Take the dirt road into Grand Wash and drive for another 1.3 miles to the end of the road. This is the point where the hike ends, and where you should leave your shuttle car or bicycle.

To get to the Cohab Canyon Trailhead, where the hike begins, return to the paved road at the head of Grand Wash and drive north, back towards the Visitors Center, for a distance of 2.3 miles. You will see a sign marking the Cohab Canyon Trailhead on the right side of the road opposite the entrance to the campground.

Sixty-five million years ago, while forces inside the earth were pushing up the Colorado Plateau, a 100-mile-long wrinkle in the earth's mantle was formed in Southern Utah. Thousands of feet of subterranean sedimentary rock was forced upward as the fold developed, twisting and buckling to form a convoluted range of mountains we now call the Waterpocket Fold. Today, after a great deal of erosion, the mountains rise less than two thousand feet above the desert floor, but what remains is a fairyland of geologic sculpture.

see map, page 305

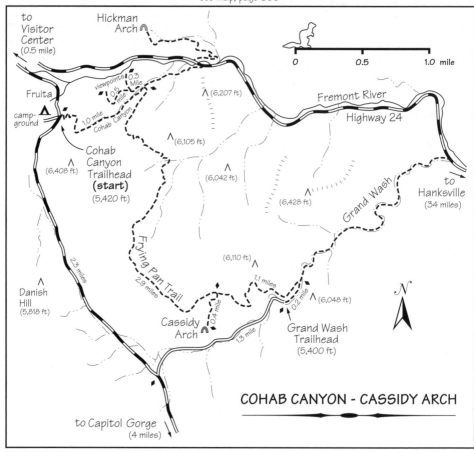

COHAB CANYON - CASSIDY ARCH

The ancient mountains, most of which are now part of Capitol Reef National Park, have been carved into a tangle of hidden canyons, monolithic spires, and towering cliffs. The hike described here starts in the Fremont River Valley, near the pioneer settlement of Fruita, and crosses a portion of the Waterpocket Fold to Grand Wash. It offers a good representation of the unique landscape of the Waterpocket Fold.

From Cohab Canyon Trailhead the path begins by switchbacking up the clay bentonite mounds of the Chinle formation. Finally, after about 0.3 mile, it arrives at the base of the reddish cliffs that can be seen above the road. These sandstone cliffs are part of the 370-foot-thick geological formation known as the Wingate Sandstone. The trail then skirts around the west side of cliffs and soon drops into a shallow, hidden drainage called Cohab Canyon. Cohab Canyon and its trail continue all the way to the Fremont River, on the east side of Capital Reef, but you won't be following it that far on this hike.

About 0.6 mile after entering Cohab canyon you will come to a trail junction with a sign indicating the way to two overlook points. You should turn left here before continuing down the canyon and make a side trip to one of them. After 0.2 mile the over-

Cassidy Arch trail junction

look trail splits again, and you are given a choice between the north and the south overlooks. If you are interested in taking photographs, take the south overlook trail (0.3 mile). It leads to a high vantage point above the Fruita area. But if you like adventure bear right to the north overlook (0.1 mile). This trail leads to a small overhang at the top of the cliffs above the Fremont River with a shear 400 foot drop below.

see color photo, page 192

When you are finished with the overlooks, backtrack to the Cohab Canyon Trail and continue onward for a short distance toward Highway 24. After just a hundred yards you will come to another trail leaving Cohab Canyon to the south. This is the Frying Pan Trail, the one that will lead you to Grand Wash. The Frying Pan Trail winds over a tortuous route along the top of the Fold, twisting between domes of sandstone and working its way around a series of gullies and ravines. In some places only rock cairns will tell you that you are still on the path, and you will probably wonder how you would ever be able to find your way through the obstacle course if you lost the trail.

Finally, after a long tiring climb, you will reach the highest point on the Frying Pan Trail and start down again toward Grand Wash. Then, 1.5 miles later, you will see a sign marking the short spur trail across the slickrock to Cassidy Arch. Cassidy Arch is a large and impressive arch only a ten minute walk from the main trail. It was named after the outlaw, Butch Cassidy, who is thought to have used Grand Wash occasionally as a hideout. The path ends on the plateau above the arch, and if you have a hiking partner and a camera it is easy to get a picture of someone standing on top of it. Getting to the bottom of the span, however, requires some rock climbing.

From Cassidy Arch junction the Frying Pan Trail continues for another 1.1 miles before reaching the bottom of Grand Wash. Once you get to the bottom of the wash turn right and walk for another 0.2 mile to the end of the Grand Wash Road, where your shuttle car is parked. If you look to the right as you drive back towards the Visitor Center you can see Cassidy Arch again from the bottom of Grand Wash. It should come into view about 0.5 mile from the end of the road.

Cassidy Arch

Chimney Rock Canyon

Capitol Reef National Park
shuttle car or bicycle required
day hike

Distance: 9.7 miles
              (plus 6.9 miles by car or bicycle)

Walking time: 5¹/₂ hours

Elevations: 250 ft. gain, 1,080 ft. loss
              Chimney Rock Trailhead (start):   6,050 ft.
              Highest point: 6,300 ft.
              Fremont River: 5,220 ft.

Trail: Most of this hike is through the sandy bottom of a desert canyon. There is no maintained trail, but the route is easy to follow. At the end of the hike it is necessary to ford the Fremont River. This is usually not a problem, but if there has been a lot of rain you should check the river before beginning the hike.

Season: Spring, summer, fall, winter. There is snow on some parts of the trail during the winter months. The trail is very hot in the summer, with temperatures often exceeding 100 degrees F. There is no reliable water along the trail, so be sure to carry plenty.

Vicinity: Capital Reef National Park, near Fruita

Maps: Twin Rocks, Fruita *(USGS)*
            Fish Lake/Capitol Reef Nat. Park *(Trails Illustrated, #213)*

Information: http://www.utahtrails.com/chimneyrock.html *(Utah Trails)*
            http://www.nps.gov/care/ *(Capitol Reef National Park)*
            phone: (435) 425-3791 *(Visitor Center)*

Drive east of the Capital Reef National Park Visitor Center on Highway 24 for a distance of 3.9 miles, where you will see a small picnic area on the south side of the Fremont River. This is where the hike ends, and where you should leave your shuttle car. The hike begins 3.0 miles west of the Visitor Center on Highway 24 at the Chimney Rock turnout on the north side of the road.

Chimney Rock Canyon is a long, narrow desert drainage on the northwestern side of Capital Reef National Park. It begins just outside the park on the eastern slopes of Thousand Lakes Mountain and meanders for some 15 miles through the Waterpocket Fold before draining into the Fremont River. This hike intersects the canyon at its midpoint and

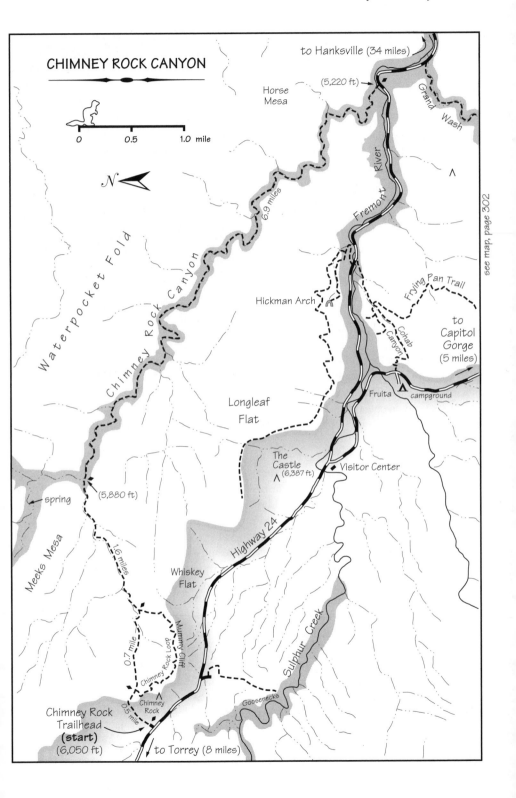

CHIMNEY ROCK CANYON

0   0.5   1.0 mile

N

to Hanksville (34 miles)

Horse
Mesa

(5,220 ft)

Grand Wash

Fremont River

6.9 miles

W a t e r p o c k e t   F o l d

C h i m n e y   R o c k   C a n y o n

Hickman Arch

Frying Pan Trail

Cohab Canyon

to
Capitol
Gorge
(5 miles)

see map, page 302

Longleaf
Flat

Fruita   campground

spring

(5,880 ft)

The
Castle
(6,387 ft)

Visitor Center

1.6 miles

Meeks Mesa

0.7 mile

Whiskey
Flat

Highway 24

Mummy Cliff

Sulphur Creek

Chimney Rock Loop

Goosenecks

Chimney
Rock

0.5 mile

Chimney Rock
Trailhead
(start)
(6,050 ft)

to Torrey (8 miles)

follows it for its last six miles.

The hike is particularly interesting from a geological point of view because it passes through so many different geologic strata. The route begins in the Moenkopi Formation, then passes through the Shinarump, Chinle, Wingate, and Kayenta Formations, and finally ends in the center of the Waterpocket Fold at the base of the Navajo Sandstone. The sequence is unusual because the Navajo Sandstone was deposited about forty million years after the Moenkopi Formation, yet here it lies a thousand feet lower.

As you descend through the canyon you will see successive layers of younger rock slanting downward along the walls to meet the older layers at the bottom. The Waterpocket Fold is a giant wrinkle in the earths crust that was formed in southern Utah about 65 million years ago. Because of the uplifting and subsequent erosion along the Fold, the exposed rock is now older on the west side than the east. The streambed of Chimney Rock Canyon cuts into the Waterpocket Fold from its western side and ends near its midpoint.

Chimney Rock Canyon was named after Chimney Rock, an impressive pinnacle of Moenkopi Shale that rises from the desert floor near the trailhead. The trail begins by winding gently upward from the parking area on the west side of Chimney Rock and then around to its north side. After walking 0.5 mile and climbing 250 feet you will come to a junction where another trail takes off to the right. This alternative route veers south again to pass by the base of Chimney Rock and then rejoins the main trail 1.7 miles later. If you have the

see color photo, page 191

time you might want take this detour for a closer look at the monolith, but doing so will add about a mile to the total length of the hike. If you take the shorter route, to the left, you will reach the point where the two

Chimney Rock Canyon

trails come together again after about 20 minutes.

After the second junction the trail descends gradually down a short, unnamed canyon for about 1.6 miles before finally intersecting Chimney Rock Canyon. To reach the Fremont River you must turn right when you reach the main canyon, but if time permits, or if you are doing this hike as an overnighter, you may want to make a side trip to the canyon's best known spring. The spring lies about 1.0 mile upcanyon to the left. It is situated in an alcove just above a small pool of water under the north wall of the canyon. You will know you are near when you see a grove of large cottonwood trees. (Cottonwood trees in the desert country of Southern Utah usually mark the presence of water.) Chimney Rock Canyon is often called Spring Canyon, because of this spring.

From the point where the trail first meets

Chimney Rock Canyon it is 6.9 miles to the Fremont River. There is no real trail, but the route is generally easy to walk. You will be following the sandy creek bed nearly all the way. There are some deer tracks in the canyon bottom, but the most interesting aspect of the hike is the geology. Much of the rock is a deep red color, and in the section of the canyon that passes through the Wingate Formation, the sandstone walls are sheer and smooth. You may be surprised to find frequent boulders of black volcanic rock. These worn boulders were washed downstream by flash floods from a volcanic area near the source of the canyon. Now they lie in stark contrast to the reddish sandstone and shale of the Waterpocket Fold.

About half way through the gorge you will enter a half-mile section of narrows, where the canyon walls converge to a mere five feet apart. There are also two ten-foot pouroffs, or dry falls, in the bottom of this stretch of canyon. These falls are relatively easy to climb down and should not be a problem unless you are carrying a large backpack. But if they do present a problem, there

is an alternative route around them. When you come to the first pouroff retrace your footsteps a few hundred feet back to a point where you can climb up to the ledge on the north side of the narrows. There you will find a primitive path that bypasses the obstacles before dropping back to the canyon bottom.

Finally, just before you reach the end of the hike, the canyon widens and becomes less arid. The walls change from the ruddy, fissured Wingate and Kayenta Sandstone to the smooth, white crossbedded texture of the Navajo Sandstone. Soon you will round the last bend in the canyon and be confronted with your last obstacle—the Fremont River.

Under normal circumstances, fording the Fremont is no problem. It is seldom more than 18 inches deep. If there has been a lot of rain, however, its depth can easily rise to twice that. Find a stout stick to help you with the crossing. Walk slowly, taking small steps, and make sure the stick and one foot are firmly planted before moving your other foot. The stick should be positioned on your downstream side, with your right side facing upstream as you walk.

View from Chimney Rock Canyon Trail

Upper Muley Twist Canyon

☆ ☆ ☆ ☆ ☆

Capitol Reef National Park
4WD vehicle or bicycle useful
day hike

Distance:	9.4 miles (loop) (plus 4.8 miles by 4WD or bicycle)
Walking time:	6 hours
Elevations:	740 ft. gain/loss Upper Muley Twist Trailhead (start): 5,860 ft. Top of Upper Muley Twist Canyon: 6,460 ft. Top of Waterpocket Fold: 6,600 ft.
Trail:	There is no developed trail for this hike, but the route is not too difficult to follow. Initially it follows the bottom of a desert canyon, then it loops back across the slickrock of the Water-pocket Fold. Where needed, the way is well marked with rock cairns. There is no water, so carry plenty.
Season:	Spring, summer, fall, winter. Capital Reef is very hot in the summer and cold in the winter. The ideal times for the hike are spring and fall.
Vicinity:	Capital Reef National Park, southern section
Maps:	Bitter Creek Divide, Wagon Box Mesa *(USGS)*
Information:	http://www.utahtrails.com/uppermuley.html *(Utah Trails)* http://www.nps.gov/care/ *(Capitol Reef National Park)* phone: (435) 425-3791 *(Visitor Center)*

Drive east of the Capital Reef National Park Visitor Center on Highway 24 for 9.1 miles until you see a paved road on the right leading to Notom and Lake Powell. Turn right onto this road and drive south for 33 miles to the junction with the Burr Trail Road. (The pavement ends after five miles, but the remaining gravel road is well maintained.) Turn right on the Burr Trail and drive for *another 3.2 miles where you will see a small sign on the right marking a dirt road that leads to Upper Muley Twist Canyon. Turn right onto this road. After 0.4 miles you will see a trail register and another sign advising you that to continue you will need a 4WD vehicle. The trailhead is another 2.4 miles down the 4WD road. Actually the road is not that bad; a 2WD pickup with high clearance should be able to make it, but not an ordinary car. The last 2.4 miles also makes a very pleasant bike ride if you don't have a high clearance vehicle.*

No other hike in Capital Reef National   Park offers as many scenic geological fea-

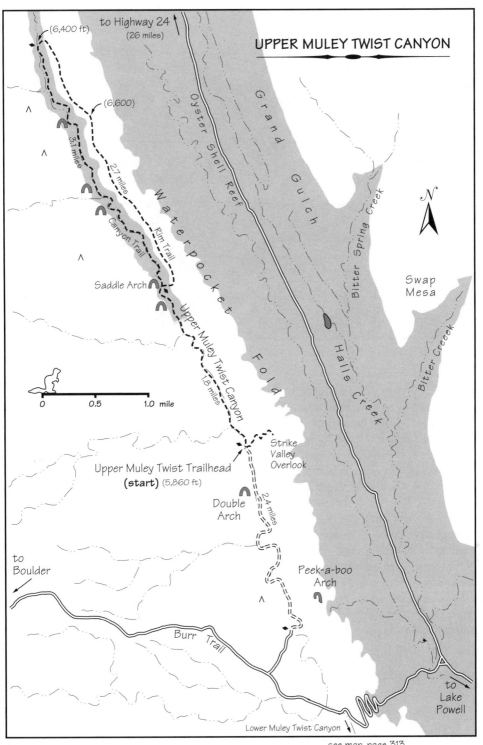

UPPER MULEY TWIST CANYON

to Highway 24
(26 miles)

(6,400 ft)

(6,600)

Oyster Shell Reef

Grand Gulch

Bitter Spring Creek

Swap Mesa

Bitter Creek

3.1 miles

2.7 miles

Waterpocket

Canyon Trail

Rim Trail

Saddle Arch

Fold

Halls Creek

Upper Muley Twist Canyon

1.8 miles

0   0.5   1.0 mile

Strike Valley Overlook

Upper Muley Twist Trailhead
(start) (5,860 ft)

Double Arch

2.4 miles

to Boulder

Peek-a-boo Arch

Burr Trail

to Lake Powell

Lower Muley Twist Canyon

see map, page 313

The Waterpocket Fold

tures as the loop through Upper Muley Twist Canyon. The canyon has been cut through a particularly interesting part of the Waterpocket Fold where the deep red Wingate Sandstone formation slopes down from the west, dipping under the eastern wall of white Navajo Sandstone. The Wingate Sandstone in this area has a tendency to erode into arches, and if you are observant you will see at least five arches on the west side as you hike up the canyon. The return portion of the hike is along a high slickrock ridge of Navajo Sandstone above the eastern side of the canyon, and the views from the top are magnificent. From this vantage point you will be able to see a

see color photo, page 192

large part of the hundred-mile-long wrinkle in the earth's crust that geologists call the Waterpocket Fold.

From the end of the road at the bottom of Upper Muley Twist Canyon you should

begin this hike by walking north along the Muley Twist streambed. Another trail on the right side of the parking area leads east to the Strike Valley Overlook, but don't be confused. This is not your trail. As you proceed be sure to scan the left side of the canyon occasionally, and after 1.6 miles you will see the first of five natural arches about 200 feet above the canyon floor. Another few hundred yards will bring you to a large crack in the canyon wall, with the second arch above it. This one is called Saddle Arch, and it is the only one of the five that has been given a name. Just below Saddle Arch you should also see a sign on the right indicating the beginning of the Rim Trail. You will be joining the Rim Trail farther up Muley Twist, and this is where you will later drop back into the Canyon.

Continuing up the wash for another 1.3 miles will bring you to a break in the red Wingate Sandstone where, again, you should be able to see two arches. The arches are about 200 yards on either side of the break, but this time they are higher up on the side of the wall. The fifth and last arch is another 0.8 miles upcanyon. This one is just at the bottom of a slot canyon joining the main canyon from the left and, unlike the others, is easily accessible.

A short distance beyond the last arch the canyon narrows and is blocked by a pouroff. In order to avoid the obstacle the trail climbs up the right side of the canyon to a shelf about 100 feet above the streambed. Watch for the rock cairns that show the way. The trail stays high for 0.6 mile before dropping back down to the bottom of the wash. Then, after only 0.1 mile more you will see another sign that says "Rim Trail". This is where you will finally leave the canyon.

It is very easy to loose the way climbing out of the canyon on the Rim Trail, so be sure to watch carefully for stone cairns. There are plenty of markers, and if you walk for more than a hundred feet without seeing one you are probably off the trail. Most of them, however, are small and hard to spot. The trail goes straight up for a while and

then doubles back through a break in the sandstone cliffs. Finally, after an altitude gain of only 200 feet, it breaks out onto the top of the Waterpocket Fold. The view comes upon you with no warning, and it is extremely impressive. One minute you are threading your way through the juniper forest, and the next minute you are on top of the world looking fifty miles down the Grand Gulch.

For the next two miles the view is nonstop. On one side of the slickrock ridge is the Grand Gulch, with Tarantula Mesa and Swap Mesa beyond, and on the other side is the Wingate Formation, containing all of the arches previously seen. In between, the top of the Waterpocket Fold seems to go on forever in both directions.

After about an hour you will come to another small sign saying "Canyon Route", and from there the trail drops back down to the bottom of Muley Twist Canyon near the Saddle Arch. Again, pay attention to the rock cairns—it is easy to loose the way. From Saddle Arch, you will have to retrace your steps back to your car or bicycle at the trailhead.

Saddle Arch

Lower Muley Twist Canyon

☆

Capitol Reef National Park
shuttle car or bicycle required
overnight hike

Distance:	18.1 miles (plus 5.0 miles by car or bicycle)
Walking time:	day 1: 6 hours day 2: 4 hours
Elevations:	1,000 ft. loss, 200 ft. gain Lower Muley Twist Trailhead (start): 5,640 ft. Cowboy Camp: 4,770 ft. The Post Trailhead: 4,860 ft.
Trail:	There is no trail for most of this hike, but the route is easy to follow. You will be walking down the streambed of a desert canyon for the first day, then 5.6 miles back to The Post along an old abandoned wagon road. The walk is easy, but unfortunately there is no water. In hot weather you should carry 1.5 gallons of water per person just for drinking.
Season:	Spring and fall. Summer hiking is possible, but it is very hot. The hike can also be pleasant during winter warm spells.
Vicinity:	Capital Reef National Park, southern section
Maps:	The Post, Wagon Box Mesa *(USGS)*
Information:	http://www.utahtrails.com/lowermuley.html *(Utah Trails)* http://www.nps.gov/care/ *(Capitol Reef National Park)* phone: (435) 425-3791 *(Visitor Center)*

After obtaining an overnight backpacking permit at the Capital Reef National Park Visitor Center, drive east on Highway 24 for 9.1 miles until you see a paved road on the right leading to Notom and Lake Powell. Turn right onto this road and drive south for 33 miles to the junction with the Burr Trail Road. (The pavement ends after five miles, but the remaining gravel road is usually *well maintained.) Lower Muley Twist Trailhead, where the hike begins, is on the south side of the Burr Trail Road, 2.1 miles west of the Notom-Lake Powell Road.*

To reach The Post Trailhead, where the hike ends, continue south on the road to Lake Powell for 2.3 miles past the Burr Trail Road. Here the road crosses over a cattle guard, beyond which you will see a small dirt road and a sign directing you to "Lower Muley Twist Trail- head". This 0.6-mile-long road ends near a large corral, where you will see another sign marking the trailhead. Leave your shuttle car or bicycle here.

see map, page 309

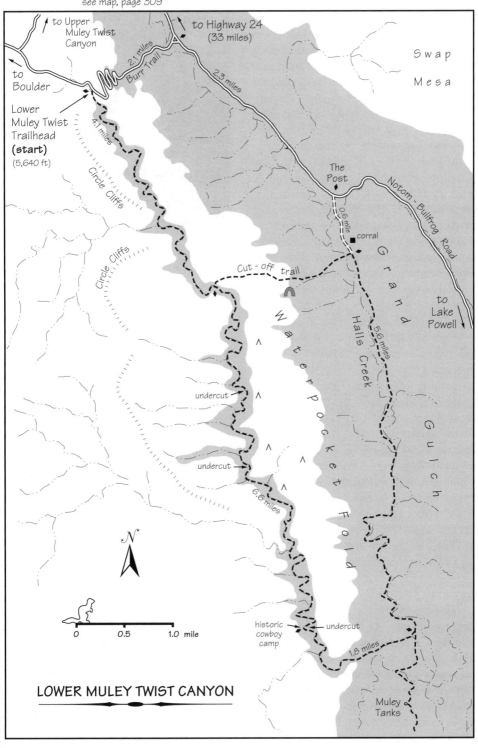

to Upper
Muley Twist
Canyon

to Highway 24
(33 miles)

2.1 miles

Burr Trail

2.3 miles

S w a p

M e s a

to
Boulder

Lower
Muley Twist
Trailhead
(start)
(5,640 ft)

4.1 miles

Circle Cliffs

Circle Cliffs

The
Post

0.6 mile

corral

Notom - Bullfrog Road

G
r
a
n
d

Cut - off trail

W
a
t
e
r
p
o
c
k
e
t

F
o
l
d

Halls Creek

5.6 miles

to
Lake
Powell

G
u
l
c
h

undercut

undercut

6.6 miles

N

historic
cowboy
camp

undercut

1.8 miles

0   0.5   1.0 mile

LOWER MULEY TWIST CANYON

Muley
Tanks

The silence of Muley Twist Canyon was briefly broken in the late 1800s, when it was discovered to be a feasible route for getting wagons through the formidable Waterpocket Fold of Southern Utah. Getting around the rugged, hundred-mile-long sandstone ridge had long been a major problem for travelers in the area—especially the Mormons, who were trying to settle the southeastern corner of the Utah Territory. On their famous Hole in the Rock expedition from Escalante to Bluff in 1879 it took the Mormon settlers six months to travel around the southern end of the Waterpocket Fold, so when Muley Twist Canyon was discovered two years later it quickly became the preferred route. The narrow canyon was said to have so many hairpin curves it could "twist a mule". Nevertheless, it was shorter and less hazardous than the notorious Hole in the Rock Trail.

Muley Twist Canyon was probably discovered by a man named Charles Hall, who operated a ferry service across the Colorado River thirty miles south of the canyon. Demand for his ferry increased dramatically for two years after his discovery, and his business thrived. However, in 1883 a new rail link across Utah was completed by the DRG&W Railroad, and communications between the eastern and western parts of the state were greatly simplified. Halls ferry service was shut down in 1884, and the winding trail through Muley Twist Canyon was rarely ever used again.

Lower Muley Twist Canyon

see color photo, page 193

Day 1 (10.7 miles)

There are many short, steep canyons running from the top of the Waterpocket Fold into the Grand Gulch on its eastern side. Muley Twist Canyon is unusual, however, because it runs in a southerly direction for a substantial distance before turning into the Grand Gulch. From its start at the Burr Trail Road, Lower Muley Twist Canyon descends down through the center of the Fold for some

eleven miles before turning east. As you walk down the canyon you will encounter two or three large side canyons coming in from the west. Bear to the left in each case to stay in Muley Twist Canyon.

After 4.1 miles you will come to a junction, where a wooden sign marks the Cutoff Trail leading to The Post. If you are looking for a shorter hike you can take this two-mile shortcut and avoid the bottom portion of Muley Twist. The most interesting part of the hike, however, is the part below the Cutoff Trail.

Continuing on past the Cutoff Trail you will notice many huge alcoves higher up the sides of the canyon. These would seem to be excellent places to find Indian ruins, but the scarcity of water makes it unlikely that Indians ever lived in the canyon. 1.7 miles below the Cutoff Trail the streambed makes a deep swing inward on the left side of the canyon, creating a huge overhang in the cliff above. For some 200 yards the trail continues under the overhang. The cave-like nature of the trail is enhanced by a 30-foot-high pile of rubble on the right side of the streambed that extends upward nearly to the roof of the overhang. This stretch of the trail feels like nothing so much as a subway tunnel. Then, 1.4 miles beyond this tunnel the trail enters another similar subway tunnel.

The cool air under the overhangs is a welcome relief. At times there may also be pools of water under them, but don't expect to be so lucky during the hot months of summer.

Throughout most of the Muley Twist Canyon there is no trace of the fact that it was once a major wagon route. Only in the Cowboy Camp, 6.6 miles below the Cutoff Trail junction can one still see a few relics of the pioneers that once passed through. The Cowboy Camp is in another large alcove that has been undercut into the west side of the canyon. This time, however, the wide, flat floor of the alcove is about ten feet above the streambed; hence it is an excellent camping area.

For over a century travelers and cowboys have broken their journeys at Cowboy Camp, and now it contains abundant signs of human occupation. The collection includes a pile of old rusted tin cans, a few leaf springs from the wagons and, above all, graffiti. There are many dated signatures on the back of the alcove from the 1920s. Unfortunately the camp floor is also liberally sprinkled with old cow pies. There haven't been any cattle in the canyon for many decades, but the normal decay of organic material occurs very slowly in this dry desert country.

Day 2 (7.4 miles)

Soon after leaving the Cowboy Camp, Muley Twist Canyon finally turns east to begin the final leg of its journey through the Waterpocket Fold to the Grand Gulch. The towering canyon walls begin to come together, then their height gradually starts to diminish, and finally the impressive canyon is transformed into nothing more than an insignificant desert gully. About 0.2 mile after leaving the Fold you will see another trail crossing Muley Twist gully. This is the trail to Brimhall Arch, and you will have to turn left at this point to get back to The Post. Watch closely for the trail crossing because

there are no signs at the junction.

After you have turned onto the Brimhall Arch Trail it is an uneventful 5.6 miles back to The Post where your shuttle car or bicycle is parked. Again, there is no water along the way.

Muley Tanks

If you are desperate for water when you reach the Grand Gulch, there are two small water holes called the Muley Tanks 1.0 mile south of Muley Twist. To get there just turn right instead of left when you see the Brimhall Arch Trail and walk south until you see a sign directing you to the Muley Tanks. Don't expect a clear mountain spring, however. The tanks are little more than two muddy potholes at the bottom of a large slickrock runoff. As their name suggests the tanks are used primarily by pack animals, and the water is usually pretty wretched. If you really plan to drink it you had better have some way of filtering out the mud first.

Lower Muley Twist undercut

The Pine Creek Box

☆ ☆

Box - Death Hollow Wilderness Area
shuttle car or bicycle required
day hike

Distance: 8.8 miles
(plus 11.1 miles by car or bicycle)

Walking time: 5 hours

Elevations: 1,300 ft. loss
Upper Box Trailhead (start): 7,740 ft.
Deep Creek Confluence: 7,010 ft.
Lower Box Trailhead: 6,440 ft.

Trail: This hike follows a small, fast running creek down a narrow, tree-lined canyon. Frequent stream crossings are necessary, so wettable boots should be worn. There is no reliable trail for the first five miles and the ground cover is thick in places, so wear long pants.

Season: Late spring, summer and fall. Access to the trailhead is usually blocked by snow in winter and early spring.

Vicinity: Box-Death Hollow Wilderness Area, near Escalante

Maps: Posy Lake, Wide Hollow Reservoir *(USGS)*
Canyons of the Escalante *(Trails Illustrated, #710)*

Information: http://www.utahtrails.com/pinebox.html *(Utah Trails)*
http://www.fs.fed.us/dxnf/ *(Dixie National Forest)*
phone: (435) 826-5499 *(Escalante Interagency Visitor Center)*

Drive north from Escalante towards Boulder on the Hells Backbone Road (a graded gravel road). After 8.0 miles you will see a sign directing you to a primitive road on the right that leads to the Lower Box access. This is where the Pine Creek Trail ends, and your shuttle car or bicycle should be left here. (Note: the primitive road to the Lower Box access is only 0.3 mile long, but *it is very sandy. You may want to leave your shuttle car beside the main road to avoid the risk of getting stuck in the sand.)*

The hike begins 10.8 miles further north on the Hells Backbone Road beside another sign that says "Upper Box access".

This hike is a very pleasant walk down an unusually scenic canyon of Pine Creek known as the Box. Conservationists fought hard to have this area included in the Utah Wilderness Act of 1984, but there was strong opposition from local ranchers and miners.

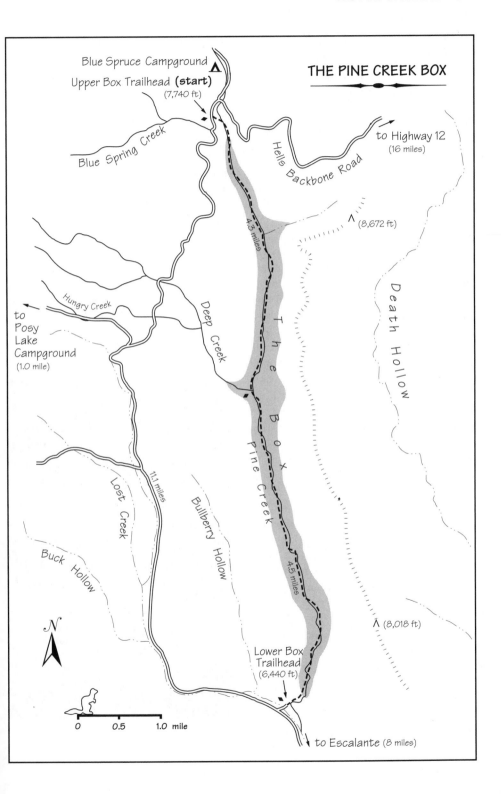

THE PINE CREEK BOX

Blue Spruce Campground
Upper Box Trailhead **(start)**
(7,740 ft)

Blue Spring Creek

Hells Backbone Road

to Highway 12
(16 miles)

Λ (8,672 ft)

Hungry Creek

Deep Creek

to
Posy
Lake
Campground
(1.0 mile)

T h e   B o x

Pine Creek

Death Hollow

11.1 miles

4.3 miles

Lost Creek

Bullberry Hollow

Buck Hollow

4.5 miles

Λ (8,018 ft)

Lower Box
Trailhead
(6,440 ft)

N

0   0.5   1.0 mile

to Escalante (8 miles)

The Box was ultimately included as part of the 25,750-acre Box-Death Hollow Wilderness Area, but only after the exclusion of the long, narrow plateau that separates the Box and Death Hollow. Now the map of the Box-Death Hollow Wilderness Area looks like a mitten,

see color photo, page 193

with Pine Creek running down the thumb. Cattle fences have been built to keep cows out of the Box, but the numerous cow pies in the canyon suggest that the effort hasn't been completely successful.

There is no trail from the road to the bottom of Pine Creek at the Upper Box access point. Just walk down the slope for a few hundred feet until you reach the creek, and then start following it downstream. There are bits and pieces of an unmaintained trail along the streambed, but for the most part you are on your own. Don't hesitate to walk across the stream if the terrain looks a little flatter on the other side, and don't work too hard at trying to keep your feet dry. You will be fording the creek many times before this hike is finished, so you might as will plunge in now and let your feet get used to the cold water.

The first few miles of the Box are particularly scenic, with steep cliffs coming down to the water's edge first on one side and then on the other. The banks of the creek are lined with spruce and occasionally Douglas fir. Fortunately no rock climbing is necessary, as there is always a passable route on at least one side of the canyon. Also, the water is seldom more that shin-deep at the crossing points.

After about 3.0 miles the canyon widens slightly and the rim becomes much higher. After 4.3 miles you will meet Deep Creek, a tiny creek flowing in from the west. At this point you have lost about 730 feet of elevation, and you are a little less than half way through the hike. The canyon rim is about a thousand feet above you. Below the Deep Creek confluence the forest gradually turns from spruce and Douglas fir to ponderosa pine, and the trail also gradually improves. You are more apt to encounter other hikers here—picnickers who have entered the Box from the lower trailhead. As the canyon widens the trail also becomes more and more sandy, the result of erosion on the sandstone cliffs that surround the Box.

Finally, 4.5 miles below Deep Creek, Pine Creek makes a sudden, dramatic exit through a slot in the cliffs out of the Box and onto Lost Creek Flat, where your shuttle car or bicycle is parked. Hell's Backbone Road is another 0.3 mile from the end of the trail.

The Pine Creek Box

Calf Creek

☆ ☆ ☆ ☆ ☆   **Grand Staircase - Escalante National Monument**
day hike

Distance:	5.4 miles (round trip)
Walking time:	3 hours
Elevations:	170 ft. gain/loss Calf Creek Trailhead (start): 5,340 ft. Lower Calf Creek Falls: 5,510 ft.
Trail:	Popular, well maintained trail. A trail guide is usually available at the trailhead.
Season:	Spring, summer, fall, winter. The trail is very hot in the summer, with temperatures often exceeding 100 degrees F.
Vicinity:	Near Escalante and Boulder
Maps:	Calf Creek *(USGS)* Canyons of the Escalante *(Trails Illustrated, #710)*
Information:	http://www.utahtrails.com/calfcreek.html *(Utah Trails)* http://www.ut.blm.gov/monument/ *(Grand Staircase-Escalante)* phone: (435) 826-5499 *(Escalante Interagency Visitor Center)*

Drive east from Escalante towards Boulder on Highway 12 for 16.3 miles to the Calf Creek Campground. The trailhead is near the back of the campground, 0.4 mile from the highway. (Note: there is a charge of $2.00/vehicle for day use of Calf Creek Recreation Area. The campground is a pleasant place to spend the night, but if that is your plan you had better arrive early. It is very popular.)

The Calf Creek Trail is the highlight of Calf Creek Recreation Area, a delightful desert oasis maintained by the Bureau of Land Management. The canyon is a haven for birds, beaver, and other wildlife, and it was also once inhabited by the Fremont and Anasazi Indians. Take a booklet with you from the trailhead to help you spot some of the Indian pictographs and two granaries that were constructed by the Indians some 800-1000 years ago. Also, be sure to take a swimming suit with you for use in the pool at the bottom of Lower Calf Creek Falls.

The Calf Creek Trail winds along the west side of Calf Creek, a small desert stream surrounded by vertical walls of white and pink Navajo Sandstone. Not surprisingly, much of the trail is covered with loose sand. As the cliffs erode, the ancient beds of sand from which the Navajo Sandstone was originally made are slowly being returned to the

CALF CREEK

Boulder Creek

Dry Hollow

∧ (5,863 ft)

Highway 12

Calf Creek
2.7 miles

to Boulder
(8 miles)

Calf Creek
Trailhead
(start)
(5,340 ft)

Calf Creek
Campground

to
Escalante
(16 miles)

∧
(5,929 ft)

Lower
Upper Calf
Calf Creek
Creek Falls
Falls
(2.5 miles)

∧
(6,227 ft)

see map, page 330

0   0.5   1.0 mile

Calf Creek

canyon floor. The dominant trees in the canyon are pinion and juniper, although cottonwoods and box elders can also be found along the stream. Many of the latter species show damage from beaver; you can scarcely walk a hundred yards along the stream without seeing a beaver dam.

About 0.9 mile from the trailhead a small stone structure can be seen near the top of the cliffs across the river. This is the remains of a granary built by the Fremont or Anasazi Indians around 1100 A.D. to store the grain they grew on the canyon floor. Another half mile upstream, closer to the canyon floor, the Fremont Indians painted three large ceremonial human figures in red. The coloring of these pictographs is remarkably well preserved despite centuries of exposure to the sun and rain. Still more pictographs and another granary are visible in a small side canyon west of the creek about 1.6 miles from the trailhead.

Finally, after 2.7 miles, Calf Creek Canyon abruptly dead ends against a 130-foot-high vertical wall of Navajo Sandstone, making it obvious that the end of the hike has been reached. Here

see color photo, page 193

the creek emanates from the base of the Lower Calf Creek Waterfall. The setting is beautiful, with a sandy shore, large shade trees, and a clear pool below the fall. Most hikers take an hour out for a swim here before heading back.

Upper Calf Creek Falls

Yes, there is also an Upper Calf Creek Falls, though it is not nearly as attractive as the lower falls and the hike to it not as interesting. Nevertheless, if you still have time and energy left after your hike to the lower falls you may want to continue your exploration by hiking to the upper falls.

To reach Upper Calf Creek Falls you must return to Highway 12 and check your odometer at the entrance to Calf Creek Campground. From that point, drive north towards Boulder for 6.0 miles where you will see a rocky dirt road taking off on the left. Follow this road for a short distance to a wide, sandy clearing on the edge of the rim. The trail to Upper Calf Creek Falls drops off the rim near a large pinyon pine tree on the edge of the clearing. It is not a developed trail, but the BLM has placed rock cairns along the route to guide you to the falls. The upper falls are only about one mile from the highway, but they are 600 feet lower in elevation and the hike out can be tiring on a hot day.

Calf Creek Trail

Escalante River

☆ ☆ ☆ ☆

Grand Staircase - Escalante National Monument
shuttle car or bicycle required
overnight hike

Distance: 14.3 miles
(plus 14.4 miles by car or bicycle)

Walking time: day 1: 4 hours
day 2: 3³/₄ hours

Elevations: 530 ft. loss
Escalante Town Trailhead (start): 5,730 ft.
Death Hollow: 5,380 ft.
Escalante River Trailhead: 5,200 ft.

Trail: The route follows along the shore of the Escalante River. There is a sandy trail most of the way, but often it is easier to walk in the gravel filled streambed so be sure to wear wettable shoes. The water is seldom more than ankle deep.

Season: Spring, summer, fall, winter. The best seasons for this hike are spring and fall. Escalante Canyon is very hot in the summertime, but you can always count on the availability of water.

Vicinity: Near the town of Escalante

Maps: Escalante, Calf Creek *(USGS)*
Canyons of the Escalante *(Trails Illustrated, #710)*

Information: http://www.utahtrails.com/escalante.html *(Utah Trails)*
http://www.ut.blm.gov/monument/ *(Grand Staircase-Escalante)*
phone: (435) 826-5499 *(Escalante Interagency Visitor Center)*

Drive east on Highway 12 from the center of Escalante Town for 1.2 miles until you see a small cemetery on your left. Turn off the highway here and continue past the cemetery on a small dirt road that leads to the city dump. After 0.4 mile you will come to a fork in the road where you must turn left for the final 0.5 mile to the Escalante Town Trailhead. Be sure to sign in at the trail register and obtain a free backcountry permit before you start.

Before beginning the hike you will need to place a shuttle car or bicycle at the Escalante River Trailhead where the hike ends. To get there drive east towards Boulder on Highway 12 for 13.5 miles past the cemetery to the point where Highway 12 crosses the Escalante River (14.7 miles from Escalante Town, or 12.7 miles from Boulder). On the north end of the bridge you will see a turnout on the left that leads to the trailhead and parking area.

Among Utah's serious hikers, the 85-mile-long Escalante River is well known. The small desert river and its dozens of side canyons contain some of the wildest, most scenic desert wilderness in the United States. It is a region of redrock canyons, sandstone arches, and Anasazi Indian ruins. The Escalante badlands contain hidden natural treasures guaranteed to give pause to even the most unenthusiastic of hikers. Sadly, none of the BLM managed Escalante drainage has yet been give the protection of a designated wilderness area, but in 1996 it was included in President Clinton's new Grand Staircase-Escalante National Monument.

Although the Escalante drains over 200 square miles of the Colorado Plateau, it is so remote that its existence wasn't even known until the middle of the last century. In 1866 it became the last major river to be discovered in the American West. It was named six years later in honor of the early Spanish explorer Silvestre Valez de Escalante who visited Utah in 1776.

There are a number of hikes in the area that touch upon parts of the Escalante River, but the 14-mile section of the river described here is the most accessible. It is also a particularly interesting section, with fine examples of the sorts of things that make the Escalante drainage so interesting: petroglyphs, Anasazi ruins, natural arches, and slickrock pools.

Day 1 (7.3 miles)

From the trailhead near Escalante Town the trail winds down a small sandy hill for about 0.2 mile before intersecting the Escalante River. The trail reaches the river very close to its source, and at this point the Escalante is little more than a muddy wash, lined with unsightly tamarisk trees and old tires that have washed down from the city dump. But don't despair. Within a mile the canyon becomes more pristine.

Escalante River

Soon after the river enters Escalante Canyon, near the junction with Pine Creek, you will pass a gauging station used for measuring the water flow. From that point the trail often splits, giving you a choice of either side of the river to walk on. Just pick the easiest side, and don't bother trying to keep your feet dry. It is futile.

If you are interested in Indian artifacts try to stay on the north side of the river as much as possible, because that is the side the prehistoric Indians along the Escalante preferred. The winter sun shines more directly on the north side of the canyon; hence it has less snow during the winter months. There are at least three small panels of prehistoric rock art within 2.2 miles of the gauging station. They are all situated on the north side of the canyon at the base of the cliffs in areas where the canyon runs due east and west. The first two sites are petroglyphs,

see map, page 325

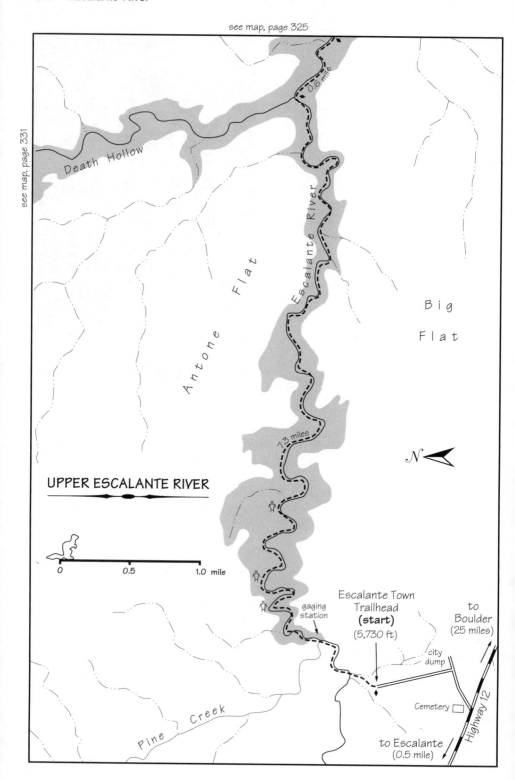

see map, page 331

Death Hollow

Escalante River

Antone Flat

Big Flat

0.6 mile

7.3 miles

N

UPPER ESCALANTE RIVER

0   0.5   1.0 mile

gaging station

Escalante Town
Trailhead
(start)
(5,730 ft)

to
Boulder
(25 miles)

city
dump

Cemetery

Highway 12

Pine Creek

to Escalante
(0.5 mile)

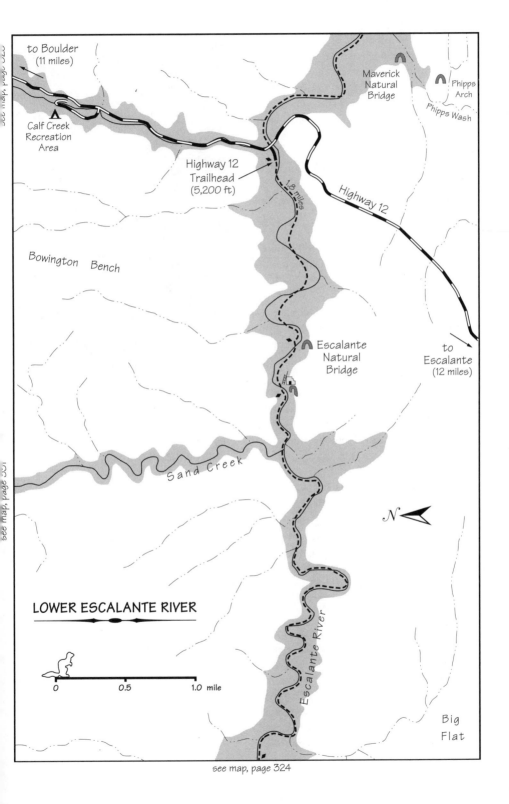

to Boulder
(11 miles)

Calf Creek
Recreation
Area

Maverick
Natural
Bridge

Phipps
Arch

Phipps Wash

Highway 12
Trailhead
(5,200 ft)

1.8 miles

Highway 12

Bowington   Bench

Escalante
Natural
Bridge

to
Escalante
(12 miles)

Sand Creek

N

LOWER ESCALANTE RIVER

Escalante River

0   0.5   1.0 mile

Big
Flat

see map, page 324

and the third is a badly damaged panel of pictographs in the back of a large alcove just above the water line.

The scenery gets better and better the farther downstream you walk. There are many good camp sites along the way, but if you plan to spend only one night in the canyon you should try to camp near the junction of Death Hollow. This side canyon is exceptionally pretty and, if time permits, you should try to spend at least a few hours exploring it before continuing down the Escalante.

Death Hollow is a 23-mile-long drainage that begins near the Hells Backbone Road between Escalante Town and Boulder. The dry upper reaches of the Hollow lie within the boundaries of Dixie National Forest and are part of the Box-Death Hollow Wilderness Area. The oasis-like Lower part of Death Hollow, however, lies within the jurisdiction of the Bureau of Land Management, and is not part of the designated wilderness area. Hopefully this situation will change in the future, but for now the most exquisite part of Death Hollow, along with the rest of the Escalante Basin, remains relatively unprotected.

Lower Death Hollow is best explored without a backpack. For the first mile the fast flowing stream rushes down the scenic canyon between patches of wild flowers and, unfortunately, poison ivy. It is best to wear long pants when walking through the foliage, or wade in the center of the streambed. After about a mile and a half the canyon begins to narrow noticeably, and you will encounter a series of pools and water slides. The best pools for swimming are about two miles upstream. The setting is idyllic: crystal-clear slickrock swimming holes, surrounded by red sandstone cliffs decorated with green foliage and yellow wildflowers. You might want to ex-

see color photos, pages 194, 195

Death Hollow

tend your hike by a day just to enjoy the attributes of the ill-named canyon.

Day 2 (7.0 miles)

From the mouth of Death Hollow, the Escalante River flows eastward for another 4.0 miles before coming to the junction of Sand Creek, another possible side trip though not quite of the same caliber as Death Hollow. Beyond that, another 0.4 miles will bring you to the first of two natural arches along this stretch of the Escalante. It is situated high on the top of the canyon wall, on the right side of the canyon. Impressive as this arch is, however, an even more thrilling sight is an Anasazi Indian ruin that lies just below and east of it. The cliff dwelling is in the back of a large alcove about 150 feet above the canyon floor.

This ruin is extremely unusual because

it lies on the south wall of the canyon and faces almost directly north. No winter sun ever shines into this alcove, yet 700 years ago it was home to a large family of Anasazis. It is quite obvious that they chose this site specifically because of its proximity to the stone arch above it. The arch must have had powerful magic for these Indians, and I can imagine that living below it must have filled them with an immense sense of well being. The location was important enough for them to forego all of the conventional wisdom of the day by living on the coldest side of the canyon.

While you are looking at the ruin notice the long jagged line that was painted on the cliff just above the largest dwelling in the alcove. One can only guess what the line represented or what its purpose was, but to me it appears to be some kind of spiritual shield separating the Indian home from the arch above. As if the arch's magic was so strong it was necessary to partially deflect it from the nearby house.

The next natural arch is located on the same side of the canyon, only 0.4 mile downstream from the first one. There are no Indian ruins near this arch and, though impressive, it is in near perpetual shade and difficult to photograph. It does have one feature, however, that makes it quite interesting. The 200-foot-high span stands directly in front of a 100-foot-deep alcove in the cliff, like the grand entrance to a giant ballroom. A small trail leads through the portal and circles around the ballroom, providing an opportunity to view the sandstone arch from a different perspective. There are also a few old cowboyglyphs carved into the walls of the room, one of which is dated 1917.

Beyond the last natural arch Escalante

Canyon widens considerably as the trail winds over the last 1.8 miles to the trailhead at Highway 12. This part of the canyon is known as Phipps Death Hollow after a tragedy that occurred here in 1878. According to local folklore two cowboys named John Boynton and Washington Phipps were partners in a ranching operation along this stretch of the Escalante when Boynton shot and killed Phipps during an argument over a woman. So distraught was Boynton over what he had done that he saddled up and rode his horse to Escalante to give himself up. The authorities in Escalante gave him ten dollars and told him to report to the county sheriff in Parowan, but he must have had second thoughts along the way because he was never seen again.

Natural Arch in Escalante Canyon

Death Hollow

☆ ☆ ☆ ☆ ☆

Grand Staircase - Escalante National Monument
shuttle car required
3-day hike

Distance: 20.4 miles
(plus 10.6 miles by car)

Walking time: day 1: 3 hours
day 2: 5 hours
day 3: 3³/₄ hours

Elevations: 1,560 ft. loss
Boulder Mail Trail parking (start):   6,760 ft.
Boulder Mail Trailhead: 6,640 ft.
Death Hollow - Escalante junction: 5,380 ft.
Escalante River Trailhead: 5,200 ft.

Trail: There is no reliable trail for most of this hike, however the route is very easy to follow. You will be walking through water much of the time, so wear wettable shoes. It may me necessary to float your backpack across a pool of water in one or two places, so you should also carry an air mattress and a watertight river bag to keep your gear dry. Also, you may occasionally have to walk through thick undergrowth, so wear long pants.

Season: Summer through fall. You will be spending a great deal of time in the water on this hike, so it should be done in warm weather. The best time is from mid-June through October. Flash floods are possible, especially at the end of summer, so stay out of the canyon if it looks like rain. There is also a great deal of water in Death Hollow during the spring runoff from mid-May to mid-June. It is still possible to go through the canyon at this time, but you will have to do some swimming to get past the obstacles.

Vicinity: Near Boulder and Escalante

Maps: Boulder Town, Calf Creek, Escalante *(USGS)*
Canyons of the Escalante *(Trails Illustrated, #710)*

Information: http://www.utahtrails.com/deathhollow.html *(Utah Trails)*
http://www.ut.blm.gov/monument/ *(Grand Staircase-Escalante)*
phone: (435) 826-5499 *(Escalante Interagency Visitor Center)*

Drive south of Boulder on Highway 12 for 3.0 miles to the Hell's Backbone Road. (If you are starting in Escalante drive east on Highway 12 for 24.8 miles.) Turn onto Hells Backbone Road and continue for another 0.2 mile, where you will see a small, unmarked road on the left leading to the Boulder Airport. Turn south here. After 0.4 miles you will arrive at the airport; continue on across the runway and in another 0.1 mile you will see the parking area for the Boulder Mail Trailhead on your left. The actual trailhead where the hike begins is another 1.0 mile down the road. Be sure to sign in at the trail register and obtain a free backcountry permit before you start.

The hike ends at the Escalante River Trailhead, which is on Highway 12 about half way between Boulder and Escalante. From Hells Backbone Road you must drive south on Highway 12 for 10.0 miles to the bridge that crosses the Escalante River. The Escalante River Trailhead and parking area is just on the north side of the bridge.

This is one of those special hikes that has something for almost everyone. The first part of the route follows the old Boulder Mail Trail, a historical trail characterized by wide vistas of slickrock desert with stunning views into Sand Creek Canyon and Death Hollow. The second part of the trail descends through the lower half of Death Hollow, a deep, wild, and watery canyon with scenery that is often spectacular. Finally, the trail leaves Death Hollow to follow a more serene section of the Escalante River, past two natural arches and an Anasazi cliff dwelling, to the trailhead near Calf Creek.

The first and last sections of the hike are easy, and can be done at almost anytime of the year. In Death Hollow, however, you will be walking in the streambed much of the time; consequently the difficulty of the hike is strongly dependent on how much water is present. Most of the year the water is never more than knee deep, but in some months hikers may have to swim to get across some of the pools. To be safe you should carry a river bag and an air mattress, just in case you have to float your pack across an unexpected pool of water. The worst time to hike through Death Hollow is during the spring runoff from mid-May through mid-June, when the creek is often flowing at 3-4 times its normal volume. There can also be problems in August, the month that receives the most rain. Never venture into the canyon if it looks like rain, since there is an ever-present danger of flash floods. But the flow rate usually drops off quickly, so if it has not rained for a few days you can generally expect good conditions.

Day 1 (5.6 miles)

After leaving the road the trail winds

Death Hollow

across the McGath Point Bench in a south-westerly direction. The vegetation is prima-rily pinion pine and juniper, although there is not enough soil to support much of a for-est. Most of the route is over slickrock, and you must depend on cairns to show you the way. Initially the grade is level, but soon the trail starts downward as it begins its long descent into the Sand Creek drainage. The creek is located 1.8 miles from the trailhead.

Sand Creek is a small perennial stream that runs through the bottom of a shallow,

see map, page 320

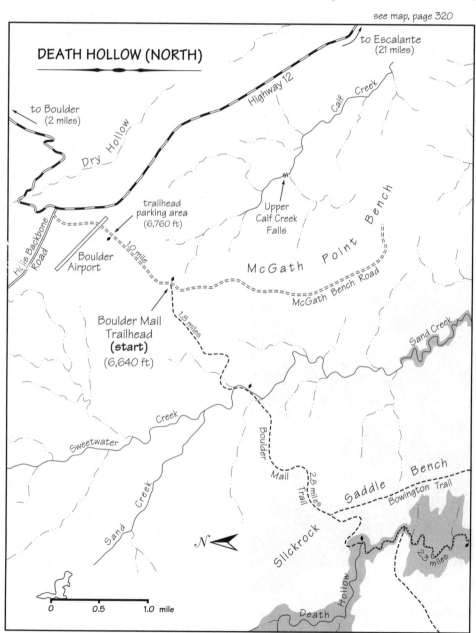

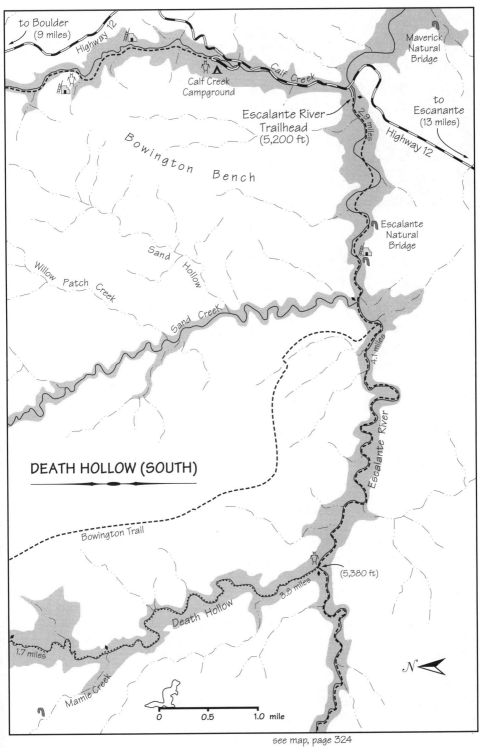

to Boulder
(9 miles)

Highway 12

Maverick
Natural
Bridge

Calf Creek

Calf Creek
Campground

Escalante River
Trailhead
(5,200 ft)

to
Escanante
(13 miles)

2.9 miles

Highway 12

Escalante
Natural
Bridge

Bowington   Bench

Sand   Hollow

Willow   Patch   Creek

Sand   Creek

Escalante River

4.1 miles

DEATH HOLLOW (SOUTH)

Bowington Trail

(5,380 ft)

3.8 miles

Death Hollow

1.7 miles

Mamie Creek

N

0   0.5   1.0   mile

see map, page 324

Boulder Mail Trail, above Death Hollow

slickrock canyon. The trail crosses the creek soon after reaching it, and then follows its west side for 0.2 mile before climbing back to the top of the plateau. If you got off to a late start there are several good places to camp along the creek.

After climbing out of Sand Creek Canyon the path begins a long meander over the top of Slickrock Saddle Bench. The Mail Trail was once an important communications link between the towns of Boulder and Escalante, and you can still see the remains of an old telegraph line that ran beside the trail linking the two towns. The line was built by the U.S. Forest Service in 1910, and it was still in use as recently as 1955. It consisted of a single galvanized iron wire, strung across the desert on poles and live trees.

2.5 miles after leaving Sand Creek you will come to a fork where the Bowington Trail departs on the left. This trail is occa-

sionally used as an alternative route to the Escalante River for pack animals. Bear to the right at the fork, and within a few minutes you will see the ground open up in front of you as Death Hollow comes into view. Unlike the more mundane Sand Creek Canyon, Death Hollow forms a deep gorge in the slickrock plateau and the view from the top is dramatic.

Just before you reach the canyon rim the trail turns sharply to the right and then begins its descent. Before going down, however, you should drop your pack and spend ten minutes enjoying the view from above. If you leave the trail just before it turns to start down (near a large ponderosa pine tree) and walk straight ahead for a hundred yards you will come to an overlook point where there is an especially fine view into Death Hollow.

see color photos, pages 194, 195

The route into Death Hollow follows a steep slickrock trail with about 640 feet of elevation loss. This section of the old Mail Trail must have been especially precarious for pack animals. It is said that the canyon received its name around the turn of the century when a mule stumbled and fell into the gorge. Near the bottom the path passes by a large alcove that is a favorite campsite for backpackers. The alcove is located near the right side of the trail, about 100 feet above the canyon bottom. There is a large flat area in the back of the recess, big enough to accommodate a small group of campers, and the site is well sheltered from the weather. If you prefer to be near the water there are also several nice sites on the canyon floor, or if you decide walk further downstream you will have no trouble finding good campsites along the entire length of Death Hollow.

Day 2 (7.8 miles)

The 7.8 miles from the Boulder Mail

Trail through Death Hollow to the Escalante River is the most exciting part of this hike. The hiker-made trail frequently plunges in and out of the streambed, dodging brush and boulders as it searches in vain for an easy way down the canyon. Occasionally you will encounter deep pools on the canyon floor, but there is usually an easy way around them. Under normal conditions you shouldn't have to cross any pools that are more than knee deep.

I have been in Death Hollow twice, and neither time did deep water present a serious obstacle to my progress. But I must add that conditions change from year to year in the canyon, and it is impossible to predict what one might encounter. Every few years a flash flood will roar down the gorge, washing all of the sand and rock from the potholes and turning shallow wading pools into deep swimming holes. So be prepared.

Death Hollow

Death Hollow is not a place you would want to be during a flash flood, so always check the weather before entering the canyon and if it looks like rain stay out. Flash floods are not particularly common, but there is ample evidence within the canyon to verify their existence (huge logs left stranded high above the streambed, flotsam stuck on the branches of trees). Most of the floods occur from mid-August to mid-September when there are more thunderstorms, so if you are hiking during these months be especially careful. Also, try to avoid Death Hollow during the spring runoff. If you are hiking between mid-May and mid-June I can almost guarantee that you will have problems with deep water.

There is one more hazard in Death Hollow that should be mentioned: poison ivy. Poison Ivy is a bright green, usually shrubby plant that grows 2-3 feet high. Its leaves

Death Hollow

always grow at the ends of the stems in groups of three, and its pea-sized berries are yellowish white in color. For some reason there is a great abundance of poison ivy growing in the lower reaches of the canyon so be careful not to walk through it.

About twenty minutes after reaching the bottom Death Hollow the trail passes by a cairn on the right that marks the exit point of the Boulder Mail Trail. The old telegraph line crosses the canyon a short distance upstream. You may have also noticed an abundance of black volcanic boulders that have washed down the canyon from an old eruption to the north. The insoluble basaltic boulders are not easily eroded by the stream and they just keep moving down the canyon with each new flash flood. They are present in all the canyons of the Escalante drainage.

After 3.8 miles and countless stream crossings the trail passes by the mouth of Mamie Creek, roughly the halfway point of the hike. Below Mamie the canyon narrows in several places to a width of only 30 feet or less. The sandy bottom of the streambed is the easiest place to walk, but be on the lookout for quicksand. Quicksand most commonly occurs is places where the water is flowing very slowly or not at all, such as on the downstream side of a large boulder or other obstruction. It is not life threatening, but it can cause you to stumble and fall.

About halfway between Mamie Creek junction and the Escalante River the canyon walls narrow around a fast flowing waterslide on the canyon floor. Sliding down the smooth sandstone chute can be a lot of fun, but getting a backpack around it presents a problem. It is usually possible to get past the waterslide by crawling along a narrow shelf at the edge of the water, but this is hard to do with a pack and if you slip you will slide in. Alternatively, you can carry your pack around the chute on a ledge above the creek and lower it back down with a short piece of rope. Or, if all else fails you can always just go down the waterslide with your gear in a river bag and hope that it doesn't get soaking wet!

Finally, 1.9 miles below the waterslide, the trail reaches the Escalante River. There is a good place to camp in the grove of cottonwood trees on the opposite side of the Escalante, or if you prefer you can camp on the sandbar near the confluence. But before it gets dark you should take some time to examine the base of the cliff on the northeast side of the confluence. This area appears to have been occupied by the Anasazi in prehistoric times. The base of the cliff contains many badly eroded petroglyphs, including an easily recognizable impression of two desert bighorn sheep. I also saw a broken grinding stone while I was there.

Escalante River

Day 3 (7.0 miles)

The Escalante River is less wild than Death Hollow, and the 7.0-mile walk to the Boulder Highway is much more serene. Nevertheless, the Escalante has its own special beauty. Escalante Canyon is more open, with a wide, flat bottom, closed in on both sides by familiar walls of Navajo Sandstone. For 50 feet on either side of the river the ground is covered with dense thickets of tamarisk, willow, and cottonwood trees. But away from the river there are wide avenues of sagebrush covered desert. The trail avoids the river most of the time, but when the canyon narrows and the trail is forced back into the trees it is often much easier to walk right in the streambed.

4.8 miles below Death Hollow the trail passes the first major landmark along this section of the Escalante River: Escalante Natural Arch. The arch sits high on the south rim of the canyon, and is completely inaccessible from the bottom. Interestingly, there is an Anasazi cliff dwelling in an alcove just below the east side of the arch. The site faces north and would have been a very uncomfortable place to stay in the winter; nevertheless it looks as though the family that occupied the alcove was very well established. 700 years ago there were many Indians living along the Escalante. With its wide flat bottom and its reliable water supply the canyon must have been an ideal place for them to grow corn. Although there are many petroglyph sites along the river, the ruin near Escalante Arch is one of the few remaining Anasazi dwellings. Most of the inhabitants must have lived in more temporary structures on the canyon floor.

The main trail continues eastward from the Escalante Arch along the north side of the river, but I suggest you pick up a lessor used trail near the Anasazi ruin on the south side of the river. This trail meets the river again 0.4 miles further downstream at the Escalante Natural Bridge, an even more impressive arch. The Natural Bridge lies in front a huge 200-foot diameter alcove that has been etched into the sandstone walls by a seep at the base of the sandstone cliff. The 15-foot-thick bridge is 200 feet high and spans across the entire width of the alcove.

East of the Escalante Natural Bridge the canyon widens out as the river makes three more long meanders before reaching Calf Creek and the Boulder Highway. The trail is well defined in this area, as many day hikers walk in from the highway to see the Escalante Natural Bridge. You should reach the Escalante River Trailhead and the end of the hike after about 45 minutes.

Escalante Natural Bridge

Coyote Gulch

☆ ☆ ☆ ☆ ☆

Glen Canyon National Recreation Area
shuttle car or bicycle useful
overnight hike

Distance: 11.8 miles
(plus 2.6 miles by car, bicycle, or foot)

Walking time: day 1: 4 hours
day 2: 4 hours

Elevations: 1,015 ft. loss, 1,110 ft. gain
Forty Mile Ridge Trailhead (start): 4,675 ft.
Jacob Hamblin Arch Trailhead: 4,770 ft.
Escalante River: 3,660 ft.

Trail: The most challenging part of this hike is the climb out of Coyote Gulch near Jacob Hamblin Arch. The climb involves scrambling up a 100-foot pitch of slickrock that ascends from the canyon floor at an angle close to 45 degrees. A 120-foot length of rope is useful here for raising backpacks. A compass is also useful for the last part of the hike, which involves a 2-mile cross-country walk from the canyon rim back to Jacob Hamblin Trailhead. Sneakers or other wettable shoes are the most practical footwear inside the canyon, as you will frequently be required to cross the stream bed.

Season: Spring, summer, fall, winter. This area is very hot in the summertime and receives some snow in the winter. The best seasons for the hike are spring and fall.

Vicinity: Near the town of Escalante

Maps: King Mesa, Stevens Canyon South *(USGS)*
Canyons of the Escalante *(Trails Illustrated, #710)*

Information: http://www.utahtrails.com/coyote.html *(Utah Trails)*
http://www.nps.gov/glca/ *(Glen Canyon Nat. Recreation Area)*
phone: (435) 826-5499 *(Escalante Interagency Visitor Center)*

Drive east of Escalante on Highway 12 for 5 miles until you come to the Hole in the Rock Road. Turn right here and drive south on this gravel road for 36.2 miles until you reach a well marked road on the left leading to Forty Mile Ridge (2.2 miles beyond Hurricane Wash). Turn left onto the Forty Mile Ridge Road and continue for 4.3 miles, where you will see another short road to a *small corral and water tank on the left. This is where the hike will end, and your shuttle car or bicycle should be left in the parking area near the corral. Continuing down the Forty Mile*

Ridge Road for another 2.6 miles will bring you to Forty Mile Ridge Trailhead where the hike begins. Be sure to sign the trail register before you start and obtain a free backcountry permit.

The Escalante River and its tributaries provide many of the most interesting hikes into the desert canyonlands of Southern Utah. Unfortunately the last 30 miles of the Escalante was flooded by Lake Powell after the construction of the Glen Canyon Dam in 1964, but enough attractions still remain to make the Escalante drainage a very special place for outdoor enthusiasts. Coyote Gulch, a side canyon of the lower Escalante, is one of the most popular hikes in the vicinity. With its impressive natural bridge, two arches, and Anasazi artifacts, it is a particularly good place to sample the wonders of the Escalante drainage.

There are at least five ways to get in and out of Coyote Gulch; hence a number of variations of this hike are possible. Most people begin and end their hike at either Hurricane Wash Trailhead or Red Well Trailhead.

The hike down Coyote Gulch to the Escalante River and back from either one of these trailheads makes a very pleasant, if somewhat long, backpacking trip for the whole family. If you are the adventurous type, however, you will probably prefer the route described here. It does require a modicum of rock climbing ability, so if that makes you uncomfortable I suggest you end your hike at Hurricane Wash Trailhead rather than Jacob Hamblin Arch Trailhead.

Day 1 (6.8 miles)

The Forty Mile Ridge Trailhead is located on the top of a small knoll in the middle of a large sandy mesa. From there a broad, well-used trail leads across the desert in a northwesterly direction towards the Escalante River. For the first half mile the sandy trail is easy to follow, but soon the

Lower Coyote Gulch

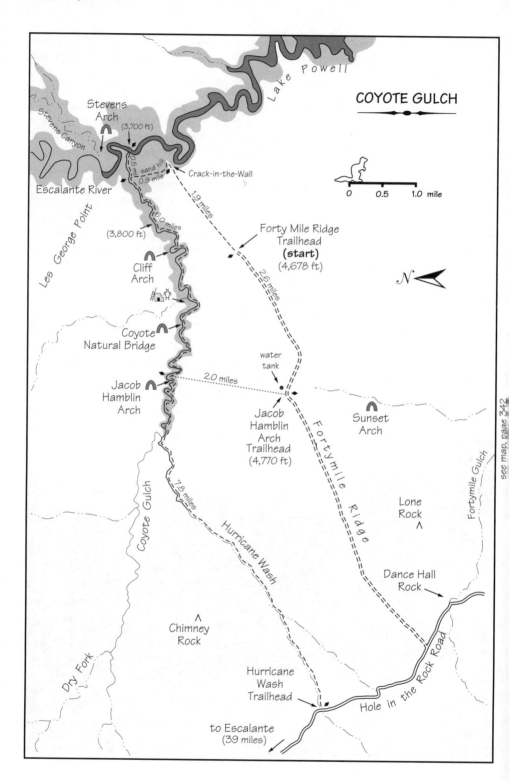

Lake Powell

Stevens Arch (3,700 ft)

Stevens Canyon

Escalante River

Les George Point

Crack-in-the-Wall

sand hill
0.9 mile

1.9 miles

(3,800 ft)

6.0 miles

Cliff Arch

Forty Mile Ridge Trailhead **(start)** (4,678 ft)

2.6 miles

N

COYOTE GULCH

0   0.5   1.0 mile

Coyote Natural Bridge

water tank

2.0 miles

Jacob Hamblin Arch

Jacob Hamblin Arch Trailhead (4,770 ft)

Sunset Arch

Fortymile Ridge

Lone Rock

Fortymile Gulch

see map, page 342

Coyote Gulch

7.8 miles

Hurricane Wash

Dance Hall Rock

Dry Fork

Chimney Rock

Hurricane Wash Trailhead

Hole in the Rock Road

to Escalante (39 miles)

sand is gone and you will find yourself walking on slickrock. There are no footprints, of course, on the slickrock, so you will be following rock cairns until you reach the canyon rim. There are occasionally spaces of several hundred feet between cairns, but the route to the rim of Escalante Canyon is nearly a straight line, so you shouldn't have any difficulty finding the way. Nevertheless, pay close attention to the cairns. If you don't arrive at precisely the right point on the canyon rim you won't be able to find your way down the Navajo Sandstone.

Your access into Escalante Canyon is through a narrow crack in a boulder just below the last cairn on the Forty Mile Ridge Trail. The crack is about 18 inches wide and fifty feet long. If you walk sideways down through this crack you will emerge at the top of an enormous pile of sand that extends nearly all the way from Coyote Gulch to the top of the Navajo Sandstone. Look down to the west and you can see the confluence of Coyote Gulch and the Escalante River about 0.6 mile away. The trail is obvious and easy to follow now. It winds downward over the sand for nearly a mile until it intersects Coyote Gulch, about a half mile west of the Escalante. As you descend a huge natural arch will soon come into view above the confluence. This is Stevens Arch.

After you reach the bottom of Coyote Gulch you will probably want to drop your backpack and take a side trip to see the Escalante River. It is only a 15-minute walk down the canyon. If you have the time and the inclination for more exploring it is also usually possible to wade or walk along the banks of the Escalante. The water is seldom more than two feet deep (although if the level of Lake Powell is higher than normal the water here may be much deeper). Five hundred yards upstream from the Coyote Gulch confluence there is another fine view of Stevens Arch. The mouth of Stevens Canyon is 1.4 miles above Coyote Gulch.

Stevens Arch

Continuing up Coyote Gulch you will pass two or three small waterfalls, and then as the streambed enters the Kayenta Formation the valley becomes wider and ascends more gently. Occasionally the trail climbs out of the streambed to circumvent a waterfall, but it never

see color photos, pages 195, 196

strays far up the side. After about an hour you will see Cliff Arch coming into view high on the north side of the canyon. As the name suggests, the arch juts straight out from the sandstone cliff, like a giant teacup handle. Slightly upstream from Cliff Arch is a gorgeous waterfall. The drop is only about fifteen feet, but the setting is magnificent.

From Cliff Arch to Jacob Hamblin Arch Coyote Gulch is at its best, with plenty of scenery and nice camp sites. This is about the halfway point in the hike, so you may want to start thinking about a camp site as you continue on.

Day 2 (5.0 miles)

Forty-five minutes or so after leaving Cliff Arch you should start watching for a particularly fine Anasazi pictograph panel on the north side of the canyon. It is located 1.6 miles beyond the Arch, about 100 feet above the trail near the bottom of the Navajo Sandstone. You will come to a small side canyon with a stream entering Coyote Gulch on the right just before you reach the site. Unfortunately, it is easier to spot the panel if you are walking in the opposite direction, so stop occasionally and look back. When you reach it you will see an obvious spur trail branching off to the right and climbing up to the panel. There is also a small Indian ruin near the pictographs. If you have sharp eyes you may see a few pottery shards and small corn cobs in the area. Please do not remove them, though. These treasures belong to the canyon, and are there for all to enjoy.

0.7 mile past the pictographs the trail passes under Coyote Natural Bridge, and 1.7 miles beyond that Jacob Hamblin Arch will come into view. Jacob Hamblin is an immense arch, cut through a fin of sandstone created by a meander in the streambed. It probably would not look so big were it on top of the mesa, but being confronted with this enormous geological sculpture in the narrow confines of the canyon makes one feel as insignificant as an ant. There are several nice camp sites near the arch, and a good spring about a hundred yards downstream on the north side of the canyon.

The route out of Coyote Gulch is also near Jacob Hamblin Arch. Walking downstream from the arch you will notice that the streambed makes a long, sweeping turn to the north as it curves around a sloping fin of sandstone that comes down from the south rim. The fin reaches the canyon floor about 150 yards below the arch, and from there it is possible to scramble up and out of the canyon. The difficult part of the climb lasts for only

100 feet, and if you can get up the first 20 feet you will have no difficulty with the rest. Look carefully at the stone face near the bottom and you will notice depressions in the stone which you can use for toe holds. You can thank the prehistoric Indians for these toe holds. They were chipped out of the stone at least a thousand years ago by canyon dwellers who used this same route in and out of the canyon. A hundred-foot length of rope will come in very handy at this point for pulling up backpacks and perhaps some of the less agile members of your party. If you don't feel comfortable with this route you can also exit the canyon through Hurricane Wash which crosses the road 7.8 miles further upcanyon.

Once you reach the rim of the canyon walk due south for two miles to intersect the road along Forty Mile Ridge. The trailhead where you left your shuttle car is on the top of a small knoll, and it should come into view after about a mile.

Anasazi pictographs, Coyote Gulch

Willow Gulch

☆ ☆ ☆   **Glen Canyon National Recreation Area**
                                                                  day hike

Distance:	7.2 miles (round trip)
Walking time:	4 hours
Elevations:	540 ft. loss/gain Willow Gulch Trailhead (start): 4,200 ft. Broken Bow Arch: 3,880 ft. Lake Powell: 3,660 ft.
Trail:	There is no trail for most of this hike, but the route is not difficult to follow. The portion of the hike below Broken Bow Arch is in a narrow canyon where there is a danger of flash floods, so don't venture beyond the arch if there is a chance of rain. Sneakers or other wettable shoes are the only practical footwear as you will frequently be walking in water.
Season:	Spring, summer, winter, fall. This area is very hot in the summertime and receives some snow in the winter. The best seasons for the hike are spring and fall.
Vicinity:	Near the town of Escalante
Maps:	Sooner Bench, Davis Gulch *(USGS)* Canyons of the Escalante *(Trails Illustrated, #710)*
Information:	http://www.utahtrails.com/willow.html *(Utah Trails)* http://www.nps.gov/glca/ *(Glen Canyon Nat. Recreation Area)* phone: (435) 826-5499 *(Escalante Interagency Visitor Center)*

Drive east of Escalante on Highway 12 for 5 miles until you come to the Hole in the Rock Road. Turn right onto this gravel road, check your odometer, and drive south. After 34.7 miles you will pass a sign marking Hurricane Wash, then Fortymile Ridge after 37.1 miles, Dancehall Rock after 37.8 miles, and Carcass Wash after 40.5 miles. When you reach Carcass Wash check your odometer again and continue south. In another 2.2 miles you will see an unmarked road on the left. Turn here and drive east for 1.4 miles to the end of the road, where you will see a sign and trail registration box marking the Willow Gulch Trailhead.

The attraction that draws most hikers to Willow Gulch is the magnificent Broken Bow Natural Arch. This improbable sand- stone formation rises boldly from a low pla- teau on the north side of the streambed, where it can be seen clearly from a distance

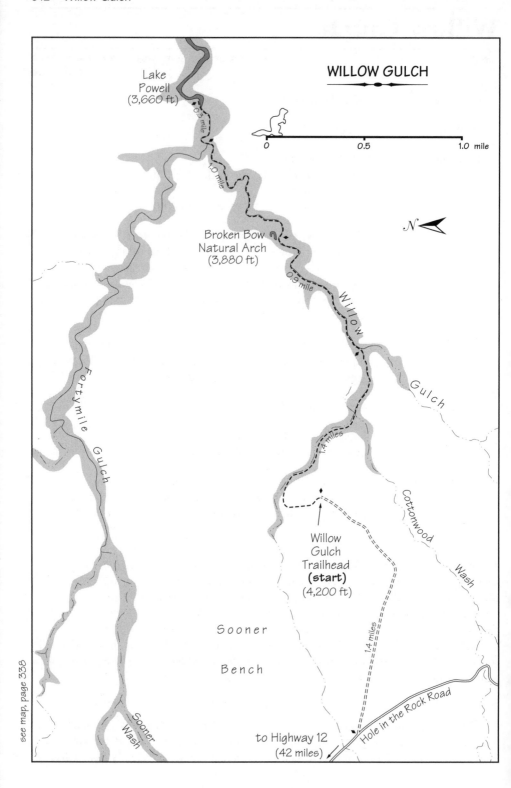

WILLOW GULCH

Lake
Powell
(3,660 ft)

0.3 mile

1.0 mile

Broken Bow
Natural Arch
(3,880 ft)

0.9 mile

Willow

Gulch

1.4 miles

Fortymile

Gulch

Cottonwood

Wash

Willow
Gulch
Trailhead
(start)
(4,200 ft)

1.4 miles

S o o n e r

B e n c h

Sooner

Wash

to Highway 12
(42 miles)

Hole in the Rock Road

N

0   0.5   1.0 mile

see map, page 338

of several hundred yards. The triangular-shaped opening easily reminds one of a bow bent nearly double, but actually that is not how the arch got its name. It was given its present name in 1930 after an Indian bow was found underneath it.

Broken Bow Arch is located only 2.3 miles from the Willow Gulch Trailhead. It is a relatively easy hike to the arch, and many hikers turn around at that point. But in my opinion the hike from the arch on down to Lake Powell is almost as interesting as the arch itself. The character of the canyon changes dramatically in a surprisingly short distance, going from an open desert environment to a constricted environment of slickrock waterslides and sandstone narrows in less than a mile. Finally the canyon opens out again at the end, where a small plateau offers a fine view of Lake Powell.

From the parking area it may be difficult to see exactly where the trail starts, but if you walk in a northerly direction from the registration box, straight down the sandy slope, you will soon begin to see the trail. Look for a large sandstone boulder that looks like an upside-down Mexican hat about 150 yards from the trailhead. The trail passes within a few feet of the boulder, and then turns east for the descent into a short side canyon that eventually leads to Willow gulch.

This unnamed side canyon is interesting in its own right. It is dry and dusty, with cliffs of Navajo Sandstone on both sides and a short stretch of nicely sculpted narrows in its center. The trail generally follows the right side of the canyon for 0.5 mile before dropping to the bottom of the streambed. Shortly after the trail reaches the bottom of the canyon you will come to an intersection where Cottonwood Wash enters from the right and another short canyon comes in from the left. You may be confused at this inter-

section, as there are three possible routes to follow. Do not turn right or left, but continue straight through the intersection into the sandy wash that continues on the other side.

At this point you are in the lower part of Cottonwood Wash. Except in very wet years the canyon is bone dry, but, interestingly, it contains signs of beaver. Notice the stunted cottonwood trees struggling to find water under the sand; many of them have been damaged by the wood-eating rodents. You can take that as an indication that there is water ahead, but it is surprising how far the beaver venture into the dry canyon.

0.4 miles after entering Cottonwood Wash the canyon widens again at the confluence with Willow Gulch. There are a great many willow trees in the area (hence the name), and you should finally see some water in the streambed. Turn left into Wil-

Broken Bow Natural Arch

low Gulch, but before continuing be sure to make a mental note of what the confluence looks like so you will know where to leave Willow on the return trip. What initially passed for a trail has long since disappeared by this time; consequently it is easy to miss the exit point from Willow Gulch when hiking out. If you do miss the turn you can still reach the Hole in the Rock Road by continuing up Willow Gulch. But if you do this you will have to walk another 2.9 miles along the road to get from the head of Willow Gulch back to the trailhead.

You will pass a half-dozen small beaver dams as you walk down Willow Gulch. The easiest place to walk is generally in the bottom of the streambed, but the dams occasionally make detours necessary. The beavers are seldom seen, but their handiwork is everywhere. It is probably the pressure of overpopulation that causes some of them to venture up Cottonwood Wash in search of another place to build a home. Finally, a half-hour after entering Willow Gulch, Broken Bow Natural Arch should come into view.

Broken Bow is surely one of the most beautiful arches in the Escalante drainage. It curves gracefully away from the wall of the canyon in a way that is reminiscent of Rainbow Natural Bridge, the world's largest natural arch. It is 170 feet high, with an opening 94 feet wide and 100 feet high. Its 70-foot-thick sides lend an element of strength to its grace, assuring us that it is going to be here for a long time to come. Best of all it lies in an easily accessible area, with no barriers on either side, so good photographic angles are easy to find. And its most photogenic side faces south, where it is in the sun for most of the day.

The Broken Bow Arch was sculpted from a fin of sandstone that once protruded into the canyon from the west wall. The stream has never actually flowed through the open-

Lower Willow Gulch

ing, and for this reason it is classified as an arch and not a natural bridge. It seems, however, that the fickle creek is intent on correcting this situation. As you walk through the streambed you can see the undercutting that has began as the water tries to straighten out its course and flow where Broken Bow now stands. The creek will probably someday be the instrument that destroys the arch.

The effects of water on sandstone become more and more apparent as you walk downstream from Broken Bow. The canyon becomes narrower, deeper, colder, and more devoid of plant life as you approach its mouth. In some | see color photo, page 197 | sections the sensation is one of walking through a 20-foot diameter pipe that has been scoured smooth by the grinding power of water and sand. In other places it feels like you are walking along a racetrack with galleries for the spectators in the huge alcoves above. There are numerous waterslides along the way where the persistent stream has cut graceful channels into the smooth sandstone. And in one part of the canyon the water has carved out a 200-foot-long section of narrows that is scarcely 4 feet wide

Thirty minutes below Broken Bow Arch you will come to Fortymile Gulch, another narrow, watery canyon that joins Willow Gulch from the north, and soon afterward the canyon ends at Lake Powell. When the lake is full the water may rise almost to the confluence with Fortymile Gulch, but by the end of summer the lake has usually receded 0.5 mile below the canyon junction. You will know you are getting close to the lake when you start seeing a thick layer of mud on the canyon floor. The mud contains the footprints of dozens of boaters who have landed and walked up Willow Gulch, but they seldom go more than a few hundred yards.

Fortymile Gulch

An interesting variation to this hike is to return to the Hole in the Rock Road through Fortymile Gulch and Carcass Wash. This route is somewhat more difficult than the walk through Willow Gulch, however, so some additional planning is needed. First, the walking distance is 3.9 miles longer, bringing the total hiking distance around the loop to 11.1 miles. Second, there is more water and more obstacles in Fortymile Gulch, so progress is slower. There are at least two places in the lower part of Fortymile where it is necessary to wade or swim through deep pools of water that block the way. For this reason the hike should only be done in warm weather, and if you are carrying a camera you should have some means of keeping it dry. Finally, the Carcass Wash Trailhead is 3.6 miles by road from the Willow Gulch Trailhead, so some kind of a shuttle is necessary to get back to the starting point.

Carcass Wash is only one of three possible exit routes from Fortymile Gulch to the Hole in the Rock Road, but it is, by far, the easiest route. If you try to exit through Sooner Wash you will find a canyon full of chock stones, and if you continue up Fortymile Gulch you will soon find yourself in a box canyon with no apparent way out. Carcass Wash is the second major canyon you will see on the left as you walk up Fortymile.

It is easy to miss the turn from Fortymile Gulch into Carcass Wash, and for that reason it is probably better to do this loop hike in the reverse direction. If you start at Carcass Wash the route simply follows the canyon downstream to Fortymile Gulch and on to Willow Gulch. Regardless of the direction you are traveling, however, be sure to pay particular attention to the weather before entering Fortymile Gulch. A flash flood in this canyon would be deadly, so don't proceed if there is a chance of rain.

Lake Powell

Hackberry Canyon

☆ ☆

Grand Staircase - Escalante National Monument
shuttle car required
overnight hike

Distance:	21.4 miles (plus 19.7 miles by car)
Walking time:	day 1: 6½ hours day 2: 5½ hours
Elevations:	1,340 ft. loss Round Valley Draw Trailhead (start): 6,100 ft. Mouth of Hackberry Canyon: 5,360 ft.
Trail:	There is no trail for this hike, but the route is easy to follow. You will be walking down the streambeds of two desert canyons. The first 2.2 miles through Round Valley Draw is in the bottom of a very narrow slot canyon and some scrambling will be necessary to get over several chock stones and other obstacles. A 30-foot length of rope will come in handy for lowering packs in a few places. Once you get through Round Valley Draw it is an easy walk down the sandy bottom of Hackberry Canyon. Unfortunately, there is no water for the first 11.3 miles of this hike, so be sure to carry plenty. Some wading will be necessary for the last 6 miles, so you should use wettable boots.
Season:	Spring, summer, fall, winter. Spring or fall are the ideal times for this hike. The canyons are very hot and dry in the summer and cold in the winter.
Vicinity:	Near Kodachrome Basin State Park, south of Bryce Canyon National Park
Maps:	Slickrock Bench, Calico Peak *(USGS)*
Information:	http://www.utahtrails.com/hackberry.html *(Utah Trails)* http://www.ut.blm.gov/monument/ *(Grand Staircase-Escalante)* phone: (435) 644-2672 *(BLM, Kanab Field Office)*

Drive east of Bryce Canyon National Park on Highway 12 to the town of Cannonville, then turn south towards Kodachrome Basin State Park and Grosvenor Arch. 7.3 miles from Cannonville you will come to a junction where the Kodachrome Basin road turns abruptly to the left. Continue straight ahead here on the smaller gravel road towards Grosvenor Arch and Highway 89. The gravel road winds across the desert for about 5 miles before climbing to the top of a ridge called Slickrock Bench, then drops down the other side. On the far side of Slickrock

Bench, 6.8 miles from the Kodachrome Basin junction, the road dips through the bottom of a small wash called Round Valley Draw, and as you climb up the other side of the wash you will see another primitive dirt road departing on the right near a sign that says "Rush Beds". Turn right here and drive towards Rush Beds. This road is seldom maintained, but most cars should be able to handle it unless there has been a recent rain. The road parallels Round Valley Draw for a while, and then, after 1.7 miles, it dips back into the draw before veering south. The hike down Round Valley Draw to Hackberry Canyon begins at this point.

Before beginning the hike you will have to leave a shuttle car at the mouth of Hackberry Canyon, where the hike ends. To get there return to the Grosvenor Arch Road and drive south. After 2.8 miles you will pass the turnoff to Grosvenor Arch. Continuing past this turnout towards Highway 89 for another 15.2 miles will bring you to the confluence of Hackberry Canyon and Cottonwood Wash, where the hike ends. (Note: if you are coming from the south, the mouth of Hackberry Canyon is 14.6 miles from Highway 89 on the Cottonwood Wash Road. The Rush Beds Road is 32.6 miles from Highway 89.)

If you don't have two cars for this hike you may want to consider leaving a bicycle at the mouth of Hackberry Canyon. Be advised, however, that the 19.7 mile ride back is very rough and has lots of ups and downs. When I did this hike in 1995 I hitchhiked from Hackberry back to the Rush Beds Road. The second car that passed gave me a ride, but I had to wait for 2¹/₂ hours. (Quite a few cars use this road during the dry months, but the great majority of them are going in the other direction.)

The Hackberry Canyon hike is well suited to those backpackers who enjoy remote areas with lots of solitude. It is in a rugged part of the state, between the Kaiparowits Plateau and the Vermilion Cliffs, where there are few good roads and fewer serious hikers. Unfortunately water is also scarce in this region, and the first 11.3 miles of the hike are waterless. Only after the gorge has cut nearly all the way through the Navajo Sandstone to the top of the Kayenta Formation, does a spring finally appear to wet the stark white sand on the canyon floor. At this point the canyon begins to undergo a dramatic change as the colors of life are added to the black and white textures of upper Hackberry. In the next few miles even the walls of the canyon change their hue from the harsh white of the Navajo Formation to the softer reddish tones of the Kayenta Sandstone.

The plateaus above Hackberry have been used by cattle ranchers since the 1800s, and traditionally they have depended on the lower part of the canyon as a source of water for their animals. A couple of trails into the canyon are still occasionally used by local livestockmen, but human activity is only a fraction of what it was at the turn of the century.

Day 1 (11.3 miles)

At the trailhead, where Rush Beds road crosses the top of Round Valley Draw, the draw is very shallow and uninteresting. The fun begins, however, about 0.5 mile further down the streambed where, in order to continue, it becomes necessary to climb down into a 20-foot-deep crack in the bottom of the gully. The crack is only 12 to 18 inches wide—too narrow to negotiate with a backpack—so you will have to lower your pack in with a short rope before climbing down. The narrows continue for about 1.7 more miles before canyon opens up again. In at least three more places you will meet inter-

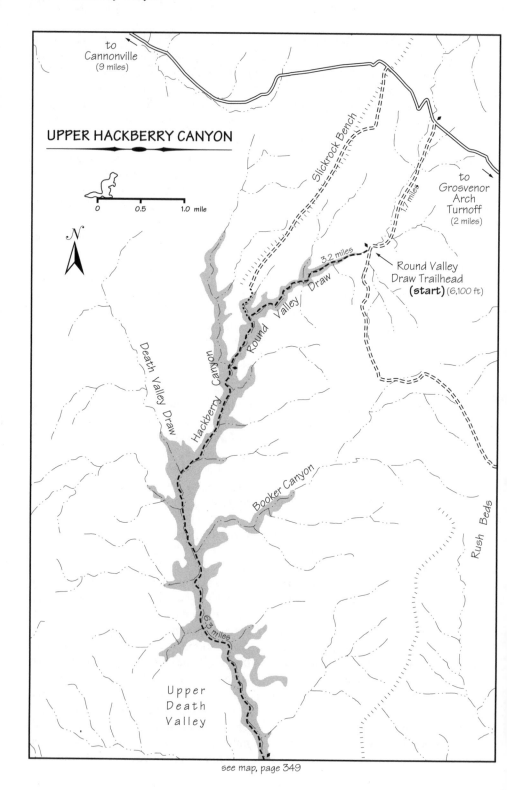

to
Cannonville
(9 miles)

UPPER HACKBERRY CANYON

0   0.5   1.0 mile

N

Slickrock Bench

to
Grosvenor
Arch
Turnoff
(2 miles)

1.7 miles

3.2 miles

Round Valley
Draw Trailhead
(start) (6,100 ft)

Round Valley Draw

Death Valley Draw

Hackberry Canyon

Booker Canyon

Rush Beds

6.3 miles

Upper
Death
Valley

see map, page 349

see map, page 348

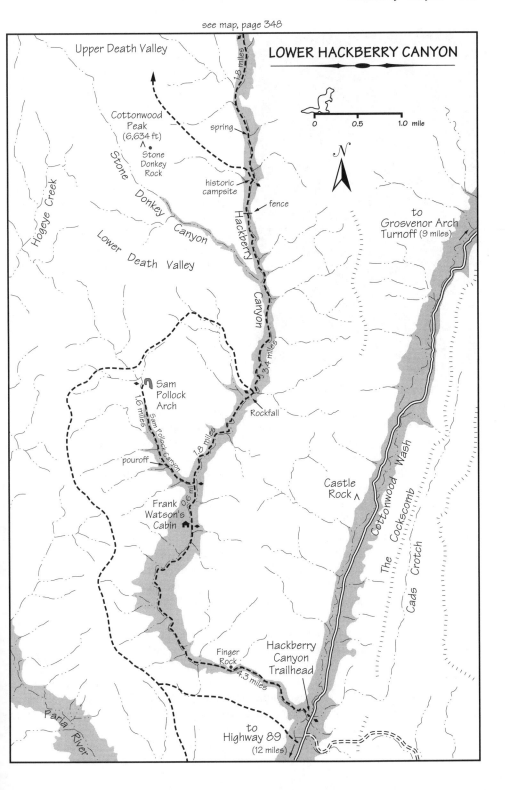

LOWER HACKBERRY CANYON

Upper Death Valley

1.8 miles

Cottonwood
Peak
(6,634 ft)
Stone
Donkey
Rock

spring

0   0.5   1.0 mile

N

Stone   Donkey   Canyon

historic
campsite

fence

Lower   Death   Valley

to
Grosvenor Arch
Turnoff (9 miles)

Hogeye Creek

Hackberry   Canyon

3.4 miles

Sam
Pollock
Arch

1.6 miles

Sam Pollock Canyon

Rockfall

1.8 miles

pouroff

Castle
Rock

Cottonwood   Wash

The   Cockscomb

Cads   Crotch

Frank
Watson's
Cabin

0.6 mi

Finger
Rock

4.3 miles

Hackberry
Canyon
Trailhead

Paria River

to
Highway 89
(12 miles)

Narrows of Round Valley Draw

esting obstacles that have to be dealt with. Again, your rope will come in handy for lowering packs. At one point it will be necessary to crawl through a small hole under a chock stone; at another your ability to get through cracks will again be tested.

2.2 miles from the trailhead you may see a large stone cairn on the north side of the canyon floor. This marks the beginning of another trail coming down to Round Valley Draw from Slickrock Bench. Day hikers can exit the draw at this point and rimwalk back to their car on the Rush Beds road. The narrows end here and the hike becomes an easy walk along the dry, sandy streambed. After another 1.0 mile you will arrive at the confluence with Hackberry Canyon.

Once you reach Hackberry Canyon turn left and proceed in a southerly direction until you reach water, 7.8 miles farther down the canyon. You will know you are getting close

when you see a few small cottonwood trees growing in the sand. Then a short ways farther the sand will turn damp, and finally you will start to see small pools of water along the sides of the canyon. At about the point where the water first starts to flow, 0.6 mile below the first cottonwoods, there is a good camp site on a sandy knoll on the right side of the canyon. This site has been used by cowboys for at least a hundred years. It is also the trailhead for Upper Trail, an old cow trail leading out of Hackberry Canyon to Death Valley. A short length of barbed wire fence at the top of the knoll, and a near-vertical cliff of Navajo Sandstone on the east side of the canyon will help you identify the site.

Like many of the place names in the West, there is an interesting story behind how Death Valley got its name. Cattlemen have long used this valley as a winter grazing pasture for their cattle. Their are no springs on the plateau, however, and the cattle depend on Upper Trail for their access to water. Oldtimers tell the story of how a cow once laid down and died on a very narrow part of the trail near the rim. The other cows were not able to get past the dead cow to go down the trail for water and, as a result, many of them died of thirst on the plateau above. Since that time the pasture has been known as Death Valley.

Day 2 (10.1 miles)

As you continue down Hackberry Canyon from the campsite the water begins to flow a little faster, but the stream is seldom more than a few inches deep. Dense vegetation lines the banks, and the easiest place to walk is in the center of the flat, sandy streambed. Wading see color photos page 196 shoes are very useful for the remainder of the hike, as you will be in the water more than half of the time.

After about ten minutes you will pass

another fence, built across the canyon floor to keep cattle from wondering downstream, and a mile farther on you will see Stone Donkey Canyon coming in from the right. Stone Donkey is a box canyon with no access to the top, but it has a nice spring near its mouth that adds to the meager flow in Hackberry.

1.9 miles below Stone Donkey Canyon there is a new feature in the canyon that was added in the fall of 1987. In that year a large rock slide came down from the west side of Hackberry, creating a dam across the canyon that backed up the stream for several hundred yards. A number of dead cottonwood trees reveal the size of the lake that was formed. The lake has subsided now, however, and it is not difficult to find your way across the rubble of the slide.

If you are observant you may see another trail descending into Hackberry Canyon from the west side a short distance upstream from the rock slide. This is the Lower Trail,

another cow trail leading up to Death Valley. Nearby, the words "W.M. Chynoweth, 1892" have been scratched into the canyon wall. The Chynoweths were a prominent ranching family in Southern Utah, and the name appears more than once in the area's cowboyglyphs.

The next item of interest is Sam Pollock Canyon, 1.8 miles below the rock slide. If you have the time and energy you might want to drop your pack here and make a side trip into this canyon to see Sam Pollock Natural Arch (1.6 miles each way). The bottom part of Sam Pollock Canyon is filled with huge boulders from the cliffs above, and a lot of scrambling is necessary to get into the canyon. After getting through a half-mile of sandstone rubble you will be confronted with a 20-foot vertical pouroff that blocks the upper half of the canyon, but don't give up yet. About 200 yards below the pouroff, on the east side of the canyon there is a relatively easy way up to a ledge above the

Sam Pollock Arch

Frank Watson's Cabin

pouroff. Once you are on this ledge you can walk upcanyon on a vague trail to a point just above the pouroff and then drop 15 feet back down to the streambed. The route is not difficult at all, but it is a little exposed at one point so be careful with your footing.

Once above the pouroff it is an easy 1.1 mile walk up the streambed to the arch, located near the top of the canyon on the north side. There are also more cowboyglyphs in the vicinity of Sam Pollock Arch. In a small cave just north of the arch you can see a glyph scratched into the rock by another member of the Chynoweth family: "Art Chynoweth, 1912".

Continuing down Hackberry Canyon, be sure not to miss Frank Watson's cabin. Watson migrated to Utah from Wisconsin at the turn of the century. Upon his arrival in Utah he changed his name, for reasons unknown, from Richard Thomas to Frank Watson, and for the next fifteen years remained completely out of touch with his relatives in Wisconsin. Many people came west at that time to begin a new life, and few newcomers were ever questioned about their past. Watson went to work for a while in the nearby town of Pahreah (now a ghost town in Paria Canyon), and in about 1914 he built his cabin in lower Hackberry Canyon. The cabin is still in surprisingly good shape after all these years.

The Watson cabin can't be seen from Hackberry creek, so it is easy to miss. It is situated on the edge of a sagebrush-covered bench, some fifteen feet above the west side of the streambed 0.6 miles downstream from the mouth of Sam Pollock Canyon. As you walk downstream watch for a large red sandstone boulder, about 15 feet in diameter, on the west side of the stream. At the foot of this boulder you should see a vague trail going up the side of the bank to the cabin, which is hidden in the sagebrush only 100 feet away.

2.5 miles downstream from Watson's cabin Hackberry Canyon makes a sharp turn to the left and knifes its way through a ridge known as the Cockscomb before converging with Cottonwood Wash. For the last 1.8 miles the canyon narrows to twenty or thirty feet, with cliffs of Navajo and Kayenta Sandstone dropping precipitously from the convoluted Cockscomb to the waters edge. It is very scenic. Finally Hackberry Creek emerges from the ridge to join Cottonwood Wash and the road back to Kodachrome Basin.

Finger Rock, Lower Hackberry Canyon

Buckskin Gulch - Paria Canyon

☆ ☆ ☆ ☆

Paria Canyon - Vermillion Cliffs Wilderness Area
shuttle car or bicycle required
overnight hike

Distance: 20.6 miles
                     (plus 15.5 miles by car or bicycle)

Walking time: day 1: 7¹/₂ hours
                     day 2: 4¹/₂ hours

Elevations: 760 ft. loss, 180 ft. gain
                     Wire Pass Trailhead (start):   4,860 ft.
                     Paria River confluence: 4,100 ft.
                     White House Trailhead: 4,280 ft.

Trail: There is no trail for this hike, but the route is easy to follow. You
                     will be walking along the bottoms of two narrow desert canyons.
                     Occasionally there are deep pools of water in the canyon
                     narrows, so be prepared with an air mattress or some other
                     means of floating your backpacks across. You will also need a
                     30-foot length of rope to help you get down a rockfall near the
                     end of Buckskin Gulch.

Season: Spring, summer, fall. Flash floods are common in Buckskin
                     Gulch, so don't attempt this hike if there is a chance of rain. Be
                     especially careful from late July through mid-September, when
                     thundershowers in Southern Utah are more frequent.

Vicinity: Near Kanab and Page, Arizona

Maps: Pine Hollow Canyon, West Clark Bench, Bridger Point *(USGS)*

Information: http://www.utahtrails.com/buckskin.html *(Utah Trails)*
                     http://paria.az.blm.gov/ *(BLM, Paria Canyon-Vermillion Cliffs)*
                     phone: (435) 644-2672 *(BLM, Kanab Field Office)*

---

*Drive east of Kanab on Highway 89 for 44 miles until you see a sign directing
you to Paria Ranger Station, 0.1 mile south of the highway. From the ranger
station there is a graded road leading to the White House Campground, 2.1
miles away, where the hike ends and where you should leave your shuttle car.*

*In order to get to the Wire Pass Trailhead, where the hike begins, return to
Highway 89 and drive back towards Kanab for a distance of 4.9 miles. After the highway
has climbed to the top of a ridge called the Cockscomb you will see an unmarked gravel road
departing on the left. Turn here and drive south for another 8.5 miles. About halfway along
you will pass the Buckskin Trailhead, and finally you will come to a large parking area and*

a sign marking the Wire Pass Trailhead.

Note: Permits are now required to hike in Buckskin Gulch and Paria Canyon, and the BLM allows only 20 people per night to camp in Buckskin. Reservations can be obtained by calling (435) 644-2672 or (435) 688-3246. The cost is $5.00/day for each person, and the maximum group size is 10 people.

Buckskin Gulch is alleged by many veteran hikers to be the longest, narrowest slot canyon in the world. There are many other narrows hikes on the Colorado Plateau, but Buckskin is exceptional because of its length. The Buckskin narrows extend almost uninterrupted for over 12 miles with the width of the canyon seldom exceeding 20 feet. The walk through the dark, narrow canyon is truly a unique hiking experience.

The key consideration in planning a trip through Buckskin Gulch is water. How much water and mud is there in the canyon? And what is the probability that it will rain while you are inside it? The canyon was created by water, and water continues to shape it and change its character. As you walk along the sandy bottom you will continually be confronted with evidence of previous floods. Dozens of logs have been wedged between the canyon walls, and piles of huge boulders

see color photo page 197

have been jammed into narrow constrictions. The characteristics change from year to year. One can never predict what the last flood might have taken away or left behind. According to BLM statistics there are about 8 flash floods a year, on the average, in Paria Canyon and its tributaries. About a third of the floods occur during the month of August, so if you are planning a trip in late summer you should be especially cautious. Flash flood danger is lowest during the months of April, May, and June.

Day 1 (13.0 miles)

It is possible to begin this hike at either Buckskin Trailhead or Wire Pass Trailhead, but if you begin at Buckskin Trailhead the hike is 2.8 miles longer. If you begin the hike at Wire Pass you will have to walk 13 miles to the confluence campsite; whereas from Buckskin Trailhead the distance is 15.8 miles—more than a comfortable day's walk for most people.

From the Wire Pass parking area the trail proceeds for a short distance along the south side of Wire Pass, then drops into the sandy bottom of the wash and descends eastward through the Cockscomb. At first the wash is so mundane it hardly seems an appropriate

Buckskin Gulch

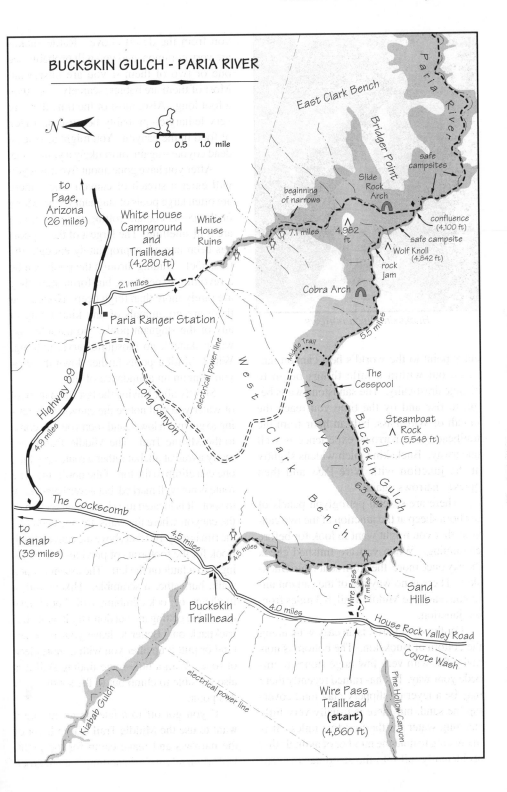

BUCKSKIN GULCH - PARIA RIVER

Paria River

East Clark Bench

Bridger Point

N

0   0.5   1.0 mile

to
Page,
Arizona
(26 miles)

White House
Campground
and
Trailhead
(4,280 ft)

White
House
Ruins

beginning
of narrows

7.1 miles

Slide
Rock
Arch

4,982
ft

safe
campsites

confluence
(4,100 ft)

safe campsite

Wolf Knoll
(4,842 ft)

rock
jam

2.1 miles

Paria Ranger Station

Cobra Arch

5.5 miles

electrical power line

W
e
s
t

C
l
a
r
k

B
e
n
c
h

Middle Trail

The
Cesspool

Steamboat
Rock
(5,548 ft)

Long Canyon

Highway 89

4.9 miles

T
h
e

D
i
v
e

B
u
c
k
s
k
i
n

G
u
l
c
h

6.3 miles

The Cockscomb

to
Kanab
(39 miles)

4.5 miles

4.5 miles

Wire Pass

1.7 miles

Sand
Hills

Buckskin
Trailhead

4.0 miles

House Rock Valley Road

Coyote Wash

Kiabab Gulch

electrical power line

Pine Hollow Canyon

Wire Pass
Trailhead
(start)
(4,860 ft)

Buckskin Gulch narrows

yon from the desert above. Rattle snakes are very common, and you will probably see one or two of them if you are observant. Most of them are babies, scarcely more than a foot long. Also, most of the time they are very lethargic—probably because of a lack of food in the canyon. You might also see a dead coyote—again, most likely a young one.

After you have gone about five miles you will enter a stretch of canyon where there are often large pools of stagnant water. Many of the pools contain rotting vegetation and are foul smelling. The largest of these pools has been named, appropriately enough, the Cesspool. Wading through the pools can be a revolting experience, but fortunately they are rarely more than thigh deep. Notice that there are no animals of any kind living in any of the stagnant pools: no tadpoles, no water skaters, no mosquito larva, nothing. Why? Similar pools farther down the canyon contain an abundance of life.

Shortly after leaving the last stagnant pool of water you will notice the canyon rim starting to get much lower, and soon you will come to the Middle Trail. The Middle Trail is not really a trail at all, but rather a route up which one can climb to the top of the north rim. The route is not well marked, but nevertheless easy to spot. It is located in a short, open section of the canyon where the walls are not steep and the rim is only 100 feet above the canyon floor. Look for the footprints of previous hikers going into a fault on the left. The assent is not a walk, but rather a scramble. Hikers with a modicum of rock climbing skill should have no trouble getting up, but don't try it with your backpack on. Better to leave your pack behind or pull it up after you with a short piece of rope. With a little route finding skill it is also possible to climb out to the south rim at this point.

If you got off to a late start you might want to use the Middle Trail to climb out of the narrows and make camp for the night. Unfortunately there is nothing but slickrock

entry point to the world's best canyon narrows, but within a mile things begin to change drastically. The sandstone walls begin to rise and by the time you reach the mouth of Wire Pass, half an hour from the trailhead, your narrows experience is well underway. Buckskin Gulch widens slightly at the junction with Wire Pass and then quickly narrows again.

There are several petroglyph panels of big horn sheep at the junction of the two canyons that you might want to look for before continuing. When you are finished check the sky once more, then turn south into Buckskin. There is no way out of the canyon until you reach the Middle Trail, 6.3 miles from the junction.

For the most part it is an easy walk along the bottom of Buckskin. The bottom is normally flat with very few large stones to impede your way. If it has rained recently there may be a layer of slippery clay mud covering the sand, but there is usually very little standing water for the first five miles. It is interesting to note the number of animals that accidentally fall into the steep narrow can-

Rock jam in lower Buckskin Gulch

and sand above the canyon, and no water. But the flash flood danger makes it unsafe to spend a night inside Buckskin Gulch.

Soon after leaving the Middle Trail the narrows close in again, and the depth of the canyon continues to increase as you approach the Paria River. There are usually no more deep wading pools below Middle Trail, but after about four miles your progress will be stopped by a pile of huge rocks that have become wedged into a tight constriction in the canyon. This rock jam is Buckskin Gulch's most serious obstacle, and most people will need a rope to get safely around it. The standard route requires that you climb about 15 feet down the smooth face of one of the boulders. Previous hikers have chipped footholds into the soft sandstone, but unless you are very agile you will still need a rope to make a safe descent. Hikers often leave their ropes tied to the top of the pitch and you might be lucky enough to find a good one already in place. But BLM rangers regularly cut away any ropes that appear

to be unsafe, so you had best have one of your own. Conditions change from year to year and, depending on what happened during the last canyon flood, you might find another easier route down the rock jam. But don't count on it.

Soon after you leave the rock jam you will pass by a series of seeps in the Navajo Sandstone walls that supply a tiny flowing stream on the canyon floor. The fresh water is a welcome change from the stagnant, lifeless pools above Middle Trail. There is plenty of life in the water of the lower Buckskin, even including small fish.

About a mile below the rock jam, or 0.5 mile above the Paria River confluence, you will come to an excellent campsite. Look for a large grove of maple and boxelder trees growing in the sand above the streambed. There are several fine places to make camp under the trees on the benches of dry sand ten feet above the canyon floor. Since this area is the only place in Buckskin Gulch where it is possible to camp you may have trouble finding an unoccupied campsite, especially during the busy months of May and June. If you can't find a place here the next closest campsite is located about a mile away in Paria Canyon below the confluence.

Day 2 (7.6 miles)

It is only a ten minute walk from the Buckskin Gulch campsite to the Paria River confluence, where you must turn north up Paria Canyon to complete the hike. The place where the two canyons come together is extremely impressive. The narrows here are much more open than the narrows of the Buckskin, but the reddish walls are shear and smooth. The presence of clean running water at the bottom of the 800-foot gorge also adds a touch of grandeur to the scene. The Paria is sometimes dry in midsummer, but there is always at least a trickle of water flowing out of Buckskin.

The next point of interest as you walk up

the Paria River is Slide Arch, located about 0.7 mile above the confluence. This is not really an arch at all, but rather a large piece of sandstone that has broken away from the east wall and slid down into the river. Beyond Slide Arch the canyon walls start to become less shear and the canyon widens until it is eventually little more than a desert wash. There are a few hard-to-find panels of petroglyphs on the west side of the canyon as you approach the White House Trailhead. The first panel is about a mile before the point where the electrical power lines cross the canyon, and the last is just above the power line crossing.

Finally, you may want to pause for a few minutes at the White House Ruins. These are not Indian ruins, as many people think, but rather the site of an old homesteader's cabin. The cabin was originally built in 1887 by Owen Washington Clark, the same man for whom the West Clark Bench was named. Unfortunately it burned down in the 1890s,

and today there is little left but a pile of stones. The ruins are located on the east side of the Paria River, opposite a small side canyon on the west side about 0.3 mile below the trailhead.

Lower Paria Canyon

Many hikers combine the Buckskin Gulch hike with a hike through the lower part of Paria Canyon to the Colorado River. If you turn south at the Paria confluence instead of north you can walk all the way down the Paria River to Lees Ferry. This 30-mile walk makes a long but rewarding backpack trip with a great deal to see. There are several abandoned homestead sites and mining camps along the way dating back to the late 1800s. You will also see several impressive panels of Indian rock art, as well as one of the largest natural sandstone arches in the world. The distance by road from Lees Ferry back to the Paria Ranger Station is about 70 miles; hence two cars are needed for the hike.

Paria Canyon narrows

Queens Garden - Peekaboo Loop

☆ ☆ ☆

Bryce Canyon National Park
day hike

Distance:	6.6 miles (loop)
Walking time:	3½ hours
Elevations:	600 ft. loss/gain
	Sunset Point Trailhead (start): 8,000 ft.
	Queens Garden: 7,600 ft.
	Bryce Creek: 7,400 ft.
Trail:	Excellent, well marked trail
Season:	Summer to mid-fall. The trail is covered with snow during the winter months.
Vicinity:	Bryce Canyon National Park
Maps:	Bryce Canyon, Bryce Point *(USGS)*
	Bryce Canyon National Park *(Trails Illustrated, #219)*
Information:	http://www.utahtrails.com/queens.html *(Utah Trails)*
	http://www.nps.gov/brca/ *(Bryce Canyon National Park)*
	phone: (435) 834-5322 *(Visitor Center)*

This hike begins in Bryce Canyon National Park at Sunset Point, 1.5 miles south of the Visitor Center on Highway 63.

Bryce Canyon National Park is one place where you can see a lot of fantastic scenery in a very short time. There are numerous trails below the rim, especially in the area between Sunrise Point and Bryce Point where most of the strange rock formations are found, and a number of variations of this hike are possible. The 6.6 mile hike I describe here is actually a combination of three separate hikes suggested by the Park Service: the Queens Garden Trail (1.6 miles), the Wall Street Trail (0.7 mile), and the Peekaboo Loop (4.8 miles). I suggest you do them all together because the only really strenuous part of any of the hikes is the climb out of the canyon. Why not see as much as possible before climbing out?

From Sunset Point the trail drops off the rim into Bryce Canyon, descending rather steeply into a forest of spires and pinnacles, or "hoodoos". You can take either of two trails for this portion of the hike, but if you have ever seen the urban canyons of New

see map, page 363

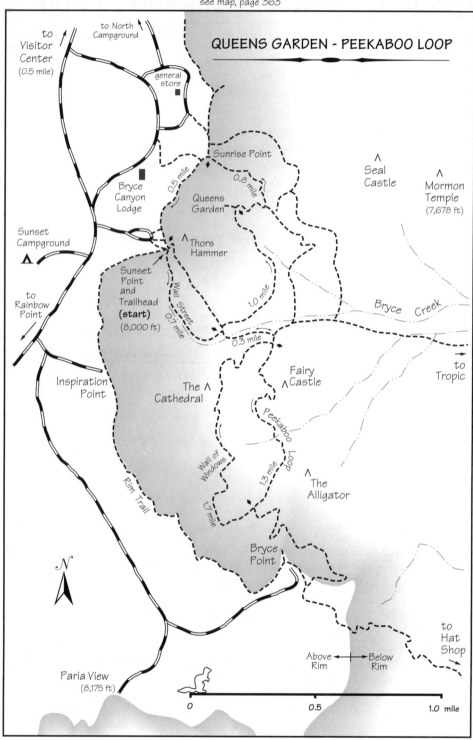

QUEENS GARDEN - PEEKABOO LOOP

York City I suggest you take Wall Street Trail on the right. This trail was metaphorically named after Wall Street Canyon in Manhattan, where New York's skyscrapers tower over the narrow road below. The Wall Street Trail lasts only 0.7 mile, but in this distance you descend 520 feet. This is close to the lowest point on the hike, so you can relax for the next 4¹/₂ miles.

Turn right at the trail junction at the bottom of Wall Street and head for the Peekaboo Loop. After 0.3 mile there is another junction where you will need to make another right turn and walk a few hundred feet to the beginning of the Peekaboo Loop. When you reach the beginning of the loop I suggest you take the left fork and walk around it in a clockwise direction. The Wall of Windows, which is the highlight of Peekaboo, should be approached from the south, its most impressive side.

As you enter the loop you will see the Fairy Castle above you on the left and Bryce Point straight ahead. If you have good eyes you will probably be able to see people on Bryce Point looking down at you. They are about a mile away and 900 feet higher. You will probably also notice that the Peekaboo Loop is a horse trail. During the summer horses can be hired at the Bryce Canyon Lodge for daily rides into the canyon; if you meet one of the riding tours stand aside and let them pass.

A little less than half way through Peekaboo Loop the path meets another trail coming down from Bryce Point. Bear to the right and stay on Peekaboo as the trail swings north and heads back along the west side of the loop. The next point of interest is the Wall of Windows, a large fin of sedimentary rock that is slowly eroding into a line of hoodoos. The uneven erosion down the sides of the fin has caused about a dozen windows of various sizes to open up in the wall, hence its name. If you are interested in photographing the Wall of Windows the best lighting is before noon, while the sun is in the east.

From the Wall of Windows the trail continues northward, passing by the Cathedral and returning to the trail junction at the beginning of the loop. From there you should retrace your steps for about 0.3 mile back to the bottom of the Wall Street Trail.

From the bottom of the Wall Street Trail, head north, past the Navajo Loop Trail, and on towards the Queens Garden. Queens Garden is one of the gems of Bryce. It is a picture postcard scene,

see color photo, page 198

perfectly decorated with trees and rock formations as only nature can do. Although Queens Garden is near the end of the hike, you should save your lunch to eat here if possible. There is no better place to relax and enjoy the tranquility of the Canyon. From Queens Garden it is 0.8 mile, and 400 feet in elevation gain, to the top of the rim. The trail exits the canyon at Sunrise Point, 0.5 mile along the Rim Trail from Sunset Point where the hike began.

Queens Garden Trail

Fairyland Loop

Distance:	8.6 miles (loop)
Walking time:	5¼ hours
Elevations:	950 ft. loss/gain

Fairyland Trailhead (start):	7,760 ft.
Fairyland Canyon:	7,150 ft.
Rim Trail:	8,100 ft.

Trail: Excellent, well marked trail

Season: Summer to mid-fall. The trail is covered with snow during the winter months. Also the road to Fairyland Point is used as a cross-country ski trail in the winter.

Vicinity: Bryce Canyon National Park

Maps: Bryce Canyon *(USGS)*
Bryce Canyon National Park *(Trails Illustrated, #219)*

Information: http://www.utahtrails.com/fairyland.html *(Utah Trails)*
http://www.nps.gov/brca/ *(Bryce Canyan National Park)*
phone: (435) 834-5322 *(Visitor Center)*

Drive north of the Bryce Canyon National Park Visitor Center for one mile, then turn right and drive for another mile to Fairyland Point. The trail begins near the parking area at the end of the road. If you are staying in the park at North Campground it may be more convenient for you to begin the hike on the Rim Trail, near the amphitheater on the south end of the campground.

The area below the rim of Bryce Canyon National Park is a fantasyland of strange and wonderful geologic formations. Stone spires and pinnacles with fanciful names like the "Chinese Wall" and "Seal Castle" surround the trails, making them delightful places to hike. The Fairyland Loop Trail provides a particularly fine opportunity to examine some of these natural sculptures and, as it is somewhat of the beaten path, it is not as crowded as other trails in the park.

The stone sculptures of Bryce Canyon, whimsically called "hoodoos", have been eroded from a thick layer of soft sedimentary rock called the Claron Formation that was deposited in Utah some 60 million years ago. As the canyon rim erodes, new hoodoos are formed. They begin first as tall thin fins, then serrate to form pinnacles and spires. The colors are caused primarily by iron and manganese impurities in the rock that oxidize into colorful hues of red, pink, orange,

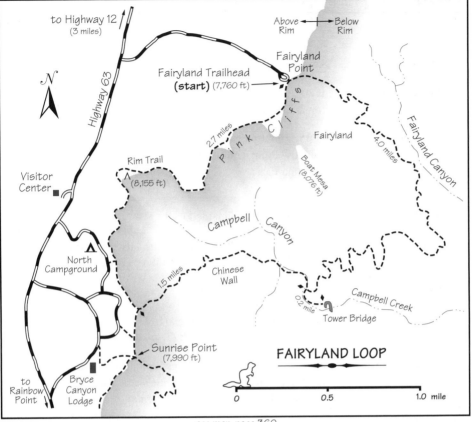

to Highway 12
(3 miles)

Above ← | → Below
Rim   Rim

Fairyland
Point

N

Highway 63

Fairyland Trailhead
(start) (7,760 ft)

2.7 miles

Pink Cliffs

Fairyland

Fairyland Canyon

4.0 miles

Visitor
Center

Rim Trail
(8,155 ft)

Boat Mesa
(8,076 ft)

Campbell Canyon

North
Campground

1.5 miles

Chinese
Wall

Campbell Creek

0.2 mile

Tower Bridge

Sunrise Point
(7,990 ft)

FAIRYLAND LOOP

to
Rainbow
Point

Bryce
Canyon
Lodge

0   0.5   1.0 mile

see map, page 360

yellow, and purple. The carving action is still continuing, and it is estimated that today the rim of Bryce Canyon is receding at the rate of about one foot in 65 years. In another hundred thousand years it will have receded by a third of a mile, and a whole new display of artwork will be ready for viewing in nature's gallery.

The trail descends immediately from Fairyland Point, winding down the north side of Boat Mesa for a distance of 1.5 miles to Fairyland Canyon, see color photo, page 198 the lowest point on the hike. From there the trail turns south and west, following the con-

tour of the land and climbing slightly for another 2.5 miles until it reaches the Tower Bridge trail junction. Tower Bridge is at the end of a short, well marked trail that branches off to the left. It is only 0.2 miles from the main trail, and it makes a nice lunch stop. From the Tower Bridge trail junction the path starts its climb back to the canyon rim. It winds to the west, with Campbell Canyon on the right and the Chinese Wall on the left, finally arriving at the canyon rim 1.5 miles later after a climb of 770 feet.

At the top of the rim the trail intersects the Rim Trail. Turn right here and walk along the rim for 2.7 miles back to the Fairyland Point parking lot.

Riggs Spring Loop

Distance:	8.8 miles (loop)
Walking time:	day 1: 3 hours day 2: 3½ hours
Elevations:	1,635 ft. loss/gain Rainbow Point Trailhead (start): 9,115 ft. Yovimpa Pass: 8,355 ft. Riggs Spring: 7,480 ft.
Trail:	Excellent, well maintained trail
Season:	Summer to mid-fall. The trail is usually covered with snow from mid-November until mid June.
Vicinity:	Bryce Canyon National Park
Maps:	Rainbow Point, Podunk Creek *(USGS)* Bryce Canyon National Park *(Trails Illustrated, #219)*
Information:	http://www.utahtrails.com/riggs.html *(Utah Trails)* http://www.nps.gov/brca/ *(Bryce Canyon National Park)* phone: (435) 834-5322 *(Visitor Center)*

This hike begins at Rainbow Point, 17 miles south of the Visitor Center at the end of the scenic drive in Bryce Canyon National Park. Before driving to Rainbow Point be sure to obtain a backcountry permit at the Visitor Center. Permits are handed out on a first-come-first-served basis and only 6 people are allowed to camp at Riggs Spring on any one night, so try to get to the Visitor Center early.

This loop hike can easily be completed in one day, but Riggs Spring is such a pleasant place to spend a night it would be a shame not to. The loop can be walked in either direction, but if you are interested in taking photographs the western half of the loop is prettiest in the morning when the eastern sun is shining directly on the Pink Cliffs. Unless you are get-

see color photo, page 198

ting an early start, save that section of the trail for the second day.

Although there are a few nice views of Bryce Canyon's famous rock formations on this hike, the main attraction is the forest itself. At the higher elevations you will be in a heavy forest of spruce, Douglas fir, white fir, and an occasional bristlecone pine. Near the bottom the forest changes to ponderosa pine. Riggs Spring is surrounded by huge

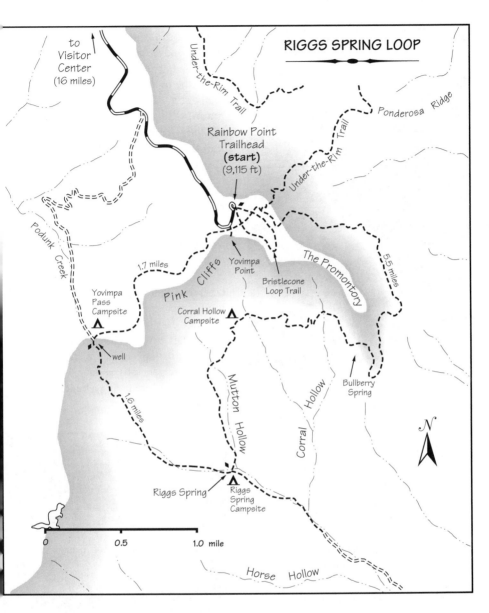

150-foot ponderosa pines, with nice grassy areas for pitching a tent. One couldn't ask for a finer spot to camp.

Day 1 (5.5 miles)

There are several trails leaving Rainbow Point and the trail to Riggs Spring is not clearly marked, so be careful not to take a wrong turn at the beginning. Start out by following the Bristlecone Loop Trail near the rest rooms on the east side of the parking area. After just a few hundred feet the path forks; take the left fork. A few hundred feet later you will come to a four-way junction with trails leading to Yovimpa Point, the Bristlecone Loop, and the Under the Rim Trail. Turn left here along the Under the Rim Trail. The trail will immediately begin loos-

The Pink Cliffs

ing elevation, and after another hundred yards you will come to the third trail junction. This time there is a sign directing you to bear right for Riggs Spring.

As the trail descends it makes a wide swing to the east to get around the Pink Cliffs, then turns west after 2.5 miles and doubles back under the cliffs. Once you are under the Pink Cliffs the trail dips in and out of three small drainages before turning south to follow the Mutton Hollow Drainage for the last 0.8 mile to Riggs Spring. You will pass by the Corral Hollow campsite 1.3 miles before you get to the spring.

Day 2 (3.3 miles)

From Riggs Spring it is 1.6 miles back to the top of the Pink Cliffs at Yovimpa Pass. The trail climbs steadily upward but the elevation gain is only 875 feet. The Park Service maintains a small well just below the pass, and you will see a dirt access road to the pass coming in from the north. The trail

turns east at the pass, and generally follows the rim above the Pink Cliffs back to Rainbow Point. There are a number of fine views along the trail; at one point you will be directly above Mutton Hollow looking south towards Riggs Spring 1.4 miles away. The Park Service has buried a pipe line under the trail to get water from the well at Yovimpa Pass to the restrooms at Rainbow Point, and occasionally you will see short sections of the pipe that are no longer buried. That is, however, only a small distraction along the scenic trail.

Be sure to watch for bristlecone pines near the edge of the rim. These ancient trees are often found in high, exposed areas where other trees don't do well, and they frequently live for more than 3,000 or even 4,000 years. They are easy to identify because of the way the needles grow all along the branches, giving them the appearance of fox tails. The needles are generally about $1\frac{1}{2}$ inches long with each bud producing a bundle of four or five needles.

Riggs Spring Trail

Rattlesnake Creek - Ashdown Gorge

☆ ☆ ☆

Ashdown Gorge Wilderness Area
shuttle car required
day hike

Distance: 9.8 miles
(plus 19 miles by car)

Walking time: 6 hours

Elevations: 3,460 ft. loss
Rattlesnake Trailhead (start): 10,460 ft.
Coal Creek: 7,000 ft.

Trail: Trail is poorly maintained, but generally easy to follow. The last 3.4 miles of the hike involve wading through a shallow, rocky creek in the bottom of the Ashdown Gorge, so be sure to wear wettable boots. Sneakers and sandals are not recommended.

Season: Midsummer to mid-fall. The higher elevations are usually covered with snow from mid-November until mid-June, making the trail difficult to follow.

Vicinity: Cedar Breaks National Monument, near Cedar City

Maps: Brian Head, Flanigan Arch *(USGS)*

Information: http://www.utahtrails.com/ashdown.html *(Utah Trails)*
http://www.fs.fed.us/dxnf/ *(Dixie National Forest)*
phone: (435) 865-3200 *(Cedar City Ranger District)*
phone: (435) 586-0787 *(Cedar Breaks Nat. Monument)*

Drive east on Center Street in Cedar City. Check your odometer as you cross Main Street and continue east on Highway 14 into Cedar Canyon. After you have driven 7.8 miles you will see a large pullout area on the left side of the road. This is where the hike ends and where you should park your shuttle car. The parking area is about 100 feet above a concrete spillway that has been constructed at the bottom of Coal Creek.

To get to Rattlesnake Trailhead where the hike begins continue driving up Cedar Canyon for another 14 miles, following the signs to Cedar Breaks National Monument. After you reach the Visitor Center drive north for another 5.0 miles, towards Brian Head Ski Resort. The well marked trailhead is located on the west side of Highway 143, just 100 feet beyond a boundary fence that marks the northern perimeter of Cedar Breaks National Monument.

This diverse hike has something for almost everyone — from high alpine wilderness to a walk through a narrow limestone river gorge. There are also several nice views of

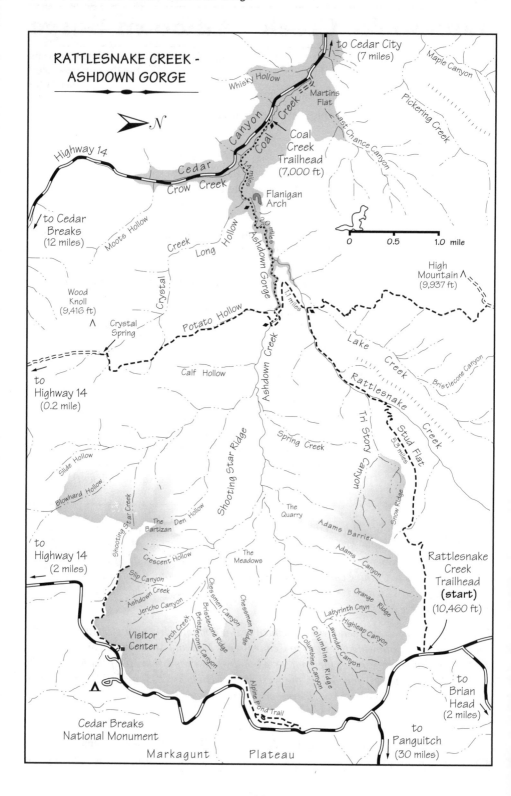

RATTLESNAKE CREEK -
ASHDOWN GORGE

the Cedar Breaks along the way. Finally, during most of the summer you will be unlikely to meet other hikers along this trail, and the solitude makes it an even more pleasant way to spend a day.

Although the hike can easily be completed in one day, many people prefer to extend it to a two or three day backpack trip. There is plenty

see color photo, page 199

to see. Ashdown Creek originates in the Cedar Breaks Amphitheater, about 1,500 feet below the Visitor Center, and a nice side trip is to walk upstream along the creek into the amphitheater. The Park Service does not allow camping in this area, however, so if you intend to do this you should establish a camp on the west side of the park boundary.

From Rattlesnake Trailhead the route meanders gently downhill in a westerly direction along the northern boundary of Cedar Breaks National Monument. The trail is faint in a few places, but it is well defined by blaze marks on the trees and occasional cairns. Short spur trails leave the main trail in at least two places for viewpoints along the rim. Be sure to take advantage of these side excursions.

After about 1.5 miles you will see Snow Ridge just south of the trail, so called because of the white rock along the top of the ridge. Here the route suddenly becomes steeper as it cuts down below the ridge on its way to Stud Flat. Stud Flat, a large rolling meadow above the confluence of Tri Story Canyon and Rattlesnake Creek, is extremely photogenic and a good place for a brief rest stop. Be sure to spend some time enjoying the view because soon you will be in the bottom of a timbered canyon.

From the western side of Stud Flat the trail continues dropping down into Rattlesnake Canyon, reaching the creek after a descent of some 600 feet. If you are interested in camping along Rattlesnake, there is

a particularly good campsite about 0.7 mile downstream from the point where the trail first reaches the water. Finally, after following the creek for 1.6 miles you will come to a trail junction where a sign identifies the High Mountain Trail on the right. Here the Ashdown Gorge Trail leaves Rattlesnake Creek, climbing slightly up the south side of the creek and swinging around in a wide turn to the east to meet Ashdown Creek. As you leave Rattlesnake be sure to start looking for a strong, straight stick to use as a walking stick over the last section of the hike through Ashdown Gorge. The trail crosses Ashdown Creek on the eastern end of the gorge, 1.1 miles after leaving Rattlesnake Creek.

As stated earlier, Ashdown Creek also forms a natural route into the Cedar Breaks Amphitheater, below the rim of Cedar Breaks National Monument. If you wish to

Ashdown Creek

make a side trip into this area it is about 4 miles upstream from the beginning of Ashdown Gorge. You can also see the remains of an old saw mill 0.5 mile upstream from the gorge. (The saw mill is on private land, so do not molest it in any way.)

Your shuttle car is positioned 3.4 miles downstream from the east entrance of Ashdown Gorge, but before proceeding into the gorge you should reassess the weather. If there is any chance of rain, stay out! Ashdown Creek drains a large area that includes the entire Cedar Breaks amphitheater, and the water level of the creek can rise very quickly during a rainstorm. There is no way out of the narrowest sections of the gorge, so if it looks like rain, don't take a chance.

If the weather looks bad, there is another route that leads to Highway 14 without entering the gorge. Just continue following the trail across Ashdown Creek. The trail soon crosses a jeep road and then continues in a southerly direction up Potato Hollow. After 2.9 miles the trail reaches Crystal Spring, where it meets another jeep road that leads to Highway 14. The total distance from Ashdown Creek to the highway by this route is 3.9 miles. Unfortunately, however, the trail meets the highway 5.8 miles upcanyon from the pullout where your shuttle car is parked.

For most people the highlight of this hike is the final 3.4 mile walk through Ashdown Gorge. From the east entrance the gorge gradually deepens until the walls on either side reach a height of 600 feet. After 1.0 mile you will pass by the junction of Rattlesnake Creek and Ashdown Creek. Notice the 100-foot-high limestone monolith, locally known as "Tom's Head" at the mouth of Rattlesnake Creek. Then another 1.0 mile of walking downstream from Rattlesnake Creek will bring you to the next point of interest, Flanigan Arch.

Flanigan Arch is a large natural arch, about 200 feet wide, positioned high on the north wall near the deepest part of the gorge. Unfortunately it is difficult to spot and many hikers miss it. If you are wading in the river it is only visible along a 100-foot-long stretch of the creek bed, and if you are walking too close to the north wall you won't be able to see it at all. Keep an eye on your watch, and after you have walked about 20 minutes downstream from Tom's Head start walking on the south side of the river and look up frequently. The stretch of river below the arch runs directly magnetic west, with a wide rocky shore on the south side.

From Flanigan Arch it is another 1.4 miles through the western portion of the gorge to Highway 14. After passing Long Hollow and Crow Creek you will see the highway above the south shore of the stream. When you reach the concrete spillway in the streambed you should see a short jeep road leading up to the pullout where your shuttle car is parked.

Tom's Head, Ashdown Gorge

Zion Narrows

☆ ☆ ☆ ☆ ☆

Zion National Park
shuttle car required
overnight hike

Distance: 17.3 miles
(plus 38 miles by car)

Walking time: day 1: 6½ hours
day 2: 6 hours

Elevations: 1,410 ft. loss
Chamberlain Ranch Trailhead (start): 5,830 ft.
Temple of Sinawava: 4,420 ft.

Trail: Except for a few miles at the beginning and the end of this hike there is no trail. You will be wading in the North Fork of the Virgin River most of the time, so be sure to wear wettable boots. Sandals and sneakers are not recommended. During the dry season the water is usually no more than knee deep, but it can get much deeper.

Season: Summer to mid-fall. It is imperative to check with the Park Service before beginning this hike. For safety reasons access to the Zion Narrows is strictly regulated and permits are required, even for day hikers. The best times of year are midsummer, after the spring runoff has subsided, and early fall. Thunder storms are more frequent in late summer; hence there is a greater danger of flash floods at that time.

Vicinity: Zion National Park

Maps: Temple of Sinawava, Clear Creek Mountain, Straight Canyon *(USGS)*
Zion National Park *(Trails Illustrated, #214)*

Information: http://www.utahtrails.com/zionnarrows.html *(Utah Trails)*
http://www.nps.gov/zion/ *(Zion National Park)*
phone: (435) 772-3256 *(Visitor Center)*

Chamberlain's Ranch, where the hike begins, is 31 miles from the Zion Canyon Visitor Center. Drive first to the Zion National Park east entrance, then continue on Highway 9 for another 2.5 miles until you see a paved road departing on the left. Take this road and drive north for 18 miles (unpaved after the first two miles) to a bridge across the North Fork of the Virgin River. Turn *left on the north side of the bridge and drive 0.3 miles to a gate on the edge of the Chamberlain Ranch property. The gate is not locked, but please be sure to close it after you. A half mile beyond the gate the road again comes to the river. Park your car here and begin your hike by crossing the stream on foot and following the road on the south side of the river.*

The hike ends at the Temple of Sinawava, 7.0 miles north of the visitor center, but the during the summer months the Park Service operates a free shuttle bus that runs frequently between the Temple of Sinawava, the visitor center, and Springdale. You should leave your shuttle car either at the visitor center or in Springdale.

Note: The Zion Canyon Transportation Company operates a convenient shuttle service for hikers to most of the national park's trailheads; the charge for a ride to Chamberlain's Ranch during the summer hiking season is $20.00/person. The shuttle leaves the visitor center parking lot at 6:00 and 9:00 every morning, but be sure to make reservations in advance as the service is very popular. For more information or reservations call (435) 635-5993.

This is probably the best known hike in Utah. The watery North Fork Virgin River Canyon offers a welcome respite from Southern Utah's hot summer weather, and the scenery within the canyon is truly spectacular. There are only about three months of the year, however, when conditions are suitable for the hike, and a fair amount of planning is required for a successful trip.

The most important consideration is the weather. Flash floods are a constant danger in narrow desert canyons like the Zion Narrows, and you shouldn't begin the narrows hike unless the forecast is good. The North Fork Virgin River drains several hundred square miles, and during a thunder storm the water level inside the canyon can rise several feet in a matter of minutes. At least five hikers have already drown in the Zion Narrows after being caught in flash floods, and because of this danger the Park Service no longer allows hikers to spend more than one night on the river. Also, it will not issue permits to walk the route before the 3:00 p.m. weather report is issued the day before the hike begins.

Another point to consider is the popularity of this hike and the limited camping facilities. There are only 12 allowed camp sites within the canyon, and they are filled almost every night during the summer. The camp sites are assigned on a first-come-first-

served basis beginning at 3:00 p.m. each day, so if you want to be assured of getting an overnight permit you should be at the Visitor Center by at least 1:00 p.m. the day before your hike. The sites are assigned according to your group size. Most of the sites

North Fork Virgin River

will accommodate 4 to 6 people, but only one site is large enough for the maximum group size of 12 people. In addition to the overnight permits, the Park Service also hands out up to 80 permits each afternoon for day hikes through the narrows.

Day 1 (11.1 miles)

Cross the North Fork Virgin River at the car parking area on Chamberlain's Ranch and continue following the jeep road on foot above the south side of the river. This is a beautiful hiking area with rolling hills, scattered trees and large grassy fields along the river, but bear in mind that it is all private property, accessible to hikers only by prior agreement with the owners. You won't actually be on National Park Service land for nearly seven miles. The owners have requested that hikers not camp on their land and not walk across their fields or disturb their cattle. If the ranchers' private property is not respected there could come a day when hikers are no longer allowed access into this area, so please follow the rules.

After walking 2.5 miles along the jeep road you will come to Bulloch's Cabin, an old abandoned homestead on the south side of the road. Remarkably, the cabin is still in reasonably good condition. There are also a few pieces of old farming machinery lying about the area. The road finally ends 0.3 mile beyond Bulloch's Cabin, and a trail continues along the river. Soon the river begins its descent into the canyon which you will follow all the way to the end of the hike. The North Fork Canyon is a canyon full of surprises, and for the rest of the day you can count on being awed and inspired over and over again. Frequently the canyon will appear to end at the base of an impenetrable cliff a hundred feet ahead, but it always turns at the last minute to find a way around the obstacle. Often you will see large trees and other debris that have been washed into the

canyon from previous flash floods. But the way around these obstructions is usually easy and very little scrambling is necessary. Because of the large number of hikers that pass through the canyon the easiest route is generally well defined.

You will come to the first long stretch of really good canyon narrows near the park boundary, about three miles after you first enter the canyon. The see color photos, page 199, 200 canyon rim at this point is 800 feet above the streambed, and the walls at the bottom are often no more than fifteen feet apart. The first campsite, Maple Camp, is also located in this area, at a well marked location on the left shore about 8 feet above the water.

The next point of interest in the canyon is a small waterfall. About 1.6 miles below Maple Camp the stream suddenly plunges over a 20-foot dam in the canyon floor. Occasionally a daring hiker will take off his backpack and jump over the fall into the pool below, but to do so is foolhardy. First of all it is impossible to see what rocks might lie below the boiling water, and second, it is hard to imagine a more inconvenient place to sustain an injury. Don't take the chance. There is an easy way around the waterfall on the south side of the canyon.

Deep Creek joins the North Fork at a wide confluence 0.8 miles below the water-

Bulloch's cabin

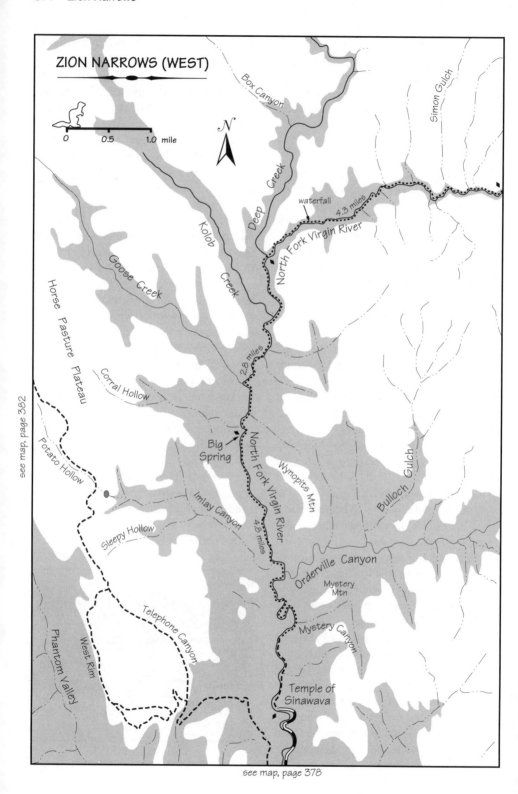

ZION NARROWS (WEST)

0   0.5   1.0 mile

N

Box Canyon

Simon Gulch

Deep Creek

waterfall

4.3 miles

North Fork Virgin River

Kolob Creek

Goose Creek

Horse Pasture Plateau

2.8 miles

Corral Hollow

see map, page 382

Potato Hollow

Big Spring

North Fork Virgin River

Wynopits Mtn

Bulloch Gulch

Imlay Canyon

4.6 miles

Sleepy Hollow

Orderville Canyon

Mystery Mtn

Telephone Canyon

Mystery Canyon

Phantom Valley

West Rim

Temple of Sinawava

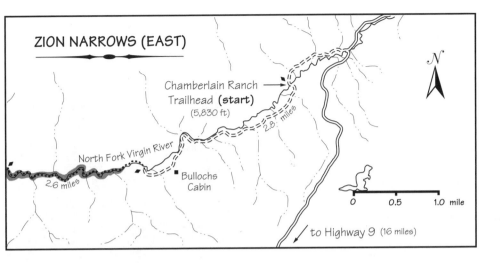

ZION NARROWS (EAST)

Chamberlain Ranch
Trailhead **(start)**
(5,830 ft)

2.8 miles

North Fork Virgin River

2.6 miles

Bullochs
Cabin

N

0   0.5   1.0 mile

to Highway 9 (16 miles)

fall. Beyond this point you will notice a large change in the flow rate of the river; about two thirds of the water flowing through the Zion Narrows comes from Deep Creek. This canyon offers a popular side trip and you may want to spend some time exploring–especially if your assigned campsite is the Deep Creek Camp, located at the confluence.

The other ten campsites are all located in the next 2.5 miles downstream from Deep Creek. Unfortunately the Park Service does not allow hikers to stipulate which site they want, but if I were given the opportunity to pick one I would probably choose the Kolob Creek Camp, 0.9 mile below Deep Creek. This campsite is located on a high shaded bench, just south of the Kolob Creek confluence. The site is very pretty, but what makes it especially attractive is its proximity to Kolob Canyon–the most interesting of all the Zion Narrows side canyons. If you have a few extra hours to spend exploring on your way through the narrows this is a good place to spend it. Kolob Canyon is one of the best examples in Utah of a deep, narrow slot canyon.

Day 2 (6.2 miles)

The next side canyon you will pass is

Goose Creek Canyon, which merges into Zion Canyon 1.3 miles below Kolob Creek. Goose Creek also provides a good opportunity for side trips. It is a wider canyon than Kolob, with more vegetation in the bottom. Goose Creek joins the North Fork on the west side of the river near campsite number 10, the Alcove Camp.

Below Goose Creek you will pass the last two campsites before coming to Big Spring, about 45 minutes away. Big Spring is a large gushing spring that cascades out of the cliff face 10 feet above the river. It is the most

Big Spring

dramatic spring you will see on this hike, but between here and the end of the trail you can count on seeing many other smaller springs. This stretch of river passes through the geologic boundary between the Navajo Sandstone and the Kayenta Formation. The Navajo Sandstone is a porous rock with microscopic spaces between the constituent particles of sand that allow water to seep down from the plateaus above, while the Kayenta Formation contains layers of clay and mudstone that effectively halt the water's downward penetration. When the water reaches the Kayenta Formation hydrostatic pressure from above pushes it out into the canyons where it is seen as spring water.

Big Spring also marks the beginning of the two-mile section of canyon commonly known as the Zion Narrows. This part of the canyon is distinguished by its sheer thousand-foot walls that rise above the river with little or no sandy shore between. There is no high ground here; hence it is not a place you would want to be during a storm. Under certain conditions the water can rise very quickly, and people have died in the past from flash floods in this section of the canyon. When no storms are imminent, however, the danger is small. Just use common sense and don't enter the narrows if the sky looks like rain.

About the time you reach the mouth of Orderville Canyon, 2.3 miles below Big Spring, the Zion Narrows widens again and you will find a well-used trail to follow on the sandy shore of the river. Also at this point you will begin to see day hikers from the Temple of Sinawava—hundreds of them. The remaining 2.7 miles of trail, from Orderville Canyon to the road, is the most popular part of Zion Canyon, and on a typical summer afternoon you will pass more than a thousand people splashing in the water along this stretch of the canyon. Finally, for the last mile you will be walking on the Gate-

way to the Narrows Trail, a paved walkway leading back to the trailhead at the Temple of Sinawava.

Zion Narrows

East Rim, Zion Canyon

☆ ☆ ☆ ☆ ☆

Zion National Park
shuttle car required
overnight hike

Distance: 17.9 miles
(plus 15 miles by car)

Walking time: day 1: 6 hours
day 2: 3³/₄ hours

Elevations: 1,190 ft. gain, 2,560 ft. loss
East Entrance Trailhead (start): 5,720 ft.
Cable Mountain: 6,500 ft.
Highest point: 6,910 ft.
Weeping Rock Trailhead: 4,350 ft.

Trail: Very popular, well maintained trail

Season: Late spring through mid-fall. The higher parts of the trail are usually covered with snow from mid-November to May.

Vicinity: Zion National Park

Maps: Temple of Sinawava, Springdale East, The Barracks, Clear Creek Mountain (*USGS*)
Zion National Park (*Trails Illustrated, #214*)

Information: http://www.utahtrails.com/eastrimzion.html (*Utah Trails*)
http://www.nps.gov/zion/ (*Zion National Park*)
phone: (435) 772-3256 (*Visitor Center*)

After obtaining an overnight backpacking permit at the Zion Canyon Visitor Center drive 11 miles east on Highway 9 to the park's east entrance. Just before you reach the entrance gate you will see a narrow road leaving on the left for the trailhead, 0.2 mile north of the highway.

The hike ends at Weeping Rock, 5.3 miles north of the visitor center, but during the summer months the Park Service operates a free shuttle bus that runs frequently between Weeping Rock, the visitor center, and Springdale. You should leave your shuttle car either at the visitor center or in Springdale.

Note: The Zion Canyon Transportation Company operates a convenient shuttle service for hikers to most of the national park's trailheads; the charge for a ride from the visitor center to the East Entrance Trailhead during the summer hiking season is $15.00/person. For more information or reservations call (435) 635-5993.

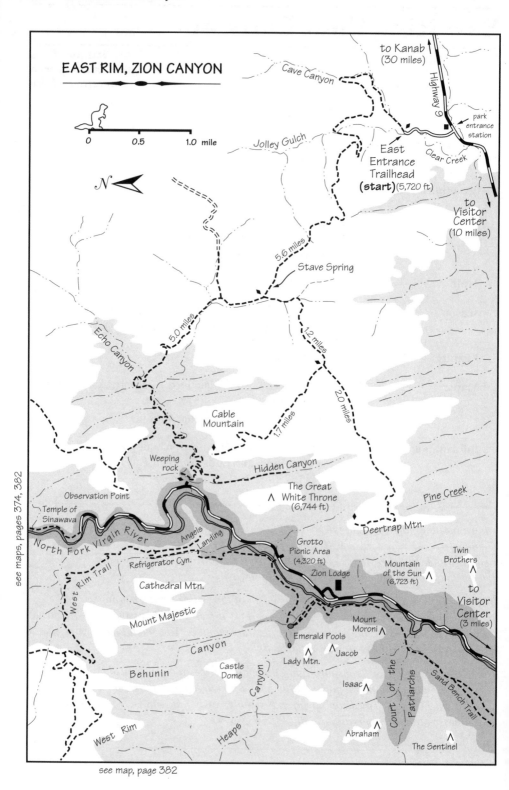

EAST RIM, ZION CANYON

0   0.5   1.0 mile

N

to Kanab
(30 miles)

Highway 9

park
entrance
station

Cave Canyon

Jolley Gulch

Clear Creek

East
Entrance
Trailhead
(start) (5,720 ft)

to
Visitor
Center
(10 miles)

5.6 miles

Stave Spring

5.0 miles

1.2 miles

Echo Canyon

1.7 miles

2.0 miles

Cable
Mountain

Weeping
rock

Hidden Canyon

Pine Creek

Observation Point

The Great
White Throne
(6,744 ft)

Temple of
Sinawava

Deertrap Mtn.

North Fork Virgin River

Angels Landing

Grotto
Picnic Area
(4,320 ft)

Twin
Brothers

see maps, pages 374, 382

West Rim Trail

Refrigerator Cyn.

Zion Lodge

Mountain
of the Sun
(6,723 ft)

Cathedral Mtn.

to
Visitor
Center
(3 miles)

Mount Majestic

Mount
Moroni

Emerald Pools

Canyon

Lady Mtn.

Jacob

Behunin

Castle
Dome

Court of the Patriarchs

Sand Bench Trail

Isaac

Canyon

West   Rim

Heaps

Abraham

The Sentinel

see map, page 382

East Rim Trail, Zion Canyon

Zion National Park is probably the best all around hiking area in the state of Utah. The trails here are very popular, so if it is solitude you are looking for this is the wrong place. But you will certainly find plenty of breathtaking scenery and interesting geological formations. The East Rim Trail, especially when walked in the direction suggested here, is a very pleasant way to sample what Zion has to offer. Very little climbing is required, the temperatures are not extreme, and the scenery just keeps getting better and better all the way to the end.

Day 1 (10.8 miles)

From the East Entrance Trailhead the hike begins by following Clear Creek for about 1.5 miles and then turns north into Cave Canyon. You will soon notice that much of the trail is along an old wagon road. Before Zion National Park was created this area was used extensively by ranchers and loggers. Once it reaches Cave Canyon the trail begins to ascend gradually to the top of the tableland that surrounds Zion Canyon, and after another mile it doubles back to give you a fine view from the mesa top down into Clear Creek Canyon. From this vantage point you can easily see the beginning of the trail, 400 feet below, threading its way along the side of Clear Creek.

Next, the trail veers again to the north to get around Jolley Gulch, and then, free of any further obstacles, it meanders along the contours of the mesa in a westerly direction towards Stave Spring. About 0.1 mile beyond Stave Spring you will see a fork in the trail, where you should turn left toward Cable Mountain. Soon you will cross a small, unnamed stream, beyond which you might want to begin looking for a camp site. There are a number of nice spots along this section of the hike. Please be aware, however, that you should not camp right next to the water and you should be out of site of the trail.

There are two interesting side trips here

to consider, either after establishing camp on the first day or before you put on your backpacks on the second day. Depending on how far from the Stave Spring trail junction you camped, Cable Mountain is about 2.0 miles away and Deertrap Mountain about 2.5 miles.

Cable Mountain, the most interesting of the two side trips, is a high promontory, about 2,100 feet above the Virgin River, with an unimpeded view of

> see color photo, page 199

Angels Landing and the West Rim. It is called Cable Mountain because in the early 1900s, before Zion National Park was formed, the Zion Cable Company operated a tram from the top of Cable Mountain to the bottom of Zion Canyon. The tram was used primarily for lowering lumber from the mesa top to the canyon floor where it was loaded onto wagons and hauled to nearby towns like Springdale and Rockville. Quite a bit of the original structure can still be seen on the edge of the mountain, although the tram hasn't been operated for seventy years.

The second side trip you might want to consider while you are on the mesa top is the walk to the Deertrap Mountain. Deertrap, which is situated high above the Zion Lodge, offers a fine view of the Court of the Patriarchs and Lady Mountain on the other side of the Canyon. You can easily walk to either one of these viewpoints and back in a couple of hours.

Day 2 (7.1 miles)

The trail from Stave Spring to Weeping Rock is one of the most scenic walks in Zion. It is all downhill and it is only 5.0 miles. It will only take a few hours to complete the trip, so if you haven't taken the side trip to Cable Mountain yet you should definitely do so before starting down. The trail to Weeping Rock passes directly beneath Cable Mountain on the way down, and it is all the more interesting if you have also seen it from the top.

The trail first heads north into the back of Echo Canyon, and then turns west to follow the canyon to the bottom of Zion. The scenery starts getting very interesting after about 1.5 miles. Echo Canyon gets narrower and narrower as you go down; in places the canyon is only 20 feet wide, and everywhere there are water-carved etchings in the rock. Finally the side canyon breaks out into the main canyon about 500 feet above the Virgin River, and the trail switchbacks the rest of the way to the bottom. 2.8 miles below Stave Spring there is another junction where the trail to the East Rim Observation Point climbs north out of Echo Canyon. Observation Point offers another possible side trip, but if you have already been to the top of Cable Mountain you will note that the view is quite similar.

Finally, 0.6 miles before you reach the bottom there is still another possible side trip that is quite worthwhile: the trail into Hidden Canyon. Hidden Canyon is another narrow slot canyon, similar to the lower reaches of Echo Canyon, that protrudes for a little over a mile from Zion Canyon into the East Rim. Depending on how much exploring you want to do, it will take from half an hour to an hour more of your time to check it out. Note, camping is not allowed in Hidden Canyon.

Hidden Canyon, Zion East Rim

West Rim, Zion Canyon

☆ ☆ ☆ ☆

Zion National Park
shuttle car required
overnight hike

Distance:	15.4 miles (plus 42 miles by car)
Walking time:	day 1: 2¹/₂ hours day 2: 5¹/₂ hours
Elevations:	3,140 ft. loss West Rim Trailhead (start): 7,460 ft. Potato Hollow: 6,780 ft. Grotto Picnic Area Trailhead: 4,320 ft.
Trail:	Very popular, well maintained trail
Season:	Late spring through mid-fall. The higher parts of the trail are usually covered with snow from mid-November to May.
Vicinity:	Zion National Park
Maps:	Kolob Reservoir, The Guardian Angels, Temple of Sinawava *(USGS)* Zion National Park *(Trails Illustrated, #214)*
Information:	http://www.utahtrails.com/westrimzion.html *(Utah Trails)* http://www.nps.gov/zion/ *(Zion National Park)* phone: (435) 772-3256 *(Visitor Center)*

To get to the West Rim Trailhead, where the hike begins, drive south from the park entrance for 14 miles on Highway 9 to the town of Virgin. In Virgin you will see a sign marking the road to Kolob Reservoir. Turn here and drive north for another 21 miles, until you see a sign directing you to Lava Point on the right. Proceed on the gravel road towards Lava Point for 1.0 mile to another junction where you must turn left on a dirt road that drops down to the West Rim Trailhead, 1.3 miles further.

The hike ends at the Grotto Picnic Area, 4.3 miles north of the visitor center, but during the summer months the Park Service operates a free shuttle bus that runs frequently between the picnic area, the visitor center, and Springdale. You should leave your shuttle car either at the visitor center or in Springdale. Then be sure to obtain a backcountry camping permit at the visitor center before driving to the West Rim Trailhead.

Note: The Zion Canyon Transportation Company operates a convenient shuttle service for hikers to most of the national park's trailheads; the charge for a ride from the visitor center to the West Entrance Trailhead during the summer hiking season is $20.00/person. For more information or reservations call (435) 635-5993.

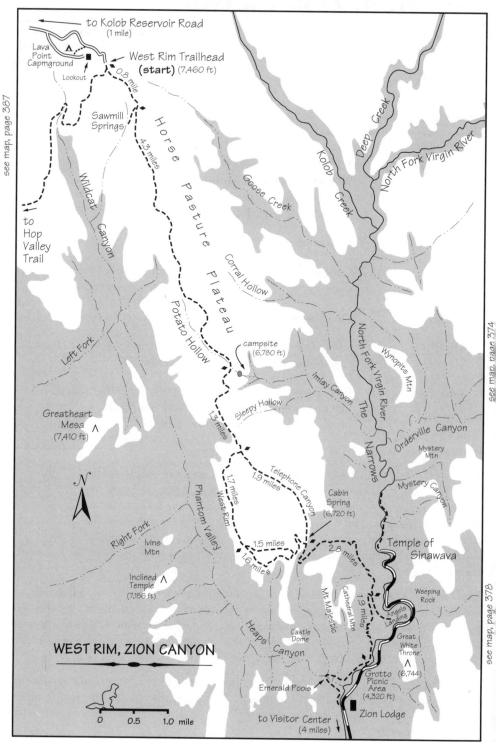

to Kolob Reservoir Road
(1 mile)

Lava Point Capmground

Lookout

West Rim Trailhead
(start) (7,460 ft)

0.8 mile

Sawmill Springs

4.3 miles

Horse Pasture Plateau

Wildcat Canyon

to Hop Valley Trail

Potato Hollow

Left Fork

campsite (6,780 ft)

Goose Creek

Corral Hollow

Kolob Creek

Deep Creek

North Fork Virgin River

see map, page 387

see map, page 374

Sleepy Hollow

1.3 miles

Imlay Canyon

North Fork Virgin River

Wynopits Mtn

Greatheart Mesa
(7,410 ft)

N

Telephone Canyon
1.9 miles

1.7 miles

West Rim

Phantom Valley

Right Fork

Ivins Mtn

1.5 miles

1.6 miles

2.8 miles

Cabin Spring
(6,720 ft)

The Narrows

Orderville Canyon

Mystery Mtn

Mystery Canyon

Temple of Sinawava

Inclined Temple
(7,156 ft)

WEST RIM, ZION CANYON

Heaps Canyon

Castle Dome

Mt Majestic

Cathedral Mtn

1.9 miles

Weeping Rock

Angels Landing

Great White Throne
(6,744)

see map, page 378

Emerald Pools

Grotto Picnic Area
(4,320 ft)

Zion Lodge

0   0.5   1.0 mile

to Visitor Center
(4 miles)

see map, page 378

The diversity of this hike, combined with the magnificent views of Zion Canyon from the West Rim, make it one of the most enjoyable trails in the park. Horse Pasture Plateau, where the trail begins, is a long flat finger of sandstone that protrudes from the Kolob Plateau, on the northern park boundary, into Zion Canyon. The path meanders gently downward through the ponderosa pine and pinon-juniper forests of the plateau, dropping 740 feet over a distance of nine miles before de- *see color photo, page 199* scending abruptly into the canyon. Spectacular views from the West Rim begin about six miles from the trailhead, where the route skirts the edge of Phantom Valley, and climax 3¹/₂ miles later at Cabin Spring. Beyond Cabin Spring the trail drops into Zion Canyon and winds through another 4.7 miles of slickrock and canyon country before reaching the North Fork of the Virgin River.

Day 1 (5.1 miles)

In contrast to the canyons below the rim the top of Horse Pasture Plateau is remarkably level. West Rim Trail meanders along the plateau for nearly ten miles, depending on your choice of routes, with little hint of the rugged terrain that lies ahead. 0.1 mile from the trailhead you will come to a fork with the Wildcat Canyon Trail branching to the right, and 0.7 miles farther another trail branches off to the right for Sawmill Springs. Keep to the left in both cases. The trail descends very gradually in a southerly direction through an open forest of ponderosa pine, turning slowly to pinion and juniper as altitude is lost.

About 3.5 miles from the Sawmill Springs junction you will begin dropping into Potato Hollow, a shallow drainage that leads to a side canyon on the west side of the plateau. A large grove of quaking aspen occupies the hollow, and the small pond near the canyon rim is a favorite afternoon watering hole for wildlife. The rim of the plateau is just west of the pond, and there are some fine views of Imlay Canyon from there.

Potato Hollow is a delightful place to make camp for the night, but in order to minimize your impact try to select a spot at least a few hundred yards from the pond itself. Also, bear in mind that open fires are not allowed. Be sure to watch the pond in the late afternoon, as you are almost certain to see deer coming for water. If it is still too early in the day to stop when you reach Potato Hollow you may want to continue on for another 4.6 miles to Cabin Spring. But Potato Hollow is such a pleasant place to spend the night it is a shame to pass it by.

Day 2 (10.3 miles)

About a mile below Potato Hollow the trail crosses Sleepy Hollow, where you will

Zion Canyon, from the West Rim

be treated to a panorama of Phantom Valley. On the opposite side of the valley you can also see Greatheart Mesa, one of the landmarks of the park. Another 0.3 mile will bring you to another trail junction where a decision has to be made. The Telephone Canyon Trail, on the left is the shorter route to Cabin Spring, but unless you are in a terrible hurry you should bear to the right here and follow the rim trail. It is 1.4 miles longer, but much more scenic.

The rim trail skirts the southeastern side of Horse Pasture Plateau and affords almost continual views of Phantom Valley and Heaps Canyon below. Telephone Canyon is a more densely forested route that cuts through the center of the plateau to meet the rim trail again at Cabin Spring. The rim trail encounters another fork 1.7 miles from the Telephone Canyon trail junction, and once again you should keep to the right. The other trail is, again, a shortcut which would save

Walter's Wiggles

you 0.1 mile, but at the cost of the scenic rim views.

Cabin Spring is a good place to stop for lunch. The spring itself is quite unimpressive. It was named after a park service cabin that once stood nearby but unfortunately burned down in the 1970s. From the rim near Cabin Spring, however, you can see a long stretch of the trail below, and it is interesting to gaze down into the slickrock canyon country and trace out the route you will follow below the plateau.

Beyond Cabin Spring the trail begins to descend almost at once, making two long switchbacks down the sandstone cliffs into the canyon below. After loosing about 900 feet you will arrive at a point directly below and to the east of the spring; look back and see the water-streaked cliffs beneath it. Immediately to your right is Mount Majestic and, behind that, Cathedral Mountain. You will spend the next two miles skirting around these two for-

Trail up Angels Landing

mations to reach Refrigerator Canyon.

After you have walked 2.8 miles from Cabin Spring you will see a spur trail on the left heading for the top of a rocky peak known as Angels Landing. If you have the time, Angels Landing is a side trip that shouldn't be missed. The top is only 0.5 mile from the main trail, and the view is absolutely incredible. The river winds around a huge 180 degree bend in the canyon, and on the road, 1,470 feet below, cars creep like ants on their way to and from the Temple of Sinawava. The Great White Throne, probably the most famous of Zion's landmarks, rises 3,420 feet above the canyon floor on the opposite side of the river. A word of caution, however, about the "trail" to Angels Landing. Some scrambling is necessary and, although the park service has installed rails and support chains on a few of the more exposed sections, the route is not for the faint of heart. Small children and people who suffer from vertigo should not attempt this hike. Angels Landing is especially dangerous when it is wet or windy. Also, the top of the ridge is frequently struck by lightning, so avoid it during stormy weather.

If you decide not to attempt Angel's Landing, at least pause to enjoy the view from Scout Lookout, near the trail junction. Leaving Scout Lookout, the trail drops straight down into Refrigerator Canyon over a series of no less than 21 switchbacks. These switchbacks, whimsically called Walter's Wiggles, were cut from the rock cliff in 1926 so that tourists could reach the viewpoints above. Viewed from a distance they look more like a rope ladder or a spider's web than a trail.

Finally, after following the bottom of Refrigerator Canyon for about a half mile, the trail emerges on the west side of the inner canyon and threads its way down to the river, 1.9 miles from Scout Lookout.

Zion Canyon, seen from Angel's Landing

Hop Valley and Kolob Arch

☆ ☆ ☆ ☆ ☆

Zion National Park
shuttle car required
overnight hike

Distance:	14.7 miles (plus 43 miles by car)
Walking time:	day 1: 6³/₄ hours day 2: 4¹/₂ hours
Elevations:	1,290 ft. loss, 1,000 ft. gain Hop Valley Trailhead (start): 6,350 ft. Kolob Arch Viewpoint: 5,400 ft. La Verkin Creek Trailhead: 6,060 ft.
Trail:	Very popular, well maintained trail
Season:	Late spring through mid-fall. Winter snows often close the roads to the trailheads from mid-November to May. Also, the trail is quite hot in July and August.
Vicinity:	Kolob Canyons Section of Zion National Park, near Saint George
Maps:	Kolob Arch, The Guardian Angels *(USGS)* Zion National Park *(Trails Illustrated, #214)*
Information:	http://www.utahtrails.com/kolob.html *(Utah Trails)* http://www.nps.gov/zion/ *(Zion National Park)* phone: (435) 586-9548 *(Kolob Canyons Visitor Center)*

Drive south of Cedar City on I-15 for 18 miles to Exit 40, then leave the highway and drive east for another 0.5 mile to the Kolob Canyons Visitor Center of Zion National Park. You will need to get a backcountry camping permit here for an overnight hike into the park. After you have obtained your permit continue driving beyond the Visitor Center for another 3.7 miles to Lees Pass, where the La Verkin Creek Trailhead is located. This trailhead marks the end of the hike, and you should leave your shuttle car in the nearby parking lot.

To get to Hop Valley Trailhead, where the hike begins, return to I-15 and drive south for 13 miles to the junction with Highway 17. Turn here and follow the signs to Zion National Park for 12 miles through La Verkin to the town of Virgin. In Virgin you will see a sign identifying the road to Kolob Reservoir. Turn left onto this road and drive for 13.4 miles, until you see the sign directing you to the Hop Valley Trailhead on your left.

Note: If you don't have two cars a shuttle between the two trailheads can be arranged with the Zion Canyon Transportation Company in Springdale, but it is quite expensive. For more information call (435) 635-5993.

see map, page 391

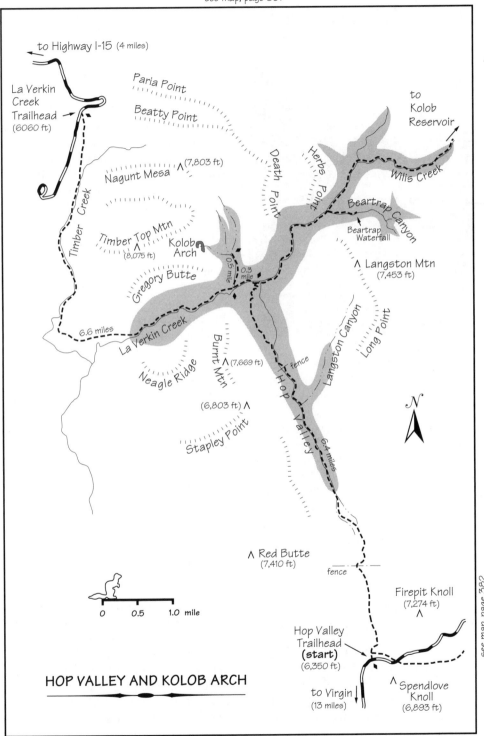

to Highway I-15 (4 miles)

La Verkin
Creek
Trailhead
(6060 ft)

Paria Point

Beatty Point

to
Kolob
Reservoir

Death Point

Herbs Point

Willis Creek

Nagunt Mesa ∧(7,803 ft)

Beartrap Canyon

Timber Creek

Timber Top Mtn
∧
(8,075 ft)

Kolob
Arch

Beartrap
Waterfall

∧ Langston Mtn
(7,453 ft)

Gregory Butte

0.5
mile

0.3
mile

6.6 miles

La Verkin Creek

Langston Canyon

Long Point

Neagle Ridge

Burnt Mtn

∧ (7,669 ft)

fence

Hop Valley

(6,803 ft) ∧

6.4 miles

Stapley Point

N

∧ Red Butte
(7,410 ft)

fence

Firepit Knoll
(7,274 ft)
∧

0   0.5   1.0 mile

Hop Valley
Trailhead
(start)
(6,350 ft)

to Virgin ↓
(13 miles)

∧ Spendlove
Knoll
(6,893 ft)

HOP VALLEY AND KOLOB ARCH

see map, page 382

La Verkin Creek

Kolob Arch is probably the largest natural arch in the world. Accurate measurement of its size is difficult because of its location, high above the canyon floor, but recent calculations place its span somewhere between 292 and 310 feet. The arch lies near the top of the Navajo Sandstone cliffs on the north side of La Verkin Creek, about 700 feet above the trail. It faces east, so the best time to see and photograph Kolob Arch is in the morning before about 10:00 a.m.

There are three possible ways to walk to Kolob Arch, but the Hop Valley Trail, suggested here, is the most scenic approach. This trail starts on the Kolob Plateau, south of La Verkin Creek, and proceeds down the colorful Hop Valley Canyon to its confluence with La Verkin. The canyon is about 200 yards wide, with a flat, grassy bottom boxed in on both sides by towering cliffs of red sandstone. A shallow stream, fed by runoff from a half

see color photo, page 200

dozen side canyons, keeps the bottom of the narrow valley green, while, in the distance, one can see the picturesque maze of mesas and canyons that surround the confluence of Hop Valley and La Verkin Creek.

Unfortunately, the Hop Valley experience is degraded by the presence of several dozen range cows. This valley was grazed long before Zion National Park was established, and cattle are still grazed there. As of this printing, 3,477 acres of land within the published boundaries of Zion National Park is still privately owned by local ranchers. The National Park Service has been trying to solve this problem for years, but like most other federal problems the solution requires money. The degree to which the Hop Valley ecosystem has been damaged by the cattle becomes obvious about a mile before La Verkin Creek, where a fence has been erected to keep cattle out of the lower end of the valley. Beyond this barrier the diversity in plant species increases dramatically, the creek bed becomes deeper and more clearly defined, and the presence of birds and other wildlife becomes noticeable once again.

Day 1 (6.9miles)

From the Hop Valley Trailhead the trail passes through 1.4 miles of open pinion-juniper forest before coming to a fence near the beginning of Hop Valley Canyon. This fence marks the beginning of an inholding of privately owned land. Beyond the fence the trail begins descending gradually into Hop Valley, finally reaching the canyon floor after about 1.5 miles. As you proceed down the canyon the floor becomes wider and flatter until, after another 1.5 miles, it reaches its maximum width of about 300 yards. Finally, 4.8 miles from the trailhead, you will cross the northern boundary of the Hop Valley grazing area, where another fence spans the bottom of the canyon to keep cattle out of La Verkin Creek. Make sure you close the gate behind you as you cross through the fence.

Soon after leaving the grazed portion of Hop Valley, the trail leaves the valley floor and climbs slightly into a forested area below the west wall. Then, 0.3 mile before reaching La Verkin Creek the trail breaks out of the trees and begins a series of switchbacks down into La Verkin Canyon. Just before reaching the creek you will see another trail coming down the canyon from Willis Creek. Turn left here and walk for 0.4 mile to the short spur trail that leads to Kolob Arch. But before going to see the arch, I suggest you continue down La Verkin Creek far enough to find a good campsite for the night. There are a lot of good sites here, so, unless it is a holiday, you shouldn't have any trouble finding one. Try to camp at least 0.2 mile from the junction with the Kolob Arch Trail–especially if you have a large group. The environment in this area has already sustained substantial damage from overuse by campers.

Day 2 (7.8 miles)

The first item of business on the second day is to see the Kolob Arch. As mentioned earlier, the best time to see the arch is in the morning, so even if you saw it the day before you should take the time to see it again before hiking out. After breaking camp leave your packs behind and walk back to the sign marking the spur trail to Kolob Arch viewpoint, 0.5 mile away. Unfortunately the viewpoint where the trail ends is still 600 yards from the arch, and because of the rough terrain it is almost impossible to get more than 200 yards closer. Without a good frame of reference the arch does not seem as big as it really is, and you may be mildly disappointed. Nevertheless, it is huge–spanning the length of a football field at its base.

From your campsite, the trail to Lees Pass continues down La Verkin Creek for about 1.6 miles before veering off to the north. The trail finally leaves the creek near the remains of an old corral that was used years ago when cattle were still being grazed here. 1.3 miles later the trail encounters Timber Creek, a tributary of La Verkin, and continues north toward Lees Pass. Finally, 0.9 mile before arriving at the trailhead, the trail leaves Timber Creek and climbs the last 470 feet to the parking lot.

Kolob Arch

Middle Fork Taylor Creek

☆ ☆ ☆

Zion National Park
day hike

Distance: 5.4 miles (round trip)

Walking time: 3 hours

Elevations: 490 ft. gain/loss
Taylor Creek Trailhead (start): 5,530 ft.
Double Arch Alcove: 6,020 ft.

Trail: Generally good trail, although parts of it are occasionally washed out by flash floods.

Season: Spring, summer, fall. The trail is often covered with snow during the winter months.

Vicinity: Kolob Canyons Section of Zion National Park

Maps: Kolob Arch *(USGS)*
Zion National Park *(Trails Illustrated, #214)*

Information: http://www.utahtrails.com/taylor.html *(Utah Trails)*
http://www.nps.gov/zion/ *(Zion National Park)*
phone: (435) 586-9548 *(Kolob Canyons Visitor Center)*

Drive south of Cedar City on I-15 for 18 miles to exit 40, then turn east onto the Kolob Canyons Road. Within 0.2 mile you will come to the Kolob Canyons Visitor Center, where you must pay a small entrance fee to enter Zion National Park. This is also a good place to buy books and maps and ask any questions you might have. The Taylor Creek Trailhead is 1.9 miles further east from the visitor center on the Kolob Canyons Road. There is a small parking lot near the trailhead on the left side of the road, and trail brochures are available at a cost of $1.00.

The Kolob Canyons section of Zion National Park offers visitors a splendid opportunity to enjoy Zion's unique redrock canyons without enduring the crowds of people that are usually present in Zion Canyon. Of particular interest to hikers are the Finger Canyons of the Kolob. These scenic canyons are deeply etched into the western side of the Kolob Plateau, and from above they look like so many fingers clawing their way into

the plateau's rouge colored sandstone. None of the canyons are more than a few miles long, but they are notable because of their sheer walls. Typically the cliffs are over a thousand feet high, rising nearly vertically through the Navajo Sandstone formation that underlies the plateau.

The Fingers can all be accessed from the Kolob Canyons Road that runs along Timber and Taylor Creeks a half mile to the west.

390

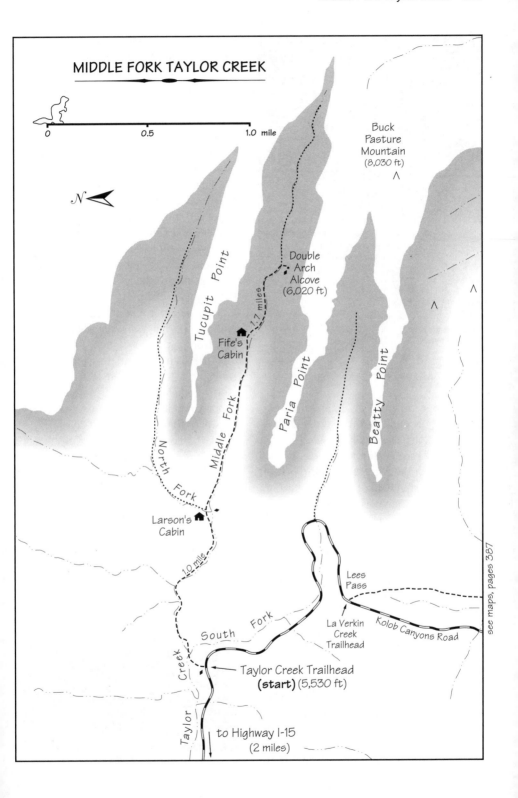

MIDDLE FORK TAYLOR CREEK

0   0.5   1.0 mile

N

Buck
Pasture
Mountain
(8,030 ft)
∧

Tucupit Point

Double
Arch
Alcove
(6,020 ft)

1.7 miles

Fife's
Cabin

Middle Fork

North Fork

Paria Point

Beatty Point

∧

∧

∧

Larson's
Cabin

1.0 mile

Lees
Pass

South Fork

La Verkin
Creek
Trailhead

Kolob Canyons Road

see maps, pages 387

Creek

Taylor Creek Trailhead
(start) (5,530 ft)

Taylor

to Highway I-15
(2 miles)

Middle Fork Taylor Creek

There are six of them in all, and their rugged beauty is enough to make the heart of any outdoorsman beat a little faster. The most popular hikes are into the canyons formed by the North, Middle, and South Forks of Taylor Creek. Of the three, Middle Fork Taylor Creek Canyon is the only one that contains a maintained trail. In my opinion this hike is also the most interesting one, and it is the one I will describe here.

From the road the trail drops down about 60 feet to the confluence of Taylor Creek and the South Fork, then continues in an easterly direction along Taylor Creek. Very soon the trail crosses to the north side of the creek, the first of many crossings to come, but it never strays far from the bottom of the drainage. There is usually at least a little water running in the streambed, although late in the summer the flow may dry up completely. You will be walking through a low montane forest of ponderosa pine, white fir, ju-

niper, and pinion pine. This area was heavily logged during the first half of this century and few of the trees are older than 50 years, but fortunately the vegetation has made a remarkable comeback and now the area seems as pristine as ever. There are few signs of the earlier destruction.

After 1.0 mile you will come to the confluence with the North Fork of Taylor Creek, where there is a primitive hiker-made trail leading off to the left. This trail goes about 2.0 miles to the back of North Fork Taylor Creek Canyon. You are likely to meet far fewer people along the North Fork of Taylor Creek, and for that reason some prefer that hike. Also, backcountry camping is allowed along the

see color photo,
page 200

North Fork, but you must obtain a permit first from the visitor center.

There is an old settler's cabin beside the trail just a few hundred feet north of the North Fork-Middle Fork confluence. The cabin was built by Gustav Larson who raised pigs here for sale in Cedar City during the early 1930s. A trip to Cedar City meant a 23-mile ride by wagon or horseback for Mr. Larson, but he did have at least one other neighbor in the area. In 1930, about the same year that the Larson Cabin was built, a professor named Arthur Fife from the agricultural college in Cedar City also built a cabin on the Middle Fork of Taylor Creek. Professor Fife's cabin is located on the left side of

Arthur Fife's cabin

Taylor Creek Trail

the creek 1.0 miles further upstream.

Middle Fork Canyon actually begins about 300 yards upstream from the Larson cabin, and by the time you reach the Fife cabin the canyon will have narrowed to just a few hundred feet. Fife raised goats on his property, and he built a fence across the canyon in order to contain his animals. There is now no trace of Fife's fence, but both his and Larson's cabins are still in remarkably good condition. The Fife cabin is right by the trail, but if you are walking in the streambed, as many people do, you might miss it. It is located about 20 feet from the left bank of the creek in a heavily shaded grove of trees.

The trail ends at the Double Arch Alcove, 0.7 miles beyond Arthur Fife's cabin. This alcove is a large cave, about 150 feet deep and 150 feet in diameter, located 20 feet above the streambed on the south side of the canyon. Like most sandstone alcoves, this one was formed by a seep in the side of the cliff. Water seeping out from the canyon wall weakens the sandstone and eventually causes

it to crumble away. A great deal of water is still seeping out of the Double Arch Alcove, and, from the size of the alcove, the seep has been active for many of thousands of years. The alcove was named after two "blind arches", or arches that have not yet been completely formed, that are located on the cliffs above.

If you still have energy left when you reach the Double Arch Alcove it is possible to continue up Middle Fork Canyon for another 0.8 mile before the walls close in and make further progress impossible. 0.2 mile above the alcove the canyon is blocked by an ancient rockslide, but if you are willing to do some scrambling you can easily climb around the right side of this obstacle. After climbing about a hundred feet to the top of the slide the canyon floor flattens out again and widens into a small hanging valley. From there you can continue another 0.6 mile or so before further progress becomes impossible.

Double Arch Alcove

Pine Valley Mountains

☆ ☆ ☆   **Pine Valley Mountains Wilderness Area**
shuttle car or bicycle useful
overnight hike

Distance: 15.7 miles
(plus 1.5 miles by foot, bicycle, or car)

Walking time: day 1: 5³/₄ hours
day 2: 8 hours

Elevations: 4,410 ft. gain, 4,580 ft. loss
Whipple Trailhead (start):   7,050 ft.
Whipple Valley: 9,320 ft.
North Valley: 9,200 ft.
Hidden Valley: 8,980 ft.
Browns Point Trailhead: 6,880 ft.

Trail: Generally well marked, easy to follow trail

Season: Early summer. Water can be a problem on this hike. In the early summer there is usually abundant water at several points along the trail, but by mid-July most of the water has dried up. You might also have problems if you attempt the hike too early in the year. Most of the snow is usually gone by June 1, but before then the route may be muddy and hard to follow. The best month is June.

Vicinity: Near Cedar City and Saint George

Maps: Signal Peak, Grass Valley *(USGS)*

Information: http://www.utahtrails.com/pinevalley.html *(Utah Trails)*
http://www.fs.fed.us/dxnf/ *(Dixie National Forest)*
phone: (435) 652-3100 *(Pine Valley Ranger District)*

Drive west from Cedar City on Highway 56 for 36 miles to the Beryl Junction. Turn left here and continue driving south for 24 miles on Highway 18 to Central, where you will see a well marked road leading to Pine Valley on your left. Turn here and drive to the town of Pine Valley 8.3 miles west of Central. Once you reach Pine Valley Town you will see a sign directing you to the Pine Valley Recreation Area. Turn here and proceed east for 1.5 miles to the recreation area entrance gate, where you must pay $2.00 per car to enter. (If you intend to use one of the campgrounds the entrance is free.)

1.3 miles beyond the entrance station you will see a paved road on the right that leads to the Pines Campground and beyond. Browns Point Trailhead is at the end of this road, 0.5 mile past the Pines Campground or 0.6 miles from the main road. This is where the hike ends. To get to the Whipple Trailhead where the hike begins you must return to the main road and continue upcanyon for another 0.2 miles until you come to the road to Blue Springs Campground. The Whipple Trailhead is on this road, 0.4 miles above Blue Springs Campground or 0.6 mile from the main road.

The Pine Valley Mountains are located in the extreme southwestern corner of Utah, on the eastern side of the Great Basin. Like most other ranges in the Great Basin they are very dry and contain no significant lakes. They do, however, contain a number of small creeks and meadows which, at least during the early weeks of summer, are extremely scenic. Unfortunately, most of the water disappears soon after the winter snow has melted. The best time to attempt this hike is during the month of June, when the meadows are usually green and full of water. As midsummer approaches they soon dry up and the hike becomes much less appealing.

Although this hike is only 15.7 miles long there is a great deal of up-and-down along the way, and many people prefer to spend a second night along the trail. If you elect to do this you will have no trouble finding good campsites along the Summit Trail between Whipple Valley and Nay Canyon. You can camp near water at Whipple Valley, South Valley, Hop Canyon, Hidden Valley or Nay Canyon.

Day 1 (5.3 miles)

From Whipple Trailhead the trail starts upward immediately, climbing steadily over the next two miles through a forest domi-

Whipple Trail, Pine Valley Mountains

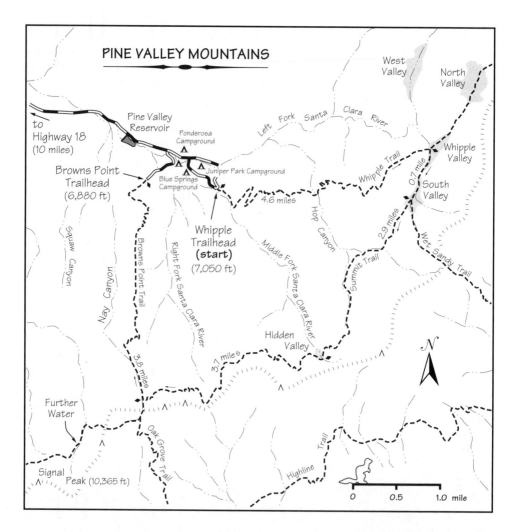

PINE VALLEY MOUNTAINS

West Valley
North Valley

to Highway 18 (10 miles)

Pine Valley Reservoir
Ponderosa Campground

Left Fork Santa Clara River

Whipple Trail

Whipple Valley

0.7 mile

Browns Point Trailhead (6,880 ft)

Blue Springs Campground
Juniper Park Campground

South Valley

4.6 miles

Hop Canyon

2.9 miles

Wet Sandy Trail

Whipple Trailhead **(start)** (7,050 ft)

Squaw Canyon

Browns Point Trail

Right Fork Santa Clara River

Nay Canyon

Middle Fork Santa Clara River

Summit Trail

Hidden Valley

3.8 miles

3.7 miles

Further Water

Oak Grove Trail

Signal Peak (10,365 ft)

Highline Trail

N

0   0.5   1.0 mile

---

nated by subalpine fir and Engelmann spruce. You will want to stop frequently to enjoy the magnificent views of Pine Valley Town below and the hills that surround it. Finally, after an elevation gain of some 1,300 feet, the trail dips 200 feet down into Hop Canyon, where you should be able to fill your canteens before continuing the climb. After Hop Canyon it is uphill again—another 1,100 feet of steady elevation gain until you reach Whipple Valley, just east of the summit ridge.

Whipple Valley is a picture-perfect alpine meadow about 100 yards wide and five times as long, with a small creek running through the middle. If you got off to a late start you might want to select a campsite on the edge of Whipple Valley. There are plenty of ideal spots along the edges of the grassy meadow. In the spring it is filled with wildflowers nourished by the melting snow, but snow is the only source of water and the meadow quickly dries out after the snow is gone. Water is plentiful in early June, but by midsummer it has usually disappeared. If there is no water in Whipple Valley try walking northwest for a half mile up the drainage towards West

see color photo, page 197

Valley. This is the headwaters of the Left Fork Santa Clara River and there is sometimes water here after Whipple Valley has dried out.

As you enter Whipple Valley you will notice a sign indicating that you have reached a trail junction. This is the point where Whipple Trail meets the Summit Trail, a 35-mile-long pack trail that runs in a northeast-southwest direction along the summit ridge of the Pine Valley Mountains. If you have an extra day to spend you might want to establish a camp here and spend some time exploring the nearby North Valley and West Valley meadows, both within a mile of the junction. In order to complete this loop hike, however, you will have to turn right at the junction and follow Summit Trail in a southerly direction until you reach Browns Point Trail, 7.3 miles away.

The Summit Trail is not as well defined as Whipple Trail and you may have trouble following it for the first mile. The route is easy, though, so don't worry too much if you can't find the trail. Just walk south along the Whipple Valley drainage until you come to the southern end of the meadow. Continue following the drainage through the trees and within 0.3 mile you will break out into another meadow called South Valley. You should be able to pick the trail up again as you continue south along the western edge of South Valley.

South Valley is every bit as beautiful as the better known Whipple Valley, and the water supply is slightly more reliable. It is another two-hour walk to the next comparable campsite, so unless you got off to a very early start you will probably want to spend the night in South Valley. Near the trail about half way through the meadow the creek bed winds around a big boulder, forming a shaded pool that seems to hold water until later in the summer. There is also plenty of flat ground in the area, making it a good place to set up camp. Furthermore, this

Summit Trail, Pine Valley Mountains

meadow seems to be a favorite evening hangout for deer, so if you are quiet and observant you will probably see some wildlife before the sun sets.

Day 2 (10.4 miles)

As you approach the southern end of South Valley the trail seems to disappear again. Finally, just before you reach the trees you will see another sign that says "Wet Sandy Trail" with an arrow pointing to the left. This is *not* the trail you want. Stop at the sign and look due magnetic south at the edge of the meadow about 100 yards in front of you. If you look carefully you will see another trail, the Summit Trail, entering the trees on the south end of the meadow. There are also well defined blaze marks on the trees where the trail leaves the meadow. Once you enter the woods the trail is again quite will defined.

Immediately after you leave South Valley the Summit Trail again begins to climb. Over the next 2.9 miles you will first gain 220 feet in elevation, then drop 420 feet, then gain 400 feet, then loose 420 feet before finally reaching what, in my opinion, is the most beautiful meadow of all: Hidden Valley. Located at the foot of a rocky outcrop near the headwaters of the Middle Fork Santa Clara River, Hidden Valley is indeed well hidden. The meadow is small, only 100 yards in diameter, and it is completely surrounded by tall, stately Engelmann spruce.

You will hardly know it is there before you walk into it. Adding to the effect, Summit Trail exits the meadow through a partially hidden five-foot-wide crack in the rock barrier on its western side—a perfect secret entrance to an outlaws' hideout. If you are looking for quiet seclusion there are no better places to camp than Hidden Valley.

Continuing its up-and-down route, the Summit Trail climbs nearly a thousand feet above Hidden Valley, and then drops 320 feet back down to Nay Canyon, wherein is located the junction with Browns Point Trail. Nay Canyon generally has water in it in early summer, and it is a good place to camp or refill your canteens.

In order to complete this loop you must leave the Summit Trail at the Nay Canyon Junction and take Brown Point Trail back to the Pine Valley Recreation Area. Again, however, if you have an extra day to spend there are a number of points of interest fur-

ther up the Summit Trail. Continuing south on Summit Trail for 1.3 miles from the junction will bring you to Further Water, a good water source and a popular camping area. Two miles from the junction Summit Trail passes within 0.2 mile of Signal Peak (10,365 ft.), the highest point in the Pine Valley Mountains. The peak is about 370 feet above the trail, and there is no trail to the summit. The climb, however, is not particularly difficult.

From its junction with the Summit Trail, Browns Point Trail follows the bottom of Nay Canyon for 0.7 mile before climbing 400 feet back up the ridge on the east side of the canyon and then following the ridge the rest of the way to the bottom. The total amount of elevation loss along the trail from the junction is a knee busting 3,120 feet, but you will be compensated by fine views of the valley below. You can see Pine Valley for almost the entire distance.

Whipple Valley, Pine Valley Mountains

Public Lands Agencies

National Park Service

Arches National Park
www.nps.gov/arch/
P.O. Box 907
Moab, UT 84532
(435) 719-2299

Bryce Canyon National Park
www.nps.gov/brca/
P.O. Box 170001
Bryce Canyon, UT 84717
(435) 834-5322

Canyonlands National Park
www.nps.gov/cany/
2282 S. West Resource Blvd.
Moab, UT 84532
(435) 719-2313 (Headquarters)
(435) 259-2652 (Hans Flat Ranger Station)

Capitol Reef National Park
www.nps.gov/care/
HC-70 Box 15
Torrey, UT 84775
(435) 425-3791

Cedar Breaks National Monument
www.nps.gov/cebr/
2390 West Highway 56, Suite #11
Cedar City, UT 84720
(435) 586-9451

Dinosaur National Monument
www.nps.gov/dino/
4545 E. Highway 40
Dinosaur, CO 81610
(970) 374-3000

Escalante Interagency Office
755 West Main Street
Escalante, UT 84726
(435) 826-5499

Glen Canyon National Recreation Area
www.nps.gov/glca/
P.O. Box 1507
Page, AZ 86040
(520) 608-6404

Hovenweep National Monument
www.nps.gov/hove/
McElmo Route
Cortez, CO 81321
(435) 459-4344

Natural Bridges National Monument
www.nps.gov/nabr/
P.O. Box 1
Lake Powell, UT 84533
(435) 692-1234

Rainbow Bridge National Monument
www.nps.gov/rabr/
P.O. Box 1507
Page, AZ 86040
(520) 608-6404

Timpanogos Cave National Monument
www.nps.gov/tica/
R.R. 3, Box 200
American Fork, UT 84003

Zion National Park
www.nps.gov/zion/
Springdale, UT 84767
(435) 772-3256

U.S. Forest Service

Ashley National Forest
www.fs.fed.us/r4/ashley/

Duchesne Ranger District
85 West Main
Duchesne, UT 84021
(435) 738-2482

Flaming Gorge Ranger District
P.O. Box 279
Manila, UT 84046
(435) 784-3445

Roosevelt Ranger District
244 West Highway 40
Roosevelt, UT 84066
(435) 722-5018

Vernal Ranger District
355 North Vernal Avenue
Vernal, UT 84078
(435) 789-1181

Dixie National Forest
www.fs.fed.us/dxnf/

Cedar City Ranger District
82 North 100 East
Cedar City, UT 84721
(435) 865-3200

Escalante Interagency Office
755 West Main Street
Escalante, UT 84726
(435) 826-5499

Escalante Ranger District
270 West Main
Escalante, UT 84726
(435) 826-5400

Pine Valley Ranger District
196 East Tabernacle Street, Room 40
St. George, UT 84771
(435) 652-3100

Powell Ranger District
225 East Center
Panguitch, UT 84759
(435) 676-8815

Teasdale Ranger District
138 East Main
Teasdale, UT 84773
(435) 425-3702

Fishlake National Forest
www.fs.fed.us/r4/fishlake/

Beaver Ranger District
575 South Main
Beaver, UT 84713
(435) 438-2436

Fillmore Ranger District
390 South Main
Fillmore, UT 84631
(435) 743-5721

Loa Ranger District
138 South Main
Loa, UT 84747
(435) 836-2811

Richfield Ranger District
115 East 900 North
Richfield, UT 84701
(435) 896-9233

U.S. Forest Service

Manti-La Sal National Forest
www.fs.fed.us/r4/mantilasal/

Ferron Ranger District
115 West Canyon Road
Ferron, UT 84523
(435) 384-2372

Moab Ranger District
2290 South Resource Blvd.
Moab, UT 84532
(435) 259-7155

Monticello Ranger District
496 East Central
Monticello, UT 84535
(435) 587-2041

Price Ranger District
599 West Price River Drive
Price, UT, 84501
(435) 637-2817

Sanpete Ranger District
540 North Main Street
Ephraim, UT 84627
(435) 283-4151

Uinta National Forest
www.fs.fed.us/r4/uinta/

Heber Ranger District
2460 South Highway 40
Heber City, UT 84032
(435) 654-0470

Pleasant Grove Ranger District
390 North 100 East
Pleasant Grove, UT 84062
(801) 785-3563

Spanish Fork Ranger District
44 West 400 North
Spanish Fork, UT 84660
(801) 798-3571

Wasatch-Cache National Forest
www.fs.fed.us/wcnf/

Evanston Ranger District
1565 South Highway 150, Suite A
Evanston, WY 82930
(307) 789-3194

Kamas Ranger District
50 East Center Street
P.O. Box 68
Kamas, UT 84036
(435) 783-4338

Logan Ranger District
1500 East Highway 89
Logan, UT 84327
(435) 755-3620

Mountain View Ranger District
P.O. Box 129
Mountain View, WY 82939
(307) 782-6555

Ogden Ranger District
507 25th Street, Suite 103
Ogden, UT   84403
(801) 625-5112

Salt Lake Ranger District
6944 South 3000 East
Salt Lake City, UT 84121
(801) 943-1794

Bureau of Land Management

Cedar City Field Office
www.ut.blm.gov/cedar_city/
176 East D.L. Sargent Drive
Cedar City, UT 84720
(435) 586-2401

Escalante Interagency Office
755 West Main Street
Escalante, UT 84726
(435) 826-5499

Fillmore Field Office
www.ut.blm.gov/fillmore/
35 East 500 North
Fillmore, UT 84631
(435) 743-3100

Grand Staircase-Escalante Nat. Mon.
www.ut.blm.gov/gsenm/
180 West 300 North
Kanab, UT 84741
(435) 644-4300

Henry Mountain Field Station
P.O. Box 99
Hanksville, UT 84734
(435) 542-3461

Kanab Field Office
www.ut.blm.gov/kanab/
318 North 100 East
Kanab, UT 84741
(435) 644-2672

Moab Field Office
www.ut.blm.gov/moab/
82 East Dogwood
Moab, UT 84532
(435) 259-6111

Monticello Field Office
www.ut.blm.gov/monticello/
435 North Main Street
Monticello, UT 84535
(435) 587-1500

Price Field Office
www.ut.blm.gov/price/
125 South 600 West
Price, UT 84501
(435) 636-3600

Richfield Field Office
www.ut.blm.gov/richfield/
150 East 900 North
Richfield, UT 84701
(435) 896-1500

Salt Lake Field Office
www.ut.blm.gov/salt_lake/
2370 South 2300 West
Salt Lake City, UT 84119
(801) 977-4300

St. George Field Office
www.ut.blm.gov/st_george/
345 East Riverside Drive
St. George, UT 84790
(435) 688-3200

Vernal Field Office
www.ut.blm.gov/vernal/
170 South 500 East
Vernal, UT 84078
(435) 781-4400

Further Reading

Hiking Guides

Ron Adkison, *Hiking Grand Staircase-Escalante & the Glen Canyon Region* (Falcon Press, Helena, Montana, 1998). Hikes in southeastern Utah, including the Cedar Mesa and Lake Powell areas.

Steve Allen, *Canyoneering the San Rafael Swell* (University of Utah Press, Salt Lake City, 1992). A detailed documentation of the roads, canyons, and hiking routes in one of Utah's most interesting geologic formations.

Steve Allen, *Canyoneering 2 - Technical Loop Hikes in Southern Utah* (University of Utah Press, Salt Lake City, 1995). A collection of 7 very challenging hiking routes through the canyons of Utah's redrock country.

Thomas Brereton and James Dunaway, *Exploring the Backcountry of Zion National Park: Off-Trail Routes* (Zion Natural History Association, Springdale, Utah, 1988). Contains comprehensive descriptions of 16 challenging backcountry hikes in Zion National Park.

Bill Cunningham and Polly Burke, *Wild Utah* (Falcon Press, Helena, Montana, 1998). A backcountry guide to Utah's wilderness areas and other lesser known wild places.

Mel Davis and John Veranth, *High Uinta Trails* (Wasatch Publishers, Salt Lake City, 1998). A detailed description of the hiking trails in the High Uintas Wilderness Area.

Michael Kelsey, *Canyon Hiking Guide to the Colorado Plateau* (Kelsey Publishing, Provo, Utah, 1995). The most useful of all of Kelsey's hiking guides. This book contains maps and descriptions of every major hiking area from the San Rafael Swell south to the Grand Canyon.

Michael Kelsey, *Utah Mountaineering Guide, 3rd Edition* (Kelsey Publishing, Provo, Utah, 1997). Route descriptions and maps for every major mountain range in the state. Kelsey's books are well known among Utah's serious mountain climbers and canyoneers.

Erik Molvar and Tamara Martin, *Hiking Zion & Bryce Canyon National Parks* (Falcon Press, Helena, Montana, 1997). A general guide to trails in and around two of Utah's most popular national parks.

Bill Schneider, *Exploring Canyonlands and Arches National Parks* (Falcon Press, Helena, Montana, 1997). Hiking and four-wheeling in Utah's two most remote national parks.

Michael R. Weibel and Dan Miller, *High in Utah* (University of Utah Press, Salt Lake City, 1999). A hiking guide to the tallest peak in each of Utah's 29 counties.

Natural History

Edward Abbey, *Desert Solitaire, a Season in the Wilderness,* (Simon & Schuster, New York, 1968). A moving and highly entertaining collection of essays about the Colorado Plateau, written by a former ranger of Arches National Park.

Stewart Aitchison, *Utah Wildlands* (Utah Geographic Series, Salt Lake City, 1987). A vividly illustrated description of Utah's designated wilderness areas and other less protected wildlands.

F. A. Barns, *Canyon Country Arches and Bridges* (Canyon Country Publications, Moab, Utah, 1987). Information on the locations, statistics, geologic history and discovery of the most prominent natural arches of the Colorado Plateau.

Halka Chronic, *Roadside Geology of Utah* (Mountain Press Publishing Company, Missoula, Montana, 1990). Utah's geologic formations and the events that formed them are told in a way that laymen will understand and geologists will appreciate.

Francis Elmore, *Shrubs and Trees of the Southwest Uplands* (Southwest Parks and Monuments Association, Tucson, Arizona, 1976). A well organized guide, illustrated with both color photographs and line drawings.

John Wesley Powell, *Exploration of the Colorado River and its Canyons* (Dover Publications, New York, 1961). A reprint of Powell's original narratives, including his expeditions down the Colorado, the Green, and the Uinta Rivers. First published in the 1870s.

David Muench and Ann Zwinger, *Utah* (Graphic Arts Center Publishing, Portland, Oregon, 1990). A photographic essay of Utah's exquisite wild lands by a world renowned landscape photographer.

Polly Schaafsma, *The Rock Art of Utah* (University of Utah Press, Salt Lake City, 1944). A comprehensive tour of the many varieties of Indian rock art in Utah, written by a leading authority on the subject.

Richard Shaw, *Utah Wildflowers* (Utah State University Press, Logan, Utah, 1995). An excellent guide to Utah's alpine wildflowers. This book is especially useful in the mountains of northern Utah.

John Telford and Terry Tempest Williams, *Coyotes Canyon* (Peregrine Smith Books, Salt Lake City, 1999). Stories and photographs that evoke the mystery and beauty of Southern Utah's desert canyons.

Ann Zwinger, *Wind in the Rock* (University of Arizona Press, Tucson, Arizona, 1978). A personal account of the author's exploration of the canyons in the Cedar Mesa area, including Grand Gulch and Slickhorn Canyon.

——————————————— **Internet Sites** ———————————————

http://www.utahtrails.com
web site for Utah's Favorite Hiking Trails

http://www.fs.fed.us/
home page of the U.S. Forest Service

http://www.nps.gov/
home page of the National Park Service

http://www.ut.blm.gov/
BLM Utah home page

http://paria.az.blm.gov/
Paria Canyon-Vermillion Cliffs Wilderness

http://www.ut.blm.gov/monument/
Grand Staircase-Escalante Nat. Mon.

http://water.usgs.gov/
data on flow rates of rivers in the U.S.

http://www.wrh.noaa.gov/Saltlake/
National Weather Service, Utah office

http://parks.state.ut.us/
Utah Department of Parks and Recreation

http://www.desertusa.com/
online adventure guide to the Southwest

http://www.americansouthwest.net/utah/
The American Southwest, Utah Guide

http://www.mountainweb.com/
an online mountaineering magazine

http://go-utah.com/
Utah travel and recreation guide

http://www.infowest.com/Utah/
information about Utah's backcountry

http://www.gorp.com/
the Great Outdoor Recreation Pages

http://www.utahadventure.com/
Utah Adventure Online Magazine & Guide

http://climbutah.homestead.com/
Mountaineering & Canyoneering in Utah

http://www.canyonquests.com/hiking/
photo tours of selected Utah hikes

http://www.trails.com/
hiking trails and maps, worldwide

http://www.sni.net/cedar_mesa/
the Cedar Mesa Project home page

http://zzyx.ucsc.edu/Comp/Bill/CandP.html
a treatise on Indian rock art in SE Utah

http://www.a1.com/pebooks/oclubs.htm
links to outdoor clubs throughout the US

http://www.csn.net/~felbel/utahsurf.html
the Utah Wilderness Surfsites home page

http://www.utahbirds.org/
bird watching in Utah

http://www.cyberseek.com/NABS/
the Natural Arch and Bridge Society

http://www.utahnature.org/
The Nature Conservancy, Utah chapter

http://www.suwa.org/
Southern Utah Wilderness Alliance

http://www.npca.org/
National Parks Conservation Association

http://www.sierraclub.org/chapters/ut/
the Utah chapter of the Sierra Club

http://www.wilderness.org/
The Wilderness Society home page

Index

V

Veranth, John: 109
Vernal: 41
Virgin River: (*see also North Fork of the Virgin River*) 380
Virgin Spring Canyon: 157, 160
Virginia Park: 247

W

Walcott Lake: 80
Wall Arch: 209
Wall Lake: 86, 87, 89, 90
Wall of Windows: 361
Wall Street Trail: 359-361
Walter's Wiggles: 384
Wasatch-Cache National Forest: 23-37, 45-71, 77-98, 105-134
Wasatch Front: 12, 35, 37, 107, 142
Wasatch Mountains: 12-14, 18, 20, 37, 110, 112, 124, 140, 145
Water Canyon: 228, 254, 261
Waterfall Canyon: 32-34
Waterpocket Fold: 192, 301-304, 306-311, 314, 315
Watson, Frank: 352
Watson Lake: 89, 90
Weber River: 86, 91, 93, 97, 98
Weber Sandstone: 44
Wedge Overlook: 156, 160
Weeping Rock: 377, 380
Weir Lake: 94
Wellsville: 28, 29
Wellsville Area Project Corporation: 29
Wellsville Cone: 28, 31
Wellsville Mountains Wilderness Area: 28-31
Wellsville Ridge: 28-31, 161
West Basin: 62, 63
West Valley: 396-397
Wetherill, Richard: 271, 273, 289
Whipple Trail: 394, 395, 397
Whipple Valley: 197, 394-398
Whirlpool Canyon: 41
White Canyon: 268, 269

White House Trailhead: 353, 358
White Pine Fork: 128, 131
White Pine Lake (Bear River Range): 4, 25-27, 161
White Pine Lake (Wasatch Range): 130-131, 175
White Pine Trail: 12, 126, 130, 131, 174
White Rim Formation: 233, 236, 255
White Rim Road: 236, 237
Wildcat Canyon Trail: 383
Wilder Lake: 80
Williams, Terry Tempest: 246
Willis Creek: 389
Willow Gulch: 197, 341-345
Willow Lakes Trail: 37
Wilson Peak: 55
Wingate Sandstone: 160, 236, 302, 306, 307, 310, 311
Wire Pass: 356
Wire Pass Trailhead: 353, 354
Wolverine Cirque: 134
Wyman Lake: 80

Y

Yellowstone Creek: 46
Youngs Canyon: 266
Yovimpa Pass: 364-366
Yovimpa Point: 365

Z

Zion Canyon: 11, 379, 380, 383
   East Rim: 377-380
   West Rim: 199, 381-385
Zion Narrows: 19, 199, 371-376
Zion National Park: 371-393

photo by Lily Day

Originally trained as an electrical engineer, David Day spent most of his first career teaching in universities in Kuala Lumpur and Penang, Malaysia. Then in 1978, after concluding that writing and photography were his real love, he resigned from teaching and moved to Hilo, Hawaii, to begin writing a series of six books on the countries of Southeast Asia. Finally, in 1991, he returned to Provo, Utah, his early childhood home, where he and his family now reside.